the Basic

Message

of the New

Testament

A Sure
FOUNDATION

Alan Cairns

AMBASSADOR
Belfast • Greenville

A SURE FOUNDATION

Copyright © 1996 Alan Cairns

ISBN 1 898787 80 8

Published by
Ambassador Productions, Ltd.
Providence House
16 Hillview Avenue,
Belfast, BT5 6JR

Emerald House
1 Chick Springs Road, Suite 206
Greenville, South Carolina 29609

C O N T E N T S

P R E F A C E

As anyone who has ever used a camera knows, a wide-angle lens misses many fine details that a telephoto lens can capture. However, it has the advantage of giving a comprehensive view of an area in a single shot. While you may miss the beauty of an individual rose, you can see the big picture of the entire landscape. Photography would be boring indeed if we were limited to one type of picture. There is a place for both the close-up and the wide-angle shot.

The same is true in Bible study. There is a need for good close-up shots of the great words and doctrines of Scripture. But there is also a need for the wide-angle shots that enable us to see the big picture of the teaching of each Bible book.

These studies are meant to be wide-angle pictures. They do not aim to give detailed structural outlines of the books of the New Testament. What they do is to present the heart of the message of each book.

There are obvious advantages in such a course. First, it enables even a new student of Scripture to grasp the essential truths of the gospel revelation. Second, it lets us see what the inspired authors considered important—it will save us from majoring on minor matters while neglecting the truly important things of the gospel. Third, it will show us just how unified is the message of the New Testament books. We will learn that each book takes the central truths of the gospel and uses them to meet the varied needs of God's people.

That leads us to the final advantage of this type of study: it is intensely practical, addressing all the real-life situations Christians face and giving the sure answers of the Holy Spirit. This is no mean advantage in a day when all too often Christians are bombarded with an endless stream of "how-to" advice from preachers and counsellors who seem to be more attuned to the latest psychological rambling of the world than they are to the gospel of Christ.

Each New Testament book is complete in itself and yet stands closely related to the books around it. The same is true of these studies. That means that this is not the kind of book you must read from page 1 to the end. You may take the chapters in just about any order you wish. For most, if not all, it may be best to start with books like Romans, Galatians, Ephesians, Hebrews, and the rest of the epistles before studying Matthew, Mark, Luke, and John. The same gospel is plainly set forth in every book, but most Christians will benefit from the simple yet profound exposition of the gospel the epistles present. The insight thus gained will make the study of the four Gospels much easier and more fruitful. However, whatever the sequence each reader may choose, the message of the New Testament books will lead him directly to Christ and thus bless his soul.

These studies were first given in our Lord's Day morning services in Faith Free Presbyterian Church, Greenville, South Carolina. They were meant to give God's people simple expositions and applications of the New Testament's revelation of the person and work of Christ. This printed version of those studies has the same aim. Thus I have kept footnotes and additional end notes to a minimum. The purpose is not to educate scholars but to instruct and edify saints.

I have to thank my wife Joan for doing the tedious work of typing the message from the original study tapes. Mary Christopher helped in that work and also did many subsequent retypings, editing, and proofreading. Her husband Stephen designed the book and prepared it for the press. To each of these willing workers I offer my sincere thanks. We have laboured to produce this book with the prayer that the Lord will be pleased to use it to show forth the glories of Christ and His gospel and to thrill and fill His people with the realization of the all-sufficiency of their Redeemer.

Alan Cairns

Why Four Gospels?

The Gospel narratives present the same Christ from

◆

four distinct perspectives. He is the central figure.

◆

Matthew shows Him as the King, Mark as the Servant,

◆

Luke as the Saviour of the world, and John as God

◆

manifested in the flesh.

THE NEW TESTAMENT COMMENCES WITH FOUR GOSPEL narratives, four individual, independent records of the person and the ministry of the Lord Jesus Christ. Some people wonder why there should be four books at the beginning of the New Testament telling what they conceive to be essentially the same story. Why is there not one exhaustive, chronological biography of the Lord Jesus Christ? The answer is very simple: these books were inspired by the Spirit of God and written by His chosen human penmen to meet specific needs. They were addressed to real people in real situations who needed some specific aspect of the person and work of the Lord Jesus Christ to be emphasized to them. It may have satisfied a certain academic curiosity if there had been one continuous biography—though I doubt it. I doubt it because the curiosity of certain critics would never be satisfied. Their quest for "the historical Jesus" proceeds from their utter rejection of anything supernatural as truly historical. So however the life of Christ had been written, they would have rejected it.

There is much advantage in having four Gospel narratives. Remember that the Lord directed these books to specific groups of people, and they are, to use a theological term, apologetic in nature. They do not aim to give a strict chronology. At times they do follow chronology. At other times they do not. At all times, however, they set forth a very clear theme, or line of thought, that was meant to convey the particular truth that was needful for the specific situation of the people addressed. Each Gospel therefore has its particular aspect of Christ that it aims to present.

The gospel—whether it is the gospel according to Matthew, Mark, Luke, or John, or whether it is the exposition of the gospel by Paul, or James, or Peter—is always essentially Christ. We cannot emphasize that enough. In these four Gospel narratives the main figure is Christ—who He is, what He did, what He said, His interpretation of the Old Testament, His application of the Old Testament, His death, His burial, and His resurrection. Everything centers on the person and work of the Lord Jesus Christ.

With Christ as his theme, each of the evangelists, Matthew, Mark, Luke, and John, is guided by the Spirit of God to treat his subject from a particular point of view. The Gospel of Matthew was originally directed to Palestinian Jews. It presents Christ as the King of Israel. In contrast, the Gospel of Mark presents Him as the Servant of Jehovah, a contrast marked even from the start by the way Mark's Gospel commences. The Gospel of Luke presents Christ as the Son of man, while the Gospel of John sets Him forth as the *Logos*, the Word, the Son of God from all eternity. This last view of Christ actually gives us the reason for the other three. Unless Jesus Christ is the Son of God then nothing that Matthew, Mark, or Luke has to say is of any value. If He is not what John says He is, then He cannot be what Matthew, Mark, and Luke say He is. It is because He is the Son of God manifested in the flesh (John 1:1, 14, 18) that He is the King who translates us out of the kingdom of darkness into His own glorious kingdom of light, love, and liberty. Because He is the Son of God He is the Servant of Jehovah who has fully obeyed the law of God, satisfied the justice of God, met the demands of God, and reconciled our souls to God. Because He is the Son of God He is the Son of man, the Saviour of the world.

CHAPTER

1

Matthew
Christ Is King

The kingdom of heaven is the rule of heaven on earth in

◆

the person and through the work of Christ the King.

◆

In one sense it is present; in another it is yet to come.

◆

In both senses it demands a response of obedient faith

◆

from all to whom its word comes.

The great theme of Matthew's Gospel is Christ the King. That is conveyed to us in various ways and in various places. John the Baptist says, "Repent ye: for the kingdom of heaven is at hand" (3:2). As soon as the Lord Jesus started preaching, He stressed the same message: "From that time Jesus began to preach, and to say, Repent: for the kingdom of heaven is at hand" (4:17). The word *kingdom* appears some fifty times in Matthew. The phrase "the kingdom of heaven" appears thirty-two times and is found nowhere else in Scripture. The other Gospels use the phrase "the kingdom of God," often in reporting the very same statements or sentiments in which Matthew uses "the kingdom of heaven."[†] This shows that the Dispensationalist idea of making the kingdom of heaven a different kingdom from the kingdom of God is without a biblical foundation. The kingdom is one, but there is obviously a clear distinction of emphasis in Matthew's unique phrase, "the kingdom of heaven." It reflects the truth of Dan. 4:26, "The heavens do rule," and of 2 Tim. 4:18, which speaks of the Lord's "heavenly kingdom." We may summarize Matthew's particular emphasis as the rule of heaven on earth by the coming and reception of the King. So the central theme of th e Gospel of Matthew concerns **the kingdom of heaven and the response it demands from men.**

THE MANIFESTATION OF THE KING

In Matthew chapter 1 the King is born. He is the Son of David and He is the Son of Abraham (v. 1). Then, He is the Son of Mary (vv. 18–25). The Son of David—that is His royal lineage. The Son of Abraham—that is His connection with the father of the nation of Israel and, as Paul says, of all the faithful. The Son of Mary—that is His virgin birth.

From these three things, we can see that the King and His kingdom stand in a very particular relationship to the Old Testament revelation. The references to David and Abraham and the reference in verses 22 and 23 to the prophecy of Isaiah all remind us of His relation to God's Word. Since David and Abraham were two of the most important people with whom the Lord confirmed His gracious covenant (Gen. 12:2–4; Gal. 3:16, 17; 2 Sam. 23:5), we must also note that the King and His kingdom stand related to God's covenant and therefore to God's people.

Now let us put all these together. The King stands in intimate relation with God's Word, God's covenant, and God's people.

He comes *to fulfil the Word of God.* In Matt. 5:17 He says, "Think not that I am come to destroy the law, or the prophets: I am not come

---

[†]See the extended note on the subject of the kingdom, p. 15.

to destroy, but to fulfil." Any system of doctrine that so divides the Old and New Testaments as to make one essentially the enemy of the other, or to make one diametrically different in its essential message from the other, misses the whole point of the message of Jesus Christ. There is one thing that ties the Old and New Testaments together. Augustine rightly stated, "The New Testament is enfolded in the Old Testament; the Old Testament is unfolded in the New Testament." The person and work of Jesus Christ is central to the whole Bible. From Genesis to Revelation, Jesus Christ is the sum and substance of the message of God to men. God has never said anything to any man about any subject without its standing in direct, definite, and essential relationship to the Lord Jesus Christ. Thus in the Gospel of Matthew there is a constant repetition of the phrase, "that it might be fulfilled which was spoken by the prophet." Remember, this was written to Jews. The Jews had the Scriptures of the Old Testament, and what Matthew set out to prove was that Jesus Christ was not like the other supposed messiahs. He was not a self-appointed messiah. He was not someone who would lead them astray. He had not come on a political mission. He was not a self-seeker. Thus Matthew emphasized that Jesus was the One who fulfilled the Old Testament.

You cannot believe the Old Testament without believing Christ. Nor can you believe Christ without believing the Old Testament. He is the substance of the Old Testament message (John 5:46; Acts 10:43), and He is the fulfiller of the Old Testament's law, type, and prophecy.

The King comes not only to fulfil God's Word, but specifically *to establish God's covenant.* Christ's covenant connection to Abraham and David teaches some very important truths. It emphasizes the unity of both Testaments. It starts off the entire New Testament revelation with the tacit acknowledgment that God always deals with men in the terms of a covenant. He never deals with any man in isolation. He deals with him either in Adam under the covenant of works, or in Christ under the covenant of grace.

Christ came to fulfil the covenant. Throughout the Old Testament period, the covenant of grace was administered in various ways in keeping with the times in which God's people lived. "But when the fulness of the time was come, God sent forth his Son, made of a woman, made under the law, to redeem them that were under the law" (Gal. 4:4, 5).

The King came not only to fulfil God's Word and covenant, but also *to rescue and to rule God's people.* Matthew 1 is a chapter of names, because Jesus Christ the King came to rescue and to rule the people of God, the Israel of God. The emphasis is on the nation of Israel. David was king of Israel. Abraham was the root of the nation of Israel. Those who try to interpret the Bible so as to cut the nation of Israel out of any current involvement or interest in God's great program for the climax of the ages, I believe, are missing the whole point of Scripture. One would have to be blind indeed to read Romans 11 and say God has no future for the nation of Israel. I am firmly convinced that God's great covenant with Abraham (Gen. 12) has not yet seen its ultimate fulfilment for the nation of Israel. God chose the Jews and has not cast them away. There is a future, a message, and an outreach to the nation of Israel.

Ultimately, however, the Israel of God goes beyond the confines of the Jewish nation. Not all Jews are true Israelites. "He is not a Jew, which is one outwardly; neither is that circumcision, which is outward in the flesh: but he is a Jew, which is one inwardly; and circumcision is that of the heart, in the spirit, and not in the letter; whose praise is not of men, but of God" (Rom. 2:28–29). Thus a true Jew is one who has his heart circumcised. That is, he has been regenerated; he has been made a new creature in Jesus Christ; he has been justified by the grace of God through faith. That is a true Israelite. The universal church of Christ is the Israel of God. That is why the Gospel of Matthew, directed to Palestinian Jews, breaks the bounds of Judaism. Notice how Matthew records that wise men from the east came to Christ. The Magi were Gentiles, and they came by divine guidance to Christ because the gospel is for the world. The Lord Jesus emphasized this worldwide scope of His mission: having healed the centurion's servant He said, "Many shall come from the east and west, and shall sit down with Abraham, and Isaac, and Jacob, in the kingdom of heaven" (8:11). In the great commission the Lord Jesus said, "Go ye therefore, and teach all nations, baptizing them in the name of the Father, and of the Son, and of the Holy Ghost: teaching them to observe all things whatsoever I have commanded you: and, lo, I am with you alway, even unto the end of the world" (28:19–20). The gospel message is the same for the Jews and for the Gentiles, and it remains the same in every age until Jesus Christ comes again.

It is entirely in keeping with this idea of the extension of covenant grace to the world that Matthew is the only one of the four Gospels that uses the word *church*. According to many Dispensationalists, the Gospel of Matthew is not for the church. It is strange that this Gospel which they say is not for the church is the only one of the four Gospels that even mentions the church (16:18; 18:17). Obviously, the kingdom is for natural-born Jews who receive Christ the King, and it is for the whole Israel of God, those who, though Gentiles in the flesh, are saved by grace.

The very first verse of Matthew 1 prepares us for this great truth: "The book of the generation of Jesus Christ, the son of David, the son of Abraham." The expression "the book of the generation of" appears only twice in Scripture. The first time is in Gen. 5:1: "the book of the generations of Adam." The second is in Matt. 1:1: "the book of the generation of Jesus Christ." This is something that is said of the first Adam and of the last Adam. Here are two great covenant heads, Adam and Christ. Jesus Christ came as the covenant head of a people for whom He appears as the King of grace. "As in Adam all die, even so in Christ shall all be made alive" (2 Cor. 15:22). That is the gospel that is gloriously suggested in the very first verse of Matthew's Gospel. That this grace extends beyond natural-born Jews is indicated by some of the names in the genealogy of Matthew 1. We find Rahab and Ruth there (v. 5)—and they were both Gentiles. That Gentiles should be included in the lineage of Christ the King is significant. It is another pointer to the worldwide scope of His saving mission.

Here, then, is the manifestation of the King. He came to fulfil God's Word. He came to establish His covenant. He came to rescue and to rule all His people by grace, whether Jew or Gentile.

To do all this He had to have a miraculous birth, a virgin birth. Without the miracle of a sinless birth from a virgin mother by the direct operation of the Holy Spirit, Jesus could not have been the King. He could not have fulfilled the prophetic word of Gen. 3:15 and Isa. 7:14. He would have been a sinner, under the dominion of sin, not the sovereign Saviour of sinners from their sins. Thus the record of the genealogy and birth of Christ in chapter 1 is carefully constructed to show that Joseph was the legal father of Jesus but not His biological father. R. C. H. Lenski remarks, "Through the entire line runs the verb 'begot—begot—begot.' Significantly it makes a halt when it reaches Joseph. He, the husband of Mary, did *not* beget Jesus, the Messiah." The King was first manifested by the miracle of the virgin birth "that it might be fulfilled which was spoken of the Lord by the prophet, saying, Behold, a virgin shall be with child, and shall bring forth a son, and they shall call his name Emmanuel, which being interpreted is, God with us" (Matt. 1:22–23).

THE MESSAGE OF THE KINGDOM

The message of the kingdom is simply and forcefully put in Christ's own words in 4:17, "Repent: for the kingdom of heaven is at hand." There is a truth of vital importance here: *repentance can be understood only in relation to the kingdom of heaven.* There are two Greek verbs that mean "repent." One of them speaks of a change of mind, and the other carries the idea of sorrow and grief and therefore of a change of how we feel about something. Now the word used in Matthew means simply a change of mind. On that basis some people glibly say that to repent means simply to change one's mind about Jesus Christ—to say with the mind, "He is the Saviour," without necessarily experiencing any change of life. That is to claim to know Christ as Saviour while denying Him as King. But that is impossible, for the word *repentance* cannot be understood apart from its relationship to the kingdom of heaven. The rethinking of repentance is not merely a mental exercise. A man may think again, and think just as foolishly and falsely as he thought the first time. He could think again, and be just as much a sinner as he was to start with. The rethinking of repentance is thinking again in the light of the coming of the King. It is thinking again in the light of the nature of His kingdom. G. Campbell Morgan said that this thinking again has in it these elements: consideration, which leads to conviction, which leads to conversion. Campbell Morgan was right. Any repentance that does not lead to conviction and conversion is not true repentance.

Consider—think again. Think again of Jesus Christ. He is not just a doctrine. He is not just an historical figure. He is God manifested in the flesh who has come to be the King of His people. Think again of His throne, of His call to "leave all and follow Me" and to "repent because the kingdom of heaven is at hand." In the light of who He is and what He did in His death and resurrection, and in the light of what He says and what He demands, think again. Consider.

Then keep considering until a deep *conviction* of sin takes hold of your heart. Under the burden of sin call on the name of the Lord. "Repent ye therefore, and be converted, that your sins may be blotted out" (Acts 3:19). Do not be like the Pharisees, who had a physical relationship to Israel and enjoyed all the advantages of the kingdom—Jesus even called them "the children of the kingdom" (Matt. 8:12)—but were rebels against the King. The Lord Jesus Christ pronounced His great series of woes upon them (chap. 23)—a solemn reminder of the doom of those who remain strangers to true repentance. Remember: repentance is a response to the message of the King and the kingdom. It is a consideration that leads to conviction that leads to conversion. Anything short of that is a total rejection of the King's message.

THE MEANING OF THE KINGDOM

This is a very deep subject that deserves extensive study. Some of the leading texts and thoughts on the meaning of the kingdom appear in the extended note that follows this chapter. Here we will summarize the meaning of the kingdom with three simple statements:

1. The preaching of the kingdom *expounds* the meaning of the kingdom of heaven.

2. The principles of the kingdom *explain* the meaning of the kingdom of heaven (chaps. 5–7).
3. The power of the kingdom *expresses* the meaning of the kingdom
   of heaven in the clearest possible terms (chaps. 8–28, the great
   miracles of Christ).

Let us consider these more fully.

*The preaching of the kingdom expounds the meaning of the kingdom
of heaven.* John the Baptist, Jesus, and then Jesus' disciples all preached
"the gospel of the kingdom." The Scofield Bible has popularized the view
that the gospel of the kingdom is essentially different from the gospel of
grace. But that is a mistake, as Acts 20:24, 25 will immediately prove. The
gospel of the kingdom is the gospel of grace with special emphasis on the
kingly office, work, and demands of the Lord Jesus Christ.

Here, however, we encounter considerable difficulty. The idea of the
kingdom is so vast that no brief, simple statement does it justice. Some
Scriptures speak of the kingdom as now present. For example, in Matt.
4:17 the kingdom of heaven is at hand. The idea there is of a present
kingdom. In 12:28 Jesus said, "If I cast out devils by the Spirit of God,
then the kingdom of God is come unto you." It is present. But then in
other places, the Scriptures speak of the kingdom as future. When Jesus
taught us to pray He told us to say, "Thy kingdom come" (6:10). In 25:34
He looked to the end of the age when He will welcome His people,
"Come, . . . inherit the kingdom." So the kingdom is still future.

We must try to put all this information together. What is the kingdom? Who is in the kingdom? When is the kingdom? These are vital
questions. *Kingdom* generally means a territory, or a realm. It has that
meaning in Scripture. In Col. 1:13, for example, we read that God has
"delivered us from the power of darkness, and hath translated us into
the kingdom of his dear Son." He has brought us out of one realm into
another. A comparison of Matt. 19:16 and 23 shows the same thing.
The rich young ruler asked, "What good thing shall I do, that I may have
eternal life?" When he went away without eternal life, the Lord Jesus
said to His disciples, "A rich man shall hardly enter into the kingdom of
heaven." Eternal life (v. 16) is equivalent to the kingdom (v. 23). So the
kingdom is a realm in which God's people enjoy eternal life.

But that is not the basic meaning of the term. When the psalmist
said, "His kingdom ruleth over all," what did he mean? He meant the
rule or the sovereignty exercised by the King. That is the kingdom. It is
the King's rule or sovereignty. That tells you not only what the kingdom
is but who is in it.

Who is in this kingdom? Remember that the kingdom is the realm
of those who have been translated out of darkness and redeemed by

blood (Col. 1:13–14). It is the realm of those who have come into eternal life having left all, set aside every hindrance, and turned away from what they know to be sin to crown Christ King of their lives (Matt. 19:16–26). They are the people who are in the kingdom. To put it even more simply, the people who recognize the personal sovereignty of Jesus Christ in their own lives, who are ruled by Christ, are in the kingdom. No one else is. That sounds like a very exclusive statement, but it is the truth. To the disciples the rich young ruler appeared a prime candidate for inclusion in the kingdom. He was rich, he was law-abiding, he could say, "I have kept the law from my youth up" and sincerely believe that he had. But Jesus revealed that he loved his money more than he loved the King. His devotion to Christ would always have been contingent upon keeping his money and all its privileges. He could not enter the kingdom. When a man comes to Christ he comes to acknowledge Him as his King. In effect, he says, "Thou art the King, I am the subject. Thou art the Ruler, I am the ruled." The people who are in the kingdom own Christ as King.

Of course there is another sense in which He is King no matter what men think. God is King. Christ is sovereign. He is going to have His way. All men—atheists or theists, Christian or heathen, nations of every tribe and tongue—are subject to the ultimate sovereignty of God. But they do not all benefit from being citizens of the kingdom. Many of them are under the rule of God as rebels. That raises an all-important question: Are you in the kingdom? Think carefully of that. Let each of us ask himself, am I in the kingdom of God's grace in Christ? It is not enough to be in some church organization, however good and biblical it may be. The question is whether we are subjects of Christ's kingdom.

What is the kingdom? It is the realm where Christ rules in grace. Who is in it? Those who have been redeemed by Christ's blood and delivered from Satan's realm to embrace Christ as their King.

When will it be? It is present. The kingdom of God is among you, Jesus said. It is here and now. In one sense we are now under His rule. We are now the recipients of His grace. We are now delivered from the power of sin and Satan. We are now walking in the light. We are now in fellowship with God. We are now justified. Paul says, "The kingdom of God is not meat and drink; but righteousness, and peace, and joy in the Holy Ghost" (Rom. 14:17). Those are things we now have. The righteousness of justification. The peace of reconciliation. The joy of glorious exaltation in Jesus Christ. The kingdom is now.

But the kingdom is yet to come. Why? Because the King is coming, and it is only when the King comes that the kingdom will be fully realized. Some speak of building the kingdom of God on earth by their efforts and service. Evangelism truly is a kingdom work (Matt. 24:14), but the earth is not to be subdued until the King returns.

So the preaching of the kingdom expounds what we mean by it. It is the realm and rule of Christ, currently in grace over all who own Him as King, and in due time in government and glory over all the world.

The principles of the kingdom explain its meaning. Space allows only a brief development of this idea. The Sermon on the Mount (chaps. 5, 6, and 7) details the principles of the kingdom. In 5:20 Jesus makes an amazing statement: "Except your righteousness shall exceed the righteousness of the scribes and Pharisees, ye shall in no case enter into the kingdom." That statement goes to the very heart of the principles of the kingdom and the moral teaching of the Sermon on the Mount. No passage of Scripture is more generally misunderstood. All too often it is represented as teaching a gospel of personal righteousness and legal obedience. Liberals embrace it as a charter of self-righteous religion: by virtue of what you do you will be a good Christian. Dispensationalists also tend to see it as legalistic and therefore divorce it from the gospel of grace and the life of the church. They postpone its use to a future kingdom age.

The statement of Christ in Matt. 5:20 shows, however, that the principles of the kingdom are the principles of the gospel. They are the principles of grace, not legal observance. They are the principles of reality and spirituality. The entire gospel is the good news of a righteousness that is better than that of the Pharisees. Christ is made unto us righteousness (1 Cor. 1:30). His obedience constitutes His people righteous (Rom. 5:17–20). That imputed righteousness leads to holy living (Romans 6)— not the mere external show of Pharisaic religion. Jesus criticized the Pharisees for a hypocritical externalism: "Woe unto you, scribes and Pharisees, hypocrites! for ye make clean the outside of the cup and of the platter, but within they are full of extortion and excess" (Matt. 23:25). He commanded them to begin by dealing with the inside (v. 26). He demands a heart religion. That is the principle of the kingdom.

The rest of the Sermon on the Mount is really a prolonged exposition of that principle. This is how the Lord Jesus explains the kingdom. Its principle is one of righteousness—a righteousness that is of a different kind from the legalism of the Pharisees. It is real righteousness. It fully meets the standards of God's law. It is, therefore, imputed righteousness, as Paul was careful to show, and it leads to true heart conformity to the will of the King.

The power of the kingdom expresses the meaning of the kingdom of heaven. Christ's message of the kingdom is not just a theory or a theology. In chapter 8 we read of a leper who came to Christ and of a centurion who sought healing for his servant who lay sick of the palsy. In both cases the Lord Jesus granted immediate healing. He spoke and bestowed instant healing. That is something that is not in the power of man or of any religious movement to do. I know there are some who claim to be doing the same kind of miracles, but their claims are bogus. That was not the case with the Lord Jesus Christ. With a word He instantly healed the leper and the paralysed man. Having done these great miracles, the Saviour immediately related what He had just done to the meaning and message of the kingdom.

Here is the power of the kingdom. It is the message of salvation. The miracles of Christ were sermons. Sinners may not be lepers in the flesh, but they are lepers in the spirit as long as they are out of Christ. They may not be paralysed in the flesh, but they are totally paralysed spiritually. There is no strength in any man without Christ. There is no ability in any man without Christ. He has no power to do anything to save his soul. But the word of the kingdom is enough to set such free. The power of the kingdom is a message of salvation.

It is also a message of prophecy. The old paraphrase of Isaiah chapter 2 says, "Behold, the mountain of the Lord in latter days shall rise." That is speaking of the millennial glory of Christ. Isa. 11:6–9 says, "The wolf also shall dwell with the lamb, and the leopard shall lie down with the kid; and the calf and the young lion and the fatling together; and a little child shall lead them. And the cow and the bear shall feed; their young ones shall lie down together: and the lion shall eat straw like the ox. And the sucking child shall play on the hole of the asp, and the weaned child shall put his hand on the cockatrice' den. They shall not hurt nor destroy in all my holy mountain: for the earth shall be full of the knowledge of the Lord, as the waters cover the sea." This is not merely figurative. It is describing an era the like of which the world has never seen since the creation, when the power of the kingdom will fully express the meaning of the kingdom of heaven.

THE MYSTERY OF THE KINGDOM

In the parables of chapter 13 the Lord Jesus speaks of the mystery of the kingdom. It is *a mystery of grace*. We do not become citizens of this kingdom by any earthly citizenship, Jewish or Gentile. It is grace that puts us there. Jesus tells the story of the Son of man planting good seed in the ground. God nurtures it and brings life. The meaning is plain. Jesus said, "He that soweth the good seed is the Son of man; the field is the world; the good seed are the children of the kingdom" (13:37–38). God's people are His plants, planted by His hand, and therefore safe and secure (15:13). Salvation is by grace alone.

13

The mystery of the kingdom is also *a mystery of growth*. The mustard seed is very small, but it grows. Similarly the seed of the kingdom produces growth in all God's people. When a soul is saved by grace all the elements of the world and of hell are against him. His home circumstances may be terrible. His physical circumstances may be trying. His finances may be in ruins. Yet his spiritual life grows and grows. That is a mystery. "The mystery which hath been hid from ages and from generations . . . now is made manifest to his saints: to whom God would make known what is the riches of the glory of this mystery among the Gentiles; which is Christ in you, the hope of glory" (Col. 1:26–27). "Christ in you." That is the key to the mystery.

Consider this mystery of growth from another standpoint. When God planted the New Testament church on the day of Pentecost it was like a tiny mustard seed or like a small measure of leaven. However, that mustard seed grew. That leaven began to penetrate and affect the world. The church grew, and it is still growing.

Growth leads to glory. In Matthew 13 Jesus speaks of His people being harvested for heaven. In chapter 25 He speaks of their inheriting the kingdom. Here is the ultimate mystery of the kingdom. What a mystery! We were born sinners. The King found us wallowing in our own blood on the road to hell (Ezek. 16:5–6). He spoke grace, gave growth, and is bringing us to glory. What a place heaven will be! There we shall inherit the fulness of the kingdom.

THE MAJESTY OF THE KINGDOM

The majesty of the kingdom is the cross of Jesus Christ. The King died. He died out of majestic love. He made a majestic atonement.

Then the King rose again, breaking the bands of death and defeating the powers of hell.

The King ascended into heaven to hear the word of His Father, "Sit thou on my right hand until I make thine enemies thy footstool."

The King commissioned His heralds. That is what gospel preachers are—heralds of the King who has come and is soon to come again. Jesus said, "This gospel of the kingdom shall be preached in all the world for a witness unto all nations; and then shall the end come. . . . Then shall appear the sign of the Son of man in heaven: and then shall all the tribes of the earth mourn, and they shall see the Son of man coming in the clouds of heaven with power and great glory" (24: 14, 30). The words of Rev. 11:15 will soon be brought to pass: "The kingdoms of this world are become the kingdoms of our Lord, and of his Christ." The Lord Jesus now rules and reigns on earth from heaven. Soon He will return to reign in glory even here on earth.

But remember that grace must precede glory. Never forget that. Grace must precede glory, and unless you are a subject of Christ in grace you will never be a subject of Christ in glory. That appears very clearly from the judgment parables of Matt. 24:45–25:46. In every case there is a separation of mere professors from the true saints of God. Only grace prepares the soul for glory.

We may sum up the response we should make to the truth about the kingdom of heaven in three brief sentences.

Enter the kingdom by repentance.

Experience or enjoy the kingdom in righteousness.

Extend the kingdom by the recruitment of others. Be an evangelist. Take this gospel of the kingdom, of the King who has come and is coming again, to a world that is lying in the kingdom of darkness and sin. Tell them the truth. Plead with them to be saved. Recruit them for Christ. God will bless the sincere efforts of sincere saints and bring poor sinners to King Jesus.

May we all fully learn the message of the Gospel of Matthew: "Repent: for the kingdom of heaven is at hand."

Additional Note on the Kingdom

The subject of the kingdom is a very complex one. To enter into a detailed discussion of the terms "the kingdom of heaven" and "the kingdom of God" is beyond the scope of this study. However, it may be helpful to note the following basic facts.

I. The two terms are often used synonymously.
   1. Matt. 19:23–24—"Then said Jesus unto his disciples, Verily I say unto you, That a rich man shall hardly enter into *the kingdom of heaven.* And again I say unto you, It is easier for a camel to go through the eye of a needle, than for a rich man to enter into *the kingdom of God."* Clearly the Lord Jesus intended the terms to be taken synonymously. Cf. Mark 10:23, 24.
   2. Matt. 4:17 records Jesus' message, "Repent: for the kingdom of heaven is at hand." Mark 1:15 uses "the kingdom of God": "The kingdom of God is at hand: repent ye, and believe the gospel."
   3. Matt. 13:11—"It is given unto you to know the mysteries of the kingdom of heaven."
      Mark 4:11-"Unto you it is given to know the mystery of the kingdom of God." Cf. Luke 8:10.

4. Matt. 13:31—"The kingdom of heaven is like to a grain of mustard seed."

   Mark 4:30, 31—"Whereunto shall we liken the kingdom of God? . . . It is like a grain of mustard seed."

5. Matt. 13:33 and Luke 13:20–21 make the same statements using *leaven* to symbolize the kingdom of heaven and the kingdom of God.

6. Matt. 18:3—"Except ye be converted, and become as little children, ye shall not enter into the kingdom of heaven."

   Mark 10:15—"Whosoever shall not receive the kingdom of God as a little child, he shall not enter therein." Cf. Luke 18:17.

7. Matt. 19:14—"Suffer little children, and forbid them not, to come unto me: for of such is the kingdom of heaven."

   Mark 10:14—"Suffer the little children to come unto me, and forbid them not: for of such is the kingdom of God." Cf. Luke 18:16.

8. Matt. 8:11–12—"Many shall come from the east and west, and shall sit down with Abraham, and Isaac, and Jacob, in the kingdom of heaven. But the children of the kingdom shall be cast out into outer darkness: there shall be weeping and gnashing of teeth."

   Luke 13:28–29—"There shall be weeping and gnashing of teeth, when ye shall see Abraham, and Isaac, and Jacob, and all the prophets, in the kingdom of God, and you yourselves thrust out. And they shall come from the east, and from the west, and from the north, and from the south, and shall sit down in the kingdom of God."

II. At times both terms mean the age to come, or eternal life.

1. Matt. 8:11–12 and Luke 13:28–29, quoted above, have clear reference to the eternal state, and the terms "kingdom of heaven" and "kingdom of God" plainly indicate the blessed state of God's redeemed forever.

2. Matt. 19:23–24 and Mark 10:23–24 are undoubted references to the state of salvation, the possession of eternal life, which is expressed by the terms "kingdom of heaven" and "kingdom of God."

III. A clue to the relation of the two terms to each other is found in the Lord's Prayer.

Matt. 6:9–10—"Our Father which art in heaven, Hallowed be thy name. *Thy kingdom come. Thy will be done in earth, as it is in heaven.*" Cf. Luke 11:2.

"Thy will be done in earth, as it is in heaven" expounds the meaning of "thy kingdom come."

This will help us grasp the meaning of the terms: "Jesus is . . . aware of a region in the universe where the will of God is at present being perfectly and universally done, and, for reasons not difficult to surmise, He elevates thither the minds and hearts of those who pray. The kingdom of heaven would thus be so entitled because it is already realized there, and is, through prayer and effort, to be transferred thence to this earth." (James Stalker)

IV. All this helps us to grasp the immense scope of the terms.

1. The kingdom has come:

Luke 17:21—"The kingdom of God is within you."

Matt. 11:12—"From the days of John the Baptist until now the kingdom of heaven suffereth violence, and the violent take it by force."

Matt. 12:28—"If I cast out devils by the spirit of God, then the kingdom of God is come unto you."

2. The kingdom is yet to come:

Matt. 6:10—"Thy kingdom come."

John 18:36—"Jesus answered, My kingdom is not of this world: if my kingdom were of this world, then would my servants fight, that I should not be delivered to the Jews: but now is my kingdom not from hence." Here *kosmos,* "world," means "the present condition of human affairs, in alienation from and opposition to God" (W. E. Vine). This is a meaning *kosmos* frequently bears (cf. John 7:7; 8:23; 14:30; 1 Cor. 2:12; Gal. 6:14; Col. 2:8; James 1:27; 1 John 4:5).

3. It is *historical*—it actually *comes* in history, and is even now at work, as in the parables of Matthew 13. It is *ethical*—it is *within* its subjects (Luke 17:21). It is *spiritual,* for it means eternal life, as in Matt. 19:23, 24. It is *eschatological,* for it is associated with the great prophetic consummation of the ages, as in Matthew 25, where the parables of the virgins and of the man going for a time into a far country direct attention to the coming of Christ at the end of the age (vv. 31–46). See also Matt. 8:11, 12; 13:24–30, 36–43—note the plain reference in 13:39 to "the end of the world" as the time when the Son of man will "gather out of his kingdom all things that offend" (v. 41) and the righteous shall "shine forth as the sun in the kingdom of their Father" (v. 43).

V. To summarize:

1. The kingdom is the rule of God, particularly through His Son.

2. It is heavenly in its origin and in its authority—but it describes the sphere and realization of its rule as being on earth.

3. It confronts men here on earth, for the King Himself has come into the world preaching repentance and the gospel of the kingdom (which Paul says is the same gospel as the gospel of free grace, Acts 20:24–25).

4. It therefore demands a strong and positive response (see Matt. 13:44ff; 11:12). Christ constantly called for a strong response to His message: Mark 9:43, 45, 47; 10:21; Luke 14:26. Those who hear it "must be willing and ready to engage in any action, however radical, in response to the presence of the kingdom of God" (G. E. Ladd).

5. Matt. 18:3; Mark 10:15: Those who now receive the kingdom as little children will enter into its great eschatological consummation—they will be among those described in Matt. 8:11. They will "sit down with Abraham, and Isaac, and Jacob, in the kingdom."

VI. The kingdom and the church are closely related.

Matt. 16:16, 18–19—"And Simon Peter answered and said, Thou art the Christ, the Son of the living God. . . . And I [Jesus] say also unto thee, That thou art Peter, and upon this rock I will build my church; and the gates of hell shall not prevail against it. And I will give unto thee the keys of the kingdom of heaven: and whatsoever thou shalt bind on earth shall be bound in heaven: and whatsoever thou shalt loose on earth shall be loosed in heaven."

And yet clearly the terms *kingdom* and *church* are not entirely synonymous. The simplest way of distinguishing them is that while the *kingdom* describes the mediatorial rule of Christ and the sphere in which He exercises it, the *church* describes the people of God. "The Church is the fellowship of men who have accepted the offer of the kingdom, submitted to its rule, and entered into its blessings." (G. E. Ladd)

2

Mark
The Divine Worker

Mark describes Christ the Worker, the Servant of Jehovah.

◆

It is a Gospel of constant movement and fast-moving

◆

events that calls us to see in what Christ did

◆

irrefutable proof of who He is.

Mark is the briefest of the Gospels. Yet in some ways it is the fullest of the four. If you were to set down the entire contents beside those of Matthew you would find that Mark is little more than half the length of Matthew. However, if you were to omit all sermonic passages and retain only those passages that detail the activities of Christ, you would find that Mark is considerably the longer Gospel. It is a wonderful book to read. It is a little book full of vivid touches. It supplies little phrases here and there, little marks about an incident that make it live, and that give this book the quality and intimacy of an eyewitness account.[†] Mark is the Gospel of constant action. Its key word is *immediately,* sometimes rendered *anon, straightway, forthwith.* In all, it occurs some forty times in this Gospel. It indicates that in the Gospel of Mark we have a veritable explosion of divine activity and of Christ at work.

This emphasis is not accidental. There is good ground to believe that the theme of the book is Christ the Worker or Christ the Servant. All the details of Mark coincide with this picture. As a matter of interest let me point out three of them. In Mark there is no genealogy of Christ. Here there are no wise men from the East looking for the King of the Jews. There are no angels with their choirs filling the skies. There is no incarnation narrative. The other three Gospels start on remarkably different notes from Mark. This Gospel omits the imposing truths with which the others commence because it is the Gospel of Christ the Servant Worker.

Then, interestingly, throughout the Gospel of Mark there is almost no reference to people addressing Christ as Lord. In chapter 1 Mark tells us of a leper saying, "If thou wilt, thou canst make me clean" (v. 40). When Matthew recounts the same incident he quotes the leper as saying, "Lord, if thou wilt, thou canst make me clean" (8:2). Mark's omission is in keeping with the overall tenor of his Gospel.

It is also interesting that in Mark alone among all the Gospels there is a strong emphasis on the hands of Christ. The other Gospels mention the hands of Christ, but Mark makes repeated reference to them. This is another indication that the theme of this Gospel is Christ the Worker. These are just some of the many features that lead to the view that Mark presents Christ the Servant or the Worker.

The prophecy of Isaiah also has the Servant of the Lord as a major theme. All the Gospels appeal to the prophecy of Isaiah and particularly to the great section on Christ the Servant of the Lord. There is,

---

[†]Many scholars take Mark to be Peter's Gospel penned under his instructions by John Mark. This theory has much to commend it and would account for the internal evidences that this Gospel is an eyewitness account of the events recorded.

however, a peculiarity about Mark's reference that sets it apart from the others. Matthew, Luke, and John use Isaiah 40 to prove that Jesus is the promised Messiah. Mark goes somewhat further. He shows that Isaiah's message of the Servant of the Lord is the gospel of Jesus Christ the Son of God. In other words, the Son of God is Isaiah's predicted Servant. Having said that, it is noteworthy that through the rest of this Gospel of Christ the Servant there is no further reference to Isaiah's Servant of the Lord. That may seem strange. The reason may well be that the two books are dealing with the subject of Christ the Servant from two very different aspects. In Isaiah the prophet presents the divine glory of the Servant to prove the value of His work. Mark, on the other hand, uses the works of Christ to prove the divine glory of His person.

The whole Gospel of Mark may be summed up in one simple sentence: Look and see what Christ has done and be convinced of who He is. That is what we are going to do. We are going to examine this message of Mark: **what Christ did proves who He is.**

THE APPEARANCE OF THE DIVINE WORKER

Let us start in chapter 1 with the appearance of the divine Worker. "The beginning of the gospel of Jesus Christ, the Son of God" (v. 1). Mark commences without any preamble. In the opening verses he immediately proceeds to make a powerful fourfold statement about Jesus Christ.

He is the Son of God (v. 1).

He is the Lord (v. 3).

He is the One mightier than John the Baptist (v. 7).

He is God's beloved Son (v. 11).

This is the Person about whom the whole book is written. Keep that fourfold statement in mind—Jesus Christ is the Son of God, the Lord, the One who is mightier than John the Baptist, and the One who is God's beloved Son. Now see what Jesus says in Mark 10:45, where He calls Himself the Son of man: "The Son of man came not to be ministered unto, but to minister, and to give his life a ransom for many." This is the essence of the gospel. This is why Mark says that this is "the beginning of the gospel of Jesus Christ, the Son of God." The fact that God became man, that the Almighty came down to earth as a worker to procure our salvation by His life and death, is what makes the gospel the glorious message it is. According to Isaiah, the Servant of Jehovah is Himself Jehovah. God's Servant is God Himself manifested in the flesh. The Gospel of Mark expounds the same marvellous mystery. It is the Son of God, the second Person of the trinity, who comes as the divine Servant to perform the work necessary to save sinners. This is what constitutes the gospel, and that is what Mark proceeds to prove.

THE ACTIVITY OF THE DIVINE WORKER

Mark is the Gospel of action. It is a book of constant movement. It records more than twenty miracles, many of which deal with casting out demons. The very first miracle of the Lord Jesus recorded in Mark is the casting out of an unclean spirit. The chapters that follow continue this emphasis. Thus Mark provides a perfect commentary on 1 John 3:8, "For this purpose the Son of God was manifested, that he might destroy the works of the devil." His Gospel is all about Christ destroying the works of the devil. Travelling throughout Galilee, Christ assailed the strongholds of hell and with His mighty word cast out devils. His powerful hand released the souls and lives of men and women from Satan's grip.

Think again of the words of Mark 10:45, "The Son of man came not to be ministered unto, but to minister [that is, to serve], and to give his life a ransom for many." In many ways, that is the key verse of Mark. It supplies a perfect division of the book. John Phillips analyses the Gospel of Mark in this way. He suggests that the book falls into two parts, corresponding to the two parts of this key verse. The first part deals with Christ giving His life in service. The second part deals with Christ giving His life in sacrifice.

He gave His life in service. As we study Mark's Gospel, we discover something wonderful about the Lord Jesus. He always had time, He always had grace, and He always had power to meet every human need. That is a sight of the Saviour we need to recapture today. We are living in a busy world. We are busy people. This is a gospel about busy-ness. It portrays the Lord Jesus in constant action. Yet in the midst of all His activity and busy-ness, He always had time for the needy. He always had a word of grace for the guilty. He always had power to exercise on behalf of those who were defeated by Satan and sin. Call to mind again the first miracle in Mark. It was the casting out of the unclean spirit from a man in the synagogue. That sets the tone for the entire Gospel. Christ has power over Satan. Let us ponder this vision of the mighty Christ, the divine Worker whose energy, power, ability, and authority are absolutely sovereign over every power of the devil and of hell. Mark sets this vision before us in many places.

One of my favourite chapters is the fifth chapter. It presents a three-fold manifestation of the power of Christ in His dealings with people in extreme need. The chapter opens with the story of the deliverance of the demoniac of Gadara. Before Jesus met him he ran wild and naked, possessed and polluted by Satan. Then the Saviour came and with a word set him free. The people were amazed when they found the erstwhile demoniac sitting, clothed and in his right mind. Christ defeated the devil and delivered the demoniac, who was depraved and dominated by him.

Then He healed the woman with the issue of blood. That poor woman was defiled and despairing. She was shut off from the privileges of the temple because of her ongoing defilement. Her life was in ruins. Her body was drained of strength. Earthly physicians could do nothing. Her condition grew constantly the worse. Then one day she met with Jesus. He cleansed her defilement and cured her despair in an instant.

Finally, in Mark 5 we read of Jairus's daughter, laid low in death at the tender age of twelve years. Depravity and domination by the devil are one thing, defilement and despair are another thing, but death is more terrible than either. The old saying is, "Where there is life there is hope." For man, death spells the end of hope. But not for the Lord Jesus Christ. In Jairus's daughter there was no life, but there was still hope because the divine Worker came to her. The Almighty God who came to earth to serve men burst the bonds of death by the power of His Word. He commanded, "Damsel, I say unto thee, arise," and she arose.

These examples from the fifth chapter are just three of the many we could cite to show that the first part of this Gospel deals with Christ giving His life in service. In Acts 10:38 Peter summed up the Saviour's entire gospel ministry in the words, "Jesus . . . went about doing good." As we read the Gospel of Mark (which is probably Peter's gospel), we see Christ constantly moving from place to place, from need to need, from sinner to sinner, and from crisis to crisis. Peter's words certainly capture the mood of His constant movement.

Yet in this Gospel of constant movement the Lord Jesus was never too busy to take time with needy or despairing souls. In chapter 10 we read of Him setting His face like a flint to go to Jerusalem. As He went on His way He met blind Bartimaeus at Jericho. The crowd had no time for that poor man. They expected Jesus to have no time for him either. They could not have been more wrong. "Jesus stood still, and commanded him to be called" (10:49). He came to serve in His life. So He took time to call and to heal the blind beggar. He is still the same. He still is constantly moving from person to person, from place to place, and from crisis to crisis. However, in all His mighty activity the Son of God always has time to stand still with a poor, darkened, benighted soul. Here is a word of hope for every poor sinner for whom the busy people of the world have no time. Though men dismiss them with hardly a thought, the Son of God will hear their cry. He is still the mighty Worker who has both the power and the heart to deliver the needy souls of men.

Mark records not only how Christ gave His life in service but how *He gave His life in sacrifice.* That is the theme of the second part of the book. He set His face to go to Jerusalem and to Jerusalem He went.

There He gave His life a ransom for many. Here is the supreme service of Christ. Theologians call the service of His life His active obedience. They call the service of His death His passive obedience. Both His life of service and His suffering sacrifice combine to present Christ as the divine Worker working out our salvation. That was His great activity.

THE ATTESTATION OF THE DIVINE WORKER

We must now see the use to which Mark puts all this. He employs the evidence of Christ's works to establish the identity of the divine Worker. The works of Christ made men see Him for who He really was. They forced them, at least on certain occasions, to confess Him as the Son of God. Remember that Mark said He was the Son of God, that God Himself spoke from heaven identifying Him as the Son of God, and that Jesus confessed Himself to be the Son of God. Clearly the deity of Christ is meant to be a major theme in this Gospel. It is with this in mind that we should note the effects of Christ's works.

In Mark 1:24 we read that the unclean spirit said, "I know thee who thou art, the Holy One of God." Verse 34 tells us that the devils knew Jesus to be the Son of God. Chapter 3:11 records how the unclean spirits, when they saw Him, fell down before Him and cried, "Thou art the Son of God." According to 5:7, the legion who possessed the demoniac of Gadara recognized Him as "Jesus, thou Son of the most high God." The nature and power of Christ's works forced the very demons to confess that He was the Son of God. Throughout His life His works elicited the same glorious and powerful testimony that He was the Son of God.

When we pass from His life to His death we find that He called forth the same testimony. Standing by His cross, the Roman centurion attested the fact of His deity: "Truly this man was the Son of God" (Mark 15:39). Surely, never man lived like this Man, and never man died like this Man.

Reading all these testimonies to the person of Christ on the basis of His mighty works, with demons and pagans uniting in recognition of Him, we may be tempted to think that the irrefutable evidence of Christ's divine person and mission had won the faith and worship of all who met or heard Him. Certainly there was no excuse for any to doubt Him. Sadly, however, despite all the clear proofs of who He was, and despite all He had done, He was hated and rejected.

THE ANTAGONISM TO THE DIVINE WORKER

The Lord Jesus drew attention to a critical time in the development of men's attitude to Him: "He began to teach them, that the Son of man must suffer many things, and be rejected of the elders, and of the chief priests, and scribes, and be killed" (Mark 8:31). That marked a turning point. From that point the antagonism to the Lord Jesus took a new direction. In reality the antagonism was there throughout His entire ministry. From the start He had suffered the opposition of the devils. Now He showed that those men who were under the control of Satan would go the whole way with their hatred and put Him to death. Here is a truth we would do well to remember. The world would rather forfeit the benefits of the ministry of Christ than bow before Him and acknowledge Him as Lord. That is true even of many people who attend the preaching of the gospel. They know the pardon which He alone can give and which He generously offers. They know the blessing of grace, the peace of mind, the cleanness of conscience, the assurance of eternal life, the open door to heaven, and the salvation from hell that Jesus gives to all who receive Him as Saviour and Lord. Yet they are willing to forgo all these blessings and benefits rather than to acknowledge Christ as Lord. That is the very same wicked antagonism to Christ that we find in the Gospel of Mark.

Throughout Mark we meet this continuing theme of confrontation. Here is an interesting thing. The first nine chapters show Christ fighting demonology. During that time He was in Galilee. After chapter 9 there is not one recorded instance of Christ casting out a devil. During that time He was in Judaea. Why should there be such a difference? The answer is that despite all its apostasy and all the wickedness of the scribes and Pharisees, Judaea was still the seat of the temple. It was still the place of the reading and exposition of the law. Jesus Himself acknowledged this. He said that the Pharisees sat in Moses' seat. Though they themselves were hypocrites, fools, and blind guides, the Word of God retained its authority and power to bless and protect. That protective power is well illustrated in the stark contrast in demonic possession in Galilee and in Judaea. Galilee, far removed from the influence of the temple—"Galilee of the Gentiles"—a place from which it was difficult even to journey down to the annual national feasts in the temple, was a hotbed of demonism. In contrast, Mark does not record one case of demonism in Judaea. That is not to say that Judaea was completely free of the plague, but there was a vast difference between the sin of Galilee and the sin of Judaea. The gospel gives a protective power even to a place like Judaea, with its apostasy. That is not to minimize the sin of Judaea; rather the opposite. Despite all the Lord's protection, Judaea rejected His Son. So while the nature of the opposition was different, Jesus faced confrontation in Judaea just as much as He did in Galilee. In Galilee He fought demonology, and in Judaea He fought apostasy.

Not only did demons and apostates oppose Him. Even His friends and His family were antagonistic. "His friends . . . went out to lay hold on him: for they said, He is beside himself" (Mark 3:21). Who were those friends? Verse 31 may supply the answer: "There came then his brethren and his mother, and, standing without, sent unto him, calling him." From this it appears that even His mother's faith wavered. That is why the Lord Jesus replied to the information that His mother and brethren were seeking Him with the question, "Who is my mother, or my brethren?" (v. 33). They had come to take Him home, charging, "He is beside Himself." That illustrates just how deeply sinners' antagonism to Christ ran. Even those who had shared His home, witnessed His sinless life, and heard His words of incomparable wisdom repeated the devil's lie, "He is beside Himself."

That antagonism, a constant theme in Mark, ultimately led to the crucifixion. That was the final step of the ceaseless opposition that met the Saviour. In procuring His death, men and devils combined to give the most glaring exhibition of their implacable opposition to "Jesus Christ, the Son of God."

THE ACCOMPLISHMENTS OF THE DIVINE WORKER

Despite all the opposition of men and devils, the Lord Jesus Christ fully accomplished what He set out to do. His work was a complete success. First, *He conquered every power of hell.* What an encouragement that is for us who are called to live for God in a day of increasing demonic activity! In a day when the whole world—its government, media, and culture—appears to lie in the lap of the wicked one, and when even the churches of Christendom have fallen into apostasy, we may be tempted to despair. But let us never lose heart. Jesus Christ is the same yesterday, today, and forever. He still breaks the power of sin and of Satan. He still defeats every power of hell. He is still the mighty Conqueror who can set men free from the destructive dominion of Satan and sin.

Second, *He meets the needs of the whole man.* The Gospel of Mark recounts how He cast out devils and healed bodies, minds, and souls. He made people right with God and with one another. He gave them power to live in this world and prepared them for eternity. He met the entire need of the entire man. He still does that.

He has presented to God the perfect ransom for His people. In the shedding of His blood He has satisfied divine justice on behalf of sinners and purchased their reconciliation and redemption.

Then *He rose again from the dead* in the body in which He was crucified. Finally, *He ascended into heaven.* That is how Mark concludes. He points us to the ascended Christ (16:19). See what this means. The Lord Jesus Christ is still the Servant. He is indeed glorified, but He is still serving His people. On earth He gave His life in service and in sacrifice.

Now in heaven He is interceding at the right hand of God.

Accordingly, Mark 16 emphasizes the glorious truth that the risen *Christ protects His people:* "These signs shall follow them that believe; in my name shall they cast out devils; they shall speak with new tongues; they shall take up serpents; and if they drink any deadly thing, it shall not hurt them; they shall lay hands on the sick, and they shall recover" (vv. 17–18). These verses have been sadly abused by fanatics. In the heat of argument we are all too likely to miss their true significance. They do not set forth the marks of every true Christian. They rather state the powerful protection the risen and ascended Christ affords to His people. Mark starts off in chapter 1 with Jesus Christ being driven by the Spirit into the wilderness to be tempted of the devil. He was surrounded by wild beasts and assailed by all of Satan's guile and power, but He conquered. In chapter 16 Mark ends with Christ's people going out into the world as His servants. They are going out into the wilderness where they will be surrounded by wild beasts and noxious serpents. They will be assailed by Satan as their Master was. But He protects them and empowers them.

Christ empowers His people to preach His gospel. Mark finishes with this glorious statement: "They went forth, and preached every where, the Lord working with them, and confirming the word with signs following" (v. 20).

This Gospel starts with Christ working on earth for men. It finishes with Christ working from heaven through men. What a wonderful climax to the Gospel of Christ the Worker!

The Lord of glory has condescended to become a servant in life and in death to save us from the slavery of Satan and sin. He alone has power to save. That is because He alone is incarnate deity. What He did proves who He is.

Luke
To All Men, A Saviour

Christ is the light of the world and the glory of Israel.

♦

The major part of this book deals with His

♦

activities to show the reach of His love for sinners

♦

of every kind, especially the outcasts, the poor,

♦

and the hopeless.

*F*rom many points of view the opening sentence of Luke's Gospel is remarkable and important: "Forasmuch as many have taken in hand to set forth in order a declaration of those things which are most surely believed among us, even as they delivered them unto us, which from the beginning were eyewitnesses, and ministers of the word; it seemed good to me also, having had perfect understanding of all things from the very first, to write unto thee in order, most excellent Theophilus, that thou mightest know the certainty of those things, wherein thou hast been instructed" (1:1–4).

Luke starts off his book by emphasizing his *message:* "Those things which are most surely believed among us." The words "most surely believed among us" literally mean, "the things which are fulfilled, confirmed, or assured." That is the message that Luke intends to emphasize throughout this Gospel.

Then he speaks of his *method* in writing. His method is to "set forth in order" the details of his message. Scholars hotly dispute which of the synoptic Gospels—Matthew, Mark, and Luke—adheres to an exact chronology in those places where they adopt a different order of events. It should be obvious from all our studies so far that the Gospel writers did not bind themselves by the modern laws of biography. It was not their intention to write a biography. They were writing by inspiration, and each of them received a unique aspect of Christ's ministry to record. Each organized his material in the light of that peculiar purpose. Luke alone says that he is setting down his material "in order." That means "in detail," and not only in detail, but with the details set forth in their proper sequence. This is his method.

His *motive* in writing was that Theophilus might "know the certainty" of the things wherein he had been instructed.

The implications of these observations are very clear. Each of these points opens up a vast field of study. We can give only a brief treatment here. From a theological standpoint this is a very important passage of Scripture. It makes it clear that apostolic teaching depends on the historical reality of the events surrounding the person and ministry of the Lord Jesus Christ. That is easily said. For many years a certain class of theologians has led people astray in their search for what they term "the historical Jesus." They hold that the Gospels do not portray the historical Jesus. They say that Matthew, Mark, Luke, and especially John, are not historical in nature. They invite us to abandon the Evangelists and to follow their newly invented schemes as they try to manufacture a history of Jesus. Any theologian who speaks of going beyond Scripture to find the historical Jesus is not a Christian but an infidel. The Gospels present the history of Christ. The doctrines of the Bible do not stand apart from the history it records. The Neo-Orthodox movement holds that either the Gospels are not historically true or it does not matter whether they are historically true or false because God does not reveal Himself in the facts of biblical history. The only thing that matters is the doctrine. This is a betrayal of the gospel. Gospel doctrine stands on gospel history. If the history is untrue we would be foolish indeed to believe the spiritual, moral, and doctrinal deductions that are taken from that flawed history. Apostolic teaching depends on the historical reality of the events recorded in the Gospels.

According to these opening verses of Luke, these events occurred in fulfilment of the Word of God. "Those things which are most surely believed among us" are believed because they are things that God has confirmed and fulfilled among us. God has spoken and acted to fulfil His Word. The events recorded in the gospel are utterly confirmed. They are not a matter of human opinion. Whatever form of literary or psychological criticism may be applied to the Gospels, if it is employed honestly, it will always yield the conclusion that here we are dealing with truth. Here we are dealing with divinely confirmed fact. Thus we are absolutely sure of the truth of what we believe. We believe what the gospel says because it is true.

Think of that. That means that the Lord Jesus Christ is all that the gospel declares Him to be. It means that He did all that the gospel declares He did. It means that Jesus Christ is where this gospel declares He is and that He will return to do what this gospel declares He will return to do.

In these opening verses Luke obviously means to stress the importance of the gospel message he is about to unveil. The question is, what exactly is the message that Luke introduces in such imposing terms? We have seen that each of the Gospels has its own particular theme, its own peculiar aspect of the doctrine of Christ. Matthew's message is of the King and His kingdom. Mark's is the Gospel of the divine Worker. Luke's theme is different again. It is established fairly early in the book.

Four Hymns of the Incarnation

The opening chapters of Luke's Gospel exhibit certain unique features. For instance, here alone among the Gospels we find the four hymns that surround the advent of the Lord Jesus Christ. In Luke 1:46–55 we have Mary's *Magnificat,* "My soul doth magnify the Lord." The theme of the *Magnificat* is God's promise to Abraham and to Israel fulfilled in Mary's virgin-born Son (vv. 54, 55). In 1:68–79 we have Zacharias's *Benedictus,* "Blessed be the Lord God of Israel." Its theme is the redemption of Israel by Christ, the "horn of salvation . . . in the house of his servant David," according to the covenant God made with Abraham. In 2:10–14 angels sound God's praise at the birth of Christ, the *Gloria in Excelsis Deo:* "Behold, I bring you good tidings of great joy, which shall be to all people. For unto you is born this day in the city of David a Saviour, which is Christ the Lord.... Glory to God in the highest, and on earth peace, good will toward men." In 2:29–32 we have Simeon's *Nunc Dimittis:* "Lord, now lettest thou thy servant depart in peace, according to thy word: for mine eyes have seen thy salvation, which thou hast prepared before the face of all people; a light to lighten the Gentiles, and the glory of thy people Israel."

The Message of Luke

Note the progress in these songs. Mary sings about the promise to Abraham and Israel. Zacharias sings about the redemption of Israel. The angels sing about a Saviour for all men. They sing about peace, not only in Israel but on earth, and about good will, not only toward Jews but toward all men. Simeon's theme is that in Christ salvation is prepared for all men. He is a light to lighten the Gentiles and He is the glory of Israel. These four songs encapsulate the message of Luke. It is a message of covenant faithfulness, redemption, grace, and peace. It is a message of good will from God to men, both Jews and Gentiles. Simeon's words go to the heart of the message of Luke: **Christ is the light of the Gentiles and the glory of Israel.** That is the great theme of Luke.

The Message Confirmed by the Genealogy of Christ

All the details of the book go to confirm this central message. Like Matthew, Luke has a genealogy of the Lord Jesus Christ. Matthew's genealogy is through the line of Joseph, who was the legal, though not the biological, father of the Lord Jesus Christ. Luke's genealogy is that of Mary, the virgin mother of Jesus. In Matthew, where the emphasis is on Christ the King of Israel, the genealogy goes back through David to Abraham and stops there. In Luke, however, it goes through David and Abraham back to Adam. That is because Luke is not a message addressed to the Jews only but to the Gentiles as well.

The Message Confirmed by Christ's Statement of His Mission

The Lord Jesus established the same point when He made His first public statement of His mission. "The Spirit of the Lord is upon me, because he hath anointed me to preach the gospel to the poor; he hath sent me to heal the brokenhearted, to preach deliverance to the captives, and recovering of sight to the blind, to set at liberty them that are bruised, to preach the acceptable year of the Lord" (Luke 4:18, 19). His hearers in Nazareth were glad to receive such a word, as long as it was limited to their Jewish nation. However, the Lord Jesus immediately showed them that God's sovereign, electing purpose extended His grace to the Gentiles. He reminded them that there were many widows in Israel in the days of Elijah but that God did not save one of them. The only widow the Lord delivered was a Gentile in Zidon. Next Jesus referred to the ministry of Elisha. There were many lepers in Israel in Elisha's day, but the Lord did not deliver one of them. However, He healed a Gentile leper, Naaman the Syrian. Though the people of Nazareth were so offended at this reminder of biblical truth that they tried to murder Him, our Lord was determined to make this fundamental point: He came to save both Jews and Gentiles.

Christ's Emphasis on the Scope of His Mission

As Luke's account proceeds it shows that while Christ did great works among the Jews He continued to lay specific and special emphasis upon His inclusion of the Gentiles. Luke is the only Gospel that records the parable of the good Samaritan (chap. 10). When He healed ten lepers and only one of them came back to thank Him, the Lord pointed out that the grateful one was a Samaritan. The point is clear: while He showed great grace and favour to the Jews, He emphasized that His gospel went beyond the Jews and reached to the Gentiles. He made sure that the disciples He commissioned as His ambassadors grasped that truth. Just before His ascension, He "opened . . . their understanding, that they might understand the scriptures, and said unto them, Thus it is written, and thus it behoved Christ to suffer, and to rise from the dead the third day: and that repentance and remission of sins should be preached in his name among all nations, beginning at Jerusalem" (Luke 24:45–47).

That is what the Gospel of Luke is all about. It is the message of Christ, the Saviour of the world. The words of Luke 2:10–11 could well stand as the theme of the entire book: "To all people . . . a Saviour."

Analysis of Luke

A simple yet comprehensive overview of Luke's outworking of this theme would be as follows:

1. The Saviour's Advent (chaps. 1–2)
2. The Saviour's Activities (chaps. 3–21)
3. The Saviour's Atonement (chaps. 22–23)
4. The Saviour's Ascension (chap. 24)

We have already noted how the songs at Christ's advent expound the central theme of the book. We have also seen that the Saviour interpreted His atonement in His final instructions prior to His ascension as a work of grace for all nations (24:47). The bulk of material in this Gospel details His activities. These activities combine to teach us a wonderful truth: the love of Christ reaches to sinners of every kind. In this book there is a special emphasis on Christ reaching out to the outcasts, the poor, and the hopeless. Additionally, Luke, above all the other Gospels, lays a particular emphasis upon the women whom Jesus reached with His grace. This is yet another evidence that He refused to be bound by the religious conventions of the day but was determined to bring His grace to people of all kinds. This fact will become indisputably clear as we consider the people whom Christ saved and delivered, as recounted in the Gospel of Luke.

THE PEOPLE CHRIST SAVED

In chapter 7:36–50 Luke records how the Lord Jesus visited the house of Simon the Pharisee. Though he had invited the Saviour to join him in a meal in his home, Simon did not extend to Him the normal courtesies. He did not wash His feet or give Him a kiss of welcome. During the meal, a woman of the streets—a fallen, immoral, wretched creature whom Simon heartily despised—came with an alabaster box of ointment. She washed the Saviour's feet with her tears, wiped them with her hair, kissed them, and then anointed them with her precious ointment. Simon was disgusted. He would never have allowed such a creature to touch him, and he could only guess that Jesus accepted her homage because He was ignorant of her true character. He could not have been more wrong. The Lord Jesus Christ welcomed the fallen woman, and when she went out of His presence she was a fallen woman no longer. Thank God, she was gloriously saved. What a picture of the Lord Jesus Christ! How we need to recapture it! Instead of turning our churches into comfortable little clubs for people who are too delicate to touch the world of lost sinners, we need to remember that Christ "receiveth sinners" (Luke 15:2).

In chapter 8:2 we read that there were certain women whom He delivered from evil spirits and infirmities. One of them was Mary Magdalene, out of whom He cast seven devils. She was another poor woman who had in some way come under the awful power of Satan. Despite the popular notion that Mary had lived an immoral life, there is no evidence of this in Scripture. However, anybody who has come under the possession and control of the devil and his legions is in a sorry, ungodly, and most miserable state. When Mary Magdalene entered the presence of Christ her life was wrecked and dominated by Satan, but the Lord Jesus cast the devils out. He healed her of her infirmities and cleansed her from every Satanic power and influence. That is the Christ we still proclaim today.

We have another great example of the reach and power of Christ's love in His release of the demoniac of Gadara (8:26–39). This man was an outcast whose only home was among the tombs. He was a shattered and broken man, separated from home and loved ones, until Jesus came and set him gloriously free.

Immediately after that narrative there is the story of the woman with the issue of blood (v. 43). She was another shattered soul, another hopeless case. Having spent all in a futile quest for deliverance, she had nothing to give to Christ. But, praise God, He had everything to give to her. He healed her in an instant. That day life began anew for her because the Lord Jesus Christ had time for a poor outcast.

There is a third outstanding example of Christ's grace to the poor and needy in chapter 8. Jairus's daughter lay dead (v. 49). She represented the ultimate in human powerlessness and need. However, she was not beyond the reach of Christ's power. With one word He raised her.

In chapter 16 we read the story of Lazarus and the rich man. Lazarus lay outside the gate of the rich man's house, a beggar. Though the world despised him and dismissed him with table scraps and dog licks, the Saviour bestowed rich grace on Him and sent His angels to bear him triumphantly to heaven.

Luke 17 recounts the cleansing of the ten lepers we have already mentioned. Those lepers were outcasts. They had to cry, "Unclean! Unclean!" any time they might come near to uninfected people. We may get some sense of the public's fear of them from reactions to the modern AIDS epidemic. Nowadays most doctors play down the danger of infection through random contact with AIDS victims. However, we recall the furor when a doctor with the 1992 Australian Olympic squad objected to the inclusion of an American basketball player who was infected with the AIDS virus. That doctor felt that that player placed all those playing around him at serious risk. Imagine the terror if all doctors gave the same warning. It is not difficult to envisage how anyone with AIDS would then become an outcast, an object of loathing and fear. That was exactly the case with lepers in ancient times. No one would touch them. But the Lord Jesus did not shun them, and when He met these ten broken, wretched sufferers He instantly healed them and sent them on their way rejoicing.

In chapter 18 we read of the blind beggar at Jericho who cried, "Son of David, have mercy on me" (v. 39). The Son of David heard his cry. In chapter 19 we read of His gracious treatment of Zacchaeus the publican. Zacchaeus was the most despised and hated man in the area, and understandably so. As a tax collector he was in the employ of the Roman forces that occupied his land and oppressed his people. He was part of a tax agency that bled the people for personal gain. In the eyes of his countrymen he was an odious character, a traitor to his people. A man cannot sink much lower than Zacchaeus. He was not only small of stature, he was mean of spirit. Then Jesus came: "This day is salvation come to this house." Zacchaeus received Him and was instantly transformed. He was no longer a mean-spirited publican, but a man of genuine godliness and generosity. Jesus had saved him.

There is one final example of Christ touching the untouchable with His grace in the Gospel of Luke. It is the story of the conversion of the dying thief, and only Luke records it. All the Gospels tell how Christ on the cross was the object of bitter scorn and mockery. Even the thieves crucified on either side of Him joined in the chorus. However, Luke records that when one of these malefactors railed on Christ, the other, who had previously done the same himself (see Matt. 27:44), was smitten with conviction. To his companion he said, "Dost not thou fear God, seeing thou art in the same condemnation? And we indeed justly; for we receive the due reward of our deeds: but this man hath done nothing amiss. And he said unto Jesus, Lord, remember me when thou comest into thy kingdom" (Luke 23:40–42). The reply of the Lord Jesus was immediate and gracious: "Verily I say unto thee, to day shalt thou be with me in paradise" (v. 43). Even on Calvary, amid the unspeakable agonies of the cross, the Lord Jesus Christ was still saving the outcast.

As we consider the people in this Gospel whom Jesus saved we are brought to realize that He is the Saviour of real sinners. We need to have that truth grip our hearts. There is hope for the hopeless. There is cleansing for the most filthy. There is deliverance for the most depraved. We tend to become discouraged by the wickedness of our society. Too quickly, we conclude many sinners to be hopeless cases and we give them up. Jesus is the Saviour of sinners. We can go to the neediest of souls with the sure message of grace. We have a message even for those whom men cast off as useless and hopeless. It is the message Luke was at pains to record: the Lord Jesus Christ receives sinners. The Pharisees of Christ's day did not like that fact. The Pharisees of our day still do not like it, but it is nonetheless true. "This man receiveth sinners."

The same gospel truth is presented in the parables Christ told. Think again of the parable of the Good Samaritan (Luke 10:30–35). A man on the road down to Jericho was overtaken by thieves who robbed him, beat him, and left him for dead. Two very religious Jews came upon him but "passed by on the other side." Then came a Samaritan who "had compassion on him," tended to his needs, and lodged him at his expense in the inn until the poor man recovered. That parable tells the gospel story in a nutshell. For people who are cast down, kicked about, robbed, beaten, left for dead, and on the verge of destruction, here is the gospel. It is not a Samaritan who has come to our rescue. It is the Son of God. He has shown compassion. He has done the work. He has paid the price. He does not pass needy sinners by on the other side. He does not leave them to perish. He has the love, time, interest, and power to save even the most abandoned of men.

The parable of the great supper (Luke 14:16–24) makes that point with unmistakable clarity and solemnity. Jesus told of a man who made a great supper and invited many guests. "Come; for all things are now ready," his servants instructed those guests. They did not want to hear about the feast and refused to attend. Then the master said, "Go out quickly into the streets and lanes of the city, and bring in hither the poor, and the maimed, and the halt, and the blind." His servants did so, but still there was room. "And the lord said unto the servant, Go out into the highways and hedges, and compel them to come in, that my house may be filled." Once again, therefore, this Gospel draws our attention to Christ's concern to bring the poorest and neediest of people into the enjoyment of His gracious provision.

In chapter 15 He tells three parables, two of which are found only in Luke. They are the parables of the lost sheep, the lost coin, and the prodigal son. It is important to realize that our Lord told these parables in response to the Pharisees' complaint, "This man receiveth sinners, and eateth with them" (v. 2). In effect, Jesus said, "I do not merely receive sinners. I go after them. I seek them and when I find them I cause rejoicing in heaven. They may be worthless in your sight, but to Me they are as valuable as a sheep to its shepherd, silver to a housewife, or a son to his father. I love those sinners you despise, and I save them."

The Saviour returns to this theme in chapter 18 with another parable, this time of a Pharisee and a publican. Both men went up to the temple to pray. The publican was obviously under conviction of sin. The Pharisee had no realization of his sin or of God's holiness. His prayer was one long boast of his own goodness. Any man who can boast before God of what he is and what he does is a fool and a sinner. While the Pharisee boasted, the publican stood afar off and would not lift up so much as his eyes unto heaven. He smote upon his breast and honestly prayed the greatest prayer a sinner can pray, "God be merciful to me a sinner." Literally, he was saying, "God be propitious to me a sinner—God be merciful to me on the merit of the atoning blood." Jesus said that that man went down to his house justified—yet another example of the people whom the Lord Jesus Christ saved.

THE PEOPLE CHRIST DID NOT SAVE

Equally significant in Luke's Gospel are the people whom Jesus did not save. He did not save the Pharisees.

In chapter 5 we read of an outstanding example of Christ's healing power. A paralytic man, whose condition was either caused or exacerbated by his sinful living, was brought to Jesus. The Lord forgave his sin and healed his body. The Pharisees were furious. "Who is this which speaketh blasphemies? Who can forgive sins, but God alone?" They were sitting in the presence of the Son of God and the power of God was present to heal. Yet all they could do was to criticize the Son of God. Even Simon, the Pharisee who invited Christ into his home, was affected with this bitter, critical spirit. He saw Christ transform the life of a fallen woman. Did it touch his heart? No. All he could do was self-righteously to condemn Christ for allowing a *sinner* to touch Him. This was the constant attitude of the Pharisees. In 11:37–38 we read, "As he spake, a certain Pharisee besought him to dine with him: and he went in, and sat down to meat. And when the Pharisee saw it, he marvelled that he had not first washed before dinner." Yet again, "It came to pass, as he went into the house of one of the chief Pharisees to eat bread on the sabbath day, that they watched him" (14:1). When He healed a man who had dropsy, the Pharisees found fault because He had done it on the sabbath day. What hypocrisy! It was fine for them to move their arms and legs on the sabbath day, but when the Lord Jesus restored that power to a poor sufferer, they labelled it as sin. We have already noted the attitude of those Pharisees who opposed Christ because He received sinners and ate with them (15:2). A Pharisee was too good, too pure, to do such a thing. He felt no need of mercy and could not bear the sight of Christ extending it to sinners.

So Christ did not save the Pharisees. They were so religious that they were doomed to perish. There are still people who are like Pharisees, so religious that they exclude themselves from the mercy of God. Pharisees, as long as they hold on to their religion of Christless self-righteousness, can never be saved.

Pharisees were not the only people Jesus did not save. He did not save triflers with religion.

In 20:20–22 we read, "They watched him, and sent forth spies, which should feign [literally, hypocritize] themselves just men, that they might take hold of his words, that so they might deliver him unto the power and authority of the governor. And they asked him, saying, Master, we know that thou sayest and teachest rightly . . . Is it lawful for us to give tribute unto Caesar, or no?" These people were doing what many continue to do today. They appear to have a question about the Bible, or about God, or about salvation. But they are trifling. They ask, not to find the truth, but to contradict the Bible, or to confuse some child of God. That is a very dangerous thing to do. To seek to find fault with God's Word, or worse, to try to use God's Word against itself, or to hinder the spiritual growth of His people, is the work of a cynical trifler. As long as men are trifling with the things of God they will not be saved.

There are other people who appear in this Gospel whom Jesus did not save. They are the lovers of wealth and of the world. In chapter 12 we read of a rich fool. He lived for what he had. He said to his soul, "Thou hast much goods laid up for many years; take thine ease, eat, drink, and be merry." God said to that man, "Thou fool, this night thy soul shall be required of thee: then whose shall those things be, which thou hast provided?" He did not save the rich fool.

In chapter 16 we read of another rich man. He fared sumptuously every day, surrounded by every earthly comfort. At his gate lay Lazarus, a poor beggar, hungry and in urgent need of physical attention. The rich man was much too busy enjoying his wealth to take much notice of Lazarus. The dogs of the street had more compassion on him than did the rich man. Then death came to both men. Lazarus died and went to paradise. The rich man died and went to perdition. Lazarus did not reach heaven because he was poor on earth. He got there by grace, for there is no other way. The rich man did not perish eternally because he possessed great wealth on earth. The real difference between the rich sinner and the poor saint does not consist in their financial position. It goes much deeper. As Matthew Henry put it, "The sinner makes gold his god, the saint makes God his gold." Here, then, is the second rich man mentioned by Luke whom Jesus did not save.

In chapter 18 we read of a third, perhaps the saddest case of them all. The rich young ruler was upright, moral, decent, and clean-living. Yet he went away from Christ sorrowful and still unsaved. Why? The Lord Jesus told him, "Yet lackest thou one thing: sell all that thou hast, and distribute unto the poor, and thou shalt have treasure in heaven: and come, follow me" (v. 22). The rich young ruler's response was tragic: "He was very sorrowful: for he was very rich." This young man wanted to have eternal life, but he wanted to have it on his own terms. He acknowledged God and His Christ, but he desired his wealth more than he desired the Lord. He was willing to do what he thought were good works to gain heaven. He was not willing to turn his heart from his gold and set it upon Christ. He left Christ a very dejected sinner, rich in goods but poor toward God. Jesus did not save him.

Christ saves some and does not save others. While we must acknowledge the sovereignty of God in this, we should also take note of this truth: none of the saved is saved because of his own merit. Everyone who is lost is lost because of his own sin. That sounds a note of hope and also of warning.

OUR RESPONSE TO THE MESSAGE OF LUKE

What should our response be to Luke's message that Christ receives sinful men? We should take it seriously. He receives sinners. That means we should cast away our pride, our hope in ourselves. We should give up our boasting of who we are, what we have done, how much we have gained, and how much we have accomplished. We should humbly take the sinner's place before Christ. We should come to Him as Mary Magdalene came, as the ten lepers came, as the demoniac of Gadara came. All who come to Christ as any of these sinners came will find that He still receives sinful men.

If, however, we trifle, or act the Pharisee, or make the world and its wealth our idol, we will find that Jesus will reject us.

This is a message to be taken seriously. Merely knowing the word is not going to save us. In this Gospel the Lord Jesus lays a very strong emphasis on discipleship. He says that if we will not take up our cross, if we will not forsake all for Him, we cannot be His disciples (Luke 14:26, 27, 33). So our first response to this message should be to take it seriously.

If we have taken it seriously and have received salvation from Christ, our response to this message should be to carry its light to those who need it most. We are never more like our Master than when giving His gospel to perishing souls. If we are ever to emulate Christ's evangelism, there is another way in which we must emulate Him. Luke speaks much of Christ in the place of prayer (3:21; 5:16; 6:12; 9:18, 28; 11:1; 22:41–44). It is no coincidence that the record of Christ's public activity stands side by side with that of His private intercessions. Public service without private prayer is mere presumption. We must be like Christ in prayer before we can be like Him in reaching the lost and needy. If we are ever to carry the message of Christ crucified to a lost world we must receive the anointing of the Holy Spirit in power as our Saviour did. The only place we will receive the power of the Spirit is in earnest prayer.

Thus our response to Luke's message should be to pray and remain praying until God gives us power for service. Indeed, Luke concludes his narrative by quoting Christ's command to His disciples to wait prayerfully for the power of the Spirit: "Ye are witnesses of these things. And, behold, I send the promise of my Father upon you: but tarry ye in the city of Jerusalem, until ye be endued with power from on high" (24:48–49). The Lord has made us His witnesses. Those who have personally experienced the love and power of Christ are the best possible witnesses to others in need. Who could have spoken of the mighty power of Christ to break the bondage of demonic powers like the demoniac of Gadara? That is why Jesus sent him home to his friends to tell them of the great things the Lord had done for him. No one could gainsay such a witness. The same thing is true of every other Christian. Let us then go and tell what we know, what we have experienced and are continuing to experience of the grace of God in our own lives. But to do it, we need His power. "Tarry . . . until ye be endued with power from on high." That is what the disciples were doing when Luke's continuation of this narrative, the book of Acts, commences. They were waiting on God and they continued to do so until the Holy Ghost finally came upon them on the day of Pentecost. Then, in the power of the Spirit, these witnesses went forth to win the world for Christ. They blazed a trail across the nations and saw the gospel established in the hearts and homes of multitudes.

Here, then, is the message of the Gospel of Luke: Christ is the light of the Gentiles and the glory of Israel. Christ is the Saviour of sinners of every kind. Let us take this message seriously and then carry it to Jew and Gentile in the power of the Spirit of God.

4

John
The Glory Of God Incarnate

The eternal Son of God became a man and declared

◆

His Father's glory by exercising His grace and truth,

◆

that is, by His incomparable works and by His

◆

incomparable words.

*T*he first three Gospels—Matthew, Mark, and Luke—are usually called the synoptic Gospels because they give a synopsis of the ministry of the Lord Jesus Christ from the same general viewpoint. The word *synoptic* literally means "with the same vision," or "with the same eyes." So while Matthew, Mark, and Luke each has his peculiar theme, they all combine to present Christ's humanity. They declare His offices and work as the Man who is our Saviour, though of course each bears some very distinct testimony on the deity of Christ. However, the general emphasis in the synoptics is on Christ our Saviour in the offices and work that He fulfilled as a man.

The Gospel of John, however, is altogether different. From its very first words it is obvious that this Gospel approaches the subject of Christ and His ministry from a very different standpoint. In the synoptics the emphasis is on the true humanity of the Saviour. In John the emphasis is on the true deity of the Saviour. Thus, whereas Matthew carries a genealogy of Christ that goes back to Abraham and Luke records one that goes right back to Adam, John dispenses with a genealogy altogether. He makes the eternal union and communion of the Son with the Father his starting point. "In the beginning was the Word, and the Word was with God, and the Word was God" (1:1). That sets the tenor and establishes the theme of the entire Gospel of John.

Every feature of this fourth Gospel contributes to the constant statement of this testimony. For example, John's Gospel records only seven incidents covered by the first three Gospels: the work of John the Baptist, the feeding of the five thousand, Christ walking on the water, the anointing of Christ at Bethany, the Last Supper, the passion of Christ, and the resurrection of Christ. Everything else in the book is unique—for example, the interview with Nicodemus; Christ's self-revelation to the woman at the well of Sychar, when He said, "I that speak unto thee am he [the Messiah]"; the healing of the man at the pool of Bethesda; the discourse on the Bread of Life; the great statements on the last day of the feast of tabernacles, "If any man thirst"; and the series of Christ's great "I am" statements. In addition to all this unique material, John uses a host of very significant words that either are unique to him or, if not unique to him, are very much more prominent here than in the other Gospels. Note, for example, John's use of such words as *abide, believe, Father, finish, judge, know, light, life, love, truth, verily,* and *world.* What the Holy Spirit is doing with the unique emphasis of the book is to declare that Jesus Christ is God manifested in the flesh. That is the grand purpose of John's Gospel.

The entire doctrine of the Gospel is summarized in the prologue. This is John's Gospel in embryo. Its great theme is "the Word," the *Logos,* the essential self-expression of eternal deity.

The opening eighteen verses of John present the following sevenfold revelation of the Word:

1. The *eternity* of the Word: "In the beginning was the Word" (v. 1). There never was a time when He *became* the Word. He is the eternal Word.

2. The *personality* of the Word: "The Word was with God . . . . The same was in the beginning with God" (vv. 1, 2). Here is a reference to the mystery of the trinity. The Word is not the Father. Though one in essence, they are distinct trinitarian Persons.

3. The *deity* of the Word: "The Word was God" (v. 1). The order of the words in the Greek text is careful to teach the true deity of the Word while making sure we do not confuse Him with the Father. "The Word was God" means that "in the beginning," that is, eternally, the Word is truly and essentially God.

4. The *activity* of the Word: "All things were made by [or, through] him; and without him was not any thing made that was made" (v. 3). He is the creative Word upon whom all creation depends. He is not a creature but the divine Creator.

5. The *glory* of the Word: "In him was life; and the life was the light of men" (v. 4). This statement could not be made of a creature. It refers to the One who is truly God.

6. The *victory* of the Word: "The light shineth in darkness; and the darkness comprehended it not [that is, overcame it not]" (v. 5).

7. The *identity* of the Word: "The Word was made [became] flesh, and dwelt among us, (and we beheld his glory, the glory as of the only begotten of the Father,) full of grace and truth" (v. 14). The Word is the Son of God who took flesh and came into the world to reveal His Father (v. 18) and bring grace to us in all its saving fulness (v. 16).

Verse 14 is the key. "The Word was made flesh, and dwelt among us, (and we beheld his glory, the glory as of the only begotten of the Father,) full of grace and truth." Thus, the central theme of John's Gospel is **the glory of God incarnate.**

THE MYSTERY OF THE INCARNATION

"The Word became flesh." Paul later called this "the mystery" of the incarnation: "Great is the mystery of godliness: God was manifest in the flesh" (1 Tim. 3:16). That is a very appropriate term. The incarnation is a truth that is far beyond the comprehension of man. We could never have discovered it. We receive it purely by divine revelation. Even then we cannot plumb its depths. Here we stand in awe before the glorious mystery that He who is eternally God became flesh. John shows us both elements in the complex person of Christ: His humanity and His deity.

He very clearly presents a Christ who is truly man. He describes Him as "wearied with his journey" sitting by the well of Sychar (John 4:6). He shows Him weeping at the grave of Lazarus (11:35).

Equally clearly, he presents a Christ who is truly God. He ascribes all the attributes of deity to Him. The fundamental attribute of deity is aseity: He has life in Himself. God's life is not a derived life. Creatures have life that is derived. God has life that is essential, eternal, and underived. He has life in Himself. The Lord Jesus Christ ascribed aseity to the Father and to Himself: "As the Father hath life in himself; so hath he given to the Son to have life in himself" (5:26). Once again we have a reference to the mystery of the trinity and to the relations of the Persons in the trinity, but the main point of this text is that Christ has life in Himself. That is true of none but God. Throughout John's Gospel there is a forceful demonstration of the omniscience of Christ. Almost every chapter presents evidence of this. For example, chapter 1 shows His divine knowledge of Nathanael. Chapter 2 tells us He "needed not that any should testify of man: for he knew what was in man" (v. 25). Chapter 3 records His divine knowledge of Nicodemus and of "heavenly things" (v. 12). Chapter 4 tells how His knowledge of the woman at the well of Sychar brought her to repentance and led her to call others to Him with the testimony, "Come, see a man, which told me all things that ever I did: is not this the Christ?" (v. 29). It is an omniscient Christ John portrays, and omniscience belongs to deity alone.

John also stresses the omnipotence of Christ. He records eight sign miracles that show absolute power and thus prove His deity:

1. Turning water into wine at Cana in Galilee (2:1–11).
2. Healing the nobleman's son in Capernaum (4:46–54).
3. Healing the impotent man at the pool of Bethesda (5:1–9).
4. Feeding the five thousand (6:1–14).
5. Walking on the sea (6:16–21).
6. Giving sight to the man born blind (9:1–38).
7. Raising Lazarus from the grave four days after his burial (11:17–45).
8. The miraculous draught of fishes (21:4–11).

All of these were performed as signs, divine proofs of Christ's deity. They show omnipotence in operation. In many cases they reveal true creative power. The turning of water to wine, the feeding of the five thousand, and the gift of sight to the man born blind were all acts of creation in the strictest sense. They are witnesses to Christ's omnipotence and therefore to His true deity.

Another divine attribute ascribed to Christ is equality with the Father: "Therefore the Jews sought the more to kill him, because he . . . said also that God was his Father, making himself equal with God" (5:18). This is not merely a human conclusion from Christ's words but His intended meaning, as we have already noted in quoting verse 26.

Here is the mystery of the incarnation. The Lord Jesus Christ is truly man but truly and absolutely God. Yet He is not two persons. He is not God humanized or man deified. The mystery of the incarnation is revealed but not explained. God the Son, the second Person of the eternal trinity, took into a union with Himself a true humanity, both body and soul. Being God and man in one Person, He is the perfect Redeemer, the only Saviour.

THE MEANING OF THE INCARNATION

Looking again at the prologue, we find the meaning of the incarnation: "The Word was made flesh, and dwelt among us" (v. 14). The word *dwelt* means "tabernacled"—He tabernacled among us. That is a most instructive verb John used. The tabernacle was God's dwelling place in the midst of Israel, the place where He covenanted to meet with His people. By this means they could approach Him and could enter into the joy of pardon through the atoning blood of the sacrifice. The tabernacle had seven major furnishings which declared God's purpose in erecting it. It was a great rectangle lying east to west, with the gate always looking eastward. Immediately inside the gate was the brazen altar, and beyond that the laver. Then came the tent of the congregation with its two compartments separated by the veil. The first was the holy place, and the second was the holy of holies. Inside the holy place, on the right side, stood the table of shewbread, and on the left side the golden candlestick. In the middle just before the veil was the golden altar of incense, while beyond the veil in the holy of holies was the ark of the covenant, over which was the mercy seat. There is a complete correspondence between the tabernacle and the Gospel of John.

We enter through the gate to this Gospel as the Jewish worshipper would have entered through the gate to the tabernacle. The first thing we see is the brazen altar: "Behold the Lamb of God, which taketh away the sin of the world" (1:29). There is no approach to God except through Christ's blood atonement. That is the message of the tabernacle, of John, and of the entire Bible.

The next piece of tabernacle furniture is the laver, which, as Paul tells us in Tit. 3:5, signifies "the washing of regeneration," literally, "the laver of regeneration." We are not left to guess what the laver means. It speaks of washing, first in regeneration, and then in sanctification. In John 3 Jesus spoke of this spiritual laver as He taught Nicodemus the truth about the new birth. "Verily, verily, I say unto thee, Except a man be born of water and of the Spirit, he cannot enter into the kingdom of God" (v. 5).

After the altar and the laver, the next piece of furniture in the tabernacle was the table of shewbread. It signifies that spiritual food which Christ described when He referred to Himself as "the bread of life" (6:35): "I am the bread of life: he that cometh to me shall never hunger; and he that believeth on me shall never thirst." Christ is the true spiritual food.

He is also the source of true spiritual illumination, fulfilling the type of the golden candlestick. Thus He said, "I am the light of the world" (8:12). In the very next chapter He demonstrated His illuminating power when He gave sight to the man born blind.

The golden altar spoke of intercession with God. That is the type. We find the antitype in John chapter 17, where the Lord Jesus Christ, the great High Priest, enters into the presence of God and prays for all His people.

The final piece of tabernacle furniture was the ark beyond the veil. The ark speaks of Christ, in whom the law of God is perfectly fulfilled. When Moses received the tables of the law from the Lord he smashed them on discovering Israel's idolatry. Then the Lord gave him two more tables, which He told him to place inside the ark (Deuteronomy 10). The ark was therefore the only place on earth where the law remained unbroken. It was a beautiful type of our sinless Saviour, who fulfilled the law in all its parts. That is why He could cry from the cross, "It is finished" (John 19:30).

On the ark was the mercy seat, or the "propitiatory," the type of acceptance at the throne of grace on the merit of Christ's blood. After His resurrection Jesus said to Mary Magdalene, "Touch me not [literally, do not be holding on to me]; for I am not yet ascended to my Father: but go to my brethren, and say unto them, I ascend unto my Father, and your Father; and to my God, and your God" (20:17). Paul expounded this in Heb. 9:12: "By his own blood he entered in once into the holy place, having obtained eternal redemption for us." On that basis we have entrance and acceptance at the throne of God: "Seeing then that we have a great high priest, that is passed into the heavens, Jesus the Son of God, let us hold fast our profession. . . . Let us therefore come boldly unto the throne of grace" (Heb. 4:14, 16).

What is the meaning of the incarnation? The meaning of the incarnation is that Christ tabernacled among us. He is God's true tabernacle for His people. In Him is the atonement. In Him is regeneration and sanctification, spiritual food, illumination, and access to God. In Him there is a perfect justification, and in Him there is acceptance at the throne of grace. It is all in Christ. In Him there is life and salvation. Out of Him there is nothing but death, condemnation, and destruction.

THE MAJESTY OF THE INCARNATION

The majesty of the incarnation is that it is the manifestation of the glory of incarnate deity. John said, "We beheld his glory." This was something that meant a great deal to the apostle John, something he always remembered. He referred again to it as he started his first epistle: "That which was from the beginning, which we have heard, which we have seen with our eyes, which we have looked upon, and our hands have handled, of the Word of life; (for the life was manifested, and we have seen it, and bear witness, and show unto you that eternal life, which was with the Father, and was manifested unto us;) that which we have seen and heard declare we unto you, that ye also may have fellowship with us: and truly our fellowship is with the Father, and with his Son Jesus Christ" (1 John 1:1–3). Notice the emphasis on witnessing, seeing, hearing, beholding, manifesting, and showing.

John says, "We beheld his glory." He beheld that glory not only with his physical sight, but with the perception of spiritual sight and faith. In this spiritual sense every Christian can bear the same testimony as John. Though we have never seen Christ in the flesh, we can say with Paul, "We see Jesus" (Heb. 2:9). This is a real sight. What we see by faith is not less real than what we see with our physical eyes. In fact, Peter says that what we see by faith is much more certain than what we see with our eyes. Our eyes can deceive us; our ears can deceive us. But faith cannot deceive us, for it perceives what God has revealed. Peter says, "We . . . were eyewitnesses of his majesty. For he received from God the Father honour and glory, when there came such a voice to him from the excellent glory, This is my beloved Son, in whom I am well pleased. And this voice which came from heaven we heard, when we were with him in the holy mount. We have also a more sure [or, confirmed] word of prophecy; whereunto ye do well that ye take heed, as unto a light that shineth in a dark place, until the day dawn, and the day star arise in your hearts" (2 Pet. 1:16–19). Do not miss the full force of the apostle's words here. The Word of God which we can grasp by faith in Jesus Christ is more dependable than the evidence of our physical faculties.

Therefore we also can say, "We beheld Him." How were we saved? We beheld Christ. That is how we were saved. How have we triumphed in every type of difficulty? By beholding Christ. How have we received strength to go on? By beholding Christ. What is the constant exhortation of Scripture? It is "Behold Christ; turn your eyes upon Christ; seek after Christ." This is the constant exhortation and emphasis in the Word of God. Christianity is real. It is not a mere theological history or philosophy. If our Christianity consists only of book knowledge, it will not save us. A saving knowledge of the gospel is not the same as learning a proposition of Euclid or a theorem of Pythagoras. It includes an intellectual grasp of necessary theological propositions, but it goes far beyond it. True Christianity is real. Beholding Christ is real. Having the glory of God dawn upon you is real. Having your life suffused with the life, the person, and the work of Christ is real. That is what we mean by the statement, "We beheld his glory."

"We beheld His glory." We beheld the glory of His person. We beheld the glory of His absolute perfections. We beheld the glory of His passion. I use that word deliberately. To the eyes of the flesh there is nothing glorious in the passion of Christ. The cross was one of the ugliest scenes that the world has ever seen. The Saviour's face was so marred as no longer even to look human (Isa. 52:14). Physically there was no beauty in the cross, but spiritually there is all the beauty of eternal deity in it. There we see God satisfied, the sinner reconciled, the law fulfilled, condemnation removed, atonement made, and, thank God, salvation purchased. We have beheld the beauty of Christ's passion. We also beheld the beauty of His power—power over sin, over Satan, over death; power for time and for eternity.

Here, then, we have the manifestation of the glory of God incarnate. It is manifested in order to give us two things, certainty and fellowship with God. That is why Christ was manifested, that we might know that we have eternal life and that we might have fellowship with God. Oh, that God today would show us something of that glory! Let us not go from this place today without praying the prayer of Moses, "O Lord, I beseech Thee, show me Thy glory."

THE MERCY OF THE INCARNATION

The Lord Jesus Christ is "full of grace and truth." *Grace* speaks of His works, and *truth* speaks of His words. Obviously those are not absolute divisions. Grace is apparent in His words as truth is in His works. Nevertheless, the phrase "full of grace" refers chiefly to Christ's works, while "full of truth" refers chiefly to His words.

Let us think of Christ's works as implied in the phrase "full of grace." First, we see His gracious works in the eight great sign miracles recorded in John's Gospel. The other three Gospels record some of Christ's miracles, but John's Gospel describes His miracles as *signs.* That is the reason for the selection of the particular miracles included in this fourth Gospel. They are signs, that is to say, evidences or proofs that Jesus Christ is God manifested in the flesh. We have already listed these eight sign miracles. Each of them provides proof that Christ is the sovereign Lord of creation. These miracles cover all areas of contingency, all the areas where events beyond human control may occur.

Christ is God incarnate, and He makes every area of contingency subject to His absolute authority. Everything that exists depends on His sovereign will and power. That is what the sign miracles of Christ testify. No mere man could ever do the things our Saviour did. However good his intentions, however strong his will, every man in the world is absolutely bound by the laws of nature. In contrast, the Lord Jesus Christ came and demonstrated that He governed the laws. That is the testimony of His sign miracles. He is the sovereign Lord of all. He has all power. Yet the beauty of the gospel is that in the exercise of His power He did not come to destroy us. He came to save us: "God sent not his Son into the world to condemn the world; but that the world through him might be saved" (3:17).

Christ's eight miracles show us the areas of life in which we need to experience His power. Think of them again. The turning of water to wine at the marriage in Cana of Galilee reminds us that we need Christ in the home. We need Christ in our marriages. Like the nobleman, we will need Christ's touch on our children. Like the man at the pool of Bethesda, in the times of our own great weakness we will need the mighty power of Christ to give us strength. We will also need spiritual sustenance and satisfaction. Only Christ will be able to give that to us and break the bread of life to us. There will be times when we are caught in the storms of life and we will need One who can walk on the top of the billows and say, "Peace, be still." We will need Him to illuminate our soul in times of darkness and to show us His resurrection power in times of death and bereavement. We will also need His power for service, if we are to have any success in doing His work. It is interesting that His last sign miracle recorded by John was the draught of fish. Matthew and Mark tell us that when He called the disciples He said, "I will make you fishers of men." With the account of the miraculous draught of fish John finishes the story. As a farewell gesture the Lord Jesus gave the disciples a great assurance of His sovereign power working with them. They had fished all night and had caught nothing. Then at the Saviour's command they cast their net "on the right side of the ship" (21:6). He filled it with a miraculous draught of fish. What He said to them by that miracle was, "I have called you to be fishers of men. It is a work you cannot accomplish by human effort or skill. I am sovereign. I can and I will fill the gospel net." That is the final sign miracle of Christ.

All eight miracles testify to Christ's person and clearly demonstrate His purpose of mercy. So also do His gifts. There are eight references to Christ's gifts in John's Gospel:

1. The water of life (4:10).
2. The Good Shepherd's life given for the sheep (10:11).

3. The Master's example of service given to His disciples (13:15).
4. The Comforter, the Holy Spirit, given to abide with God's people (14:16).
5. The peace of Christ (14:27).
6. The very words of God (Greek, r*hema)* given to Christ's disciples (17:8).
7. The Word of God (Greek, *logos)* given to them (17:14).
8. The glory given by God to Christ given by Him to His disciples (17:22).

It is noteworthy that Christ's first gift is the gift of grace, and His last is the gift of glory. In addition He gives everything we need between grace and glory. What mercy there is in the incarnation!

Christ's sign miracles declare His grace, and His gifts declare His mercy. There is an even greater work that demonstrates His mercy, and that is the work of Calvary. The Gospel of John is insistent on this theme. "Behold the Lamb of God, which taketh away the sin of the world" (1:29). "For God so loved the world, that he gave his only begotten Son, that whosoever believeth in him should not perish, but have everlasting life" (3:16). "The good shepherd giveth his life for the sheep" (10:11). All these point us to the work Christ did on the cross where He accomplished our redemption. His cry "It is finished" (19:30) crowned the greatest exhibition of the mercy of God ever given to the world.

Christ is "full of grace," in His works, in His gifts, and in His death. He is also "full of truth." This focuses our attention on His words. Remember what the officers who were sent to arrest Him said: "Never man spake like this man" (7:46). They were right. The unique character of the words of Christ is a recurring theme of John's Gospel. In 7:16 Jesus says, "My doctrine is not mine, but his that sent me." In 14:6 He says, "I am . . . the truth." In 5:32 He declares, "There is another that beareth witness of me; and I know that the witness which he witnesseth of me is true." In 7:18 He claims to seek the glory of Him that sent Him and notes that this is a proof that He is true. In 8:14 He says, "My record is true," and in verse 16, "My judgment is true." This repeated emphasis is not accidental. One of the great lessons John's Gospel intends to teach us is that the words of Christ are true and divinely attested. We may summarize Christ's words recorded in John under five categories.

Significant Words

We have already noted some words that are unique to John or more prominent in this Gospel than in any of the others. Take the noun *love*. Greek literature does not use it, but John makes it one of the key words of his entire Gospel. What is the meaning of the incarnation? It is a demonstration of God's love. "God is love" (1 John 4:8). How do we know the love of God? "In this was manifested the love of God toward us, because that God sent his only begotten Son into the world, that we might live through him. Herein is love, not that we loved God, but that he loved us, and sent his Son to be the propitiation for our sins" (1 John 4:9–10).

Other significant words are *life* and *light.* These are the great results of God's love in Christ. How do we enter into life and light and the love of God in Christ? By *faith,* another key word in John's Gospel. So there are significant words in this Gospel. Ponder them carefully.

Sovereign Words

Twenty-three times in this Gospel Jesus uses that mighty statement of Exodus 3, "I AM." The "I AM" is a declaration of His absolute deity. He is Jehovah, and seven times He attaches to that "I AM" a glorious metaphor: "I am the bread" (6:35); "I am the light" (8:12); "I am the door" (10:7); "I am the good shepherd" (10:11); "I am the resurrection, and the life" (11:25); "I am the way, the truth, and the life" (14:6); and "I am the true vine" (15:1). These are sovereign words by which Christ claimed and established His true deity.

Saving Words

The words of Christ are wonderful words of salvation. Chapter 3 records His words to a Jewish ruler. What were they? First, He spoke a word about regeneration by the Spirit: "Ye must be born again," born "of the Spirit." Then He spoke a word about redemption by the blood: "As Moses lifted up the serpent in the wilderness, even so must the Son of man be lifted up; that whosoever believeth in him should not perish, but have eternal life" (vv. 14–15). There is God's word to a religious Pharisee, regeneration and redemption. As His interviews with two openly sinful women (chaps. 4 and 8) indicate, Christ's message to notable sinners was the same as He gave to Nicodemus. He presented to them the very same message of God's gift of gracious pardon. Chapter 7 records His invitation to the entire nation of Israel: "If any man thirst, let him come unto me, and drink" (v. 37). That is the gospel. That is the invitation. If you are a religious person you must be born again, you must be washed in the blood, for you are a sinner. If you are a poor fallen sinner, if you are as immoral as those two women, the Lord Jesus gives you the same message. The gift of God is offered to you, even eternal life through Jesus Christ our Lord. Whether you are religious or irreligious, Christ has words of salvation for you: "If any man thirst, let him come unto me, and drink."

Sympathetic Words

Chapters 13 through 17 tell us how the disciples were in a despondent mood. It was a difficult time for them, but the Lord Jesus came, sympathized with them, and strengthened them. He washed their feet (chap. 13), showing that *He serves and He sanctifies His people.* Furthermore, *He settles us and He sends us His Spirit* (chap. 14). *He selects us and sends us as His servants* (chap. 15). *He secures and He strengthens us* (chap. 16). Finally, in chapter 17 *He brings us within the veil.* He intercedes specifically for us and assures us of our arrival in glory. What a comfort the words of Christ bring to our hearts in every period of gloom and need. He still refreshes us, washes our feet, and prepares us for further steps in our Christian walk. He still knows how to speak the word that will settle our hearts and assure us of His Spirit's power to strengthen us and use us. There is still no voice like the voice of Jesus to speak sympathy and strength to God's people in the hard places of life.

Sustaining Words

Chapters 20 and 21 record Christ's words of revelation when He showed Himself alive to His disciples. They record His words of *reassurance* when He breathed on them and said, "Receive ye the Holy Ghost." They record His words of *restoration* when He spoke to Peter, "Lovest thou me? . . . Feed my sheep." Finally, they record words of His *return,* "If I will that he [John] tarry till I come, what is that to thee?" Christ's meaning was, "I am certainly going to return. In the meantime, whatever circumstances you may face, follow Me and keep your eye upon the certainty of My return."

So ends the message of John's Gospel. It commenced with Christ's first coming, "The Word was made flesh." It ends with Christ's second coming. Here are the two poles around which all the events of history revolve. At the first coming the cry was, "Behold the Lamb." That is still the call of God to every man, woman, and child. Soon the second coming will be upon us, and then the world will discover the meaning of the words of Pontius Pilate, "Behold your King."

"Behold the Lamb. . . . Behold your King." Everything in this book is calculated to turn your eyes upon Christ. John clearly states the fundamental purpose for writing this Gospel: "These are written, that ye might believe that Jesus is the Christ, the Son of God; and that believing ye might have life through his name" (20:31). Let us ponder deeply this record of the glory of God incarnate until God in His grace quickens our faith to behold His Son as our Saviour and our Sovereign.

C H A P T E R
5

Acts
Church Ablaze!

The Lord makes His church militant and triumphant

♦

in its witness for Christ by the power of the Holy Spirit.

♦

No power of men or devils can stop the progress of the

♦

gospel under the ministry of such Spirit-filled witnesses.

The book of Acts is well named. Though our Bible titles it "The Acts of the Apostles," many think that it should be "The Acts of the Holy Ghost Through the Apostles." Still others suggest that it would be better termed "The Acts of the Risen or Glorified Christ Through the Apostles." I think it was the Bantu translation of the Scriptures that titled it "Words About Deeds." In all these the idea of action is central, and I think that makes Acts a well-titled book, because from chapter 1 to chapter 28 it is a book of constant action.

Yet it is not a book of frenetic activity. We find no evidence here of mere busy-ness on the part of the early Christians—that is, doing things merely because they felt they must be doing *something*. Rather we find in this book that there was waiting before working. There was praying before preaching, and there was power before practice. Here we learn the difference between doing the business of the kingdom and merely being busy. We learn the value of waiting upon the Lord. Only through prayer can we obtain the power we need if we are to do anything of lasting significance for God. That is a primary lesson of the book of the Acts.

The action we see in this book is not primarily human. There is, indeed, abundant human endeavour. Mighty men of God do mighty works for God. However, in the book of Acts the activity we see is not primarily human, but divine.

This divine action flies in the face of all human conventions and wisdom. See how the Lord goes about the work. In chapter 1 the Lord Jesus Christ is about to launch a programme that will change the history of the world. Yet He starts in a private upper room with a little group of people, not one of whom has a scintilla of political or social standing in the world. Here is the first picture in the book: men alone with the Saviour. The lesson for us in the first chapter of Acts is clear: every great work of God commences in the private place, in our upper room with the Lord. The same lesson appears in the last chapter of the book. Placed under house arrest by the Romans, Paul is left alone, a prisoner of the state, but even more a prisoner of Jesus Christ. As the narrative closes, we see him alone with his Saviour.

In the body of the book we discover that God does not court the influence of the world's great capitols. He does not reveal His Word in the world's great temples. He does not work through the world's great armies. Rather, His focus is upon a people who are few and despised. They are opposed. They are persecuted. They are weak. But they are unstoppable. If ever any book of the Bible proved the principle of Zech. 4:6, it is the book of Acts: "Not by might, nor by power, but by my spirit, saith the Lord." God's work is not accomplished by human power or strength. It is not advanced by armies or vast numbers. It is carried on by the power of God's Spirit alone, through the instrumentality of His people.

The instruments the Lord used were His *chosen people.* Acts is one prolonged exposition of Paul's words in 1 Cor. 1:26–29: "For ye see your calling, brethren, how that not many wise men after the flesh, not many mighty, not many noble, are called: but God hath chosen the foolish things of the world to confound the wise; and God hath chosen the weak things of the world to confound the things which are mighty; and base things of the world, and things which are despised, hath God chosen, yea, and things which are not, to bring to nought things that are: that no flesh should glory in his presence."

They were a *prepared people.* Acts opens with the disciples in the school of Christ and, after His ascension, in the school of prolonged waiting on God. Then, after Pentecost, the new converts continued in the school of the apostles, learning their doctrine and practice (2:42). Nowadays we tend to be in too much of a hurry to launch ill-prepared people into ill-conceived schemes. The Lord wants us to be well prepared to serve Him according to His Word. One of the Bible's symbols of Christians in a state of blessing is the cedar tree. The cedar of Lebanon spends years putting down roots that run deep. Only when its roots are well established can it grow to its proverbial stature and strength. The same thing holds true for God's people. To grow strong and fruitful they must be "established in the present truth" (2 Pet. 1:12).

The people God used were a *Spirit-filled people.* Acts is full of references to this fact. Only after receiving power by the Holy Ghost coming upon them could Christ's apostles fulfil the great commission (1:8). The power of the Spirit, so wonderfully demonstrated on the day of Pentecost, was what made their ministry so successful. That is a truth we must not only believe but experience. Too many orthodox preachers and churches have all but abandoned the doctrine of the fulness of the Holy Spirit for fear of sounding like Charismatics. The position of the Charismatic movement has little or nothing to do with the apostolic experience of the fulness of the Holy Spirit. We must not allow any counterfeit to discredit the reality of the biblical doctrine. We can no more do the work of the gospel without being filled with the Spirit's power than the early church could. God used—and still uses—Spirit-filled people.

In Acts, the people He used were also *praying people.* Praying and being filled with the Spirit always go together. The Gospel of Luke reveals a twin emphasis in the ministry of the Lord Jesus Christ. First Luke emphasizes His prayer life, and second His experience of the power of the Spirit. These two things are inseparable. The people God used in Acts were a Spirit-filled people because they were a praying people, and they were a praying people because they were a Spirit-filled people.

They were also a *preaching people*. That was the great climax. Their preaching was the natural outflow of what God had done within them. Having come to know Christ, they felt the burden of reaching the world's lost for their Saviour. The love of Christ constrained them (2 Cor. 5:14). These were the people the Lord used.

Acts is the story of the conquests of the gospel. It is therefore a book of history. But it is much more than that; it is a book of working theology. It is a book of vision, a vision that encompassed the whole world. This book will expand our vision and stir us to serve Christ wherever there are sinners in need of His gospel. So the book of Acts is an ideal book for today. Then, as now, God's people were fascinated by the thought of Christ's return to set up His kingdom in Israel. "Wilt thou at this time restore again the kingdom to Israel?" they asked (1:6). The Saviour's answer is very illuminating: "It is not for you to know the times or the seasons, which the Father hath put in his own power [or, authority]. But ye shall receive power [or, ability], after that the Holy Ghost is come upon you: and ye shall be witnesses unto me both in Jerusalem, and in all Judaea, and in Samaria, and unto the uttermost part of the earth" (1:7–8). In effect He says, "The times and the seasons of God's prophetic programme are not in the realm of your authority. The Father holds them in His own hand. He has not given any of this authority to you. What He does give you, however, is ability to be My witnesses, not through any personal talent, but through the mighty power of the Holy Spirit filling you."

Three motifs that run throughout the book of Acts appear in 1:8—God's power, purpose, and programme for evangelism. Power is the enabling of the Spirit to witness effectively for Christ in the world. The purpose of the Spirit's power is clear: it is to make us Christ's witnesses in the world. All too often nowadays Christians are deceived into thinking that the purpose of the fulness of the Holy Spirit is to enable them to speak in tongues, or some such thing. Since John the Baptist did not speak in tongues, and the Lord Jesus Christ did not speak in tongues, we are left to conclude either that they did not have the Spirit's fulness (which we know is not true), or that the proof of the fulness of the Spirit is not speaking in tongues. Paul stated emphatically, "Tongues are for a sign, not to them that believe, but to them that believe not" (1 Cor. 14:22). It is even more obvious that the ecstatic effusions of the modern Charismatic and Pentecostal movements, which are not even distantly related to the biblical gift of speaking in foreign languages, are no sign of the power of the

Holy Spirit. The true purpose of the Spirit's power—and the proof of its reality—is effective witnessing to Christ in all His saving fulness.

The third motif that runs through Acts is God's programme for evangelism. Christ's witnesses were to start in Jerusalem and proceed to Judaea, to Samaria, and then to the ends of the earth (1:8). Chapter 2 records how the apostles began preaching in Jerusalem. Chapters 3–7 show the gospel spreading to all Judaea. In chapter 8 it reaches into Samaria and other areas. In chapters 13–28 it extends to the uttermost parts of the earth.

In some ways, the story of the extension of the gospel to the world is tinged with sadness, for it is the story of the cutting off of Israel because of her rejection of Christ. From a human perspective it may appear that the cause of the gospel in the world would have been greatly advanced if the Jews had embraced Christ. The apostles would not have had to struggle against the bitter opposition of their unbelieving countrymen all over the empire. However, this human perspective is flawed. Paul testifies in Rom. 11:12 that Israel's fall has actually brought rich benefits to the rest of the world. We can see that in operation in Acts. Jewish rejection of Christ and subsequent antagonism ensured that the apostles quickly reached out to the Gentiles. This sudden spread of the gospel meant that any effort, as by the sect of the Pharisees in chapter 15, to limit the gospel by Jewish nationalism was bound to fail. The gospel could never stagnate as a subset of Judaism.

Thus the story of Acts is one of positive development. Even the apparently dismal aspects of the story are in reality evidences of God's good and benevolent purpose. His programme was to reach the world, and He did.

God gave His Spirit to empower His people, to witness to the person and work of His Son, and so built His church, His kingdom, in the world. He has never withdrawn that gift. The Holy Spirit remains with the church and will do so until the consummation of the kingdom in the return of the Lord Jesus Christ.

The theme of the book of Acts, then, is that **the Lord makes the church militant and triumphant in its witness for Christ by the power of the Holy Spirit.** Acts develops this theme by making three basic points.

CHRIST'S MESSENGERS IN THE WORLD

The first point is that the church of Christ alone has the message the world needs. In the time of the book of Acts there were many voices clamouring to be heard. Various philosophies and religions asserted that they had the light. But none of them had the message the world needed. None of them had any word of hope for a poor sinner. Only the church of Jesus Christ had that, because God had given her the message. The message was a universal one, for the Jews, for the Gentiles, for the Barbarians, for the bond and for the free. It was a divine message with all the authority of heaven behind it. It was a Christ-centred message.

Having God's message, how could the apostles do anything but preach? Thus Acts is a book of great preaching. It records for us portions of some powerful apostolic sermons: chapters 2, 3, 7, 10, 13, 20, 24, 26, 28. Wherever the early Christians preached, the message was always the same: "The Lord Jesus was rejected by men and crucified. God raised Him from the dead. Therefore He is both Lord and Christ. In His name we preach the forgiveness of sins, full salvation by grace through faith without works." That was the message. Paul summed it up in chapter 20 verses 24–27: "But none of these things move me, neither count I my life dear unto myself, so that I might finish my course with joy, and the ministry, which I have received of the Lord Jesus, to testify the gospel of the grace of God. And now, behold, I know that ye all, among whom I have gone preaching the kingdom of God, shall see my face no more. Wherefore I take you to record this day, that I am pure from the blood of all men. For I have not shunned to declare unto you all the counsel of God."

Notice, by the way, that to the apostles to preach the gospel of the grace of God meant preaching the kingdom, and to preach the kingdom meant preaching the gospel of the grace of God. They knew nothing of the Dispensationalist dichotomy between the gospel of grace and the gospel of the kingdom. To the apostles the kingdom had come in Christ. They were already enjoying the kingdom in Christ, and they looked forward with the expectation that the kingdom would be consummated at His return. It seems a natural conclusion from 1:6–7 that they fully expected Christ to reign on earth after Israel has been regrafted into the olive tree of God's one indivisible church. Good men disagree on that point. Time will soon prove if this is accurate exegesis. In the meantime we need to stress again that it is not for us to spend our time speculating about times and seasons which God has reserved in His own authority. We are called to be witnesses to Jesus Christ. We have a message for the world. We are the only ones with a message for the world. Amidst the Babel of confusion that is all around us, we have the message the whole world desperately needs to hear. It is the old message of the gospel of Jesus Christ crucified and risen from the dead and able to save. That is the message. The early church preached it uncompromisingly. We need to learn their secret in this age that centres so much on man—man's rights, man's ideas, man's technology, man's ability, man's autonomy, man's power. We need to return to the focal point of Peter's first sermon in Acts 2: "the wonderful works of God" (v. 11).

In Acts, the preachers make no secret of their belief in God's sovereignty. On the one hand they preach human responsibility, but on the other they strongly assert the utter sovereignty of God: "Him, being delivered by the determinate counsel and foreknowledge of God, ye have taken, and by wicked hands have crucified and slain" (2:23). They especially relate this doctrine to their message of salvation. "As many as were ordained to eternal life believed" (13:48). That is why they had such confidence in the success of their message. They knew the strength of the opposition they faced. They fully recognized their own weakness and inability to overcome it. But they went forth with the assurance that God has a sovereign purpose to bring His ordained people to faith in Christ through the preaching of the gospel. Thus gospel preaching cannot fail because God cannot fail.

When God did His sovereign work He left no room for the pride of man. No apostle could lay claim to any secret method for achieving success, which he could then impart to lesser brethren in the church. That is the sort of thing men do today. Someone imagines he has discovered the secret of success in some area of service and before you know it he has formed an organization, or a seminar, with his superior stature looming large over the participants. The early church knew nothing of such things. Neither men nor methods received any glory or credit for the success of the apostles. In 3:9–13 they gave all the credit to the person, the work, and the merit of the Lord Jesus Christ. He alone received the glory.

The apostles preached the wonderful works of God, especially His greatest work, the sending of His Son. Therefore their message was Christ: "Lord and Christ" (2:36). He is "a Prince and a Saviour, for to give repentance" (5:31). "He is Lord of all" (10:36). This is the Christ they preached. To their sin-cursed age they proclaimed, "Through this man is preached unto you the forgiveness of sins" (13:38). That is the message the world still needs today. When you see people hurting, their hearts and their homes broken by sin, estranged from God and lying in the lap of the evil one, remember that this is the message they need. As Peter told Cornelius and his household, God is "preaching peace by Jesus Christ" (10:36). The world is vainly searching for peace. Politicians cannot provide it. Nor can economists, nor psychologists. The only people on earth who have a message of true peace are the people who know the Prince of peace, who paid the price of peace and who can establish the reign of peace in the lives of all who trust Him.

With that message the apostles set forth to evangelize the world. To such a message they demanded a response. Paul summarized his preaching in his farewell address to the Ephesian elders: "Testifying both to the Jews, and also to the Greeks, repentance toward God, and faith toward our Lord Jesus Christ" (20:21). Peter had demanded the same response on the day of Pentecost: "Repent, and be baptized every one of you in the name of Jesus Christ for the remission of sins" (2:38). Paul had told the Philippian jailer, "Believe on the Lord Jesus Christ, and thou shalt be saved" (16:31) and had boldly asserted the claims of the gospel to the Athenians: "[God] commandeth all men every where to repent: because he hath appointed a day, in the which he will judge the world" by the Lord Jesus Christ (17:30–31). This is the message the world needs, and the church of Christ alone has it.

THE OPPOSITION OF THE WORLD TO THE GOSPEL

The second point Acts makes to establish its theme is that the world obstinately opposes this message of the gospel. It shows how both Jews and Gentiles opposed it. The Jews opposed it because of their attachment to dead tradition. Stephen addresses this is 7:48–53. Speaking to the Sanhedrin he says: "Howbeit the most High dwelleth not in temples made with hands; as saith the prophet, Heaven is my throne, and earth is my footstool: what house will ye build me? saith the Lord: or what is the place of my rest? Hath not my hand made all these things? Ye stiffnecked and uncircumcised in heart and ears, ye do always resist the Holy Ghost: as your fathers did, so do ye. Which of the prophets have not your fathers persecuted? and they have slain them which showed before of the coming of the Just One; of whom ye have been now the betrayers and murderers: who have received the law by the disposition of angels, and have not kept it." In effect, Stephen says that though they loved the temple they were constant rejecters of God's truth. The Jewish leaders understood perfectly where he was going with his argument and stopped him immediately. The application was all too obvious: the real reason for their rejection of the Lord Jesus Christ was their attachment to dead tradition. In 24:6 Tertullus, the advocate the Jews employed against Paul, charges Paul with profaning the temple. To the Jews the choice was stark: the temple or Christ, tradition or the gospel. That is why they opposed the apostles' message.

Some of the Gentiles opposed the gospel because it undermined their heathen idolatry. For instance, in Ephesus a riotous mob yelled their defiance of the Christian message, crying, "Great is Diana of the Ephesians!" Other Gentiles opposed it because it insulted their heathen philosophy. Festus heard the doctrine of the resurrection. He was an educated man. He knew that dead bodies do nothing but decompose. So when he heard Paul preach that the Lord Jesus Christ had risen bodily the third day from the dead he cried, "Paul, thou art beside thyself;

much learning doth make thee mad" (26:24). His heathen intellectual-ism was insulted by the gospel. The same was true in Athens, the centre of worldly learning. Other Gentiles hated the gospel because it deprived them of their wicked gains. Acts 16 tells the story of the pythoness, the girl who was a Satan-controlled soothsayer. There were people who made money out of her Satanism, and therefore they did not like the gospel. Men and nations still oppose the gospel for the same reasons—dead religions, vain traditions, the teachings of the flesh, and the tyranny of greed. Those remain the crucial elements in the opposition to the gospel of Jesus Christ today. The church has the message. The world opposes it with all its might.

THE POWER OF THE SPIRIT

The final line of truth that Acts uses to establish its central theme is that the Holy Spirit's power overcomes the opposition of men, builds the church, and starts the cycle of the book all over again. Acts tells us how God gave His people the power of His Spirit to enable them to *preach with persuasion.* That is what we need today. Preachers today probably enjoy greater educational opportunity and greater access to the various tools of their trade (books, commentaries, lexical aids, etc.) than at any time in the past. Sadly, however, we cannot claim that preaching is in a healthy state in most churches. Christians complain of not being fed, except on a diet of empty words and cute stories. Many preachers never preach on the person and work of Christ, or on justifi-cation, the imputed righteousness of Christ, or any of the essential doctrines of the gospel. And many who do seem to do so in a dead, dry academic manner that is bereft of spiritual power. We need preachers like those in Acts, people who spent time alone with God, who waited before working, who prayed before preaching, and who received power before they tried to perform their ministry. The Holy Spirit gave His peo-ple power to preach with persuasion.

He also gave them power to *suffer with patience.* They needed that. That is an aspect of the work of the Holy Spirit that is greatly over-looked. He gave them, when they needed it, the power to *die in peace.* Did anybody ever die better than Stephen did? Acts 7:59–60 says, "They stoned Stephen, calling upon God, and saying, Lord Jesus, receive my spirit. And he kneeled down, and cried with a loud voice, Lord, lay not this sin to their charge. And when he had said this, he fell asleep." It is easy for us to read these words and miss the painful reality of the scene they describe. They describe a man being roughly thrown up against a wall. An enraged mob hurls great rocks at him. They smash sickeningly against his body. His bones are crushed. Gaping wounds appear; his blood flows; every muscle aches. His face is disfigured, his skull is crushed, and at last his life is extinguished. Yet through all of this Stephen never lost the angelic demeanour he had displayed at his trial. He was never more heavenly or Christlike than in the hour of his death. His last words were a prayer for his murderers: "Lord, lay not this sin to their charge" (7:60). How could he suffer and die like that? It was not by will power. It was not even by strength of character. Only the power of the Spirit of God could enable Stephen to die as he did.

We need that power today. Think of what the Holy Spirit did. He came upon a praying people. He brought three thousand people to Christ in a single day. He performed great acts of power that the world could not ignore. He gave very ordinary people boldness to stand true to Christ despite violent opposition. He brought more and more people to Christ every day. He opened the door to the Gentiles and won whole communities to the Saviour. He planted churches in every kind of place, including some very unlikely ones. Those new churches took root and bore fruit.

That is what God did, first among the Jews and then, increasingly, among the Gentiles. The gospel found the Roman empire pagan and it did three things: It evangelized it. It civilized it. It Christianized it. These are terms about which there is much dispute among Christians. Some deny that we should Christianize the nation. They say, "Evangelize, not Christianize." There are others who seem to do little evangelizing but who have very grandiose ideas about Christianizing the "culture," as they like to call it. Surely no Christian can really feel indifferent to the moral state of his nation. He cannot be anything but deeply grieved at the abominable practices that flourish with legal sanction, things such as the wicked perversions flaunted by sodomites and the mass killing of the unborn to fulfil a radical feminist agenda. It is right and proper for Christians to desire to see their nation civilized and Christianized. The point of the book of Acts is that we cannot accomplish those goals by political or social action. These have their place, but we can really change a society for good only if we set about it in God's way. Evangelize it, and the gospel will civilize it and Christianize it.

That is how God worked through the early church. It is still His way of working. When God through the gospel saves a person, He makes him a new creature in Christ. When He repeats that work in large numbers of cases, is it not natural that those multitudes of new creatures in Christ will radically affect their nation? Christians cannot be mere onlookers in the affairs of their nation. They have the God-given right and responsibility to exert an influence for God and for good among men. However, the great job of the church is not political or social action. We cannot

Christianize what we have not evangelized in the power of the Holy Spirit. It is only as the result of such evangelism that God's people will civilize and Christianize their society. Any time the church has tried to civilize and Christianize apart from the soul-saving results of Spirit-filled evangelism, it has become politicized and has lost its spiritual power.

The book of Acts is clearly a very appropriate book for today. God has never withdrawn the Holy Spirit from His church. He is still the Father's gift to fill His people with power, to bless their witness, and to overcome the attacks of the world and the devil. The entire cycle of waiting in prayer, being filled with the Spirit, going forth with the gospel, and winning the lost for Christ at home and abroad may still be the experience of God's people. We have the message. The world opposes it, but we have the Holy Spirit, whose power will fill us and make us His militant and triumphant witnesses for Christ.

Romans
God's Way Of Salvation

The gospel is the message of the free justification of

◆

sinners by the imputation of the righteousness of Christ,

◆

received by faith without works. Expounding this,

◆

Romans points the way of freedom from the guilt and

◆

power of sin and provides believers with spiritual

◆

motivation to serve the Lord with a desire for His glory.

The gospel had been spreading throughout the Roman world for some quarter of a century when Paul wrote this epistle. As it spread it had great success, and many Christian churches came into existence. Inevitably, with the spread and success of the gospel, many important questions arose among the new converts. For example:

If pardon and salvation are all of grace—if God freely, graciously pardons wicked men—what are we to believe concerning the righteousness of God? How can God be infinitely just and still pardon the ungodly?

Again, if salvation is by faith without works, does not the gospel destroy the law? And if that is the case, what are we to do with the words of the Lord Jesus, "I am not come to destroy the law, but to fulfil it"?

A third question arose. If the Gentiles are admitted to an equal standing before God with the Jews, does this not nullify the Lord's covenant with Abraham and his seed? Does the gospel therefore not imply that God has broken His covenant with Israel and cast them away? And if God has cast away that people with whom He entered into a covenant engagement, how can Christians be sure He will not cast them away, despite all the promises of the gospel?

Perhaps most pressing of all was the question, if salvation is all of grace without any law-works, and if grace superabounds over our sin (Rom. 5:20), will believers not be encouraged to live in sin? Will they not draw the logical conclusion that the more we sin, the more the grace of God will be glorified in pardoning our sin?

These were some of the questions that stirred the early church. Some people asked them in all sincerity. Others asked them in an effort to misrepresent the teaching of the gospel and confuse the saints. One way or another these were the questions that agitated the church, and they were the questions Paul set out to answer in writing the book of Romans.

In doing so Paul gives us the most formal, thorough, and logical statement of God's way of salvation in all the Word of God. An eminent man of letters called Romans "the profoundest piece of writing in existence." Martin Luther said that it is the chief book of the New Testament and that it deserves to be known by heart, word by word, by every Christian. A great Scottish preacher described it as "the charter of evangelical Christianity." The gospel is clear throughout the Scriptures. It is especially clear in the New Testament. However, its clearest exposition is set forth in all its many aspects and in all its multiple relations in the epistle to the Romans. Romans centres on the very heart of the gospel message of salvation, which is a free justification of ungodly sinners in the sight of a righteous God. That is the heart of the gospel.

Describing, defining, and expounding that message, this epistle relates the truth of justification to the historical facts of the birth, life, death, resurrection, and ascension of the Lord Jesus Christ. It presents Christ as the perfect Mediator. It emphasizes that all the blessings of justifying grace are through our Lord Jesus Christ: "Being justified by faith, we have peace with God through our Lord Jesus Christ" (5:1). Again and again Paul makes the point: Christ is the perfect mediator. Later he shows that as mediator He is the perfect covenant head of His people, so that in union with Him, the people of God possess a perfect righteousness and enjoy a perfect reconciliation with God. The apostle goes on to establish that the only means whereby the ungodly can actually receive this blessing of acceptance with God is by faith, without any admixture of their own merit. The only means of laying hold of salvation is by faith without works. That is the grand doctrine of the epistle.

As I have indicated, Paul had to answer some objections. Particularly he had to repel a very wicked misuse of his doctrine. Those who opposed his doctrine argued that since salvation is by God's grace through faith without works, and since that grace is magnified by justifying wicked and ungodly people, we may logically conclude that we are free to sin without restraint. Indeed, they insisted, thereby we will be glorifying the grace of God. To make it clear that that was a perverse misrepresentation of his doctrine, the apostle sets forth in detail the intimate relationship between our justification and our sanctification. He shows how the objective work of Christ, that is, what He did for us as our substitute and surety, inevitably leads to the work of the Holy Spirit subjectively within us. We cannot have one without the other. Thus justified men are debtors to grace, not to sin, to live in holiness through faith in the Lord Jesus Christ.

The apostle proceeds to show how this justification yields the peaceable fruit of assurance and gives us a solid basis for the truth of the eternal security of the saints. Finally, Paul shows that this gospel so questioned, so maligned, so despised by the Jews as something altogether new, is in fact the very gospel that is witnessed by the law and the prophets. It is the gospel that is set forth throughout the Old Testament Scriptures. According to Paul, God never had any other way of salvation for sinners. Abraham was justified by grace through faith. David was justified by grace through faith. Moses taught justification by grace through faith. Habbakuk the prophet taught justification by grace through faith. Isaiah taught justification by grace through faith. The apostle is at great pains, and he goes to great lengths, to show that this gospel, which was being so questioned by Jewish opponents, is not something foreign to the Old

Testament. On the contrary, it is the inevitable and logical consummation of the Old Testament revelation.

That is why Paul includes the profound section on Israel (chaps.
9–11), which so many commentators have had great difficulty relating
to the general theme of Romans. Many treat it as a parenthetical section. It is far from being parenthetical. Having demonstrated that the
Old Testament is the basis of his gospel, Paul goes on to show that
God's eternal purpose for Israel and for the church can be understood
only in the unity of the gospel of Jesus Christ. It is to misunderstand the
gospel to deny God's unbreakable purpose for Israel. To deny all distinction between the national (Old Testament) and multinational (New
Testament) bodies of God's people, so that all the Old Testament blessings on Israel are transferred to the church, but all the curses remain on
the nation, even when blessing and curse appear in the very same
verses, is to handle the Scriptures in an unwarrantable way. However,
while it is wrong to deny that Israel and the church in some sense are
treated distinctively in Scripture, Romans 11 shows that it is equally
wrong to divorce them eternally, to make them two elects, two essentially and eternally separate bodies, one a heavenly people and the other
an earthly people, as Dispensationalism does. Paul teaches something
very different. He pictures God's Old Testament and New Testament
peoples united in one olive tree, in one root, in one Saviour, and in one
salvation. God has a future for Israel. Romans 11 cannot be adequately
dealt with if we deny a future for national Israel. However, the glory of
that future is that Israel will be brought into the very blessings that
Christians now have in Jesus Christ. Their distinctive national future
should not obscure the truth that they will be brought back into their
own olive tree, the one into which we have already been grafted. This,
then, is the argument of the book of Romans.

This is a book with a vast scope. We will take the central theme,
which is **God's way of salvation.** We will set forth the theme of God's
way of salvation in four developing steps. We will first consider the heart
of the gospel, the truth of justification by grace through faith. Our second step will be to show that justification establishes our union with
Christ. Our third step will be to show that our union with Christ produces holiness of life. Finally, we will note that holiness of life fits us for
Christian service. These four simple points sum up the central teaching
of the entire book of Romans.

JUSTIFICATION BY GRACE THROUGH FAITH

Let us start at the beginning. The heart of the gospel is the truth of
justification by grace through faith in the Lord Jesus Christ. In Rom.

1:17 we read, "Therein [that is, in the gospel] is the righteousness of God revealed from faith to faith: as it is written, The just shall live by faith." We must pay particular attention to the expression, "the righteousness of God." It is a key to understanding the entire epistle to the Romans. What does it mean? It may mean God's attribute of righteousness, or justice. In 3:5 that is what it means: "If our unrighteousness commend the righteousness of God, what shall we say?" Again, 3:26 says that in the gospel God declares His righteousness that He might be just, or righteous, and the justifier of him who believes in Jesus. In these references "the righteousness of God" clearly refers to God's eternal attribute of righteousness or justice. However, that is not the case in 1:17. One moment's consideration will make that very clear. Faith in the mere fact that God is just will never save anybody. Never once in Scripture does the Holy Spirit tell us that by believing that God is just we will be saved. Those who embrace Christ as Saviour do believe God is just, but the object of saving faith is not the attribute of divine justice. Thus when Paul says that the righteousness of God is revealed from faith to faith, he is not speaking of the attribute of divine justice. Rather, he means "the righteousness which is of God"—a God-righteousness as distinct from a man-righteousness, the righteousness which God provides as the sole ground of acceptance with Him for all His people. As chapter 5 makes very clear, it is specifically the righteousness of Christ's perfect obedience in His life and in His death, which is imputed freely to, or graciously made over to the account of, all who believe in Him. That is what Paul means by the term "the righteousness of God."

The Righteousness of God

Many people imagine that Paul sets the righteousness of God, this God-righteousness, in contrast to man's sin. There is some truth in this, but the great truth of Romans goes much further. Paul contrasts the righteousness which is of God not only with man's sin, but also with man's righteousness. There is a great deal of spiritual pride in us all. It is very easy to look at certain kinds of sinners, some of whom are mentioned in Romans 1, and say, "Thank God I am not as they are." Without doubt, the righteousness of God stands in contrast with their awful wickedness, but that should not dull the conviction of our own sin. This book deals a death blow to the pride man takes in his own righteousness. It brings the self-righteous, self-satisfied religionist down into the dust and shows him to be as unclean and guilty, as vile, and as deserving of hell, as the poor, wicked heathens mentioned in the first chapter. This God-righteousness, then, stands against every attempt of man to make himself righteous in the sight of God.

It is called God's righteousness because its source is in God. It is all of grace. "Being justified freely by his grace through the redemption that is in Christ Jesus" (3:24). The word that is translated "freely" is translated in John 15:25 "without a cause." That is a beautiful thought. When God looks for a cause in us to justify us, He finds none. The cause of the righteousness that justifies us is in God Himself. He is the sole source of our justification. Therefore it is free to us. That is the major message of this epistle. Justification is free. Though it is free to us, it cost God everything, for it is "through the redemption that is in Christ Jesus." It does not come to us without the payment of a great price. It required the payment of the greatest price that heaven could afford, but it is free to us. We do not work for it, either before, at, or after our conversion. We do not help toward our justification. It is free. It is a gift bestowed by grace. Paul piles up strong words to make this point: we are "justified freely *by his grace.*" Free justification provided by free grace. The righteousness that is of God has its source in Him.

This righteousness satisfies God's attribute of righteousness, or justice. We see that in 3:26. God is just even while He justifies the ungodly. This gracious way of salvation, this "righteousness of God," does not in any way violate the character of God. It does not run contrary to His justice. Rather it fully and absolutely satisfies it. It satisfies God's justice, first, because it takes full note of man's sin, and, second, because it shows how Christ paid the penalty for that sin. Let us consider these truths carefully.

God's way of salvation satisfies His justice by taking full note of man's sin. This is not a way of salvation that goes light on sin. Romans 1 deals with the Gentile world and says, "The wrath of God is revealed from heaven against all ungodliness and unrighteousness of men" (v. 18). Notice carefully what the wrath of God is revealed against: "all ungodliness and unrighteousness of men." There is a view of sin today that is altogether too shallow. Sin is defined as merely acts of unrighteousness. But the apostle insists that the wrath of God is revealed against *ungodliness*—that is, the root of sin—and against *unrighteousness*—that is, the fruit of sin. In a peculiar way in this epistle Paul deals with how the gospel treats two very closely related things: *sins,* plural, and our *sin,* singular. The wrath of God is against both. The gospel, therefore, does not cover over man's sin by denying its existence or by denying that it is as bad as other Scriptures paint it. No, Romans 1 is every bit as devastating, perhaps even more so, in its description and denunciation of sin as Isaiah 1. Isaiah described Israel as a diseased body. From the crown of the head to the sole of the foot, there was no soundness in it, only wounds, bruises, and putrefying sores that had been neither mollified with ointment nor bound up. That is a picture of a total depravity. Romans 1 is just as plain in its denunciation of sin: "[They] changed the glory of the uncorruptible God into an image made like to corruptible man, and to birds, and four-footed beasts, and creeping things. Wherefore God also gave them up to uncleanness through the lusts of their own hearts, to dishonour their own bodies between themselves: who changed the truth of God into a lie, and worshipped and served the creature more than the Creator, who is blessed for ever. Amen. For this cause God gave them up unto vile affections: for even their women did change the natural use into that which is against nature: and likewise also the men, leaving the natural use of the woman, burned in their lust one toward another; men with men working that which is unseemly, and receiving in themselves that recompence of their error which was meet. And even as they did not like to retain God in their knowledge, God gave them over to a reprobate mind, to do those things which are not convenient; being filled with all unrighteousness, fornication, wickedness, covetousness, maliciousness; full of envy, murder, debate, deceit, malignity; whisperers, backbiters, haters of God, despiteful, proud, boasters, inventors of evil things, disobedient to parents, without understanding, covenantbreakers, without natural affection, implacable, unmerciful: who knowing the judgment of God, that they which commit such things are worthy of death, not only do the same, but have pleasure in them that do them" (vv. 23–32).

God does not pardon sinners by going easy on their sin. Nor does He allow them to hide behind a façade of self-righteousness. If chapter 1 exposes the depths of Gentile depravity, chapter 2 does the same to Jewish depravity. In 1:20 Paul says that the Gentiles were inexcusable for their ignorance of God. In 2:1 he uses the same word of the Jews who boasted in their knowledge of God and His law and yet remained sinful and disobedient. Mere head knowledge of the truths of revealed religion provides no escape from the judgment of God against sin. Nor does ritual observance of religious ceremonies, even those that are biblical in origin. Indeed, such religious advantages add to the Jews' weight of responsibility. As they are first in privilege, they will be first in judgment (2:9, 10).

The opening chapters of Romans bring all men under the just judgment of God. "We have before proved both Jews and Gentiles, that they are all under sin; as it is written, There is none righteous, no, not one . . . . There is no difference: for all have sinned, and come short of the glory of God" (3:9–10, 22–23). "All the world," Jew and Gentile, stands indicted as "guilty before God" (3:19).

Having taken full note of man's sin, God's way of salvation satisfies His justice because it tells how Jesus Christ paid the penalty for that sin.

"God hath set forth [Christ] to be a propitiation" (3:25). What does that mean? By propitiation Paul means Christ's sacrifice to appease the wrath of a sin-hating God by bearing it Himself. Perhaps the simplest way of showing the absolute sufficiency of the sacrifice of Christ is to say that throughout the Old Testament on every altar the fire consumed the sacrifice. When we come to Calvary, where the wrath of God burned in all its fury, the sacrifice consumed the fire. Jesus Christ satisfied the wrath of God. That is why Paul could say, "There is therefore now no condemnation to them which are in Christ Jesus" (8:1). Why is there no condemnation to all who are in Christ? The answer is that in Christ the fire of the wrath of God has forever burned itself out. There is no fire, no wrath in Christ because He satisfied the justice of God.

Not only does the righteousness of God have its source in God and render satisfaction to His justice, but *it has its substance in the actual obedience of Christ.* The substance of this righteousness is not what we do, but what Christ did. Chapter 5:17–19 shows clearly that by His obedience we are made, or constituted, righteous: "For if by one man's offence death reigned by one; much more they which receive abundance of grace and of the gift of righteousness shall reign in life by one, Jesus Christ. Therefore as by the offence of one judgment came upon all men to condemnation; even so by the righteousness of one the free gift came upon all men unto justification of life. For as by one man's disobedience many were made sinners, so by the obedience of one shall many be made righteous." 2 Cor. 5:21 sums it up beautifully: "[God] hath made him to be sin for us, who knew no sin; that we might be made the righteousness of God in him." The Scottish theologian Hugh Martin paraphrased that text in a lovely way: "God made Him, who knew no sin, to be sin for us, who knew no righteousness, that we might be made the righteousness of God in Him." He did this in order that His righteousness should become ours, imputed to us—that is, that the actual obedience of Christ and all His merit should be placed to our account. That is the substance of this righteousness of God. Paul says that this God-righteousness is our righteousness as believers in Christ, so that we now stand before God as righteous, not partially righteous, not even mostly righteous, but entirely, totally, irrevocably righteous, as righteous as Christ, because Christ is our righteousness. "[He] is made unto us . . . righteousness" (1 Cor. 1:30). The ten commandments have not lost their voice, the thunders of Sinai are as loud as ever, but now there is a Man in the glory who points to each believer and says, "This person stands in the righteousness of a perfect obedience. For him, no law remains unfulfilled, no penalty unpaid. I have freely imputed My righteousness to him." Paul means all that by his phrase "the righteousness of God."

The Revelation of God's Righteousness

In 1:18 the apostle also says that the righteousness of God has been "revealed." This is an important word. It signifies that this righteousness comes from heaven. It comes from the outside. It is something totally foreign to man's way of thinking. That is very easily proved. An examination of the religions of man shows that this doctrine of the gospel is in complete opposition to all their teaching. There is not a religion in the world, be it heathen, Judaistic, or professedly Christian—Roman Catholic, Protestant, or Eastern Orthodox—that naturally agrees with this doctrine. That is why the battle for the Reformation has to be fought in every generation. It is why there must be a prophetic voice that constantly calls evangelical Christianity back to its doctrinal foundation. The truth of a free justification by the imputed righteousness of Christ is so foreign to man's way of thinking that even in evangelical circles there is an ever-present tendency to obscure it. The gospel is about a righteousness revealed.

The word *revealed* indicates something made known to our minds and hearts. But it means more than simply "made known." This revelation is what we may call a dynamic revelation—a revelation that is moving dynamically and actively to bring us into acceptance with God. In other words, it does not merely present the information about justifying grace, it applies justifying grace to our hearts. According to 3:21 this revelation of righteousness was historically given: "But now the righteousness of God without the law is manifested, being witnessed by the law and the prophets." The words "but now" isolate a point in time. That point is the historical ministry of the Lord Jesus Christ, His incarnation, life, death, and resurrection. Rom. 4:25 bases our justification on the death and resurrection of the Lord Jesus, "who was delivered for [that is, on account of] our offences, and was raised again for [on account of] our justification." The justifying faith of the next verse rests on this historical foundation: "Therefore being justified by faith, we have peace with God through our Lord Jesus Christ." So God's righteousness was revealed in time. But it is also revealed personally and savingly. Every justified person can testify with perfect truth, "The righteousness of God is revealed to me, not merely as a theory, or a theology, but dynamically to bring me into the personal possession of perfect acceptance with God."

The Reception of God's Righteousness

Rom. 1:17 adds that in the gospel the righteousness of God is revealed "from faith to faith." That little phrase has caused much discussion among learned men. What does it mean? Some say it simply means that it is all of faith. There is a lot of truth in that, but if that is all it meant, Paul would have stated it in those terms. The simplest way to understand the phrase "from faith to faith" is to combine it with 3:22, where we read that the righteousness of God is "unto all and upon all them that believe." "Unto all" and "upon all" are not two ways of saying the same thing. "Unto all" denotes the scope or reach of this righteousness. "Upon all" speaks of the reality of its reception. The righteousness of God is first of all "from faith," or by faith. This justification is a justification by faith. But it is also "to faith," which is the same as "unto all them that believe." In other words, justification is always conferred upon faith. To say that justification is by faith is one thing, but it is a much greater statement to say that everyone who has faith is justified. Those are the two statements Paul intends to convey in 1:17. Justification is by faith, and it is conferred upon every believer. What a wonderful truth that is! The revelation of God's righteousness in the gospel is a dynamic, personal revelation. God revealed it to us. We did not work it up or dream it up. We did not labour for it or pay for it. God revealed it to us personally.

That truth magnifies the sovereignty of God in salvation. It demonstrates the strength and guarantees the success of God's grace in salvation. His revelation of righteousness works effectually. It lightens our darkness. It overcomes our wickedness. And it shows the special nature of our justification—it is one revealed to us, imputed to us, and given freely to us, not wrought by us. This righteousness is received by every believer by faith alone. There is no place for any meritorious work of ours. The addition of works for salvation denies the very essence of the gospel.

The Result of Receiving God's Righteousness

The fundamental result of this righteousness is that "we have peace with God" (5:1). Peace with God means reconciliation. With the enmity between God and us removed, we are made nigh to Him. We are brought into fellowship with God. That is the privileged position of the justified.

By now I hope it is clear why I say that justification is the heart of the gospel. It is Paul's major concern in Romans to define and expound this justification. It is vital that we understand his doctrine on this subject. If we do not, we will certainly not grasp his meaning in the rest of the epistle. Everything else in Romans grows out of this fundamental truth. The heart of the gospel is justification. It is by failing to understand justification that so many have misunderstood and misapplied what appears later in the book. This is especially the case with the many erroneous schemes of sanctification supposedly based on Romans 6 and 7.

JUSTIFICATION ESTABLISHES OUR UNION WITH CHRIST

Rom. 5:12–21 is a complex portion. It is also, in many ways, the key section of the book. Anyone who understands that section will understand the whole message of Romans. Anyone who does not understand that section will miss the book's essential teaching. It is that important.

This section teaches us that in Adam, and because of his one sin, we all stand condemned. By nature we are in Adam, sinned in him, and stand condemned because of his one sin. There is such a thing as original sin. Some teach that God does not condemn anyone for Adam's sin. That is simply not true. Adam's sin is our sin. We were in him when he sinned. We were in Adam physically and federally, for he is both the root and the covenant head of the entire human race, as the Westminster Confession of Faith teaches. The race was complete in Adam. Adam sinned, and the race sinned in him. Because of its solidarity with Adam, it stands condemned.

The second strand of Paul's teaching in the section 5:12–21 is that in Christ, because of His righteousness, we have justification. Notice that our legal standing before God, whether for condemnation or for justification, reflects our solidarity, our union, either with our first father Adam, or with the last Adam, the Lord Jesus Christ. Our legal standing reflects our union with one of those two great federal heads. Believers are one with Christ in His perfect righteousness and acceptance with God. They are accepted as He is accepted.

This is a truth that yields powerful and immediate benefits (5:1–11). It yields the benefit of assurance. The justified cannot fail to be glorified. In 5:1–2 Paul proceeds directly from justification to glorification: "Therefore being justified by faith, we have peace with God through our Lord Jesus Christ: by whom also we have access by faith into this grace wherein we stand, and rejoice in hope of the glory of God." In 8:29–30 Paul again proceeds directly from justification to glorification: "For whom he did foreknow, he also did predestinate to be conformed to the image of his Son, that he might be the firstborn among many brethren. Moreover whom he did predestinate, them he also called: and whom he called, them he also justified: and whom he justified, them he also glorified." There is no slip betwixt the cup and the lip. Justification always ends in glorification. We have that absolute assurance. That is the first benefit of our justification.

The second is closely related—*security*. "Much more then, being now justified by his blood, we shall be saved from wrath through him. For if, when we were enemies, we were reconciled to God by the death of his Son, much more, being reconciled, we shall be saved by [or, in] his [resurrection] life" (5:9–10). We have assurance; we have security. Is this security not what chapters 8 to 11 in Romans are all about? Paul expounds it in chapter 8. Believers stand under no condemnation. Who shall separate us from the love of Christ? If God be for us, who can be against us? Who is he that condemneth? Who will lay anything to the charge of God's elect? Such things are impossible. We have perfect security.

Chapters 9 to 11 deal with an apparent objection to this doctrine of security. Did not Israel have a covenant with God that secured their position and blessings as God's chosen people? They had the very security Paul now ascribes to believers. Yet, did not God cut them off? And if they have been cut off, what assurance or security can we have? That is the question Paul answers in chapters 9 to 11. He points out—and this has a very solemn application to the visible church today—that not all who were born into the nation of Israel were real Israelites. That is, not all who were natural-born Jews were the elect of God. None of God's elect has ever been cut off. Furthermore, God will yet save all His true people in Israel. "All Israel shall be saved" (11:26). Not everyone who is of the natural line of Abraham, but every one of God's covenant people in the nation of Israel will assuredly be brought to Christ.

Another reason not to use God's dealings with Israel as an objection to the doctrine of the security of His covenant people in Christ is that the cutting off of Israel is part of His sovereign purpose. He has cut off the nation of Israel for a while, for the benefit of the Gentiles. However, we should not judge anything before the time. God has not yet finished with Israel. She will yet be grafted back in to the olive tree, the symbol God uses to describe her living union with Abraham, and with all believers in Christ. There is one root and one olive tree. In its final form, the olive tree will be complete, with Old Testament believers, New Testament believers, and the yet future remnant of Israel brought together in Christ by the grace of God. God's dealings with Israel prove that His purpose never fails. We are secure in that purpose. We are in Christ. Can Christ perish? Can God ever say to His Son, "Depart from Me into everlasting fire"? Can He ever say, "I repudiate Your life; I repudiate Your death; I repudiate Your blood; I repudiate Your resurrection; I deafen My ears to Your intercession"? The very idea is impossible. So He can never cast away any who are in Christ. It is not enough to be in Abraham. It is not enough to be in Israel. It is not enough to be in Protestantism, or Presbyterianism, or Baptism, or any other *ism*. We can perish in any of those things. But we can never perish if we are in Christ.

UNION WITH CHRIST PRODUCES HOLINESS OF LIFE

Mark well the development of the apostle's argument. Justification is the heart of the gospel. Justification proves our union with Christ. Now he shows that our union with Christ produces holiness of life.

Paul constantly had to face objections to his doctrine of justification. The same kind of objections are as plentiful and popular today as in his day. They go as follows: "If you say you are saved without works, then your works do not matter. How you live does not matter. If you say that God justifies the ungodly (4:5), how can you escape the conclusion that we can live in whatever way we like?" In chapters 6 and 7 Paul gives his answer. Justification in union with Christ and our security in Christ are not an excuse to sin. Why? Because we are in *Christ*. When He died to sin on the cross, we died. When He arose, we arose. "How shall we, that are dead [literally, who died] to sin, live any longer therein?" (6:2). That is what makes it impossible for a believer to use his position in Christ as an excuse to sin. We are legally one with Christ. We are not under the law, which would condemn us. We are under grace (6:14). Those who are under grace "delight in the law of God after the inward man" (7:22). The logic of the believer is, "I am in Christ. In Him I died to sin. How can I continue to live in sin? I am in Christ. In Him I arose in newness of life. How can I continue to live my old life?"

Moreover, as Paul goes on to show, legal union with Christ is the basis of the indwelling of the Spirit of God within us. The great objective work of the Saviour leads to the Spirit's work within us. Christ purchased the activity of the Holy Spirit for all His people. "If any man have not the Spirit of Christ, he is none of his" (8:9). Any man who says he is justified to live as he likes, and who likes to live in sin, has not the Spirit of Christ. Paul says that such a man is not justified, because a justified man, on the ground of what Christ has done for him, experiences the internal work of the Holy Spirit. The Holy Spirit is just what His name suggests, the Spirit of holiness. The Lord always gives His Spirit to those whom He justifies—and the Spirit always produces holiness in those whom He indwells. So our union with Christ leads us to holiness.

HOLINESS OF LIFE FITS US FOR SERVICE

Finally, Paul argues that holiness of life fits us for service: "Neither yield ye your members as instruments of unrighteousness unto sin: but yield yourselves unto God, as those that are alive from the dead, and your members as instruments of righteousness unto God" (6:13). The word *instruments* is a military term meaning "weapons." In other words, this repudiation of sin and consecration to God are what constitute true, practical holiness. Justified men must not yield their members as weapons to be used against the work of God, the glory of God, or the law of God. They must yield themselves so that every particle of their being will be a weapon in the hand of God. That is what it means to live in holiness.

How does this work out in everyday life? According to chapters 12 to 16, it works out in a life of service. "I beseech you therefore, brethren, by the mercies of God, that ye present your bodies a living sacrifice, holy, acceptable unto God, which is your reasonable service. And be not conformed to this world: but be ye transformed by the renewing of your mind, that ye may prove what is that good, and acceptable, and perfect, will of God" (12:1–2). We are not under law. Therefore we are not slaves to sin. We do not serve sin. We are under grace. We are slaves of righteousness. That is true freedom. Justified men are free to serve Christ in the liberty of true holiness.

Immediately after the text just quoted from 12:1–2 there is a section that describes Christians as the body of Christ. In other words, we are to function in union with Him, and with one another as members of His body. Union with Christ leads to holiness of life, and holiness of life is the proper function and service of every member of the body of Christ. Romans 14 shows how this works out in the church. Instead of majoring on things the Bible treats as minor, instead of dividing the body of Christ along the lines of personal, racial, or cultural prejudice (to name just some of the baggage we bring with us from the world into the church), we should recognize our union with Christ as members of His body. In the unity of the body of Christ, we should aim to serve one another as we serve the Lord. Every aspect of our service is to be a reflection of our justification and union with Christ.

Here, then, is Paul's message in Romans. The central message of the gospel way of salvation is justification by God's free grace received through faith in the merits of Christ. Justification establishes our union with Christ. Our union with Christ leads us into holiness. And holiness fits us for service. This is how Paul expounds the way of salvation in Romans. It is both an exposition and an exhortation. It shows us how to be free from the guilt of sin. It shows us the way of freedom from the power of sin. It gives us the proper motivation to serve Christ with fervour—something Christians urgently need to experience. Too many churches and preachers know no way to try to motivate their people to serve but guilt manipulation. We need to regain the biblical motivation to serve Christ with fervour. How can we obtain it? By understanding this gospel. The gospel fixes our purpose on the glory of the One who gave us such a salvation. A grasp of His love for us will inflame our love for Him, and we will serve Him gladly.

The closing words of Romans set before us the only purpose that is worthy of a person who has known the grace of a free justification in Christ: "The grace of our Lord Jesus Christ be with you all. Amen. Now to him that is of power to stablish you according to my gospel, and the preaching of Jesus Christ, according to the revelation of the mystery, which was kept secret since the world began. But now is made manifest, and by the scriptures of the prophets, according to the commandment of the everlasting God, made known to all nations for the obedience of faith: to God only wise, be glory through Jesus Christ for ever" (16:24–27). The only purpose that is worthy of a justified person is to live for the glory of Him who gave His Son for us. That is a perfect way for Romans to end.

7

1 Corinthians
Reclaiming The Church From Sin And Failure

The gospel of Christ is God's answer to every problem of

◆

faith and practice. Since Christ died, rose from the dead,

◆

ascended, and is soon to return, there is no need for His

◆

people to be defeated by sin and the problems it brings.

*P*aul was the first to preach the gospel in Corinth. He arrived there after his very brief witness in Athens, the centre of Greek culture and philosophy, where he had preached not only for a short time but with less than his usual success. The Lord is sovereign as to where and when He builds churches, and as to whom He saves and how soon He saves them. So in Athens Paul did not see many people saved. When he left Athens and proceeded to Corinth he felt a great sense of fear and deep foreboding. After Athens, he kept certain fundamental truths in mind. More than ever he was convinced of the folly and uselessness of human philosophy. He had confronted all that in Athens, and he had seen the vanity to which it led. He was also aware of his own weakness to overcome such a situation, so much so that he feared and trembled. In 1 Cor. 2:3 he says concerning his arrival in the city, "I was with you in weakness, and in fear, and in much trembling."

There was another thing in his mind. He was determined that he would preach the gospel with bold simplicity. He would not embellish it in any way with the wisdom or philosophy of the world, and he would wait upon God to make it fruitful by the demonstration and power of the Holy Spirit. That is how Paul went to Corinth.

From the beginning the Lord signally blessed his visit. There was the usual opposition orchestrated by the Jews, but the Lord gave Paul special encouragement. Paul was not only fearful but also deeply aware of the deficiency of his skills as a public speaker. There is evidence in the New Testament that while he was a great missionary, a great teacher, a great preacher, a great theologian, a great thinker, a great church builder, and a great soulwinner, by the standards of men he was not a great orator. The strength of his preaching was not in the polished sentence. Especially in Greece, which was so proud of its orators, Paul felt that his attempts at public speaking were miserable. But the Lord said, "Be not afraid, but speak, and hold not thy peace: for I am with thee, and no man shall set on thee to hurt thee: for I have much people in this city" (Acts 18:9–10). Anyone who does not believe in the sovereignty of God and the doctrine of election should ponder that statement. While some Corinthians had been saved when the Lord said this, the vast majority of those who would form the church in Corinth had not yet been reached for Christ. While they were still in their heathenism and sin, God said to Paul, "I have much people in this city." With that encouragement the apostle laboured in the city of Corinth for a year and a half. The results of that labour were the crown of his second missionary journey. He saw a living, thriving church established in the city of Corinth.

Later, when Paul had moved on to Ephesus and established a church there, Apollos visited Corinth. He made a deep impression on the Corinthians, not only by his orthodoxy but by the preaching of the gospel with consummate oratory.

The church in Corinth was blessed with greatly gifted people. "In every thing ye are enriched by him, in all utterance, and in all knowledge; even as the testimony of Christ was confirmed in you: so that ye come behind in no gift; waiting for the coming of our Lord Jesus Christ" (1 Cor. 1:5–7). The Corinthian church had people whose lives had been dramatically transformed by the power of God's grace. In chapter 6 the apostle speaks of many kinds of wicked sinners—fornicators, idolaters, adulterers, effeminate, sodomites, thieves, covetous, drunkards, revilers, and extortioners. Then he adds, "And such were some of you: but ye are washed" (v. 11). They were a changed people. They were a new people. While they were not the kind of people proud religionists would have chosen as candidates for sainthood or as the material with which to build a new church, they were the people God chose to be saints, living stones in the temple He was building. So in the city of Corinth a church was established on a solid foundation, built by a wise master builder, as Paul describes himself, enriched by the ministry of Apollos, and mightily endowed with all the gifts and graces of the Holy Spirit to carry on the work of God. It was a great beginning. Never did Paul see a greater work done in any place than in Corinth.

Then came the problems. The new converts were gloriously transformed people. They were spiritually gifted. They were on fire for God. They were blazing a trail for Christ throughout all the region of Achaia. They were widely known because of what God was doing for them. All this was wonderful, but there were serious problems. The devil got in among them. Soon sin began to express itself, and fleshliness began to be accepted as the norm among them. There is evidence in 1 Corinthians that they misused the gospel and its doctrines as a cloak for their wicked living. They were proud rather than ashamed of their sins. They split themselves into factions, little warring groups and cliques, so causing havoc in the church and jeopardizing its entire witness.

When these sad tidings reached Paul in Ephesus he was deeply grieved. From Acts 19:21–22 it would appear that the apostle formed the purpose of visiting Corinth on the way to Jerusalem. Although that visit never materialized, he did send Timothy and Erastus to seek to bring the Corinthians back, as he puts it in 1 Cor. 4:17, "into remembrance of my ways which be in Christ." From 16:10 it would appear that before Timothy and Erastus reached Corinth some messengers, a deputation of leading Corinthian Christians, came to visit Paul. They brought him their personal account of what was happening in the church, informing him of just how bad the situation was. They also brought a letter in which they laid before the apostle some of the questions that were perplexing the church. With this account and written request for answers, the apostle's immediate and inspired response was to write this first epistle to the Corinthians.

In some ways it is a tragedy that such an epistle had to be written at all. It seems a shame that the apostle had to take time away from preaching the gospel to the Ephesians to deal with the sins of the Corinthians. But in other ways it was not a tragedy. We can only rejoice that the Lord in wisdom and grace, right at the very inception of the church, gave to the entire body of Christ an inspired treatment of many of the problems and questions that have troubled local churches in every age. Corinth's problems and questions make it sound like a twentieth-century church. G. Campbell Morgan, the great English Congregational preacher and teacher, pointed out that in 1 Cor. 1:2 Paul began the epistle by emphasizing the church of Corinth and the city of Corinth: "Unto the church of God which is at Corinth." It is very clear that there was every kind of wickedness in the city. Corinth was a city of luxury and lasciviousness. The expression "to Corinthianize" implied whoredom. In later times a Corinthian came to mean a polished rake. In Corinth all sorts of ungodliness flourished. The trouble was that the city was infecting the church more than the church influencing the city. That was the problem. That remains a great problem for us. We still have the city and the church. The church ought to be influencing the city. Every time that happens—and to some degree it is happening—we must rejoice. But to an increasing degree the city is infecting the church. The things that are done in the city are being brought into the church. The wickedness that is acceptable in the city is becoming acceptable in the church. That is what happened in Corinth.

The Sins of Corinth

An examination of 1 Corinthians reveals just how widespread was this infection. First, there was the adoption of *human philosophy* in the place of the theology of the cross. The Corinthian Christians did not give up the Bible—at least, not in so many words. They professed to continue to believe the gospel and to stand for its truths. But they wanted to express the gospel in the terms of Greek philosophy. They wanted to clothe the body of divine truth with the robe of the wisdom of the city. In doing so they obscured the theology of the cross.

Things have changed very little. If there is one thing that is at the root of most of the problems in evangelical churches nowadays, this is it. It is not that evangelicals have come out and said, "We no longer believe the Bible." There are "New Evangelicals" and "Young Evangelicals" who effectively deny the true inspiration of the Bible. Such people are not really evangelicals at all. But while most evangelicals claim to adhere to Scripture, many of them have embraced human philosophy. The ideas of worldly, wicked psychologists and philosophers have been imported into many a church, with a Bible text tagged on to make them sound orthodox. The old theology of the cross is conspicuous by its absence. Corinthian sin is flourishing.

The church in Corinth also suffered from *divisions*. There were cliques among the people of God, little groups in the church isolated from one another. The Corinthians tried to put a spiritual face on their sin. Some said, "We are Apollosites. We follow Apollos." Others said, "We are Paulites. We follow Paul." Others said, "We are Cephasites. We follow Simon Peter." Then there were others who said, "We are *the* church of Christ. We are Christites. We alone are Christ's ones." Such were the cliques into which the Corinthians divided themselves. There was no division among Paul, Peter, and Apollos, but the Corinthians divided themselves into exclusive groups in their names. To this day, when Christians form factions, they invariably attempt to put a spiritual face on it. They try to make their schism look biblical. They delude themselves that there are good, scriptural reasons for what they are doing. There is a world of difference between biblical separation and carnal schism. When churches split into factions, it is always carnal.

The Corinthians even went so far as to have church members suing one another at law before the ungodly. There was no judgment in the church. The leadership of the church had lost control. They would not judge sin. Worse still, the evidence is that the Corinthian Christians were more afraid of the law of man than of the law of God, of the sentence of a human judge than of that of the Judge of all the earth. They were more afraid of losing a little money than of losing the blessing of God. How tragic it is when division reaches that stage in a church!

Even then we have not plumbed the depths of Corinth's divisions. Those Christians even brought their schism to the Lord's Table (chap. 11). In the early church, a social meal often preceded the actual observance of the Lord's Supper. It was the Greek custom that each would bring his own provisions. In the church of Corinth the rich brought lavish meals, and they ate all they brought without regard for the poor of the congregation who had little or nothing and were left to go hungry. One Christian lorded it over another, and because of social, educational, or economic distinctions, one would have nothing to do with the other. Such divisions caused deep wounds in the body of the church.

Then there were *immoral practices*. People who had been saved from fornication and adultery went back into their former sin. It is easy to read too much into what is recorded in chapter 5 as if gross immorality were the norm among the Corinthian Christians. Chapter 5 indicates that there was one man, a certain "one," as Paul says, who was guilty of a kind of fornication that even the heathens would not have allowed. However, immoral practices were tolerated in the church. There was no judgment of sin. The guilty could still come to the Lord's Table. Their hypocrisy was a desecration of the Table, but that did not seem to matter.

Do we not find a similar lack of church discipline today? People can carouse all week and still take their place at the Lord's Table without raising a question. There is little judgment of sin in churches today. When any man brings the name of the Lord Jesus Christ into public disrepute, he should come under biblical discipline. This is particularly essential in the case of fallen preachers. Let them be restored to God. Let them work with humility, but let them accept discipline so that the cause of Christ will not be further sullied by a tolerant attitude toward sin by the church.

The church at Corinth had yet another problem: a *radical feminism,* as the opening chapters show. Feminism is no new thing. Like many another modern movement, it has ancient roots. How did feminism in Corinth show itself? First of all, it was professedly based on the apostolic teaching of the equal worth of the woman with the man. Many people misread 1 Corinthians and imagine that Paul rejected this doctrine. Nothing could be further from the truth. He showed that in the church the woman shared with the man a place of equal dignity and worth before God, though she fulfilled a different function. That is what Paul taught. He said that the covering a woman was required to place on her head in worship was the "power" of God (11:10). William Ramsey, an expert on ancient Eastern customs, disagreed with the idea that the covering was merely a sign that she was under authority. In his opinion it meant the very opposite. He said that in the Eastern world when a woman wore a covering on her head it was her protection. It was her power. Even the most abandoned wretch would not touch a woman who was wearing her covering. It was for her a power, and it enabled her to walk safely in any place. According to Ramsey, that was the background from which Paul made the statement that the covering on a woman's head in worship was her power. It is a very interesting idea. The head covering, which almost all modern Christian women mistakenly reject as demeaning, is actually a proclamation of privilege, protection, and power. Far from implying any inferiority in the woman, it declares her equal acceptance with God in Christ.

As we have noted, equality of dignity does not mean sameness of function. The difference of function may be illustrated by another reference to head covering in worship. According to Paul, the man must not wear a covering, while the woman must do so. Those are entirely opposite actions. Yet by fulfilling the command of God in this matter, both the man and the woman perform the same fundamental service. They equally declare the glory of Christ. The man worships with uncovered head to acknowledge the glory of his Saviour. The woman's covering covers her hair, which is her "glory." By covering her glory she joins the man in proclaiming that in the assembly of the saints, Christ has all the glory. Thus the woman is accepted in Christ just as truly as the man is and has equal worth, though her function is different.

How did the Corinthian women take that message? In effect, they said that since they were equal with men they were going to act as the men did. Thus they set about rejecting the peculiarly Christian ordinance that men must worship with their heads uncovered and women with theirs covered.

Nowadays, Christian women evade the plain teaching of 1 Corinthians 11 on head covering by relegating it to the level of a local custom. The truth of the matter is that Jews did not, and to this day do not, believe in men worshipping with their heads uncovered. The heathen also insisted that the men cover their heads in worship. So Paul's teaching was not a local custom at all; it was a specific Christian ordinance given by the inspiration and the power of the Holy Ghost: in order to express the glory of Christ, the man must not cover his head, while the woman, whose hair is her glory, must cover her head in order to join the man in expressing the glory of Christ. That was the ordinance of the Holy Ghost, but the Corinthian women said, "Why should the men be allowed to worship with their heads uncovered and we have to have ours covered? We are as good as they are. We demand equality." Radical feminism is a great enemy of womankind. That is what was raising its head in the church in Corinth and, alas, still holds sway in most churches.

The next problem in Corinth was a certain *false Pentecostalism,* what we may term a false charismatic movement. The Corinthians placed great emphasis on the *charismata,* the gifts of the Spirit. Undoubtedly there were genuine exhibitions of the gifts of the Spirit in the church in Corinth. Some people were given special gifts by God, and they used them in a wonderful way. However, there were others who practised a counterfeit of the Spirit's gifts. They were more enamoured of signs than they were of the Saviour. They professed to be moved by the Holy Spirit, but they turned the meetings of the church into a bedlam of confusion, and some even called Christ accursed. This is the obvious inference from 12:3. Some clearly lost control of themselves. Others could apparently exercise their supposed spiritual gifts at will.

Is this not similar to what we find today? False Pentecostalism, a spurious claim to the apostolic gifts, is once again spreading confusion among Christians. In contrast to Paul's clear assertion that "the spirits of the prophets are subject to the prophets" (14:32), we discover a carnal ecstasy in which the person professedly moved by the Holy Spirit loses conscious control of his thoughts, words, and actions. There are others who can turn their claimed spiritual gift on and off like a faucet. There is usually a high degree of emotionalism and psychological manipulation. All of this reflects the error of Corinth's false charismatism. It is as deadly today as it was then.

We may mention one more sin of the church in Corinth. It was the sin of *tolerating, and in many cases adopting, heresy,* especially on the subject of the resurrection (chapter 15). Clearly, some in Corinth denied that there was to be a resurrection from the dead, but their theological deviation did not cause their exclusion from the church. The very people who were quick to divide over frivolous and carnal things would not practise the biblical doctrine of separation on matters of fundamental importance to the gospel. Perhaps, like all too many today, they could tolerate all kinds of sin and heresy under the banner of the professed experience of the Spirit's charismatic gifts. Certainly in the last number of years we have witnessed the demotion of theological orthodoxy to a place of little or no consequence on the ground of a common charismatic experience. When a professed charismatic experience, rather than fidelity to the gospel, is made the test of true Christianity, the church becomes a prey to an array of disorders, just as the church in Corinth did.

Here, then, were the sins of Corinth. They were many. They were serious. Not surprisingly, they caused enormous problems.

The Pastoral Problems of Corinth

The Corinthians addressed a letter to Paul asking about *marriage and divorce.* Essentially the question was, when a man becomes a Christian and his wife remains unsaved, and things are far from pleasant at home, has he the right to divorce his wife and marry a Christian? That was a real problem in Corinth, and it remains a real problem for many today. Take the following example. A woman receives Christ as her Saviour and joins the church. Her husband remains unsaved and refuses to attend church with her. Naturally, that woman starts finding her company in the church. As she fellowships with other people, she drifts apart from her husband. She begins to rationalize that it may be all right to divorce her husband and to take a Christian husband. It is not all right; it is all wrong. That is what Paul told the Corinthians, and his answer still stands.

However, there was another aspect to the question. What if the unsaved partner refuses to live with the saved partner? What if the unsaved partner divorces the saved partner? What is the Christian to do then? Is the Christian bound to that marriage, or is he free to take a Christian spouse? According to many today the Christian is bound to that marriage, but Paul is blunt and says, "A brother or a sister is not under bondage in such cases" (7:15). They are free. Divorce and remarriage is one of the most contentious subjects in the church today. It would help a great deal if people would set aside their own personal prejudice and simply accept what the Bible says, without trying to impose their own preconceived notions on it.

Another problem in Corinth involved *eating things offered to idols.* That may not appear to be much of a problem for most of us, but in fact it has far-reaching ramifications. The Corinthian Christians lived in a heathen society. The question was, how far may a Christian integrate into the heathen society that is round about him? To what extent must he isolate himself from it? Put in those terms, the question is very relevant today. So is Paul's answer. We may summarize the apostle's reply in four ways. First, maintain a total separation from what promotes the cause of the devil. To the Corinthians this meant refusing to eat what they knew to be a sacrifice to idols (10:20–21). Second, in matters that are indifferent, seek to do what is spiritually profitable and edifying (10:23). Third, in all things maintain a good testimony and be particularly careful not to lead a weaker brother astray (8:9–13). Finally, whatever you do, do all to the glory of God (10:31).

The Corinthians also had a problem with *Paul's apostolic authority.* By what right did he presume to command them? It was really the question of any authority in the church versus spiritual anarchy. That is a very modern problem. We are living in a day when people recognize little or no real authority in the church. To a large extent authority has broken down in the modern church. Frequently, when a church imposes discipline on an erring member, he will simply go to another church, which will receive him without making contact with the first church. They simply ignore the issue of discipline. In other cases, a person disciplined for sin rebels and challenges the elders. "Who are you to judge me?" he asks. "I will defy your judgment." Very often such a person will seek to raise support for his cause among other church members, all with a view to challenging the elders' right to rule the church as the Scripture commands. We are living in a day of virtual anarchy. Every man does that which is right in his own eyes. That is one reason I believe that in order to be biblical, Christians should have church membership. Every Christian, preachers included, must be spiritually responsible and accountable to men ordained of God to the leadership and good government of the church. It is anarchical for Christians to set themselves up as individuals with the attitude that they can attend and use the church but refuse to live under its discipline. That was the attitude of some of the Corinthians, and it was, and is, entirely wrong.

All the sins of Corinth are the sins of the twentieth century. The questions are the questions of the modern church. What was not contemporary was Paul's answer. Nowadays the usual pastoral response to such a situation as confronted Paul is to emphasize psychology. His answer was altogether different. It was theological, not psychological. In fact, we can go even further and say that it was Christological, or in other words the preaching of Christ. This approach to the problems of Corinth supplies us with the key to the message of 1 Corinthians. That message may be stated very simply: **Reclaiming the Church by a Return to Christ.** Paul works this out by expounding three great truths.

First he shows us that the Satisfaction of Christ—i.e., His entire work on our behalf: His life, His death, His resurrection, and His intercession—gives us the principles to deal with every problem of faith and practice.

Second, Paul shows us that the Spirit of Christ gives us the power to deal with every problem of faith and practice.

Finally, at the very end of the book he shows us how the second coming of Christ gives us the prospect of full and final deliverance from every problem of faith and practice.

THE SATISFACTION OF CHRIST GIVES US THE PRINCIPLES TO DEAL WITH EVERY PROBLEM OF FAITH AND PRACTICE

The Corinthian church's problems must have pained Paul beyond words. Their discovery must have fallen on him like a hammer blow. But not for a moment did he allow his pain to cloud his judgment. So what did he do? In the very first chapter of his epistle he brought them immediately to Christ and to the cross. That showed great wisdom. What was his answer to the sins, questions, and problems besetting the church? It was the gospel. Paul wanted to get the Corinthians on to a firm foundation to receive the great appeal to holiness he was going to make to them. Thus in chapter 1 he brings them to Christ crucified. In verse 30 he says to them, "Of [God] are ye in Christ Jesus, who of God is made unto us wisdom, and righteousness, and sanctification, and redemption." Notice those four aspects of the work of Christ. I think I could make a strong case to prove that the whole of 1 Corinthians is really an exposition of those four things. Chapters 1 to 4 deal with Christ our wisdom. Chapters 5 to 7 deal with Christ our righteousness.

Chapters 8 to 14 deal with Christ our sanctification. The book ends by expounding Christ our redemption. Christ is made unto us wisdom, righteousness, sanctification, and redemption. In other words, He is a complete Saviour to us, we are complete in Him, and He is therefore the complete answer to our situation. The work of Christ on our behalf establishes the principles upon which we can face the sins and the questions that agitate the church. Take these four great truths and apply them directly to the things that troubled the Corinthians.

These people were troubled about the *message.* They wanted wisdom. They wanted philosophy. They wanted learning. In effect, they were complaining, "Paul, you are not giving us those things. You never do anything but preach the fundamentals." What is Paul's answer? He brings them to the cross. He shows them that God is satisfied with Christ and that we are justified and reconciled to God through Christ. In effect, he argues, "Can one really understand the gospel and still desire the wisdom of the world?" Let me put it this way. How many people ever got to heaven by reading Aristotle? None. How many people ever got to heaven by reading Plato? None. How many people ever got to heaven by attending the Greek schools? None. Let me bring it up to date. How many people ever got to heaven by studying Freud? None. How many people ever got to heaven by the sceptical science of Carl Sagan? None. Why then would anybody desire to turn from the message of the cross of Jesus Christ to the philosophy of the world when the cross saves everybody who comes to it and the wisdom of the world damns everybody who comes to it? That is Paul's answer to the Corinthians' trouble with his message.

They had trouble also with their *members.* There were strifes and schisms, divisions and contentions. The rich would not fellowship with the poor. The educated were too intellectually proud to have anything in common with the uneducated. Church members did not see some minor matters in exactly the same way, and so they split the church. Christians will always have differences of emphasis and of interpretation on nonessential matters, but to make those differences a cause of division is sin. What is the answer to division? The work of Christ for us—that is the answer. Paul says, "Ye see your calling, brethren" (1:26). He says, in effect, "As you see your calling, understand that you are complete in Christ. That is equally true of the rich man who is saved and of the pauper who is saved. It is true of the slave who is saved. It is true of the free man who is saved. He is free and he is complete in Christ. See your calling. Instead of despising one another, understand your common calling and completeness in Christ. Let the church in its life express the true position of each of its members in the body of the

Lord Jesus Christ. You are all brethren. Look at one another in Christ."

What a difference it would make if Christians looked at one another in Christ! If husbands and wives were to look at each other in Christ—especially when one feels the need to criticize the other—how much better their home life would be. The same holds good for the church. What a glorious thing it would be in the church if we did not look at people and say, "He is white, or black, or brown, or yellow," but "He is in Christ." We know we are seeing straight when we see our brethren the way the Lord sees them. When the Lord sees them clothed in His righteousness, we are wickedly foolish when we divide ourselves from them because we refuse to look at them in the same way.

We may also take these truths and apply them to *morals.* Christ is made unto us *both* righteousness and sanctification (1:30). That is the literal force of the original. Seeing that truth is the answer to the moral problems mentioned in chapters 5 and 6. Six times in chapter 6 (vv. 2, 3, 9, 15, 16, 19) Paul asks, "Know ye not?" In other words, "Do you not know what it is to be complete in Christ? Do you not understand what it is that He is your righteousness and your sanctification? See what you are in Christ, and live in the light of it." How can a man have his mind fixed on what he is in Christ, how can he consider the cross, how can he contemplate the completeness of Christ's saving work for him, and live in sin? He cannot do it. Christians fall into such wickedness only when they fail to think through the gospel. That was the Corinthians' fundamental failure. The answer to moral problems starts with how a Christian thinks. I am not referring to what the world terms positive thinking. I am speaking of thinking the gospel, thinking Christ. When a Christian thinks right he will live right, in the church, in the home, in his marriage, and in the world.

Paul applied this same truth to the Corinthians' problems in their *meetings.* They had some real trouble in their meetings. We have seen that the idea of their equality made some women feminists. Social position made other people factional. Once again Paul's answer was, "See your calling, brethren. You are complete in Christ. If you are all complete in Christ, you cannot be separated one from another." In chapter 12 he uses the illustration of the body. The hand cannot say to the foot, "I have no need of you." What use would hands be without feet, eyes, ears, and all the other parts of the body? The church is to be an expression of the unity of the body of Christ. In our church meetings we must remember that. We are one in Christ. We cannot do without one another.

He goes on to apply this same truth to the *ministry.* Some in Corinth were making false claims to spiritual gifts. These false claims were full of self-promotion and self-gratification. What is the only answer to such a false charismatic movement? It is a gospel theology. We must lay low man's pride at the cross and teach Christians to glory in salvation, not in showmanship. The ministry of the Spirit is to exalt the Lord Jesus Christ. Six times in the opening verses of 1 Corinthians Paul uses the expression "the Lord Jesus Christ." He adds four more references later in the book. He lays another emphasis on Christ as the Lord some forty-seven times. That makes more than fifty references to the Lordship of Christ in sixteen chapters. That is what motivates and governs a Christian. Indeed, that is the touchstone of the reality of our profession. "If any man love not the Lord Jesus Christ, let him be Anathema" (16:22). It does not matter what gifts he professes; if he does not love our Lord Jesus Christ he is damned. That is what Paul teaches. The ministration of the Spirit is to exalt the Lord. It is to expound the gospel. It is to edify the saints and to evangelize sinners.

Here then are the principles, the great doctrinal truths, by which we are to deal with the problems, the sins, and the questions raised in 1 Corinthians.

THE SPIRIT OF CHRIST GIVES US THE POWER TO DEAL WITH EVERY PROBLEM OF FAITH AND PRACTICE

We have seen the principles, but we must have them applied by the Spirit of Christ actually giving us the power to live as Paul here directs. All these things are only words and theories until the Holy Spirit applies them to us. Christian living is not a mechanical observance of so many precepts and principles. We need the ministry of the Holy Spirit to apply the work of Christ to our hearts. A key verse, not only to 1 Corinthians but to the whole Christian life, is 2:12: "Now we have received, not the spirit of the world, but the spirit which is of God; that we might know the things that are freely given to us of God." That is the key verse for the point I am making.

The Holy Spirit is the Spirit of *light* (2:10): "God hath revealed them unto us by his Spirit." He enlightens the minds of Christians that they may know their completeness in Christ. He applies the theological truth and translates it into practical power. It is one thing to say we believe in justification by faith; it is quite another thing to have the Holy Spirit so apply it that we can live in the light of it.

He is the Spirit of *life* (3:16): "Ye are the temple of God, and . . . the Spirit of God dwelleth in you." He lives in us. He sustains spiritual life in us. He maintains us in vital union with Christ. He imparts spiritual power for life and service (2:4).

He is also the Spirit of *liberty,* but He is the opponent of license and lust. He brings us into the liberty of the gospel but not into liberty to live in lust. He does not give Christians liberty to leave their spouses who are willing to live with them in the bonds of marriage. He does not give us liberty to run amok in the church and cast off authority. The liberty He gives is liberty from the dominion of sin.

The Holy Spirit is also the Spirit of *love.* Love is the "more excellent way" of which Paul speaks in chapter 13. When Christians live in the lust of the flesh they are effectively saying that they do not love the Lord as they ought to and as they once did. Those who really love the Lord cannot live in immorality or wicked worldliness. Those who really love the Lord cannot deal with their fellow Christians in the church without the love of Christ. All who love the Lord will have His love for His people. The same is true in the home. It is impossible to live in bitterness and contention with your husband or wife if you have the love of Christ for him or her ruling your heart. Love is the more excellent way. Wickedness, worldliness, and schism among God's people ultimately express a failure of love. That is Paul's message.

Love for our Lord, and through Him for all His people, is the paramount Christian grace. Without it all religion is vain. Some people disguise their lack of love under great swelling words. They talk a good religion. But Paul says, "Though I speak with the tongues of men and of angels, and have not love, I am become as sounding brass, or a tinkling cymbal" (13:1). Others cover their lack of love with great religious zeal or with claims of miraculous spiritual gifts. Still others replace love with mere money, as if giving to the poor and needy could make up for their cold hearts toward God and men. To all such Paul says, "Though I have the gift of prophecy, and understand all mysteries, and all knowledge; and though I have all faith, so that I could remove mountains, and have not love, I am nothing. And though I bestow all my goods to feed the poor, and though I give my body to be burned, and have not love, it profiteth me nothing" (vv. 2–3).

We must have love. The question is, how do we obtain it? How do we come to love the Lord? How do we come to love people? We obtain such love only at the cross when the Holy Spirit applies to our hearts the wonder of the love of Christ for us. That is the key. Christ's love for us will beget a love for Christ in us and a love from Christ through us. As the Spirit of love, the Holy Spirit must apply the principles of the gospel to our hearts and thereby give us the power to deal with the problems and needs of the Christian life.

THE SECOND COMING OF CHRIST GIVES US THE PROSPECT OF A FULL AND FINAL DELIVERANCE FROM EVERY PROBLEM OF FAITH AND PRACTICE

Happily we can finish our study as Paul finished the epistle—with the truth that the second coming gives us the prospect of final deliverance (15:23). Christ is coming. Chapter 15:49–58 tells us what is going to happen when He comes. We are going to be like Him. What a glorious day that will be when this mortal puts on immortality, when this corruptible puts on incorruption, and when sin is totally eradicated from both body and soul! That is the prospect of full and final deliverance. That is the "blessed hope" (Tit. 2:13) of every Christian. In effect Paul says, "Keep that thrilling prospect in view and it will enable you to live in Christian victory over the problems that afflict you." Having instructed the Corinthians to live looking back to what Christ did for them, the apostle now tells them to live looking forward to what He is going to do at His return.

It is critical for Christians to live with the backward look, the upward look, and the forward look. Here is the way to overcome the problems that so often afflict us. Here is how both individuals and churches may escape the failures of the Corinthians while emulating their successes. Here is God's way to ensure that the church affects the city and the city does not infect the church. By living in the light of Christ's cross and coming we will share Paul's joyous assurance: "Thanks be to God, which giveth us the victory through our Lord Jesus Christ. Therefore, my beloved brethren, be ye steadfast, unmoveable, always abounding in the work of the Lord" (1 Cor. 15:57–58).

2 Corinthians
Successful Spiritual Warfare

The glorious message of the gospel always triumphs

♦

over the opposition of malicious men. It overcomes

♦

the threat posed by enemies outside the church and

♦

enemies on the inside.

I can sympathize with the apostle Paul and how he felt as he wrote 2 Corinthians. His message in his first epistle had had a mixed reception. Most of the Corinthian Christians had received it well. 2 Cor. 2:5–11 indicates that these people had acted upon what Paul had written to them as he exposed their sin and corrected their deviations from God's truth and from the practice of the gospel. Their repentance was deep and genuine and was not to be repented of (7:9f). It led to an ongoing change of life so that they began to live as Christians ought to live. So there was a section of the congregation in Corinth that embraced the word. Though it had wounded their consciences it had also healed them. However, there were others who did not welcome the word. They strove against it, and in fighting against the message they fought against the messenger. There was a viciously anti-Paul group in the church in Corinth. These people attacked the apostle in a very wicked way. First they denied his apostleship. Then they attacked his character, going so far as to call him a liar. They accused him of making empty promises which he wantonly failed to fulfil. That is the meaning of the apostle's statement, "Our word toward you was not yea and nay" (1:18).

Why did they accuse him? It appears that Paul changed his announced plans for a visit to Corinth. In 1 Cor. 16:5–6 he informed the church that he would visit Corinth after he had been to Macedonia. At the time of writing Paul was in Ephesus, where his work was being blessed by God and viciously opposed by men. To make his situation worse, he received very discouraging news from Corinth. He even made an emergency visit to the church there. It is probable that it was then that he informed the Corinthians of a change of plans. Now he thought it best to return to Corinth for his third visit as soon as he had finished his work in Ephesus. He would go to Corinth before Macedonia. However, he was obliged to change his plans again. The continuing bad news out of Corinth led Paul to feel it would be better for him to send Titus to seek to help the church through its difficulties. Paul felt that if he had gone personally the results for some of the Corinthians would have been severe. So "to spare" them, he sent Titus and arranged to meet him in Troas, from where they would travel to Macedonia and then on to Corinth. This latest change of travel plans stirred up the apostle's opponents to new levels of fury. Forgetting his extreme danger in Asia (1:8) and his desire to postpone having to deal with them, for their own good, his Corinthian detractors assaulted his character as if he were a changeable, untrustworthy, and untruthful man.

They attacked not only his office and his character but also his message. They concluded that since his word was not to be trusted, neither was his doctrine. Such was the assault on Paul by one faction of the church in

Corinth. These people were led astray by Judaizers who hated Paul's doctrine of grace. Judaizers lay under the condemnation of God (Gal. 1:8, 9). Notwithstanding the fact that they were under God's curse, these preachers received a ready hearing from the anti-Paul faction in Corinth.

This difference of response to Paul's first epistle between those who welcomed the word and those who warred against it explains a very difficult feature of 2 Corinthians. When you read this book you cannot help but be impressed by the sudden differences in tone that Paul adopts. At one moment he is tender, conciliatory, thankful, and full of praise for the Corinthians. The next moment he denounces their obstinacy and rebellion. These sudden variations in tone can be confusing to the reader unless he recognizes that this is not meant to be a cool theological treatise. Rather, Paul, carried along in the mighty torrent of his passion for the church in Corinth, deals first with one group and then with the other. The result of all this is that 2 Corinthians gives us a unique view of a number of subjects.

First, it gives us a unique view of Paul himself. This is the most autobiographical of all his epistles. There is more of Paul himself in this epistle than in any other part of the New Testament. All his epistles reveal Paul the worker. 2 Corinthians goes further. It not only shows us the hands of Paul at work and the feet of Paul tramping the missionary trails of this world, it draws aside the veil and shows us the mind and heart of Paul. It uncovers the deep motions that moved within him and made him what he was in the work of God. That is why 2 Corinthians is such a vital book for every preacher. There is more to preaching than facility of speech. There is more to preaching than knowing Hebrew, Greek, systematic theology, and the other courses that are properly part of a minister's training. There is more to preaching even than having the ability to analyse and outline a text of Scripture and set forth its message in a cogent fashion. A true minister of Jesus Christ must attend to all these things but not stop short at such accomplishments. He must be a man whose heart and soul are aflame with the love and power of his Saviour. That is what makes 2 Corinthians so important to preachers: it reveals the heart of the greatest of all Christ's ministers.

This epistle also provides a unique view of the Christian ministry, of church discipline and the spirit in which it is to be administered, of the Satan-inspired opposition that God's people endure, and of the constant battle for the faith that must be waged against that opposition. These are some of the things with which Paul deals in 2 Corinthians. He does so very positively. Though there is strong denunciation in it, this is not an epistle of bitterness. It is not an epistle of frustration. It is an epistle of consolation and instruction. The aim of 2 Corinthians was first to strengthen the faithful and then to win back those who had been deceived by Judaizers. The good news is that it was entirely successful. How do we know that? There is a letter that is not part of the New Testament but that deserves close attention. It was written some forty years after this by Clement of Rome. Clement was an elder in the church in Rome, and he wrote to the church in Corinth. Such was the success of Paul's intervention that even after such an interval Clement could celebrate the unity of the church in Corinth and testify to its fidelity to the gospel of the Lord Jesus Christ. Evidently Paul's epistle was effective and successful. The threatened subversion of the church by Judaizers came to nothing. Therefore I think we can say that in 2 Corinthians we have what I will call **a gospel manual for successful spiritual warfare.** It is not my intention to present a detailed analysis of the epistle but to lay bare the message that lies at its heart. However, since many people find 2 Corinthians a difficult book to outline, it may be of benefit to some if I gave a simple outline of it. There are four sections:

1. Paul's explanation of his motives and ministry (chaps. 1–5).
2. Paul's exhortation to godly living and Christian fellowship (chaps. 6–9).
3. Paul's vindication of his apostleship (chaps. 10–12).
4. Conclusion: Paul's expectation to visit Corinth and his final benediction (chap. 13).

In considering 2 Corinthians as a gospel manual for successful spiritual warfare I will make three simple observations.

First, the gospel presents a glorious message.

Second, malicious men oppose that message.

Third, a spiritual ministry always defeats those malicious men.

THE GLORIOUS MESSAGE OF THE GOSPEL

The gospel presents a glorious message. 2 Corinthians contains some of the most memorable texts and declarations of gospel truth in all of the New Testament. It is not a formal theological treatise like the book of Romans, but it is a glorious statement of evangelical truth nonetheless. The focus of the whole message of 2 Corinthians is Christ, His person and His work. We recall that lovely verse, "Ye know the grace of our Lord Jesus Christ, that, though he was rich, yet for your sakes he became poor, that ye through his poverty might be rich" (8:9). Because of that wondrous grace the glory of God in its mighty fulness shines to us in Jesus Christ. In 4:3–4 we read, "If our gospel be hid, it is hid to them that are lost: in whom the god of this world hath blinded the minds of them which believe not, lest the light of the glorious gospel of Christ, who is the image of God, should shine unto them." Why is

Satan so anxious to blind the minds of unbelievers? What does he fear more than all the armies of Christendom? He fears "lest the light of the glorious gospel of Christ . . . should shine unto them."

Let that penetrate our souls. There are many tasks facing God's people in this world of need. There is a social work for Christians to do. There is the work of helping the poor. There is a need to care for the victims of war and tyranny. There is a work of Christian education. These are all legitimate things that Christians may do, but let us never be derailed from our main task. The devil is not afraid of all the sociological and educational programs in the world. There is only one thing of which he is afraid, and that is the light of the glorious gospel of Christ illuminating the subjects of his kingdom of darkness. Why then do so many of God's people waste their time with things that are of little importance, while neglecting the great work of letting the gospel shine? I am not advocating isolation. I do not believe that God's people are to withdraw from human affairs. What I am saying is that we must not make those affairs an end in themselves. Rather, we must make them a vehicle to spread the gospel of Christ, for that is what the devil is afraid of. He blinds men "lest the light of the glorious gospel of Christ, who is the image of God, should shine unto them."

Notice the source of this glorious light: "Christ, who is the image of God." Nowhere else does the light of divine grace shine. "God, who commanded the light to shine out of darkness, hath shined in our hearts, to give the light of the knowledge of the glory of God in the face of Jesus Christ" (4:6). If you would see the glory of God, says the apostle Paul, turn your eyes upon Jesus. If you desire your mind to be suffused with the glory of God, meditate on the person and work of Jesus Christ. Considering the filthiness and rubbish of the world that so many people are putting into their minds, is it any wonder that they cannot see the glory of God and are blind to the great realities of eternity? Is it any wonder they have no vision for souls? A man who cannot see the glory of God cannot see anything. As the psalmist said, "In thy light shall we see light" (Ps. 36:9). Oh, that we would long to see the glory of God! I cannot believe that a man is genuinely saved who has no desire to see the glory of God. Let us cry with Moses, "I beseech thee, show me thy glory" (Exod. 33:18). We see that glory only as we meditate and focus upon the person of the Lord Jesus Christ. In Him shines all the fulness of the glory of God. Thus—as Paul argues through the third and fourth chapters of 2 Corinthians—the gospel far surpasses the law. In 3:7ff he argues that though the law was a ministration of death and condemnation, it was attended by great glory at the time of its revelation. Indeed, the face of Moses shone with that glory. However, Moses put a veil over his face. Why did he do that? Paul cites two great reasons. First, to teach the Israelites once and for all that men cannot face the glory of God on the basis of law. If you ever try to come face to face with the glory of God on the basis of your legal obedience, that glory will consume you in judgment. No man on the basis of law keeping and self-righteousness can look upon God and live. That was the first reason Moses placed a veil over his face.

The second reason was that that glory was fading away. "The ministration of death, written and engraven in stones, was glorious, so that the children of Israel could not [or, should not] steadfastly behold the face of Moses for the glory of his countenance; which glory was to be done away" (3:7). According to 3:13 Moses put a veil over his face so that the children of Israel should not steadfastly look to the end of that which was being abolished. That glory was a fading glory. Why was it fading? Because the dispensation of the law was purely temporary. It was not meant to be permanent. Paul says that where people cling to Moses they still have a veil upon them. Thus he teaches that if we would see the glory of God we must see it in the face of Jesus Christ, because in Him alone does that glory shine forth in all its unfading fulness.

Moreover, if we see the glory of God in the face of Jesus Christ we see it in the face of a Saviour and not of a judge. We see it in the face of Him who has fulfilled the law and left not one iota of it unaccounted for. God is satisfied with Christ and what He did for us. On that ground of Christ's glorious person and gracious work we stand reconciled to Him. This is the gospel, and it is greater than the law because it is a ministration of life and salvation. That is Paul's argument.

Despite all this, he tells the Corinthians, Judaizers want us to give up Christ and return to Moses. They want to make that temporary legal dispensation permanent. They want to superimpose it on the gospel and make the law an instrument of salvation. They want to deny the sole sufficiency of the righteousness of Christ and either replace or supplement it with our own legal obedience. To rebut such heresy Paul sounds the two great keynotes of this epistle: "The grace of our Lord Jesus Christ" (8:9) and "the glory of God in the face of Jesus Christ" (4:6). Around these notes of grace and glory Paul plays the whole symphony of the gospel.

What a message he has to give! In Christ we have wondrous gospel blessings. First, in Christ we have *union with Christ,* because we are *in* Him. God identifies Christ with His people and His people with Christ. Legally, spiritually, and eternally they are one. Oh, that we could grasp what identification with Christ really means! Oh, that we would live our lives in the light of that identification! It is the most potent force for holiness and spiritual fulness we can know. The second blessing we have in Christ is *regeneration:* "If any man be in Christ, he is a new creature" (5:17). That is regeneration. Then we have *confirmation,* not in the sense Roman Catholicism and Episcopalianism have given to the term, but in the sense that He seals us with the Holy Spirit (1:22). The seal of the Holy Spirit is the mark of confirmed ownership. It is God's assurance to us that we are His; it is His guarantee that we will be in glory. The next blessing we have in Christ is *reconciliation.* "God ... hath reconciled us to himself by Jesus Christ" (5:18). The enmity between us and our God is gone. Our rebellious hearts have been subdued. God has wrought repentance within us. He has created in us a new disposition of will, and He receives us in friendship with Himself. Furthermore, we have *justification.* God "hath made him to be sin for us, who knew no sin; that we might be made the righteousness of God in him" (5:21). Here is one of the most profound texts in all of Scripture. It describes a forensic, or purely legal, transaction, not a moral transaction. Christ never became personally sinful or defiled. When God made Him to be sin for us, He imputed all our sin to Him and made Him the object of His wrath against that sin. When He makes us "the righteousness of God in him," He imputes Christ's righteousness to us and makes us the object of all the favour due to that righteousness. That is what it means to be "justified freely by his grace" (Rom. 3:24).

Then we have *consolation.* At the very beginning of the epistle Paul states that God, "the Father of our Lord Jesus Christ [is] the Father of mercies, and the God of all comfort; who comforteth us in all our tribulation" (1:3, 4). It is good to be saved and to enjoy the comfort of the gospel. As Christians, we have the Lord with us as "a very present help in trouble," as the psalmist puts it (Ps. 46:1). The gospel brings great comfort, whatever afflictions or difficulties we may have to face. The greatest consolation is that all this leads to *glorification.* In 2 Cor. 4:17 we read, "Our light affliction, which is but for a moment, worketh for us a far more exceeding and eternal weight of glory." That glory is certain for every justified believer. "We know that if our earthly house of this tabernacle were dissolved, we have a building of God, an house not made with hands, eternal in the heavens" (5:1). For every Christian there is glory on ahead.

Now, says Paul, here is the message of the gospel. Others come with their little theories and theologies, but here is the message of the gospel: grace and glory in and through Jesus Christ. What a message! It is worth preaching. To those who have personally experienced its power, God has committed this word of reconciliation. They are ambassadors for Christ (5:18–20). Let us give ourselves to the proclamation of this glorious gospel. Let us never be diverted from that task. It is not an easy task. As Paul discovered, and as we will find, the gospel message is opposed by malicious men.

THE OPPOSITION OF MALICIOUS MEN

In Paul's case there were two groups of opponents, one professedly Christian and the other confessedly heathen. His opponents within the church were of two kinds. First, there were in the church those who opposed Paul because they loved their own wicked lifestyle. Then there were the Judaizers, who hated the message, and therefore the messengers, of free grace. They set out to undo the apostle's work. By slander they sought to ruin his reputation. Such was their antagonism that though they were professed defenders of the law, they made common cause with the most audacious and unrepentant of lawbreakers just to defeat Paul's ministry of grace. What hypocrisy!

The other source of opposition was the heathen. They strove viciously against the gospel and its preachers and caused Paul much suffering. The apostle describes this bitter persecution very fully in 2 Corinthians. In the first chapter he writes, "We would not, brethren, have you ignorant of our trouble which came to us in Asia, that we were pressed out of measure, above strength, insomuch that we despaired even of life: but we had the sentence of death in ourselves, that we should not trust in ourselves, but in God which raiseth the dead" (1:8, 9). Such was the opposition Paul encountered that he had been brought to the point of death by the enemies of the gospel. He returns to this theme in chapter 4. He refers to himself as an earthen vessel (v. 7), a simple pot made of clay. In other words, Paul says he is just an ordinary man. He was not a superman who had no feelings. He suffered deeply. "We are troubled on every side . . . we are perplexed . . . persecuted . . . cast down . . . always bearing about in the body the dying of the Lord Jesus" (vv. 8–10). True, he did not succumb to all those pressures, but he suffered nonetheless.

In chapter 11 Paul gives another deep insight into his suffering. In verses 23–27 he lists the afflictions he bore at the hands of sinners: "Are they ministers of Christ? (I speak as a fool) I am more; in labours more abundant, in stripes above measure, in prisons more frequent, in deaths oft. Of the Jews five times received I forty stripes save one. Thrice was I beaten with rods, once was I stoned, thrice I suffered shipwreck, a night and a day I have been in the deep; in journeyings often, in perils of waters, in perils of robbers, in perils by mine own countrymen, in perils by the heathen, in perils in the city, in perils in the wilderness, in perils in the sea, in perils among false brethren; in weariness and painfulness, in watchings often, in hunger and thirst, in fastings often, in cold and nakedness."

So from outside the church there was opposition. From inside the church there was opposition. The same is true in every place. It is true to-day. There is an unrelenting battle against the truth of God. It comes from the outside under many guises, some of them political, some of them social, some of them pseudoscientific, some of them military. There are forces at work against the church of Jesus Christ. There are politicians, and judges, indeed people of all sorts who, given the chance, will do their best to crush the messenger of the gospel and the message he bears. In addition to those who challenge the gospel from the outside, there are those who seek to corrupt it from the inside. Paul constantly warned of this. He warned the Ephesian elders that after his departure there would arise out of their own midst grievous wolves who would not spare the flock (Acts 20:29–30). To Timothy he wrote that there would arise in the church seducing spirits who would preach the doctrine of demons (1 Tim. 4:1).

What makes 2 Corinthians such a valuable epistle for us today is that it is a manual for Christian warfare. For us the battle is raging. To-day as in Paul's day there are false prophets who preach another gospel that presents another Jesus, and they are energized by another spirit (11:4). As Paul says, Satan appears as an angel of light, and his ministers pretend to be ministers of light (11:13–15). You will find such false prophets in the church. They are sowing confusion and false gospels. Here is the true significance of the Romanizing, ecumenical (the drive for one world church), and charismatic theories and practices so prevalent today. These are not the gospel. They are another gospel, of another Jesus, by another spirit. When you get Roman Catholic Charismatic priests, even cardinals, claiming that they have received the baptism of the Spirit and it has given them a greater devotion than ever to the mass and to Mary, you know that it is another gospel, and another Jesus, and another Spirit. The mass is under the curse of God's Word. You cannot believe the Bible and believe the mass. Mary, the mediatrix of Rome, is not the mother of the Lord Jesus Christ; she is an invention of the popes for the damnation of souls. Yet today practically all Christendom unites to welcome the "Christian unity" now promoted between Rome and evangelical believers. This is what is going on today. Satan's ministers have come inside the church, and they are gaining the ears of the people while God's true messengers find it difficult to gain a hearing at all.

THE VICTORY OF A SPIRITUAL MINISTRY

We do not need to become despondent, for 2 Corinthians is a manual for victory. Therefore we must finish our study by noting that a spiritual ministry always defeats malicious men who oppose it.

God's faithful people in Corinth could take Paul's statement in 1:9–10 as an expression of their own confidence in the midst of the spiritual battle that raged around them: "But we had the sentence of death in ourselves, that we should not trust in ourselves, but in God which raiseth the dead: who delivered us from so great a death, and doth deliver: in whom we trust that he will yet deliver us." To all appearances Paul was doomed to death, but he trusted his God to deliver him, and He did. That is our hope, our confidence, in this day when we are apparently being engulfed by apostasy. I believe in revival. God has delivered the church in the past. He can do it again today. There is victory and deliverance for God's people.

That deliverance does not come through fleshly methods. We cannot fight God's battles with the devil's weapons. That is made clear in 10:3–5: "Though we walk in the flesh, we do not war after the flesh: (for the weapons of our warfare are not carnal, but mighty through God to the pulling down of strong holds;) casting down imaginations, and every high thing that exalteth itself against the knowledge of God, and bringing into captivity every thought to the obedience of Christ."

What are these mighty spiritual weapons? *"The sentence of death"* (1:9) is one. A strange weapon, is it not? God brings His people to the end of themselves. He lets us see we have no power, and no ability, that we have no power to stand. He lets us feel this "sentence of death" in order that we may not trust in ourselves but in our God. A second spiritual weapon is *supplication:* "Ye also helping together by prayer for us" (1:11). Another weapon is *sincerity* (2:17; 4:2). *Spreading the gospel* is yet another weapon (4:3–7). By refusing to hide our gospel, because we realize that gospel is the only hope of the world, we employ a weapon that causes Satan to tremble. A fifth weapon is our *separation:* "Be ye not unequally yoked together with unbelievers: for what fellowship hath righteousness with unrighteousness? and what communion hath light with darkness? And what concord hath Christ with Belial? or what part hath he that believeth with an infidel? And what agreement hath the temple of God with idols? for ye are the temple of the living God; as God hath said, I will dwell in them, and walk in them; and I will be their God, and they shall be my people. Wherefore come out from among them, and be ye separate, saith the Lord, and touch not the unclean thing; and I will receive you, and will be a Father unto you, and ye shall be my sons and daughters, saith the Lord Almighty. Having therefore these promises, dearly beloved, let us cleanse ourselves from all filthiness of the flesh and spirit, perfecting holiness in the fear of God" (6:14–7:1). What a weapon biblical separation is!

We have yet another weapon for successful spiritual warfare: *support of the work of God.* God's people enjoy true fellowship with their fellow believers. We are not in this battle alone. Corinth was separated geographically from the church in Macedonia and from the church in Jerusalem, but they were one in Christ. Thus Paul exhorted them to support one another and so benefit from the fellowship and the oneness of the church of Christ. The final spiritual weapon we mention is a *sowing* (9:6–11). Paul here is talking about giving money, about investing in God's work. But he includes much more than that. He uses the example of the Macedonian Christians, who gave themselves to God's work and therefore gave liberally, though they were chronically poor, to support the cause of Christ. Here is the true apostolic model of spiritual sowing. Invest yourself and then invest what you have in God's work. What a weapon against the kingdom of darkness is a man (or a church) who has dedicated himself and his substance to the work of the gospel.

We are in a real spiritual warfare. We cannot fight it according to the wisdom or ways of the flesh. But the Lord has provided us with potent spiritual weapons—the sentence of death on all self-sufficiency, supplication, sincerity, spreading the gospel, separation from sinful alliances, support of God's work, and sowing spiritual seed by investing ourselves and our substance in the work of God. These are the weapons the Lord has provided for us. He means us to use them. Wielded by the power of the Holy Spirit they will guarantee us a spiritual ministry that will defeat every power and plan of hell. If we use these we will be more than conquerors, and however hot the conflict will live and serve in the enjoyment of the wonderful trinitarian blessing with which this manual for successful spiritual warfare ends: "The grace of the Lord Jesus Christ, and the love of God, and the communion of the Holy Ghost, be with you all. Amen" (13:14).

9

Galatians
Standing Fast In Gospel Liberty

Salvation by God's free grace received by faith in the

◆

merits of Christ without additional works of our own is

◆

the only gospel. So important is this truth that Paul

◆

pronounces God's curse on any, even an apostle or an

◆

angel from heaven, who would preach any other gospel.

◆

We must therefore maintain this charter of true

◆

Christian liberty against all shades of legalism.

*T*he churches of Galatia were formed as a result of Paul's missionary labours. They were then *de*formed as the result of the activities of certain Judaizers, probably from the church in Jerusalem. These
Judaizers sought to convince the Galatians that to be saved Gentiles had
to submit themselves to circumcision and to the rest of the ritual observances of the Jewish law. The entire apostolic band had met in Jerusalem
to consider this matter (Acts 15). Under the inspiration of the Holy Spirit
they had utterly repudiated the dogma of the Judaizers and had emphatically endorsed Paul's teaching of the gospel of free grace received
by faith without the works of the law. Despite this the Judaizers persisted
in a pernicious campaign of opposition to Paul's ministry. They flatly
contradicted his great theme of salvation by grace alone through faith
alone. They gave the impression that the Jerusalem apostles—Peter,
John, and James the brother of our Lord—stood behind them. They
alleged that Paul was not one of the pillars of the church. He was a second-class teacher who was running contrary to the opinion of the true
apostles. That was the general tenor of their message as they attacked
Paul's person in order to attack his message. In Galatia they met with
startling success, succeeding in subverting all the churches of the region.
That is what led Paul to write this brief but very intense epistle.

Galatians is the sharpest of all the epistles Paul wrote. Even when
he wrote 1 and 2 Corinthians to condemn great sin in the church, he
sounded a note of thankfulness for the people who were standing faithful. He acknowledged the response of many spiritually minded people
to his word of rebuke. In the epistle to the Galatians, however, he makes
no reference to anything in the Galatian churches for which he thanks
God. That is an amazing thing for Paul, who always seemed to find
something in the churches for which to be grateful. Such was the sin of
the Galatians that they had afforded him no occasion to give thanks to
God for anything in them. They had broken his heart because they had
turned from grace to law and from faith to works. They had turned from
Christianity to Judaism, though still retaining the name of Christian.
The apostle's response was a stern rebuke.

From the very beginning of the epistle he goes to the heart of the
controversy. In one of the most lucid and concentrated theological expositions in the Bible, he utterly demolishes the false gospel of the
Judaizers. That is what it was, a false gospel. It was a total perversion of
the truth, and as such it came under Paul's scathing indictment. He says
this so-called gospel is "another gospel: which is not another" (1:6–7). It
was another (Greek, *heteros*) gospel with no identity with, and little resemblance to, the gospel of Christ. It was not merely another (Greek,
allos) view of the same gospel. In fact, the Judaizers themselves knew

that very well. Paul spells out their motives very clearly: "[They] trouble you, and would pervert the gospel of Christ" (1:7). Such a perversion of divine truth merits the strongest possible denunciation, and Paul issues it: "Though we, or an angel from heaven, preach any other gospel unto you than that which we have preached unto you, let him be accursed" (1:8). On the issue of salvation by free grace through faith in the merits of Christ without any works of man Paul was not willing to compromise one iota. There were many issues over which he would let every man follow his conscience. In matters of indifference—that is, matters about which Christians may adopt different views without hurt to the teaching or the testimony of the gospel—Paul would have all Christians seek to do the will of God as they understood it, with love for differing brethren. But on the matter at issue in Galatia he left no room for compromise. He would withstand anybody on this issue. When even Peter on a visit to Antioch in Syria preached the same gospel Paul preached, but compromised what he taught by yielding to the pressure of some Jews zealous for circumcision and withdrew himself from eating with his Gentile brethren, Paul withstood him to the face. Peter fully believed the gospel but was afraid to face the anger of the Judaizers (2:12). Even Barnabas, Paul's closest friend and co-worker, was scared into submission by these Jews. But Paul refused to yield to them. He was dealing with a matter so vital to the gospel that he would have been willing to separate from even Peter and Barnabas rather than to detract from the essential truth of the gospel: justification by free grace through faith without works, Christ's merit alone being the ground of our acceptance with God.

There can never be fellowship between light and darkness, between heaven and hell, between God and the devil, between truth and outright error. There can never be fellowship between the gospel and the perversion of the gospel. We cannot have Christian fellowship with those who are preaching the devil's gospel that Paul opposes in Galatians, or with those who are preaching a mixture of law and grace as the way to heaven. According to Paul we are to oppose and separate from such perverters of truth and troublers of the church. That is the clear teaching of the New Testament. Nowadays people tend to dismiss the doctrine of separation as schismatic. Sometimes the charge is well grounded. Too many sectarians use the doctrine of separation as an excuse for indulging their own narrow prejudice. That misuse, however, should not be allowed to obscure the fact that under the circumstances set forth in Scripture, separation is a Christian duty. The issues in separation are those truths that form the heart of the gospel. Where the gospel is faithfully believed and proclaimed in its biblical purity, there is no ground for separation. Where it is not, there is no ground for fellowship. Paul recognized that and was determined that the Galatians also would recognize it. That is what makes his Galatian epistle such an important book.

The six chapters of the epistle fall into three sections of two chapters each. The first two chapters are personal narrative, the second two chapters are a doctrinal argument, and the final two chapters are a practical exhortation. The central theme is that **the message of free grace is the only true gospel.** In working out this theme Paul makes four points.

First, free grace is the vital principle of God's one and only gospel of salvation.

Second, this gospel of free grace is the charter of Christian liberty.

Third, this gospel of grace which gives us our liberty is under constant threat.

Fourth, we must therefore stand fast in gospel liberty and refuse the yoke of bondage.

THE VITAL PRINCIPLE OF THE GOSPEL

Free grace is the vital principle of the only gospel of salvation God has ever revealed to us. Clearly, chapter 1 is the basis of the entire Galatian epistle. In it the apostle Paul is at pains to point out certain very important truths. First, he emphasizes that the message he preaches is not his message at all. He did not originate it. There is a class of religious authors who talk about Paul's theological genius, as if he had produced his own gospel. Paul was undoubtedly a genius. He had a brilliant intellect. However, the gospel he preached was not the product of his genius. He did not modify a message conveyed to him by Peter or some other teacher. Paul says that he did not receive his gospel "of man, neither was I taught it, but by the revelation of Jesus Christ" (1:12).

The next point he is at pains to make is that this gospel had utterly and totally changed his own life. He gives his testimony to the power of the gospel: "Ye have heard of my conversation [or, manner of life] in time past in the Jews' religion, how that beyond measure I persecuted the church of God, and wasted it: and profited in the Jews' religion above many my equals in mine own nation, being more exceedingly zealous of the traditions of my fathers. But . . . it pleased God, who separated me from my mother's womb, and called me by his grace, to reveal his Son in me, that I might preach him among the heathen" (1:13–16). What a statement of grace! Paul's testimony was that he was converted to Christ by the free grace of God.

When a man has experienced full, free, sovereign, saving grace in its all-sufficient fulness, he will be totally opposed to any gospel that belittles the grace of God. People who talk about salvation by works, by doing the best they can, obviously have never felt what Paul felt. When

Paul felt the grace of God, he forever repudiated works as a means of salvation. He was intolerant of the entire notion of human merit. He did not consider his message as an aspect of the truth. He did not present it as his view of the gospel. No, what he preached was God's gospel and the whole gospel. That is why in 1:8–9 he issues a very strong denunciation of any who would preach any other gospel: "But though we, or an angel from heaven, preach any other gospel unto you than that which we have preached unto you, let him be accursed. As we said before, so say I now again, If any man preach any other gospel unto you than that ye have received, let him be accursed." In this ecumenical age such a statement sounds extreme. It is not "moderate," and we all know that to be a theological moderate is the pinnacle of goodness and love!

But Paul was not extreme. Nor was he lacking in love. In fact, we see from 1:4–5 that he made his statements because he was moved by a great love for Christ. He describes the Lord Jesus Christ as the One "who gave himself for our sins, that he might deliver us from this present evil world, according to the will of God and our Father: to whom be glory for ever and ever." Here is why Paul made such strong statements against false gospellers. It was because he had the real gospel, which he preached for the glory of His Lord. Note carefully the fundamental teaching of Paul's gospel.

The free will of God is the source of the gospel. It is "according to the will of God and our Father." The only reason there is any gospel is the absolute sovereign will of God, whereby in eternity He chose to save a people for the glory of His name.

The free obedience of Christ is the substance of the gospel. Christ "gave himself for our sins." As Paul says in another place, He "became obedient unto death, even the death of the cross" (Phil. 2:8). Perfect legal obedience is necessary for a man to enter heaven, that is, an obedience which fulfils the precept and the penalty of God's law. The message of the gospel is that it is not our personal obedience that merits heaven for us, but Christ's obedience. Christ owed nothing to the law; we owe everything to it. From the moment our life is conceived in the womb we are in debt to the law of God. No act of obedience on our part can ever erase that debt. It can only add to it, for even "our righteousnesses are as filthy rags" in God's sight (Isa. 64:6). But the free obedience of Christ is the substance of the gospel. In His life He satisfied the precept, and in His death He paid the penalty, of the law of God, and thereby redeemed us unto God.

The free deliverance of sinners shows the strength of the gospel. By faith in Jesus Christ's finished work sinners are immediately and eternally delivered from sin, saved from the wrath of God, freely justified, and made joint heirs with Christ. Some time ago I saw film coverage of a Christian television personality's visit to part of San Francisco. She took her camera crew along as she went "soulwinning" among drunkards and drug addicts, many of whom were lying in the street. Her message was, "I love you, and Jesus loves you. Would you allow me to pray with you? Would you pray and ask Jesus into your heart?" In all I heard there was not even a reference to the glad tidings of the gospel. One man said he was "gay." The visitor told him, "Ask Jesus; He'll take it away." The man was lying on the pavement, either drunk or drugged. Fiercely he replied, "No, He won't. I have asked Him a hundred times." The lady's reply saddened me beyond words. She said, "Ask Him the hundred and first time, *and then you have got to do your best.*" Is that the gospel which is the power of God? Is that good news for a sinner whose will is depraved, whose mind is darkened, and whose whole being is enslaved by sin? The gospel is not the message that God will support men in some program of self-help. It is rather the word of all-powerful grace that He who gave Himself for our sins actually delivers us from this present evil world.

The free worship of those delivered is the song of the gospel: "To whom be glory for ever and ever." Those who have experienced God's saving grace have every cause to sing. Theirs is no worldly song of self-congratulations but a carol of praise to their all-powerful Redeemer.

That is Paul's gospel, and it utterly excludes all law works, or impressing God by doing the best we can, or gaining His favour by anything we can perform. That is why Paul says he constantly placarded Christ before the Galatians: "O foolish Galatians, who hath bewitched you, that ye should not obey the truth, before whose eyes Jesus Christ hath been evidently set forth [literally, placarded], crucified among you?" (3:1). Everywhere Paul went he preached Christ crucified. He placarded Him. Christ crucified was his only message. He knew no other gospel. "Christ hath redeemed us from the curse of the law, being made a curse for us: for it is written, Cursed is every one that hangeth on a tree: that the blessing of Abraham might come on the Gentiles through Jesus Christ" (3:13–14). This is Paul's gospel. He restates it in the next chapter: "When the fulness of the time was come, God sent forth his Son, made of a woman, made under the law, to redeem them that were under the law, that we might receive the adoption of sons" (4:4–5). In 6:14 he says, "God forbid that I should glory, save in the cross of our Lord Jesus Christ."

Here then is the gospel. It is the message of free, saving grace bestowed on us on the ground of the merit of Christ's person and work. This is the starting point of the gospel. It is also its finishing point.

The gospel never wavers from this message. This is the substance and sum of God's saving message. We must not trim it. We must not add to it or take from it. It is the perfect creation of God. As the Lord said to Moses of His altar, "If thou lift up thy tool upon it, thou hast polluted it" (Exod. 20:25).

Free grace, then, is the vital principle of the gospel.

THE CHARTER OF CHRISTIAN LIBERTY

In the light of all this, the gospel of free grace is the charter of the Christian's liberty. Liberty is one of the major themes of Galatians. Eleven times in this epistle Paul raises the theme of liberty, more than in all his other epistles combined. That means that eleven times he implies a reference to bondage. He adds another seven explicit references to bondage. Clearly these allusions to liberty and bondage are not accidental or incidental. Therefore it is vital for us to understand exactly what Paul means by them.

What does liberty mean? Nowadays the phrase "Christian liberty" usually means the freedom some Christians assert to smoke, or drink alcohol, or play cards—the freedom to cut loose from the restraints of "pietism." That is the extent of Christian liberty in many people's minds nowadays. That is not what Paul means by Christian liberty. What Paul means by liberty is the liberty of not having to establish our own righteousness before God by our own works, the liberty of not having to merit acceptance with God. By liberty Paul means a standing of perfect acceptance with God. That is true liberty. To be accepted by God, and free from all condemnation, that is liberty. By liberty Paul means a free and perfect righteousness. To be counted perfectly righteous by God because of the imputed righteousness of Christ, that is liberty. By liberty Paul means such things as produce genuine rest of conscience. No man enjoys liberty if his conscience is in turmoil and constantly condemns him.

Here, then, is the meaning of liberty: perfect acceptance with God, perfect righteousness, and genuine peace. It is the glory of the gospel that it meets all three requirements for the enjoyment of liberty. It assures us of acceptance with God. It reveals to us our perfect righteousness in Christ in the sight of God. When those truths grip our hearts they create in us true rest of conscience and silence every voice of blame and accusation. That is true liberty.

By bondage the apostle means a servile submission to the rites and rituals of religious observance as a means of obtaining favour with God. The notion of impressing God and earning His favour by virtue of how well we perform engenders bondage. It is destructive of all Christian assurance and peace. Anyone who thinks that God will accept him on the basis of what he does can never attain to any assurance of his acceptance because he can never know when he has done enough. Indeed, can any man ever say he has done enough to satisfy the standards of the infinitely holy God? If God offered to accept us on condition that we love Him enough, or trust Him enough, or obey Him enough, or give enough to Him, how could we ever meet the required standard? A religion of salvation by works condemns sinners to the judgment of God and leaves them without hope. Even if it were possible for a man to merit acceptance with God (and it is not), he could never enjoy the assurance of that acceptance because, as we have noted, he could never reach the place of knowing that he had done enough. That is why Paul calls works-religion "the yoke of bondage" (5:1). He says that works-religion "gendereth [bears children] to bondage" (4:24). Those who trust in the works of the flesh are slaves.

They are slaves to guilt. Those who try to remove the gnawing feeling of sin's guilt by personal penance or atonement will always remain slaves of guilt. The only power that can deal with the guilt of sin is the power of grace through the blood and righteousness of Jesus Christ—and that grace is received by faith without works.

Those who trust in a religion of works-righteousness are not only slaves of guilt, *they are slaves to the flesh.* Works-righteousness can never make a man holy. We do not obtain victory over sin by will power or by mere human effort. Victory over sin comes only by grace through faith as we live in fellowship with Jesus Christ. Those who substitute the works of the flesh for the merit of Christ received by faith condemn themselves and their followers to slavery to passion and lust of the worst kind. Paul gives us an insight into what the flesh produces. It is not holiness but wickedness. "Now the works of the flesh are manifest, which are these; adultery, fornication, uncleanness, lasciviousness, idolatry, witchcraft, hatred, variance, emulations, wrath, strife, seditions, heresies, envyings, murders, drunkenness, revellings, and such like: of the which I tell you before, as I have also told you in time past, that they which do such things shall not inherit the kingdom of God" (5:19–21). These are not merely the works of pagans. Paul means us to see that these are the works of the very people he has identified as false gospellers. They boasted of their works as the ground of their acceptance with God and their entrance into heaven. But what is the true nature of the works of the flesh? It is as Paul describes. Far from being satisfactory to God, they are not even satisfactory to man. Works-religionists are slaves to the flesh.

And, of course, *they are slaves to uncertainty.* Only the gospel of free grace in Christ can produce the liberty of true peace and assurance. Paul gives us four great reasons for that.

First, the gospel of free grace gives us peace and assurance because *it satisfies the law.* Gal. 2:19 says, "I through the law am dead to the law." What does that mean? It clearly means, "I am legally dead to the demands of the law as the ground of my justification and therefore to its claims and curse against me as a lawbreaker." How can any man make such an assertion? How could even Paul make such a claim? The answer is simple yet sublime. In the person of Jesus Christ his Saviour, who kept the precept of the law for him and bore its curse for him (3:13), he fully and finally satisfied the law. Christ is our Representative. We were chosen in Him. We obeyed the law in Him. We say with Paul, "I am [have been] crucified with Christ: nevertheless I live; yet not I, but Christ liveth in me" (2:20). When He died, we died. When He arose, we arose in Him. When the law exhausted its condemnation against Him, it exhausted its condemnation against all His people in Him. Now the law is satisfied. It is not abrogated. It is not curtailed. It is satisfied. We do not get to heaven by God's dropping the standard; we get to heaven by Christ's meeting the standard. So the gospel of free grace produces liberty because it satisfies the law.

Second, this gospel of free grace gives peace and assurance because *it justifies the believer.* "Knowing that a man is not justified by the works of the law, but by the faith of Jesus Christ, even we have believed in Jesus Christ, that we might be justified by the faith of Christ, and not by the works of the law" (2:16). We are justified. What glorious news this is! When God looked at our Saviour on the cross, He saw not only Jesus of Nazareth as one individual. He saw Him as the legal head of all His people. He saw all believers representatively bear the curse of the law and exhaust its every demand. No condemnation remains for them to endure. The law has been satisfied. They have been justified. That gracious truth brings peace. When we know that we are justified, that our sin is pardoned, and that our righteousness is the very righteousness of Christ, we are as sure of heaven as if we were in it. God could no more keep a believer in Christ out of heaven than He could keep Christ Himself out of heaven. Nothing is more calculated to impart peace and assurance than a heart knowledge of the doctrine of justification.

Third, the gospel of free grace yields peace and assurance because *it sanctifies the believer.* In 3:5 Paul asks a revealing question: "He therefore that ministereth to you the Spirit, and worketh miracles among you, doeth he it by the works of the law, or by the hearing of faith?" Note the expression, "ministereth to you the Spirit." The word *minister* means "supply." God supplies the Spirit to His people, and He does so not "by the works of the law," but by grace through faith. The Spirit is God's gift of grace to believers on the merit of Christ. By the working of that Spirit believers are made holy. "But the fruit of the Spirit is love, joy, peace, longsuffering, gentleness, goodness, faith, meekness, temperance: against such there is no law. And they that are Christ's have crucified the flesh with the affections and lusts. If we live in the Spirit, let us also walk in the Spirit" (Gal. 5:22–25). When God saves a man, He supplies him with the continuing ministry of the Holy Spirit. That is the force of the present tense in 3:5. God constantly supplies the Spirit to His people, and the Holy Spirit working in the justified believer produces spiritual fruit. We are not saved by what we do or how we do it. But when we are justified, we do work, we produce true holiness, because the Holy Spirit is within us. The gospel is not only the message of our justification. It is also—indeed, we could say, *consequently*—the message of our sanctification. That truth is a vital element in our enjoyment of the liberty of peace and assurance. That liberty and true holiness go together. Christian liberty is not licence. "Ye have been called unto liberty; only use not liberty for an occasion to the flesh" (5:13). Christian liberty is freedom to be holy. It is not an excuse for sin. Tolerated sin is destructive to true liberty, for it robs us of the peace and assurance that belong to God's people. It is by its sanctifying power, as much as by its justifying power, that the gospel produces this liberty in believers.

We should perhaps emphasize the utter consistency of the gospel. It does not preach grace through faith for justification and then abandon us to works for our sanctification. Legalism never produces sanctification. Many people go wrong here. Even a leading Reformed journal carried the statement that while justification is by faith, sanctification is by law. That is dangerous nonsense. Paul brings justification and sanctification together in 2:20: "I am [have been] crucified with Christ: nevertheless I live; yet not I, but Christ liveth in me: and the life which I now live in the flesh I live by the faith of the Son of God, who loved me, and gave himself for me." How do we live a life of holy obedience that does full justice to God's law as our recognized rule of duty? "By the faith of the Son of God, who loved me, and gave himself for me." In other words, the believer constantly lives by faith. He allows what he believes concerning Christ to dictate his behaviour. That is true gospel holiness, and it brings the blessing of peace and assurance.

Fourth, the glorious gospel of grace gives us the liberty of peace and assurance because *it clarifies the nature and function of the law.* Chapters 3 and 4 show that the law was never meant to be the means of justification. The law demands a redemption by blood, so it cannot preach salvation by works. It came four hundred years after the promise of grace, and it cannot annul that promise. It was only a temporary addition to the promise, not a permanent replacement or appendix.

In trying to understand the relationship of the law to the promise we should note the words of 3:20, one of the most difficult verses in all the Bible. It is said that there are at least 250 different interpretations of this verse. We will take the meaning that is most consistent with the context: "A mediator is not a mediator of one, but God is one." Paul is speaking of the promise and the law. He says the law was "ordained by angels in the hand of a mediator" (v. 19, the Greek text has the definite article, *"the* mediator"). Then he goes on, "Now a mediator is not [merely] a mediator of one [of these, i.e., of law and promise], but God is one [and the same under both]." Christ is the only mediator between God and men (1 Tim. 2:5). Paul says He mediated both the promise and the law. Therefore the law is not the enemy of grace.

It was given as a schoolmaster to lead God's people to Christ that they might be justified by faith (Gal. 3:24). Once they are justified by faith they are no longer under a schoolmaster (3:25). They are like people who have passed from childhood to full age. That is how Paul views the period when the spiritual heirs of Abraham were held under the law. They were true sons of the Father, but they were still in the time of their minority, not yet invested with all their filial rights. Subjection to the law denotes childhood, not maturity; servitude, not liberty. Once God's people have come to faith in Christ and entered upon all the rights and privileges of their sonship, why would they want to go back to the law? That is Paul's argument.

He goes even further. He likens law worshippers to Ishmael; they are the spiritual sons of Hagar. Believers in Christ are like Isaac, the sons of promise. How then could any Christian ever go back to the law? Shall we give up free grace for the bondage of substituting our work for, or adding it to, the work of Christ?

THE THREAT TO THE GOSPEL

Despite Paul's powerful statement of the liberty the gospel brings to believers, there are always legalists who pose a threat to the gospel of grace. "False brethren unawares brought in . . . came in privily to spy out our liberty which we have in Christ Jesus, that they might bring us into bondage" (2:4). The false brethren to whom Paul referred were Judaizers. They were not true Christians. They were those on whom he placed his anathema (1:8, 9). Yet they were in the church, parading themselves as guardians of the truth of God. That is what made them so dangerous to the Galatian churches.

The legalistic attack on the gospel of free grace has never slackened. Throughout church history legalism, with its dogma of works-righteousness, has sought to subvert the gospel of grace, with its message of free justification through the imputation of the righteousness of Christ to His believing people. Indeed, the Council of Trent enshrined as Roman Catholic doctrine the very thing Paul anathematized in Galatians. The recently published *Catechism of the Catholic Church* confirms Trent's doctrine. Thus Rome's central doctrine is a system of works-righteousness. It is a false gospel. Nor is the threat to the gospel confined to the Roman Catholic church. It has taken over many of the churches of Protestantism. Have most Protestant denominations not effectively moved to some form of salvation by works?

Even where salvation by grace through faith is espoused the danger to the gospel is often real. In 2:11–13 we read of how Peter, who undoubtedly believed in the gospel of grace, weakened that gospel and endangered the liberty of God's people. All too often good men weaken the gospel of grace by ill-considered beliefs or practices. For example, when evangelists make God's election depend on His foresight of our faith, do they not make a human work the basis of salvation? When they make regeneration a joint work of God and man, do they not weaken the doctrine of free grace? When they make regeneration the result of faith—that is, of the action of one still dead in sin—and not the cause of that faith, are they not adopting a key element in the very system Galatians was written to oppose? These views have become so entrenched in Bible-believing churches that to question them exposes one to the suspicion of heresy—the exact opposite of the position Paul adopted in writing Galatians. Any attempt to mix legalism with the gospel of grace will produce a kind of guilt theology. Guilt theology destroys Christian peace and assurance. It kills Christian liberty and Christian life. It is the enemy of the gospel of Christ. Yet many Christians are labouring under it. In the face of the threat of legalism our watchword should be Gal. 2:19–20: "I through the law am dead to the law, that I might live unto God. I am [have been] crucified with Christ: nevertheless I live; yet not I, but Christ liveth in me: and the life which I now live in the flesh I live by the faith of the Son of God, who loved me, and gave himself for me." As Christians, *we are legally free from the law.* Recognizing that glorious truth we are ready for Paul's call to combat legalism.

STAND FAST!

Let us not give up our liberty in Christ. Paul sounds the call to arms: "Stand fast therefore in the liberty wherewith Christ hath made us free, and be not entangled again with the yoke of bondage" (5:1). Later he adds the command to "run." "Ye did run well; who did hinder you that ye should not obey the truth?" (5:7). Finally, twice he gives the instruction to "walk in the Spirit" (5:16, 25).

"Stand" is a call to fidelity to the gospel of grace. The faith of the gospel is under attack from a false gospel that bewitches men (3:1) and leads them astray. We must have such a firm grasp of the truth that we will be impervious to the witchery of every false gospel. However unpopular it may make us, we must take our stand for the gospel of the all-sufficient grace of God received by faith in the merits of Christ.

"Run" is a call to fervency. In 5:7 Paul equates running well, that is, living by the faith of the gospel, with obeying the truth. The faith of the gospel is not merely some dead intellectual assent. It includes intellectual assent, but it goes far beyond it to produce a fervent obedience to the truth of God. This fact is something legalists never grasp. The grace that justifies and sanctifies us through faith in the merits of Christ produces a life that honours the law of God and rejoices to do the will of God. Repudiating the yoke of legal bondage sets believers free to be holy with a fervent obedience to their Lord.

"Walk" is a call to fellowship. Amos asked, "Can two walk together, except they be agreed?" (Amos 3:3). The Christian walks in fellowship with his Lord because he walks in the Spirit—that is, he lives by faith in Christ and His merits. He does not walk in the flesh, either to seek acceptance with God by its works, or to gratify it by indulging its lusts.

Here, then, is the way to combat the threat of legalism to the gospel of grace—fidelity, fervency, and fellowship on the sole basis provided in the gospel. In a word, the answer to legalism is a scriptural understanding of Christ and His atoning work. As Paul said, "God forbid that I should glory, save in the cross of our Lord Jesus Christ, by whom the world is crucified unto me, and I unto the world" (Gal. 6:14).

Legalism always betrays itself by providing something other than Christ and His finished work to glory in. Those who sought to subvert the Galatians gloried in their circumcision, the mark of a dead religion. Paul had better marks in which to glory, for he bore in his body the brand marks of the Lord Jesus Christ (6:17). Five classes of people bore brand marks. Criminals, slaves, the abhorred, soldiers, and people who were devoted to a religion all wore them. Paul bore the marks of Christ for all five reasons. He was Christ's prisoner (Eph. 4:1). As the slave of His Saviour (Rom. 1:1) he was abhorred and reproached. However, he remained a faithful soldier of Christ, entirely consecrated to His service. For Christ he lived. For Him he was willing to die (Acts 20:24). He bore many scars on his body to testify of his unflinching faithfulness to Christ. Yet he found nothing in them to boast about. They were Christ's brand marks. They simply said that he was the Saviour's prisoner, slave, soldier, and worshipper, who bore the reproach of Christ's foes. All Paul could glory in was in Christ. He needed nothing else. He wanted nothing else. Neither should we.

CHAPTER

10

Ephesians

The Unsearchable Riches Of Christ

God has formed His church and filled it with all His

♦

fulness in Christ so as to make it His triumphant

♦

witness to heaven, earth, and hell.

*E*phesus was a very important city, the capital of proconsular Asia, or what we somewhat inexactly term Asia Minor. In many ways Ephesus was like Athens. It had borrowed many features from the Greek capital. It was a centre of culture and of architecture, noted for its literature, arts, and learning. It was the site of one of the seven great wonders of the ancient world, the temple of the fertility goddess Artemis, or Diana, as she is called in Scripture. The temple of Diana brought much more than architecture to Ephesus. It became Asia's most secure bank, and many of the region's rich and famous felt it safe to store their wealth there. It was also a commercial centre, as Paul found out when he went to Ephesus. Then as now, great numbers of people were willing to spend enormous amounts of money on all sorts of religious paraphernalia, producing a bustling trade around the temple of Diana. In addition, like all centres of heathen worship, the temple of Diana brought to the city unspeakable lewdness, immorality, and vice.

To the religious significance of Ephesus was added an ideal situation which made it a city of trade that made it wealthy and of art that won it renown. Dean Farrar said, "Its seas and rivers were rich with fish; its air was salubrious; its position unrivalled; its population multifarious and immense. Its markets [glittered] with the produce of the world's art."

This was the city to which the apostle Paul took the gospel of the Lord Jesus Christ and in which he established the church that was to become the third great capital of Christianity, after Jerusalem and Antioch. Paul's first visit to Ephesus was extremely brief, but when he returned he found "a great door and effectual" opened unto him (1 Cor. 16:9). He spent three years of concentrated evangelistic effort and church building endeavour there and saw much fruit for his labour. Along with the fruitful opportunity he soon discovered that there were "many adversaries." As the Lord mightily blessed the ministry of His servant and saved many souls with whom He established a strong church, the enemies of the gospel rose up in fury. So hot was the conflict that Paul spoke of it as fighting with wild beasts (1 Cor. 15:32). The craftsmen who made a fat living out of the worship of Diana stirred up a riot against him, but they altogether failed to stop the powerful movement of the Spirit of God through Paul in Ephesus. Despite all their opposition the Ephesian church flourished as a centre of eminent piety amid pagan depravity and earned a reputation for faithfulness to the Lord Jesus Christ. This was the church to which Paul addressed this letter. (It would appear that Paul wrote this epistle as something of an encyclical letter to a number of the churches in the region. The epistle to the Laodiceans mentioned in Col. 4:16 was probably their copy of the epistle we know as Ephesians. The encyclical nature of the epistle would also explain why the words "at Ephesus" in 1:1 are missing from some of our Greek mss. while found in others.)

In many ways Ephesians is the deepest and most sublime of all the letters Paul wrote. It may also be the most difficult. In places it pours forth in a veritable torrent of words on subjects so elevated that they beggar our understanding. Ephesians seems to start where Romans leaves off. In Romans Paul speaks of believers as identified with Christ in His death, resurrection, and ascension. In Ephesians he describes them as seated in heaven with Christ their Head. Having stated the position of believers in Christ, Paul proceeds to discuss everything else in the light of it. In Romans the emphasis is upon the personal standing of the believer, albeit with various applications to the church as a body. In Ephesians, while there are references to the individual believer, the main emphasis is on the church as a body. Ephesians is the great church epistle.

It is an epistle that is full of glory. It glows with the light of heaven. Here we see the smile of God and feel the joy of grace. The triumphs of the cross, the empty tomb, and the throne of Christ meet us on every page. That Paul should have written such an epistle from a Roman prison while he stood in jeopardy of his life speaks volumes for the power of the gospel. The joy and peace he felt in Christ far outweighed the gloom of his circumstances. Paul did not languish in prison. He was not frustrated. His faith was in the victorious Christ. His knowledge of the sovereignty of God taught him that the God who had given him an open door in Ephesus was the One who would now use him from behind the closed doors of a Roman prison. Paul knew that the Lord was working out every detail of his life "unto the furtherance of the gospel" (Phil. 1:12). So Ephesians is a glowing testimony to the victory of grace through faith in Christ.

That makes it a book of immense importance to us all. We all must face trouble and suffering. Unless we know the same victory of grace through faith in Christ that Paul knew, such circumstances are likely to crush our spirits. Human philosophies and theories are a broken reed. We need the peace and joy that come from a personal knowledge of Christ and a deep assurance of our acceptance in Him. Our present suffering cannot change God's love for us or the security of our position as the redeemed of His Son. It is the full persuasion of these things that will make us, like Paul, more than conquerors.

Any study of Ephesians must take note of certain pivotal expressions in the epistle. The phrase "in Christ" may be used as the key to the entire book. It refers to the mystical union of believers with Christ. No study of Ephesians, or Colossians, for that matter, can be complete without a thorough grasp of this truth. Another pivotal phrase is "accepted in the beloved" (1:6). A heart appreciation of this truth is the key to living in the peace, joy, and victory of the gospel. A third pivotal phrase is "in heavenly places," or "in the heavenlies." God "hath blessed us with all spiritual blessings in heavenly places in Christ" (1:3). As Christians, we are living in the world, but our joy, peace, security, and eternal salvation—that is, the things that truly define life for us—are not in or of this world. They are located in heaven. Whatever our temporary experience on earth, we are blessed in heaven in Christ.

Closely related to this heavenly blessing is another favourite expression of Paul's, "fulness." *Fulness* means communicated fulness. Christ communicates His fulness to His church (1:23). He desires all Christians to "be filled with all the fulness of God" (3:19), that is, to live up to what God has given them in Christ. While we remain in this body, our experience of Christ's fulness always falls short of perfection. Nevertheless, we should be continually filled with the Spirit (5:18). Soon our experience of Christ will be perfect, when "we all come in the unity of the faith, and of the knowledge of the Son of God, unto a perfect [or, full-grown] man, unto the measure of the stature of the fulness of Christ" (4:13).

Another pivotal expression is "the mystery" (3:3), around which Dispensationalists have woven some very fanciful, but erroneous, theories. We will consider Paul's "mystery" a little later. Perhaps we may take one more expression to sum up all we have mentioned, indeed all that we will yet mention: "the unsearchable [or, untraceable] riches of Christ" (3:8). That is what Ephesians is all about, grace so marvellous that "in all the universe there was no track or trace by following which men's minds could ever have discovered these riches of Christ. Revelation brought them, revelation alone" (R. C. H. Lenski). Ephesians reveals "the breadth, and length, and depth, and height" of God's gracious love in Christ (3:18).

It is a book not only of pivotal expressions but of unforgettable texts. I will list a few of them. These are texts every Christian should know by heart and be able to use in meditation, prayer, and witness: 1:3–7; 2:1–7; 2:8–10; 3:20; 4:4–6; 4:32; 5:18; 5:22–28; 6:1–4; 6:10–20. Ephesians records two wonderful prayers, 1:17–23 and 3:14–21. These are among the greatest prayers to be found in Scripture, and they will repay not only our closest study but our honest adoption of them as our own cry to the Lord.

Ephesians lends itself to simple outlining. The famous Chinese preacher Watchman Nee entitled his studies in Ephesians "Sit, Walk, and Stand." That sums up the book very nicely (see 2:6; 4:1, 17 and 5:2; 6:11, 13, 14). Another simple outline that traces the development of the epistle is Our Wealth (chaps. 1–3), Our Walk (chaps. 4–5), and Our Warfare (chap. 6). It is inviting to consider the book in this way, but our purpose in this study must be to go beyond a bare analysis and grasp the central theme of Paul's message. We have noted his reference to "the unsearchable riches of Christ." We have also noted that this is an epistle that speaks mainly about the church and what Christ has given to it. Combining these fundamental ideas, we arrive at the theme of Ephesians: **God's grace has formed and filled His church as His triumphant witness to heaven, earth, and hell.** In expounding this theme I will make three very simple statements: First, the church is exalted to heaven. Second, the church is effective on earth. Finally, the church is empowered over hell.

THE CHURCH EXALTED TO HEAVEN

God "hath put all things under his [Christ's] feet, and gave him to be the head over all things to the church, which is his body, the fulness of him that filleth all in all" (1:22–23). As we have noted, *fulness* has the idea of a communicated fulness. The teaching is that Christ has communicated His fulness to His church. All the fulness of the Godhead bodily dwells in Christ (Col. 2:9), and He has communicated His fulness to His church. In other words, Christ's church is not something separate from Him. God never considers the church apart from Christ. He never considers any individual member of the church, any believer, apart from Christ. Furthermore, Christians are so united to Christ that He lives vitally in the church and communicates His fulness to it. Paul describes something of what that means in Eph. 2:5–7: "When we were dead in sins, [God] hath quickened us together with Christ, (by grace ye are saved;) and hath raised us up together, and made us sit together in heavenly places in Christ Jesus: that in the ages to come he might show the exceeding riches of his grace in his kindness toward us through Christ Jesus."

All this is a wonderful statement of what the church of Christ *is:* it is His body. There is also a statement of what the church of Christ *has:* it has His fulness. Then there is a statement of what the church of Christ *is going to attain:* in the ages to come the Lord will show it the exceeding riches of His grace.

For the present, God is administering His plan of grace in Christ according to His own eternal counsel, and with a view to His own eternal glory. That is why chapters 1–3 contain such glorious statements about the Christian's exalted position in Christ. In chapter 1, for example, Paul heads his enumeration of the believer's blessings in Christ with his *predestination* by his sovereign Lord. "According as he hath chosen us in him before the foundation of the world, that we should be holy and without blame before him in love: having predestinated us unto the adoption of children by Jesus Christ to himself, according to the good pleasure of his will" (1:4–5). We must not try to avoid or evade the full force of this statement. Recently I heard a preacher quote Eph. 1:4 and explain it as follows: "At Calvary Jesus chose all the world without exception. He chose us all at Calvary." Despite the fact that there is no mention of Calvary in the text, and not the slightest basis for his explanation, he went on, "But we have a choice, and by our choice we can nullify the choice of God." According to that preacher, salvation depends ultimately on our choice, not God's choice. That is not the gospel Paul preached. It is not the message of Ephesians. And I suggest that it is not a gospel that would bring the slightest peace or joy to any needy soul. When God's eternal choice can be negated by the decision of a moment, it is neither eternal nor divine. When God's purpose is overthrown by man's purpose, it is no longer an omnipotent purpose. And when God's purpose is not omnipotent, there is nothing certain in this world, and there is nothing certain in eternity. How different is Paul's statement about our predestination. "He hath chosen us"—not because we are Israelites or because we are Gentiles, not because we are white or because we are black, not because we are good or because we are rich. No, He has chosen us in Christ. That is a sovereign determination. The sovereignty of God's choice is clear from when and why He chose us. When did He choose us? He chose us "before the foundation of the world." Why did He choose us? He chose us "according to the good pleasure of his will."

In Ephesians Paul places a strong emphasis on God's eternal purpose. He predestinated us "according to the good pleasure of his will" (1:5). He "made known unto us the mystery of his will, according to his good pleasure which he hath purposed in himself" (1:9). Again, we have obtained an inheritance in Christ because we were predestinated "according to the purpose of him who worketh all things after the counsel of his own will" (1:11). Finally, in 3:11 Paul shows that the entire purpose and destiny of the church is "according to the eternal purpose which he purposed in Christ Jesus our Lord." So Paul places the believer's predestination at the head of the list of blessings we enjoy by grace. We must not be among those who fear to allow these statements to have their full and natural force. But equally we must not be among those who glory in predestination without regard to personal holiness. God's purpose is not only sovereign. It is also saving and sanctifying. He chose us "that we should be holy and without blame before him" (1:4). A true appreciation of the scriptural doctrine of predestination always leads to humble purity of life before God, never to a proud antinomianism.

Paul follows his mention of the saints' predestination with an emphasis on their *position*. It is "in Christ." Throughout chapter 1 the apostle repeats this thought: chosen in Christ (1:4), "accepted in the beloved" (1:6), and redeemed in Christ through His blood (1:7). Paul continues to use this phrase at every opportunity: God will ultimately head up all things "in Christ" (1:10), "in whom also we have obtained an inheritance" (1:11), "in whom" we trusted (1:12, 13), and "in whom also after that ye believed, ye were sealed with that holy Spirit of promise" (1:13). In 2:10 he says, "We are his workmanship, created in Christ Jesus unto good works." All these emphasize the saints' position, which is perhaps best summed up in the words of 2:13: "Now in Christ Jesus ye who sometimes were far off are made nigh by the blood of Christ."

Paul also speaks of our *possessions.* "Blessed be the God and Father of our Lord Jesus Christ, who hath blessed us with all spiritual blessings in heavenly places in Christ" (1:3). That is one of the most important statements in the Bible. We have in our possession every spiritual blessing necessary to live on earth in the enjoyment of our exalted Head. Despite this rich provision, because of unbelief or disobedience many Christians are living impoverished lives, staggering from one crisis to another. This is not a criticism of people for having crises in their lives. It is a criticism of Christians' inability to apply the gospel to their crises and thus of their inability to live in the joy of the Lord. Some Christians live as if they possessed little or nothing. They have very little power over sin, very little power to witness, very little joy in the Lord, and very little peace in believing. Christians who have been blessed with the fulness of Christ should not be living the lives of spiritual paupers. How can we live up to our inheritance? Instead of majoring upon our subjective feelings, we must understand the gospel and apply it to our circumstances. We must let the fact of the fulness which is ours, the unsearchable riches of Christ, grip our hearts. We must think upon those riches until the thought sets our hearts on fire. Then, realizing what we have in Christ, we must reckon upon it by faith. As we take our stand upon it we will begin to live as the sons of God in victory over the frustration and impoverishment that enervate the life and witness of so many of God's people.

This is not some kind of mind game. It is not merely positive thinking, at least as the world understands that term. We have great possessions. We have adoption into the family of God (1:6). Our heavenly Father has invested us with all the legal rights of sonship and heirship. We also have redemption, deliverance from sin by the blood of Christ (1:7). We have an inheritance (1:11). We have even received the earnest, or initial pledge or token, of that inheritance (1:14). In other words, heaven has begun in the life of a Christian. Oh, it is not complete. We are not yet perfect, but, thank God, we have already entered into great possessions.

That leads to the thought that we have glorious *prospects*. This is a vast idea that Paul introduces to the Ephesians. In 1:10 he says, "That in the dispensation of the fulness of times he might gather together in one [or, that He might sum up under one head] all things in Christ, both which are in heaven, and which are on earth; even in him." Here is our destiny: to belong to a redeemed people enjoying the rule of Christ our Head over a new heaven and a new earth without any "alien and discordant elements" (J. B. Lightfoot). The Holy Spirit who now seals us is the "earnest [the pledge or guarantee] of our inheritance until the redemption of the purchased possession" (1:14). What does that mean? By His blood Christ has purchased us as His possession. Our redemption is, as far as the payment is concerned, complete. Christ will pay no more. As far as our experience of it is concerned, however, our redemption is ongoing. We are redeemed, and daily we are entering into the meaning of that redemption. And as to its fulness, our redemption is yet future. The day of redemption is at hand, when the children of God, being perfectly conformed to Jesus Christ, both physically and spiritually, and absolutely without sin, will enter into the everlasting joy of their Lord. This is what Paul means when he prays, "The eyes of your understanding being enlightened; that ye may know what is the hope of his calling, and what the riches of the glory of his inheritance in the saints" (1:18).

What a glorious prospect we have! Eph. 2:7 speaks of the ages to come. Only a Christian can honestly look forward to the ages to come. People without Christ have nothing to look forward to in this life but drifting ever farther away from God. And they have nothing to look forward to in the life to come but being cast out into outer darkness where there is wailing and gnashing of teeth. By contrast, Christians can look forward to the ages to come knowing that God is going to unfold to them the exceeding riches of His grace. Throughout eternity He will heap upon His people the exceeding greatness and indescribable fulness of all that His grace and kindness can devise.

These prospects are all tied in to God's *purpose* for His people. God's purpose for us is that we should express His glory (1:6, 12). We are not saved merely to be safe from hell. In Christ we have that safety, but God's purpose in saving us goes beyond this. We are not saved merely to raise the comfort level of our lives. Salvation does that, but that is not its ultimate purpose. We are saved that we should be to the praise of the glory of His grace. Our lives are to be songs of praise to God's glorious grace. Not only is this so of Christians as individuals, but the church is intended by God to be His witness to the principalities and powers (3:10–11). Angels and devils should look upon the church and be able to see the wisdom and power of grace in us. Peter tells us that the angels of God desired to look into God's purpose of grace in Christ (1 Pet. 1:12). Now Paul shows us how the Lord gives them that knowledge, namely, by His church. Here then is the church's highest purpose: to be a testimony to the glory of her Lord, declaring His "many-splendoured wisdom," as F. F. Bruce translates the phrase in Eph. 3:10. We should keep that purpose in mind when we speak of our pre-destination, position, possessions, and prospects. God has exalted His people to heaven, even while they live on earth, that they may glorify Him before heaven, earth, and hell.

THE CHURCH EFFECTIVE ON EARTH

From all this it is clear that Christ's church must be effective on earth. The effectiveness of the church of Christ arises, first, out of its spiritual nature, expressed by Paul's teaching of "the mystery"; second, out of its spiritual ministry; and finally, out of its spiritual morality.

The Mystery of the Church

We will have to pay most attention to the first of these, the mystery, because it has become such a contentious issue on account of the ex-treme views adopted by Dispensationalists. They make the mystery to mean that the New Testament church was something completely un-known in Old Testament prophecy, something that has no organic conti-nuity with Israel. According to Dispensationalism, Israel and the church are two eternally separate entities. This theory has enormous repercus-sions and seriously affects one's view of the gospel.[†] Since it depends so largely on a false exposition of Paul's mystery, we must be clear on what that mystery really is. In a word, the essence of the mystery is the forma-tion of Jews and Gentiles as one body in Christ (2:14–22; 3:6). The Dis-pensational theory is that this was the very first time God revealed this truth. It was something entirely new. This entirely new thing, the church, is a totally distinct entity, essentially different from anything that went before. Its people have no connection with the people of God in the Old Testament, and its promises are totally different from all the Old Testa-ment promises of God. Most Dispensationalists will say that after the rejection and death of Jesus Christ, God interposed a parenthetical pe-riod, the church age, and He is going to resume His original purpose with the Jews after He has raptured the church. Some modern

---

[†] For a full treatment of this subject see *The Gospel According to Dispensationalism* by Reginald C. Kimbro (Toronto: Wittenberg Publications, 1995).

Dispensationalists go even further. They hold that the church age is not a parenthetical age; it is an intercalation. In other words, it is something that stands unrelated to anything that went before or comes after. God's purpose in the church is something entirely new, essentially different from what He did in the Old Testament and from what He is going to do with and through the Jews in the tribulation period and in the millennium.

It is a tragedy this theory ever gained acceptance in Bible-believing churches. It is absolutely without foundation. A close investigation of chapter 3 will prove that. It is not true that the mystery of which Paul was writing in Ephesians was being revealed for the very first time. God revealed it to the apostles and prophets, or to the apostolic prophets. These are the apostles of the Lord Jesus Christ (3:5). So all the apostles received this revelation; it was not only Paul. Further, Paul explicitly states that this mystery was not made known in former ages "as it is now revealed unto his holy apostles and prophets." Note the force of the words "as it is now revealed." The word *as* means simply in like manner or in the same way. This truth was revealed in former times, but not to the same degree, not with the same clarity.

So, what was being revealed for the first time? The answer is, "That the Gentiles should be fellowheirs, and of the same body, partakers of his promise in Christ by the gospel" (3:6). Paul goes on to state that a major purpose of his ministry is "to make all men see what is the fellowship [or, dispensation] of the mystery, which from the beginning of the world hath been hid in God" (3:9). Through Paul God is now revealing what had previously been hidden. What is that? It is the dispensation of the mystery. *Dispensation* means the plan of administration. This is what long lay hidden and was revealed through Paul, the administration of the mystery that included all believers, Gentile as well as Jewish, in one body in Christ. The fact of the conversion of the Gentiles was not new. There are numerous Old Testament prophecies of that blessing. What was not revealed was how they were to be brought in. The Jews always thought that when the Gentiles were brought in, they would be Jewish proselytes. That was the thinking behind the contention of those who said, "Except ye be circumcised after the manner of Moses, ye cannot be saved" (Acts 15:1). They were happy to have the Gentiles converted, but they thought that in order to be in the church they had to become Jews. "Absolutely not," said Paul. This is what was brand new. This was the apex of the gospel revelation. This is the dispensation of the mystery, that the Gentiles are brought in to the same body, are made fellow heirs and joint partakers of the promise, but do not have to become Jews. Jewish and Gentile believers form one body in Christ.

Paul clearly states that this body includes the Old Testament saints. He calls the converted Gentiles "fellowheirs," members "of the same body," and "[joint] partakers" of God's promise (3:6). The question is, joint heirs, joint members, and joint partakers with whom? The expression "partakers of his promise" supplies the answer. They are fellow heirs and joint partakers with those who received the promise. Who received the promise? Heb. 11:17 states categorically that Abraham received the promises. All the Old Testament saints did, for they saw them "afar off, and were persuaded of them, and embraced them" (Heb. 11:13). Christians are joint partakers with all who have received the promise. They are members of the same body as the Old Testament saints, because they are partakers of the same promise.

Dispensationalists deny this. They tell us the church is so distinct from anything in the Old Testament that even Abraham is not in the church. The Bible says that Abraham received the gospel (Gal. 3:8), saw and rejoiced in the day of the Lord Jesus Christ (John 8:56), was justified by faith (Rom. 4:1–10), is the "heir of the world" (not just of the Jews, Rom. 4:13), and is "the father of all them that believe" (Rom. 4:11), but somehow or other, according to Dispensationalism, he is not in the church. Gal. 3:14 explicitly states that it is "the blessing of Abraham" that comes on the Gentiles through Jesus Christ. How anyone can interpret Paul's mystery in Ephesians so as to exclude New Testament believers from any identity with Abraham is a mystery indeed. The notion that the church is something that began at Pentecost and will end at the rapture, so that the saints of the Old Testament and of the great tribulation period are not in the church, is totally erroneous.

Here is the mystery of the church: by grace through faith without works, the Gentiles enter into the full blessing of the Abrahamic covenant, without having to become Jews. The middle wall of partition between Jews and Gentiles is removed in Christ (Eph. 2:14–22).

This mystery denotes the spiritual nature of the church. It is unlike anything else on earth. That is the secret of its effectiveness. We must not try to make it like earthly organizations. It is a grave mistake to import the practices and promotions of the business world or of the entertainment world into the church with the idea that "it works for them and therefore it will work for us." Christ's church is a spiritual organization of redeemed people united to Him, indwelt and sealed by the Spirit of God. Treat it as such. That is the key to its effectiveness. The spiritual body of Christ can be effective only as it operates according to its spiritual nature.

The Ministry of the Church

The second key to the church's effectiveness is its ministry. Paul deals extensively with the subject of the church's ministry, its aims and its operations, in 4:8–16: "Wherefore he saith, When he ascended up on high, he led captivity captive, and gave gifts unto men. (Now that he ascended, what is it but that he also descended first into the lower parts of the earth? He that descended is the same also that ascended up far above all heavens, that he might fill all things.) And he gave some, apostles; and some, prophets; and some, evangelists; and some, pastors and teachers; for the perfecting of the saints, for the work of the ministry, for the edifying of the body of Christ: till we all come in the unity of the faith, and of the knowledge of the Son of God, unto a perfect man, unto the measure of the stature of the fulness of Christ: that we henceforth be no more children, tossed to and fro, and carried about with every wind of doctrine, by the sleight of men, and cunning craftiness, whereby they lie in wait to deceive; but speaking the truth in love, may grow up into him in all things, which is the head, even Christ: from whom the whole body fitly joined together and compacted by that which every joint supplieth, according to the effectual working in the measure of every part, maketh increase of the body unto the edifying of itself in love."

The word *for* in verse 12 means unto. God gave apostles, prophets, evangelists, pastors, and teachers *unto* the perfecting, or maturing, of the saints. This perfecting is *unto* their participation in the church's ministry, and this ministry is *unto* the edifying of the body of Christ. That is a picture of the effective working of the church. It is like a healthy body working in all its varied parts (4:16). When every Christian is a witness and a worker, when every Christian takes his full share of responsibility, the church will be effective as Christ's witness on earth.

The Morality of the Church

The third vital key to the church's effectiveness is its morality. In chapters 4–6 Paul describes the church walking, worshipping, serving, and standing for God in the world. In a sentence, his call to God's people is to exhibit the moral standards of the gospel. He tells us to put off the old man and to put on the new, and thus to walk worthy of Christ before men (4:22–24). In the church also our behaviour must be according to God's standard revealed in the gospel. In 4:3–6 Paul shows us that because there is one body, one Spirit, one hope of our calling, one Lord, one faith, one baptism, and one God and Father, we should endeavour to "keep the unity of the Spirit in the bond of peace."

This practice will have dramatic effects on our dealings with one another: "Be ye kind one to another, tenderhearted, forgiving one another, even as God for Christ's sake hath forgiven you" (4:32). When we come together in the church we are not just so many disparate individuals, parading our different cultures, backgrounds, jobs, and talents, all of which tend to divide us one from another. We should realize that despite all our earthly differences we are members of the body of Jesus Christ. That is the standard of our behaviour in the church. We should submit ourselves one to another (5:21), thereby crucifying the flesh and edifying the body. That concern for the body will lead to separation from sin and apostasy: "Have no fellowship with the unfruitful works of darkness, but rather reprove them" (5:11). It will also lead to service (5:16, 17). And it will lead to spiritual fulness. "Be not drunk with wine, wherein is excess; but be filled with the Spirit" (5:18).

The morality of the gospel makes God's people effective not only in the world, and in the church, but also in the home. All too often the church's effectiveness is marred by problems in the homes of its members. In many cases, Christians adopt the philosophy of the world toward their roles and attitudes in their home life. They allow the godless theories of men to define their proper place in the home. This is bound to frustrate and impoverish them. Paul sets forth the sure basis for believers in their home life in 5:22–6:4. He shows that Christian marriage is a reflection of the relationship of Christ and His church. When Christians grasp their true relationship to their Saviour and let that dictate their relationship with their spouses, they will have a happy and effective marriage. It will be a testimony to Christ. When a husband loves his wife with the selfless, sacrificial, sanctifying love of Christ for His church, he is an effective witness to Him. When a wife respects her husband and obeys him with the submission the church shows to Christ, she will be an effective witness to her Saviour. Husbands and wives who thus portray Christ in their homes will see the fruit of such an effective witness in their children. Christians who by faith maintain the gospel morality of chapters 5 and 6 in their home life will find that not only is God's way the right way, it is the way that works.

In 6:5–9 Paul ends his exposition of the effectiveness of gospel morality by dealing with business relationships. He refers particularly to the relationships and actions of servants (slaves) and masters. He did not set out a social agenda to change the prevailing system, but he showed how the gospel affected the dealings of masters and slaves. In due time his message would undermine the evil of slavery, but only as the gospel prevailed. The church's effectiveness in changing the evils of society depends on its power to proclaim the gospel. Its work is never to degenerate into that of social revolutionaries or of the political pressure group. On the other hand, when God's people bring their faith to the work place and live by the standards and power of the gospel, their witness will be effective.

Though the world recognizes other organizations as the centres of power on earth, the church of Christ is God's instrument for doing His mighty works of grace and power. It is not obsolete or effete. It is the body of Christ, and He will continue to make it effective as it recognizes and acts upon its true spiritual nature, its spiritual ministry, and its spiritual moral standards in the world, in its own fellowship, in the home, and in the business realm.

THE CHURCH EMPOWERED OVER HELL

If Christ's church is truly exalted to heaven and effective on earth, it must have great power to subdue the powers of hell. Those powers are real.

In 6:12 Paul speaks of the *engagement,* or battle, God's people have with the powers of darkness: "For we wrestle not against flesh and blood, but against principalities, against powers, against the rulers of the darkness of this world, against spiritual wickedness in high places." Christians who aim to be effective for God cannot escape this conflict, but they do not fight it in their own strength.

Their Lord promises them an *enduement* of spiritual power: "Be strong in the Lord, and in the power of his might" (6:10). "Be strong" literally means to be endued or to be empowered. The Lord not only commands us to stand (6:11, 13, 14), He provides the power for us to do so.

He also provides the *equipment* we need, what Paul calls "the whole armour of God." He details this armour for us (6:14–18) and shows how our appropriation of the fulness that is in Christ provides us with all we need to overcome every power of hell.

It is no mean privilege to be a member of the church of Christ, that is, of His body. He lavishes the fulness of His grace and gifts upon His church. He has, by virtue of its union with Himself as its Head, enthroned it in heaven.

Let us grasp that truth. It, more than anything else, will make us bold and effective witnesses for Christ on earth, vanquishing by His power every power of hell that opposes us. This is our calling. By grace we are our Saviour's triumphant witness to heaven, earth, and hell.

11

Philippians
A Joyous And Victorious Christian Life

When the church at Philippi was threatened by divisions,

◆

legalism, and sensualism, Paul's answer was to help

◆

God's people understand and enjoy the gospel.

◆

Thinking through the gospel is the key to a joyful life

◆

of service and fellowship.

*T*he church at Philippi was a miracle of grace. It had both a very auspicious and a very inauspicious beginning. The auspicious part was that Paul went there at the direct command of God through a vision of a man of Macedonia who implored him, "Come over and help us." Assuredly gathering that the Lord would have him and his companions go there, Paul set out for Philippi, the chief city of Macedonia. However, when he got there he did not see a very auspicious start to the work of church planting. Acts 16 informs us that his first meetings were with a few women at a prayer meeting conducted beside a river bank. It was not a Christian prayer meeting but a meeting of some who desired to seek the Lord. At first Paul saw only one woman convert, Lydia, a seller of purple. Then another woman convert of a very different type felt the transforming power of grace. She was a demonized girl whom Paul set free by the authority of Christ. That miracle raised all sorts of opposition. Paul was beaten with rods and thrown into jail. At midnight he and his companion Silas sang and made the prison ring with the mighty sound of the praises of God. While they sang there was an earthquake. The prison doors burst open. The keeper of the prison, whose life depended on keeping these notorious prisoners safe under his control, was on the point of suicide. Instead of seizing the opportunity of escape, Paul showed his concern for the prison guard and said, "Do thyself no harm." That night he led the guard and his family to Christ.

These were the first few converts of a work to which Paul had had such an auspicious introduction. Despite the unique form of direction that had led him there, his efforts did not appear to meet with any outstanding success. Appearances, however, were deceptive, for the conversion of those few souls marked the birth of one of the greatest of all the New Testament churches. Unlike other churches, it stood fully and without apology in support of Paul's ministry. It supported him far more liberally and often than any other. Its commitment to him and his gospel never wavered. It stood resolutely with him in the defence and confirmation of the gospel even when he suffered imprisonment and it was dangerous to be closely associated with him. Undoubtedly it was a great church.

Yet it is evident that Paul was deeply concerned about the Philippian church. In writing to the saints at Philippi, with the elders and deacons (1:1), he draws attention to some incipient dangers.

First there was the constant danger of *division*. He alludes to this in chapters 2 and 4. He warns against "strife" and "vainglory" (2:3). He pleads with these saints to "do all things without murmurings and disputings" (2:14). In 4:2 he writes, "I beseech Euodias, and beseech Syntyche, that they be of the same mind in the Lord." Clearly division had not reached the stage it had in Corinth, but it was still posing a real threat to the work and witness of a great church.

Paul saw a second danger: the constant threat from *legalists, or Judaizers.* They were not strong in Philippi, and it is very clear from the tone of the letter that the people at Philippi had not succumbed to them. However, they were there trying to insinuate themselves into the church and to move it away from the simplicity and purity of the gospel—and particularly to turn it away from Paul. The Judaizers always wanted the Gentiles to feel that they were not real Christians until they had submitted to circumcision and to the other observances of the Jewish religion. They were unremitting in their efforts to subvert the gospel of grace and posed a very real threat to the Philippian church.

The third danger to the church may have arisen either through them or in answer to them—it is difficult to say. This was the danger of *sensualism* or *antinomianism.* Chapter 3:18, 19 shows just how immediate the danger was: "Many walk, of whom I have told you often, and now tell you even weeping, that they are the enemies of the cross of Christ: whose end is destruction, whose God is their belly, and whose glory is in their shame, who mind earthly things."

These three things are the abiding dangers for every church that would seek to do a work for God: division, drifting from the purity of the gospel, and worldly living. Paul wrote this short letter to the Philippians from his Roman prison to encourage them in the face of these dangers.

None of his letters is more heartwarming than this. Perhaps that is the reason commentators find Philippians difficult to analyse. How do you analyse a love letter? This is the outpouring of the apostle's heart to a people who had a genuine love for him. They expressed their love by sending their gifts for his support (4:10, 14–16). That thrilled Paul's heart, not because it made life a little easier for him, but because it indicated increasing spiritual fruitfulness in them (4:17). He desired them and their fellowship more than he desired their money. When Epaphroditus arrived as their gift bearer, he was all the more welcome because he was a little piece of the church in Philippi. However, the apostle could not enjoy his fellowship for long. Not long after his arrival in Rome, Epaphroditus became dangerously ill. Though the Lord mercifully healed him, the Philippians heard of his illness and were deeply concerned, for they held him in high regard. So Paul decided to send him back. He was so concerned about the dangers facing the Philippian church he determined to send Timothy also. He would sacrifice the fellowship of two men who were very near and dear to him, indeed even essential to him as he lay in his Roman prison (2:19, 27–28).

That was good news to the Philippians, but even better news accompanied it. Paul believed the Lord had given him an assurance that He would set him free so that he could go personally to Philippi (1:25–26; 2:24). Paul recognized that this visit was necessary for the welfare of the church, though for his own part he would rather the Lord would speedily take him home to Himself. He had such a vision of the Lord and of glory, such an assurance that for him to be absent from the body was to be present with the Lord, that he said, "I am in a strait betwixt two, having a desire to depart, and to be with Christ; which is far better: nevertheless to abide in the flesh is more needful for you" (1:23–24). Since, however, it would be some time before he was free to visit them, he sent this letter to direct them how to deal with the areas of difficulty he perceived as threats to the church. He wanted them to deal with the difficulties before they became crises.

That is a point worth considering. There are two extremes to avoid in facing problems. One is the philosophy that you should make little things into big things so that they never actually become big things. In other words, make mountains out of molehills. That is usually a disastrous error that keeps churches and individuals in constant crisis and ultimately breeds division and cynicism. The other extreme is to ignore mountains as if they were molehills, hoping they will simply disappear. They usually do not. In fact, they often become insurmountable obstacles to further spiritual growth and fruitfulness. The longer they are ignored the more painful and difficult it will be to deal with them at all. The best approach is that which recognizes each difficulty for what it really is and deals with it accordingly, not creating a crisis where there is none and not ignoring one that needs urgent or radical attention. That is what Paul wanted the Philippians to do, and he gave them this letter to show them how.

His answer to the three dangers confronting the church—divisions, the drift from the gospel, and the promotion of sensual living—is still the only answer to the same problems today. Bible believers find nothing controversial in that statement—but often they do not live by it. The problem-solving principles so popular among Christians today are not the solutions Paul gave. His answer to the problems the Philippians were facing was simply the gospel understood and enjoyed. That is a vital statement. There are three terms in that statement.

First, *the gospel.* In this epistle Paul refers by name to the gospel nine times, six of them in the very first chapter. When Paul specifically mentions an important term nine times in four chapters, he obviously means us to understand that this is a major theme of the book.

The second term in our vital statement is *the gospel understood.* That introduces the idea of the mind, and there are ten places in this little epistle where Paul refers explicitly to the mind of the Christian. In other places he makes implied references. So the Christian's ability to think clearly about the gospel is one of the important issues that Paul deals with in this epistle.

The third term in our vital statement is *the gospel enjoyed.* Paul writes of joy five times in Philippians and uses the word *rejoice* seven times. In our English version a different Greek word, which means glorying or boasting, is also translated "rejoicing" (1:26).

This piling up of texts about the gospel, about understanding, and about rejoicing is not accidental. It reveals the core message of the epistle. In a word, Paul is saying that the answer to all the needs of the church is the gospel understood and enjoyed. If you keep that in mind, you will be able to understand the oft-quoted words of 2:12-13: "Work out your own salvation with fear and trembling. For it is God which worketh in you both to will and to do of his good pleasure"—as Paul's instruction to understand and enjoy the gospel. It is only as you understand and enjoy the gospel that you will be able to work out your salvation. This is crucial. It is Paul's constant theme: living by faith in Christ. Failure to grasp this truth leads to all sorts of complications in the Christian life. Christians who try to "work out" their salvation by resolution, will power, and self-effort usually fall into legalistic bondage or deep frustration or both. Unless what we do or refrain from doing is the direct result of our understanding and enjoyment of the gospel, it will not be done by "faith which worketh by love" (Gal. 5:6). And Christians are supposed to live their lives by that faith (Gal. 2:20).

All that lends a special urgency to the message of the epistle. We will call our study of that message **Thinking Through the Gospel as the Key to a Joyful Life of Service and Fellowship.** When Paul says, "Work out your own salvation," he uses a word which literally means to work down. As the context clearly shows, his emphasis is upon cause and effect. "God is working in you. Therefore you should work down and out into your life what He has done and is doing in you." This is the uniform witness of the epistle: God has begun a good work in you (1:6), He is continuing to work within you (2:13), and He will complete His work in you until the day of Jesus Christ (1:6). That divine activity is the basis for our "working out" our own salvation. John Calvin interpreted the verb translated "work out" in the sense of continuing on to completion. The Christian's progress unto completion is the effect of which the Lord's work for him and in him is the cause. In other words, our progress—and that means the ability to cope successfully with the various dangers and difficulties that confront us—is by grace. Grace operates through faith. Thus, thinking through the gospel is the key to a complete and victorious Christian life.

OVERCOMING SUFFERING

First, it is the key to overcoming suffering. Suffering is a major theme in Philippians. In chapter 1 we read of Paul suffering in prison. Chapter 2 speaks of Christ's suffering and humiliation, and later mentions Epaphroditus's near-fatal illness. Suffering is as prevalent in life as in our epistle. What is the answer to it? Few of us are good at suffering, and the Philippians were no different. Suffering is one of Satan's most potent philosophical tools to contradict the revelation of the love of God in Jesus Christ. How often we have heard the question, "If God is a God of love, why is there so much suffering in the world?" The kind of philosophy that poses such a question is a dead-end street. It has no answers. True philosophy never starts by questioning reality. True philosophy accepts the revelation of God and deals with facts in the light of that revelation. So when someone says, "If God is a God of love—" he voices the deception of the devil, who cruelly uses human suffering to blind men to the truth and love of God. Of course, many people do not think or speak in philosophical terms. They put the question in much more intimate and personal terms. Even Christians at times ask, "If God really loves me, why am I suffering as I am?" Thus our pain becomes an argument against our faith.

How are we to deal with this? The answer is that we can do so only as we think through the truth of the gospel. Paul makes this very clear. In each of the cases of suffering mentioned in this epistle, the suffering one fixed his mind on the glorious reality of the gospel. These believers focused, not on their immediate circumstances, but on what God was working in and through them and their circumstances. Knowing God's ultimate purpose of grace, they recognized that their sufferings did not contradict that purpose of God but were a vehicle for its furtherance. Much of the joy of life depends on our understanding and experiencing this truth. Once we truly understand it we will enjoy it. Can you experience joy even when you are suffering? The Bible says you can: "Wherein ye greatly rejoice, though now for a season, if need be, ye are in heaviness [deep depression, distress, or disconsolation] through manifold temptations" (1 Pet. 1:6). The word *wherein* refers to the glorious truths of the gospel with all its present grace and prospective glory. Peter's readers were in heaviness as to their circumstances but were rejoicing in their God and His gospel. It is the same story in Philippians. That is why Paul places such an emphasis on rejoicing. Paul rejoiced. Right at the very beginning of this epistle he says he is continually "making request with joy" (1:4). Again, in 1:18 he says, "Notwithstanding, every way, whether in pretence, or in truth, Christ is preached; and I therein do rejoice, yea, and will rejoice." Even in prison, with his life under constant threat, Paul rejoiced. His suffering was very real, but it did not rob him of his joy. How could he rejoice under the circumstances he had to endure? There are two reasons, both of which show why understanding and enjoying the gospel is the key to overcoming suffering.

First, Paul understood that he could rest his soul on the gospel he preached. Second, he recognized that the gospel he preached could never be stopped. Consider these for a moment.

First, Paul knew that *the gospel is completely trustworthy.* That is why when he faced the choice of life or death, his personal preference was to die. He knew that the gospel is just as good in death as it is in life. To him that was not a philosophy or a hypothesis. It was not an opinion of man. It was the revelation of God. Paul knew the gospel and rejoiced in it. No suffering of life could dim its glorious light. Christ our Saviour is the Son of God manifested in the flesh. He who was eternally God became man and went all the way to the cross in obedience to God. He died, the Just for the unjust, made an atonement for our sin, and rose again from the dead. To Paul this was the ultimate reality. This gospel was something he could live by and something he could die by. No pains of earth could change what Christ had done for him.

This gospel faith is the key to overcoming suffering. Here is how Paul explained it: "To me to live is Christ, and to die is gain" (1:21). John Calvin's interpretation captured the apostle's thought beautifully: "Both in life, and in death, Christ is my gain." That is what buoyed Paul up and gave him joy. "If I live, Christ is my gain." He speaks of this in chapter 3: "I count all things but loss for the excellency of the knowledge of Christ Jesus my Lord: for whom I have suffered the loss of all things." In other words, "Once I thought I was gaining a lot in the world. I had prestige; I had position; I had learning. But what value are all those things? What are they in comparison to the excellency of the knowledge of Christ? Far from having lost anything by receiving Christ, I have gained." That is not how the world saw the situation. To the carnal mind, Paul lost everything by becoming a Christian—money, position, popularity, and the opportunity to achieve national acclaim. In place of these, all he received now was pain. The world might have said to Paul, "You have been lashed, you have been stoned, you have been left for dead, you have been shipwrecked, and now you are thrown in jail. You have been forsaken by your friends; you have lost everything for the sake of Christ. Christ has been a loss to you." But he would have replied, "No, no. I have gained everything, for I have Christ." There is an old hymn that says,

> In land or store I may be poor,
> My name unknown, my place obscure,

Of this I have the witness sure,
Oh, bless the Lord, I have Jesus.

That was Paul's testimony. What a gain he had! That was the realization that kept him rejoicing even in the midst of great suffering.
A clear sight of Christ always makes the burdens lighter and the
prospects brighter.

Second, Paul rejoiced because *the gospel which sustained him can-*
not be stopped. He may be imprisoned, but no one could imprison the
gospel. The Roman and Jewish authorities could stop Paul's mouth, but
they could not stop God's mouth: "Christ is [still being] preached;
and I therein do rejoice." That thought always comforted Paul. He
wrote to Timothy from prison not long before his martyrdom, "I suffer
trouble . . . even unto bonds; but the word of God is not bound" (2 Tim.
2:9). Our suffering does not alter the gospel. It does not change Christ. It
does not hinder God from blessing and using us. He may bless and use
us by delivering us from our suffering. He did that for Paul for a while.
Or He may bless and use us by giving us grace to endure the suffering.
Whichever course the Lord adopts, let us understand and enjoy Christ
in the gospel. That is the key to overcoming our suffering.

OVERCOMING STRIFE

Understanding and thinking through the gospel is also the key to
overcoming strife. As we have seen, strife was a problem that was beginning to affect the Philippian church. In 2:2 Paul implores the people to
be "likeminded, having the same love, being of one accord, of one
mind." In 4:2 he mentions two women in particular whose personal differences were threatening the unity of the church: "I beseech Euodias,
and beseech Syntyche, that they be of the same mind in the Lord." The
situation was not yet out of control, but if it went uncorrected, it would
soon make Philippi like Corinth for strife. That is always a danger for
churches. We bring so many differences with us into the church from
the world—differences of background, culture, education, outlook, and
opinion. All these have the potential to cause strife and division. That is
why they must be constantly corrected in the very same way Paul corrected the strife in the church at Philippi.

What was his answer to the problem? He gives it three times in this
epistle in the repeated command, "Mind the same [or, the one] thing"
(3:16; 2:2, "be likeminded"; 4:2, "be of the same mind"; Paul's words in
each case are the same in the Greek text). Here is his answer to strife.
"Mind the one thing." What is "the one thing"? Paul makes it clear that
"the one thing" is the gospel of Jesus Christ. He does not merely tell

Christians to agree. He tells them to get their minds on the gospel. That will put an end to petty bickering and carnal division. Being mindful of the gospel will lead us to what Christ has done for us. It will show us His selflessness. And it will inspire us with desire to be like Him. The call to striving parties in any church must always be, "Let this mind be in you, which was also in Christ Jesus" (2:5). When the mind that was in Christ—the mind that took Him from the throne of God down to the depths of Calvary's shame and led Him to suffer for the salvation of His church—is in control of us, we will not be proud and selfish, demanding our "rights." We will not be motivated by the philosophy of the world that takes humility for weakness. Humility is not weakness. Lowly-mindedness is not weakness. Turning away from a belligerent brother is not weakness. Curbing our tongue and our natural reaction to unjust attack is not weakness. It is Christ-likeness, and Christ-likeness is the greatest strength Christians can ever know or show. Let that be our guide; let that be our guard. In other words, let our consideration of the gospel overshadow all our dealings with God's people. As Paul instructed the Ephesians, "Be ye kind one to another, tenderhearted, forgiving one another, even as God for Christ's sake hath forgiven you" (Eph. 4:32). That is how we behave when we apply the gospel to our relationships with our brethren. The gospel understood and enjoyed is the sure answer to strife.

OVERCOMING SEDUCERS

Thinking through the gospel is also the key to overcoming seducers. In chapter 3 Paul deals with the Judaizers and the sensualists who were troubling the church. Apparently they represented two opposite extremes. In fact, one always produces the other. Legalism always produces sensualism, either as its own natural result or as a reaction to it. And sensualism in the church very often produces legalism as a cover-up for guilt or again as a reaction to it. So legalism and sensualism often go together. They are twin attacks on the church's faith and practice. While legalism corrupts the distinctive testimony of the church's gospel message, sensualism corrupts the distinctive testimony of her gospel morality. Legalism seeks to destroy the gospel by denying the sufficiency of faith in Christ for salvation. Sensualism seeks to destroy the gospel by denying that the faith that saves necessarily produces the fruit of holy works. On both counts, the gospel is denied with the inevitable result that sin runs rampant in the church. We see all too much evidence of this all around us. The gospel of free grace is largely unpreached and unheard, and consequently sin spreads almost unchecked. Every year hundreds of pastors have to leave the ministry because of gross sin. The picture is no more encouraging among people in the pew. Infidelity, marriage break-up, moral perversion, and a host of other sins are at epidemic levels in professing Christian churches. It is a bleak picture. Seducers have done a deadly work in drawing many away from the old paths of biblical truth and righteousness.

What is the answer to the problem caused by seducers? It is one thing to analyse or describe the problem. It is quite another thing to give the answer to it. How should we evaluate men, movements, and messages? The answer: by the gospel of Jesus Christ. Bring everything to that touchstone. There are two simple statements we may make from Philippians 3 to sum up our duty in this regard.

First, *reject all that exalts the flesh:* "We . . . have no confidence in the flesh" (3:3). That will deal with false gospels and legalistic messages.

Second, *reject all that gives expression to the flesh.* That will deal with sensualism. In other words, as we evaluate and deal with men's theories and practices in the light of the central message of the gospel of Jesus Christ, we will overcome seducers.

OVERCOMING STRESS

Clear thinking on the gospel is also the key to overcoming stress. In 4:6, 7 Paul says, "Be careful [anxious or worried] for nothing; but in every thing by prayer and supplication with thanksgiving let your requests be made known unto God. And the peace of God, which passeth all understanding, shall keep your hearts and minds through Christ Jesus." The Philippians were worried about many things. They were worried about Paul. They feared he was about to be killed. They were worried about Epaphroditus. They thought he was about to die. They were worried about the difficulties in their church and the forces that were arrayed against them. In the face of all these concerns Paul bluntly commands them, "Do not worry." Normally when people give that advice it is inane and utterly unhelpful. When you are deeply worried and someone comes along, pats you on the back as he hurries on his own way, and says, "Don't worry," he really means, "Keep your worries to yourself. Don't bother me with them. I don't really have the time, interest, or inclination to listen." However, here Paul is certainly not giving inane advice. He did not merely tell the Philippians not to worry—he gave them good reasons why they had no need to worry. He not only told them they should not worry, he told them how to stop worrying. He gave them the key to overcoming stress.

How should we face the things that cause distress and introduce tension into our lives? Paul's answer is, think through the gospel.

First, says the apostle, *rejoice in the Lord.* Think of all His glorious grace. Do not allow any concern of the moment to dim your enjoyment of the eternal salvation He has given you. Has God chosen you in

Christ? What you are worrying about will never undo that election. Has God given Christ to be your Redeemer? What is worrying you will never change it. Has Christ died to redeem you? Has He reconciled you to God? Has He justified you freely by His grace? Has He brought you into vital union with Himself? Has He given you the assurance of heaven? Has He given you His Holy Spirit, the down payment of eternal glory? Has He gone to prepare a place for you? Then rejoice in those things. Start giving the Lord thanks for them, and you will have taken the first big step toward dealing with the problem of worry.

Then *pray.* Pray with submission and with sincere desire. That would be a fair paraphrase of what Paul says in 4:6: "By prayer and supplication." When under great pressure, many people deceive themselves that they are praying when what they are really doing is endlessly reciting their worries to themselves. Far from finding relief, they merely feed their fears and concerns. They are so focused on their trouble that they forget the gospel, at least as it touches upon their immediate situation. True prayer admits the difficulties, brings them to the Lord, and submits them to Him. It puts right anything in our lives that may contribute to those difficulties. It accepts from the hand of God the discipline that may be causing us much distress, and it cries to Him for His intervention. Such prayer obtains the Lord's answer. He gives His promise. When you cease using up your energy in worry and use it to pray with submission and sincere desire, "the peace of God, which passeth all understanding, shall keep your hearts and minds through Christ Jesus." The word *keep* is a military term. It means that God's peace will stand guard over you. It will be like a garrison of soldiers guarding your heart and mind. You can worry only on account of the things that you entertain in your mind. Control of the mind, then, is essential to overcoming stress and worry. That is what gives such urgency to Paul's argument here. If you think through the gospel, it will place so many sentries around your mind that it will establish a defence force that debilitating stress cannot penetrate. The gospel gives us the peace of God, and the peace of God keeps our minds. That is God's promise.

To enjoy this peace you must *exercise your mind,* says Paul. "Finally, brethren, whatsoever things are true, whatsoever things are honest, whatsoever things are just, whatsoever things are pure, whatsoever things are lovely, whatsoever things are of good report; if there be any virtue, and if there be any praise, think on these things" (4:8). The peace of God does not just drop out of nowhere into blank minds or into minds set upon wrong things. If you have your mind exercised on the wrong things, you will not have the peace of God. But if your mind is exercised on Christ and His gospel, you will have peace.

Such mental exercise on the gospel will produce holy living that will produce a deepened sense of peace. Thus in 4:9 Paul says that those who live out the gospel in their lives will enjoy the real presence and fellowship of the God of peace. The ultimate guarantee of the peace of God is a living, ongoing contact with the God of peace. This is the key, then, to overcoming stress in life.

AN OVERCOMING LIFE OF SERVICE

Thinking through the gospel is the key to a useful life of service. "Work out your own salvation" (2:12). That is each Christian's individual responsibility. How are we to discharge it? Paul makes the answer plain: "As ye have always obeyed, not as in my presence only, but now much more in my absence, work out your own salvation with fear and trembling." In other words, the Philippians' spiritual life was not dependent on Paul, but on the Saviour and the salvation He gave them. As they recognized that truth and lived in the light of it, they would increase in holy obedience. As faith continued to lay hold of Christ it would take what He had wrought in them and work it down and through every part of their lives. They would go on with God and be good servants of Christ. They would "shine as lights in the world" (2:15). That is the essence of successful witnessing. Christians have the light of Christ burning within them. Their witness is not merely a matter of theory or of opinion. They are in continual, vital contact with Christ. The light of their fellowship with Him is real and visible. That is how they are to hold forth the word of life (2:16). Philippians sets before us three vivid examples of such dynamic Christian testimony: Paul himself (1:17), Timothy (2:19–22), and Epaphroditus (2:25). Their zeal sprang from their grasp of the gospel. So will ours.

Of course we each have a very limited sphere of service. That was true of the Philippian church. That was why Paul commended them for showing interest in and support for God's work in places far removed from their own particular field of service (4:10–19). They had a missionary vision and gave sacrificially to the Lord's work in foreign places. Missionary interest is an important part of our service for God. We must never become so engrossed in our own field of service that we lose the larger vision. The way to ensure a lively missionary interest is to have such a personal enjoyment of the gospel that we burn with the desire to have its light penetrate every dark corner of the world. Christians who have a vital understanding of the gospel will give of themselves and their substance to bring its message to the world. They will do it without fear of impoverishing themselves, knowing the truth of Paul's words: "My God shall supply all your need according to his riches in glory by Christ Jesus" (4:19); therefore "I can do all things through Christ which strengtheneth me" (4:13).

The issues Paul addresses in this epistle touch all Christians in a most intimate way—suffering, strife, seductive heresies, and personal stress. His answer to each and all of them is, think through the gospel, let its truth possess your mind, and it will lead you into the joy of Christian service and fellowship. Let us, then, get a grip of the gospel. Rather, let the gospel get a grip of us.

Colossians
The Fulness Of Christ

Under attack from a mongrel philosophy that was part

♦

legalism, part mysticism, and part asceticism, the

♦

Colossian church needed answers. Paul's answer to every

♦

false doctrine was a pure Christology. He taught the

♦

Colossian Christians a lesson for Christians of every age

♦

and condition: the fulness of God dwells in Christ and

♦

through Him flows to all His people to enrich every

♦

area of their lives.

S ome argue from Col. 2:1 that Paul had never been to Colosse and therefore could not personally have founded the church there. They suppose that after Philemon and Epaphras had been saved through the apostle, probably at Ephesus, they went on to Colosse and commenced preaching the gospel. The church was the fruit of their labours.

Other interpreters argue that Paul must have visited Colosse because his journey from Galatia to Ephesus (Acts 18:23–19:1) would have taken him straight through it. Though he did not spend much time there it was long enough to see Epaphras and Philemon saved and a small church established. However, almost none of the Colossian Christians knew the apostle by sight.

The church in Colosse was well ordered. It presented Paul with the pleasing picture of many converts from heathen darkness developing into strong Christians. But there was a danger. If it was not already in the church it was making strenuous efforts to gain admission. This danger came from a strangely mixed-up philosophy. It appears to have had a strong Judaizing tendency along with some very mystical elements that either advocated a kind of angel worship or, more likely, claimed to enter the same humility the angels manifested in their worship. That seems to be the best interpretation of Paul's references in chapter 2 to a "show of wisdom," the worship of angels, and "will worship." The reference to the worship of angels is admittedly difficult to understand. There is no record of the Jewish people worshipping angels. Some commentators believe that the Essenes, an ascetic Jewish sect, practised some sort of angel worship. However, there is no evidence that the Essenes ever travelled as far as Colosse, and it is unlikely that they established angel worship there. As I have indicated, it is questionable if Paul intends to say that there was any actual angel worship at all in Colosse. There is good reason to believe that he meant that the people he was describing professed to be superspiritual. Hence they claimed to have some special knowledge, some exalted religious experience, and to partake in some mystical way of the humility of the angels as they worshipped Jehovah. They brought to Colosse strict standards of asceticism: "Touch not; taste not; handle not" (2:21). They promoted a monkish withdrawal from the world as if that were the essence of true holiness. What they were seeking to impose on the believers at Colosse, then, was a mixture of legalism, mysticism, and asceticism, all on the presumption of an esoteric knowledge.

That this mongrel philosophy was seriously threatening the Colossian church is clear from the fact that Epaphras hastened to Rome to seek Paul's guidance in dealing with it. The apostle immediately recognized the danger of this Christless philosophy and saw through its spurious holiness. Not for a moment was he deceived by the outward show of superior piety. Nor was he intimidated by the claims of special knowledge. A man who had been with God as he had been, who had been exalted to the third heaven, whether in the body or out of the body he could not tell, and who had seen and heard such things as were unlawful to speak about (2 Cor. 12:1–4) was not likely to be impressed by the foolish tittle-tattle of vain zealots who sought to impose themselves, their philosophy, and their religion on immature converts. The Colossian epistle was his response to their attack on the church.

Paul's central theme is the person of Jesus Christ and the relationship which He sustains to His people. It is as if he were saying to the Colossian Christians, "Grasp the truth of who Christ is; understand your relationship to Him, and you will never need a deeper or higher knowledge, or a deeper or higher holiness."

That message makes Colossians a very timely epistle for us today. Notice the things Paul particularly mentioned as matters of concern. First, there was "philosophy and vain deceit" (2:8). Then there was sinful investigation of the unseen world (2:18). Finally, there was the promotion of human theories that proceeded from the mind of the flesh and did not hold fast to the central revelation of the gospel (2:18, 19). These are the very things that are causing havoc in Bible-believing churches today. Consider the situation we face.

Once again vain philosophy has invaded the church and has largely replaced biblical theology. "Beware lest any man spoil you through philosophy and vain deceit" (2:8). That is an up-to-date warning. Literally Paul warns, "Beware lest any man make a spoil of you (or, make you his prey) through his philosophy, namely, his vain deceit." In many branches of the professing church we have an intellectualism that obscures and is ashamed of the simplicity of the gospel of Jesus Christ. Intellectualism that is ashamed of the gospel of Christ is not light; it is darkness. It makes a spoil of souls. It is a vain deceit that robs and defrauds all who embrace it.

Again, nowadays we are inundated by profitless speculation, especially into occult and evil matters. In 2:18 Paul warns against any man whose practice may be described as "intruding into [or, investigating, as the verb *embateuo* means] those things which he hath not seen." In the light of such a plain warning, why is it that in most Christian book shops some of the most popular subjects are demonism, the occult, and every dark side of the affairs of men and devils? There is apparently endless speculative research into such matters. This is totally unbiblical. In Rom. 16:19 Paul says, "I would have you wise unto that which is good, and simple concerning evil." Christians are not to be experts on the occult. They are to be experts on Christ. They are not to be experts on the filthiness and ungodliness of this dark world. Nor do they need anyone to give them a seminar on demonism to enable them to recognize and defeat the devil. The apostle Paul says to people who walk with God, "We are not ignorant of his [Satan's] devices" (2 Cor. 2:11). When a man is walking in the light, he does not need a seminar to teach him what darkness is. He recognizes the darkness, because when he looks at it in the light of the gospel of Christ's person and work he sees it for what it really is. Profitless speculation into the dark world of Satanic activity brings darkness, not light. It brings bondage, not liberty.

Then again, in the church today we have human theories that are supposed to bring people fulfilment. They claim to take Christians beyond the point where faith in the gospel can take them. That is why we have so little real Bible exposition and so many psychology-based seminars in the church. Hosea's lament is all too applicable today: "My people are destroyed for lack of knowledge" (Hos. 4:6). Today there is no lack of futile psychological gimmicks but a real vacuum of fundamental gospel theology. I often wonder how the early church did without the modern seminar movement. How did they ever conquer the world without the psychological inventions modern Christians have been deceived into thinking are essential to spiritual wellbeing? Let us learn that these things do not fulfil, they frustrate. They have usurped the place of the gospel. "Beware of such things" is Paul's advice (Col. 2:8). So widespread has been the departure from apostolic Christianity, and so comprehensively have human theories replaced gospel theology, that nowadays Paul's teaching sounds to most Christians like a dangerous and oversimplified innovation. That is the sad pass to which we have come in the church today.

However, the answer to every heresy, and to anything else that would spoil or defraud God's people, is still a thoroughly sound Christology. That is where Paul starts. Notice carefully how he deals with the danger to the Colossians posed by worldly philosophy and Judaistic heresy. He does not match speculation with speculation. He does not follow his opponents up every blind alley into which their own argument takes them. Instead he establishes the truth regarding Christ. Right at the very beginning of the epistle he speaks of "the word of the truth of the gospel" (1:5). Again, at the end of the next verse he says, "Ye . . . knew the grace of God in truth." So he starts with the truth as it is in the Lord Jesus Christ. But he goes further. In 2:6 he says, "As ye have therefore received Christ Jesus the Lord, so walk ye in him"—literally, "As ye have therefore received the Christ, Jesus the Lord, so walk in Him." As Bishop Ellicott noted from this text, Christ is the sum and the substance of all teaching. Paul uses a powerful argument, an argument that must be conclusive to all true Christians. In effect, he says, "As ye have received the Christ, who is Jesus the Lord, so walk in Him. No matter what Jews and Judaizers say, the Lord Jesus is the true Messiah. You have received Him as your Lord, your Christ, and your Saviour. Walk in the light of that truth. The person of Christ and His Lordship over all who have trusted Him must govern all you believe and do."

Consider Paul's words in 2:6 very carefully. "Ye have received . . . Christ Jesus the Lord." There is clearly an intellectual aspect to this reception. The truth of the gospel captures the minds of believers. There is also something that goes beyond the merely intellectual. In capturing our minds the gospel has changed our hearts. We believe with the heart (Rom. 10:10). In other words, there is something theological here. What we truly believe with our mind moves our will. The conclusion from such a premise is inevitable: walk in the light of the truth you profess to believe. Bishop Handley Moule said that in 2:6 Paul was warning the Colossians against the danger of an "unapplied orthodoxy." That is an apt phrase. An unapplied orthodoxy. It is not enough to have our heads full of biblical information. It is not enough to be able to recite proof texts for doctrinal propositions. It is not enough to learn by rote the answers to certain theological questions. We need more than mere theory to live for Christ. The truth of the gospel must get into our souls so that we walk in the light of what we believe concerning the Lord Jesus Christ. That is what Colossians is all about—Christology taught and applied.

One text goes to the heart of this message and spells out every major point the apostle wants to make: "In him [Christ] dwelleth all the fulness of the Godhead bodily. And ye are complete in him, which is the head of all principality and power" (2:9, 10). In the Greek text the word *fulness* in verse 9 is the noun form of the verb translated "ye are complete" in verse 10. Literally, Paul's statement reads, "In Him dwelleth all the fulness of the Godhead bodily. And ye are made full in Him." Here is the central theme of the epistle: **the fulness of God dwells in Christ, and through Christ flows to all His people.** That is the basis for the exhortation of 2:6—Christians should govern all their belief and behaviour in the light of this central truth. Follow the apostle's argument very carefully: The fulness of God fills Christ. The fulness of Christ fills His people. Therefore, the fulness of His people entirely fits them for life both now and forever—they live in the light of the fulness of Christ. In a nutshell, that is the message of Colossians.

GOD'S FULNESS FILLS CHRIST

Let us take the apostle's argument one step at a time. We will start at the beginning: the fulness of God fills the Lord Jesus Christ. There are three vitally important texts in Colossians on this subject. First, "It pleased the Father that in him should all fulness dwell" (1:19). Second, "In whom [Christ] are hid all the treasures of wisdom and knowledge" (2:3). Third, "In him [Christ] dwelleth all the fulness of the Godhead bodily" (2:9). The word *fulness* carries the thought of a communicated fulness. In other words, it is the fulness God gave to His incarnate Son. This fulness does not describe that essential, eternal relationship which the Son has with the Father in the trinity. As God the Son, our Saviour possesses all the fulness of eternal deity. It is His naturally. It is not the result of a decision or decree by His Father. As God, He is what He is by eternal necessity. As the Christ, the mediator between God and men, however, our Saviour possesses a fulness given to Him by His Father to equip Him for His task of saving His people.

Paul is careful to draw the distinction between our Lord's eternal fulness and His communicated fulness, particularly in chapter 1. He makes some statements that clarify his meaning. First, the Son is truly God. Chapter 1:15 says, "[He] is the image of the invisible God, the firstborn of every creature." He is the image of the Father. The word *image* does not mean a mere likeness. We think of an image as what we see when we look in a mirror. That is not what Paul means by an image. Even a photograph would not satisfy his idea of an image. What the mirror and the camera produce are merely representations produced by rays of light. A perfect image is much more than that. The more perfect an image is, the more equality there is between it and the original. When we look in a mirror or at a photograph, we see a mere outline. We do not see our ego, our mind, our real self. We see a partial likeness, not a true image. A true image shows not merely the likeness of the thing represented, but its essence. In other words, the thing represented and the image that perfectly represents it are equal. That is Paul's thought in calling the Son of God the image of His Father. He not only resembles God, He is God. Moreover, as the image of the Father He is the manifestation of God to every intelligent creature. No creature, be he angel, devil, or man, has ever seen God or communed with Him except in and through the person of the Son of God. God has never revealed Himself except in His Son. That is a vital truth that underlies the exclusive position of Christ as the mediator between God and men. Apart from Him no man can know God or approach God. God has nothing to say to anyone except in and through His Son. "No man hath seen God at any time; the only begotten Son, which is in the bosom of the Father, he hath declared him" (John 1:18). Jesus said, "All things are delivered unto me of my Father: and no man knoweth the Son, but the Father; neither knoweth any man the Father, save the Son, and he to whomsoever the Son will reveal him" (Matt. 11:27).

Paul's second statement in Colossians 1 is that the Son is eternal (1:15, 17). He says that not only is He "before all things," but He is "the firstborn of every creature." Some heretics take this to mean that He is the first creature God made. That is not Paul's meaning. The word *firstborn* here means that God's Son is eternally begotten and is the One through whom all created things were brought into being. Apart from Him there could be no creation.

Paul's third statement about the Son follows naturally: He is the Creator (1:15–17). All things were created in Him, through Him, and for Him. That is why 1:17 says, "By him [or, in Him] all things consist." The word *consist* means cohere, or hang together in organized dependence. That is an immensely important statement. We now know that the created universe is unimaginably vast and complex. Even its smallest components are incredibly complicated. Yet the entire creation "hangs together." It is not a haphazard jumble of disorganized parts. It is an organized system composed of an almost endless number of smaller organized systems. What Paul says is that the whole and all its parts hang together in organized dependence on Christ. He holds the whole together and gives to each part its proper place, purpose, and meaning. It is therefore utter folly to seek the truth and the meaning of creation, whether it is in astronomy, or in biology, or in physics, or in chemistry, or in any other discipline, apart from Christ. All creation coheres, occupies its own peculiar place and has its meaning in the Lord Jesus Christ.

The point of all this truth is that our Lord Jesus is truly God, and as such He possesses all fulness. Fulness belongs to Him.

However, the eternal Son of God became our Saviour. To fulfil that office He became a man, and as a man He needed to receive the fulness of grace and ability to accomplish His purpose. Thus the Father gave Him all He needed to be our perfect Redeemer. Here we touch upon the mystery of the incarnation. We cannot comprehend that mystery. At best we can describe it. The Shorter Catechism sums up the biblical data: "The only Redeemer of God's elect is the Lord Jesus Christ, who, being the eternal Son of God, became man, and so was, and continueth to be, God and man in two distinct natures, and one person, for ever." As our Redeemer, the Lord Jesus Christ acts in both His natures, but His deity and His humanity are never fused or confused. As God He naturally possesses all the fulness of deity, but as man He receives from His Father all the fulness of grace to fit Him for His work. The Scripture speaks clearly about God bestowing grace on Christ the Saviour. In John 3:34 we read, "God giveth not the Spirit by measure unto him." In Luke 4:18 the Lord Jesus quotes from Isaiah 61 and says, "The Spirit of the Lord is upon me, because he hath anointed me to preach." Matt. 12:18 quotes from Isaiah 42 as saying, "I will put my spirit upon him." According to the words of Isa. 42:6 the Father promises the Son His help: "I . . . will hold thine hand, and will keep thee." In Isa. 50:4 the Son says, "The Lord God hath given me the tongue of the learned, that I should know how to speak a word in season to him that is weary." All these texts of Scripture present a common truth: that God gave His Son as the Mediator the fulness of the gifts and graces that made Him the perfect Saviour. It is this communicated fulness of which Col. 1:19 and 2:3, 9 speak. John Owen, the great Puritan theologian, beautifully summed up the teaching of these texts: "There is no grace that is not in Christ, and every grace is in Him in the highest degree." That is the first element in Paul's central theme in Colossians: the fulness of God fills the Lord Jesus Christ.

CHRIST'S FULNESS FILLS HIS PEOPLE

The second element is this: the fulness of the Lord Jesus Christ fills His people. Remember the literal force of 2:9, 10: "In him dwelleth all the fulness of the Godhead bodily. And ye are made full in him." This means that Christ is the sole channel and mediator of divine grace to us and that He actually confers the fulness of saving grace on all His people. It is Christ who died, it is Christ who rose from the dead, and therefore it is Christ alone who can convey fulness and grace. All the saving fulness of God is in Him. There is no grace of God for any man outside of Christ. There is no mercy outside of Christ. There is no love outside of Christ. God has concentrated everything of His fulness and His grace in the person of Christ and imparts His saving health solely through the merits of Christ. He is the only mediator between God and men, the sole channel of God's goodness to men. In this ecumenical age there are many who assure us that there are many ways to God and that Jesus Christ is just one of them. They tell us that the love of God is so great that it reaches all mankind, whether in Christ or out of Christ. Recently I was reading a book by a prominent Roman Catholic theologian. He was trying to prove that Christ-rejecting Jews are still the covenant people of God, not merely in a national sense but individually. According to the writer they are in covenant with God and will get to heaven despite their rejection of Christ. He maintained that there is a world of difference between saying that all the grace of God reaches men through Christ and that every man must receive Christ in order to be saved. What he meant was that Christ gives His grace to everybody, Jew or Gentile, whether they receive Him or not. What does the Bible say? It puts the matter very bluntly: "He that believeth not shall be damned" (Mark 16:16). That is the old-fashioned biblical position. In

Christ we have life, salvation, and fulness of grace. "Without Christ," on the other hand, men are said to be "without God" and therefore without hope (Eph. 2:12).

Christ's fulness belongs to all His people and is actually bestowed upon them. It belongs to them collectively, as His church. It also belongs to them individually. Col. 1:18 says that He is our Head. Psalm 133 gives us a lovely picture of what this means. It describes how the precious ointment that was poured upon the head of Aaron, the high priest, flowed down upon his beard and right down to the skirts of his garments. Aaron is a type of the Lord Jesus Christ as the head of His body, the church. God poured His fulness, His gracious anointing, upon Christ our head, and from the head it reaches to the very skirts of His garment—that is, it reaches to the entire body that is covered by the garments of His imputed righteousness. Christ's fulness belongs to the whole church only because first it belongs to every individual Christian. Paul says, "Ye are made full in Him." That fulness brings every spiritual blessing to the people of God. We are "blessed . . . with all spiritual blessings in heavenly places in Christ" (Eph. 1:3).

In Colossians Paul gives a full exposition of this fulness of grace that we receive in and from Christ. In 1:14 he says, "In whom [Christ] we have *redemption* through his blood." Redemption means release from sin through the payment of a ransom price. What a wonderful truth! Christ shed His blood and thereby purchased for all His people a full release from the slavery and sentence of sin. In Christ we also have *reconciliation* (1:19–22). No longer are we alienated from God in our minds by wicked works, for Christ has reconciled us in the body of His flesh through death. As 1:20 puts it, He "made peace through the blood of his cross."

Then, in Christ we have *justification* (2:11–15). There are some lovely terms in this passage. It says that in Christ His people are "circumcised with the circumcision made without hands, in putting off the body of the sins of the flesh by the circumcision of Christ." This circumcision is a spiritual work; it is "without hands." There is no reference here to the fleshly rite of circumcision. It is the spiritual reality that lies behind the rite that Paul means. According to verse 11 this spiritual work was accomplished "by [or, in] the circumcision of Christ." This is one of Paul's many references to our union and our legal identification with Christ. He says that we were circumcised in the circumcision of Christ. In the act of His circumcision as an infant, the incarnate Son of God submitted Himself to the law of God to satisfy its claims against us. In that act, therefore, God provided the ground for our justification. In Christ's circumcision, we have been circumcised. We have put off the body of the sins of the flesh. Col. 2:11 stresses our union with the infant Christ. Verse 12 stresses our union with the crucified Christ. We are "buried with him in baptism," into His death. And, united to Christ in His death, we now live by the faith of God, that is, faith in the resurrecting power of God. As possessors of life in Christ, we have liberty and enjoy a perfect pardon from God. Col. 2:14 says that Christ has blotted out the handwriting of ordinances that was against us. That means that we have pardon because Christ perfectly satisfied the law on our behalf. We are clear of all charge and guilt before God's law. What fulness of grace is this! The law of God reveals His awesome holiness and His immutable justice. If we seek to bring our own self-righteousness to God, His law condemns us. Thus any works of ours that aim to establish a legal righteousness to gain acceptance with God cannot justify us. "But," says the apostle, "stand on redemption ground, stand on the ground of the shed blood of Christ, and you will see that the handwriting of ordinances, the awful condemnation of the broken law, is now taken out of the way. It is nailed to the cross. The law is satisfied; we are justified."

What is more, we are not only set free from the condemnation of the law, but we are set *free from Satanic dominion,* for Christ has "spoiled principalities and powers" (2:15). The people who were trying to subvert the Colossian Christians were evidently taken up with supernatural beings, what Paul calls "principalities and powers." The apostle's message is that Christ has freed His people from the dominion of all such spiritual beings. He is the Head of principalities and powers and has made a show of them openly, triumphing over them in His cross.

The fulness of Christ fills us and brings us the fullest possible range of spiritual blessings, namely, redemption, reconciliation, justification, and liberty from all Satanic dominion. It is vital for us to realize that we have all these things in Christ our Head. That is why Paul lays such emphasis in this epistle on the subject of holding fast the headship of Christ (2:19). It is also why we should maintain the same emphasis. Let Christians grasp this truth of the fulness of Christ conveyed to them and it will forever enrich their lives and service. That leads us to the final element in Paul's development of his central theme.

CHRIST'S FULNESS FULLY EQUIPS US FOR LIFE

The fulness of Christ in His people fits them entirely for life now and forever. We may condense a major section of Paul's argument in this epistle by noting three propositions he lays down.

First, the fulness of Christ in His people excludes every other claimed way of spiritual life and growth.

Second, it empowers Christians in every sphere of life.

Third, it finally exalts them to heaven.

These are the three proofs that the fulness of Christ fits His people for life now and forever. We must follow Paul's arguments in some detail.

An Exclusive Message

First, the fulness of Christ excludes every other claimed way of spiritual life and growth. In Col. 2:4–8 Paul speaks of the wisdom of the flesh and labels it "vain." That vain wisdom stands in stark contrast with the real wisdom available to Christians (1:9). They can "be filled with the knowledge of his will in all wisdom and spiritual understanding." That is true wisdom; the *wisdom* of the world is vain. The *works* of the flesh are also vain (2:16–17, 21–22). Paul bids us beware of people who come with man-made rules and regulations which they seek to impose on us as some sort of superior spirituality. He says, "Which things have indeed a show of wisdom in will worship, and humility, and neglecting of the body; not in any honour to the satisfying of the flesh" (2:23). He means that ascetic observances are of no value as remedies against the flesh. When Martin Luther went into an Augustinian monastery, he did so to discipline his body and mind and to endure privation in order to burn out the lust of the old man. He found that the old sins were worse in the monastery cell than they were in the outside world. Ascetic behaviour, indeed, all the invented standards of men, do not actually make us holy. They may make us proud or pharisaical, but they will never make us holy.

Do not misunderstand me. There are clear standards for Christian living. They are God's standards, not man's. People who understand the gospel are not antinomian. The gospel of free grace sets them free to be Christ's slaves in holy living. Some people misunderstand Christian liberty as licence to sin instead of power to live in victory over sin. However—and this is Paul's point here in Colossians 2—that victory is not to be gained by fleshly works. The works of the flesh, just like the wisdom of the flesh, are vain.

The *worship* of the flesh is also vain (2:18–23). The opponents of the gospel in Colosse boasted of some mystical communion with angels. Christians, however, have a communion that is infinitely superior to any contact with the angelic world. They have fellowship with God Himself, and access to His throne, through Christ. Why then would they stoop to the follies of trying to make contact with, pray to, or hold communion with angels? Such so-called spirituality has a fatal fascination for gullible people—witness its acceptance in Roman Catholicism and in the modern Charismatic movement. It does not promote spiritual life and growth. Only the fulness that is in Christ can do that.

An Enabling Message

Paul's second proposition is that the fulness of Christ empowers Christians in every sphere of life. Colossians gives us a fourfold statement of the full relationship we have with Christ. We have a full Christ, not an impoverished Christ. And we have a full relationship with that full Christ. In 1:27 Paul speaks of *Christ our hope:* "Christ in you, the hope of glory." In 2:10, 19, he speaks of our being in Christ—*Christ is our Head.* In 3:1, 3, 4, Paul speaks of believers being "with Christ," and the idea is *Christ is our life.* Then, at the end of chapter 3 into chapter 4, he speaks of our being unto, or for, Christ (3:23) so that *Christ is our Master* (4:1). This is the fourfold relationship that we have with Him, and this is what governs our beliefs and behaviour. According to 1:10, this is what produces fruitfulness in the life of a Christian. We are rooted in Him (2:7), and this root will produce fruit in every sphere of our experience. It will give us the power to do right in every area of life.

Take our personal life. Paul speaks of two things: our wisdom and our walk, that is, our thoughts and our actions. In 1:9 he speaks of our being "filled with the knowledge of his will in all wisdom and spiritual understanding." The word *knowledge* means a full, developed, spiritual knowledge. The word *understanding* means reflective thought, the ability to comprehend. Christ imparts to His people such a transformation of mind that their minds are filled with deep, true spiritual knowledge, enabling them to comprehend the will of God. This transformation is apparent in the working of the spiritual mind, something of which Paul writes a great deal in his epistles. Christians have the power to think straight because they can set everything in the light of the gospel. They can govern all their thoughts by the fulness of Christ. That is true wisdom. And it produces glorious results. In 2:2 Paul mentions "the full assurance of understanding, to the acknowledgment [or, to the full spiritual knowledge] of the mystery of God, and of the Father, and of Christ." The wisdom Christians have in Christ—a mind to think through the gospel and apply it to every area of life—produces "full assurance." Here is the answer to doubt and fear. It is a precious thing. That is why we must take Paul's admonition very seriously: "Beware lest any man spoil you through philosophy and vain deceit" (2:8). We must not imbibe the foolish theories of the world and its false religions. We must fill our mind with Christ and His fulness.

Such thinking will affect our walk. Paul tells us two things about our walk. We should walk worthy of Christ (1:10), and we should walk wisely (4:5). What does it mean to walk worthy of Christ? It means that our union with Christ should dictate how we walk. "If ye then be risen with Christ, seek those things which are above, where Christ sitteth on the right hand of God" (3:1). Those who reckon that they are risen with Christ will not be found grovelling in the mire of worldliness. They will set their affections on the things that are above and not on the things of earth. They will "mortify . . . [their] members which are upon the earth; fornication, uncleanness, inordinate affection, evil concupiscence, and covetousness, which is idolatry" (3:5). This is what it means to let our life be reflective of our union with Christ. We will "put off" the old man and his "anger, wrath, malice, blasphemy, filthy communication" (v. 8). And we will "put on the new man, which is renewed in knowledge after the image of him that created him" (v. 10). Notice that this putting on is related to knowledge. It is only as we know Christ that we have the power to put off the old man and put on the new. The words of 3:10 are very instructive. The new man is created in knowledge "after the image of him that created him." Col. 1:15 describes Christ as the image of the Father. Col. 3:10 describes the Christian as the image of Christ. In other words, we are to be a manifestation of Christ, just as Christ is the manifestation of the Father. That is what it means to walk worthy of Christ.

We are also to walk wisely. How may we walk wisely? Col. 2:6 supplies the answer: "As ye have therefore received Christ Jesus the Lord, so walk ye in him." The fulness of Christ will give us the power to walk wisely. So much for our personal life.

The fulness of Christ will also give us power in our church life. How we look at Christ's church and how we treat His people should be established by our union with Him. In 2:19 Paul castigates the troublers of the church in Colosse for not "holding [fast] the Head." He gives a wonderful description of the church. From Christ the Head "all the body by joints and bands having nourishment ministered, and knit together, increaseth with the increase of God." In 3:11 Paul speaks of the church as those who are new creatures in Christ, "where there is neither Greek nor Jew, circumcision nor uncircumcision, Barbarian, Scythian, bond nor free: but Christ is all, and in all." How are those who are united to Christ to act toward the church of Christ, which is made up of people in union with Him? The apostle supplies the answer in 3:12–17. They should live in *unity*, as functioning parts of the same body. They should also show true *humility*: "Put on . . . humbleness of mind, meekness, longsuffering; forbearing one another, and forgiving one another, if any man have a quarrel [literally, a grievance] against any: even as Christ forgave you, so also do ye" (vv. 12–13). They should also "put on *charity*" (v. 14). In verse 15 Paul adds another injunction: "Let the peace of God rule in your hearts." Christians are to walk in *serenity* in the church. The word *rule* is a unique word. This is the only place it appears in the New Testament. It is the word *brabeuo,* and it means to umpire. Paul's command is, "Let the peace of God umpire in your hearts." He uses a very closely related word in 2:18: "Let no man *beguile you of your reward.*" This is a single word in the Greek text *(katabrabeuo),* and it means to defraud of a prize. A *brabeus* was one who regulated and superintended public games, acting as a judge in the distribution of prizes. When Paul says, "Let the peace of God *rule* in your hearts," he conveys the idea, "Let the peace of God adjudicate in your dealings with one another, so as to settle every question and lead you to enjoy the prize or reward of Christ."

This is how the fulness of Christ should govern our behaviour in the church. However, as we all know only too well, there is a vast difference between what should be and what actually is. The vital question is, how are we to find the grace and strength to live together in unity, humility, and charity? How are we to live serenely with the peace of God ruling our hearts? We have to deal with some people who are not very lovable characters. Is there a way for us to live as we ought in the face of the challenges such people pose? There is a way. "Let the word of Christ dwell in you richly in all wisdom" (3:16). When that gospel word dwells in us we will be able to teach and admonish one another "in psalms and hymns and spiritual songs, singing with grace in [our] hearts to the Lord." The way for any church to enjoy the kind of unity and love Paul describes is for God's people to saturate their souls with "the word of the truth of the gospel" (1:5) so that it gets into their very being, dwells richly in them, and conforms them to Christ their Lord.

The fulness of Christ will affect our lives in another vital area, our family life. The fulness of Christ empowers husbands, wives, parents, and children to live right in the home. Submissive wives, loving husbands, obedient children, and wise parents are not mere abstractions, or unattainable ideals. They are not the products of humanistic psychology. They are the result of a living union with Christ, whose fulness of grace will not only show us our family duty but give us the desire and the power to do that duty. In a word, when Christ presides over our family relationships, we will treat one another in the light of how Christ treats us. Remembering our union with Him, and all the benefits that union has conferred on us, we will treat our families as those who also enjoy union with Him, with all its attendant blessings. Husbands and wives who look on each other as those whom Christ has saved and united to Himself will treat each other right. The gospel of Christ's fulness of grace empowers us to live as we ought in the family.

Finally, it also empowers us to live right in the business world, whether we are employers or employees (3:22–4:1). Employees who live in the light of their union with Christ will do their work "heartily, as to the Lord," and will labour for His reward, not merely their earthly wages

(3:23, 24). Employers who live in the light of their union with Christ will remember that He is their Master and will treat their employees righteously and equitably (4:1). People who live in the enjoyment of Christ's gracious fulness cannot live to defraud their fellow men.

An Exalting Message

Such is the power of the fulness of Christ to enable us to live in every sphere of life. But its power extends even beyond this life, for, as Paul taught the Colossians, it exalts us to heaven. As to our spiritual position in Christ, we are already in heaven (Eph. 2:6). However, heaven is not only our present spiritual position, it is our joyful and imminent prospect. In Colossians 1 we learn three things about this hope. It is a *guaranteed hope:* it is laid up, or stored away, for us in heaven (1:5). It is a *gospel hope:* "Ye heard [of it] in the word of the truth of the gospel" (1:5). It is a *glorious hope:* "Christ in you, the hope of glory" (1:27).

The fulness of Christ will never leave us short of heaven. Until then we should redeem the time (4:5). What does that mean? It means we should buy up the opportunity. But what does buying up the opportunity mean? It means that we should live our lives in the enjoyment of the fulness of Christ until the day we enter heaven. We should live in the fulness of Christ *intellectually,* filling our minds with the things we have been considering in this study. We should live in the fulness of Christ *theologically,* letting the truth of the gospel fire our souls and compel our service. We should live in the fulness of Christ *practically,* with the truth of the gospel provoking us to holiness. Last but not least, we should live in the fulness of Christ *evangelistically,* letting the truth of the gospel set us ablaze with zeal to spread it abroad to the whole world.

In a word, we should live in the light of the key text of Colossians: "In him dwelleth all the fulness of the Godhead bodily. And ye are made full in him."

13

1 Thessalonians

Living In The Light
Of Christ's Return

The doctrine of the second coming of Christ is a truth

♦

of great comfort and immediate usefulness to God's

♦

people. It touches every area of their lives so that

♦

Christians should live, work, and worship in the

♦

light of their Lord's return.

*A*fter the controversy of their imprisonment at Philippi, Paul and Silas journeyed to Thessalonica. As usual, Paul went first to the Jewish synagogue to preach Christ, and for three sabbath days he continued, "opening and alleging, that Christ must needs have suffered, and risen again from the dead; and that this Jesus, whom I preach unto you, is Christ" (Acts 17:3). "Opening and alleging" means "effectually opening the Scriptures and demonstrating from them" that Jesus is the Christ whose death and resurrection are the great subjects of Old Testament prophecy. A few Jews believed the message, but they were greatly outnumbered by the throngs of "devout Greeks," as Acts calls them, who responded to the gospel. Devout Greeks were pagans who had left their temples to seek the truth in the loftier concepts of Jewish monotheistic worship. On hearing the gospel, great numbers of them recognized its truth and joyfully received Christ.

The response of the unbelieving Jews was predictable. They immediately went into action to stem the success of the gospel by enlisting the services of "certain lewd fellows of the baser sort" (v. 5). These were evil men from among the market loungers, the kind of people we would call idlers, ruffians, ne'er-do-wells, or troublemakers. They did nothing but lounge about the marketplace looking for some wicked thing in which to be involved. The Jews employed these rowdies to gather a noisy crowd and to commence a riot in the city. They attacked the home of Jason, where they hoped to find Paul and Silas. Failing to find them, they dragged Jason before the magistrates. Their accusation actually shows just how powerful the ministry of Paul and Silas was, because they said, "These that have turned the world upside down are come hither also" (v. 6). That is the kind of ministry Paul had. He turned people upside down. He turned communities upside down. He certainly turned Thessalonica upside down. So the unbelieving Jews hauled his friend Jason before the magistrates, who bound him over to keep the peace under payment of a very substantial bail. It may have been to relieve Jason's particular and pressing problems that Paul agreed quietly to move on at once to Berea. From Berea he made his way to Athens, from which he intended to proceed to Corinth. Before leaving Athens, however, he decided to send Timothy back to Thessalonica to check on the wellbeing of the church and to see how the believers were coping with all the pressures they were enduring. When Timothy brought his report to Paul in Corinth, the apostle was moved to write this epistle.

This is probably the first epistle Paul wrote to a New Testament church. Reading it, we find that he was obviously encouraged by Timothy's report, though there were a few things that concerned him. We may note five clear purposes Paul had in writing.

First, he wrote to commend the Thessalonians for their great missionary zeal: "Remembering without ceasing your work of faith, and labour of love, and patience of hope in our Lord Jesus Christ . . . . Ye became followers of us, and of the Lord, having received the word in much affliction, with joy of the Holy Ghost . . . . From you sounded out the word of the Lord not only in Macedonia and Achaia, but also in every place your faith to God-ward is spread abroad" (1 Thess. 1:3, 6, 8). Notice how he speaks of their work of faith, their labour of love, and their patience of hope. Faith, hope, and love are the central virtues of the Christian faith (1 Cor. 13:13), and these new Christians richly manifested them. They did so in two ways, discipleship and service. They bore the evident marks of saving grace in their lives and had a great missionary zeal to spread the gospel. As a result, they were suffering affliction and persecution. Far from stopping them, persecution merely added oil to the fire of their love so that they blazed more brightly than ever with missionary zeal. When Paul wrote this letter he was in Corinth. There he had heavy burdens to bear, but news of the Thessalonians' prayers, zeal, and missionary effort brought great comfort to his heart (3:6–10). What a joy it is to see a people who are saved, who are glad they are saved, and who are ready to spread the gospel of Christ.

Second, Paul wrote to repel the slander of the Jews against his character and motives. In chapter 2 he defends his ministry and calls the church to witness "how holily and justly and unblameably we behaved ourselves among you that believe" (2:10). The object of the Jews' attack on Paul was clearly to draw his converts away from their new faith. Paul could see through their ploy and used their attack rather to encourage the Thessalonians to remain steadfast. "Ye, brethren, became followers of the churches of God which in Judaea are in Christ Jesus: for ye also have suffered like things of your own countrymen, even as they have of the Jews" (2:14). Suffering was the common lot of Christians. "No man should be moved by these afflictions: for yourselves know that we are appointed thereunto" (3:3). Paul had warned them of this when he presented the gospel to them (3:4). He had been concerned lest they should wilt before the fire of persecution but rejoiced to hear from Timothy that they were unmoved (3:5, 6). Now he wanted to encourage them to remain faithful, despite the slanders the Jews heaped on the one who had won them for Christ.

Third, Paul wrote because he desired to establish the Thessalonians in holiness. He was very much aware of the pagan background from which they had been converted. He was in Corinth after all, that pagan stronghold, and though he saw one of the greatest revivals in history there, he experienced tremendous difficulty in freeing the Corinthian Christians completely from their pagan practices. It is easy for us to condemn their lapses, but converted pagans in a pagan culture, with all the pressure family, friends, and society could bring to bear on them, were very vulnerable to the lure of pagan practices. Paul was aware of that, and so he prayed that the Lord would establish their hearts "unblameable in holiness before God, even our Father, at the coming of our Lord Jesus Christ" (3:13). He wanted them to remember that though they were in Thessalonica, they were no longer of it. He wanted them to live, not as Thessalonians, but as Christians. How much we need to learn that. We also live in an increasingly pagan society. It is all too easy for us to be simply a reflection of the age and culture in which we live. Paul's epistle to the Thessalonians makes it clear that being "unblameable in holiness" is the standard Christians must aim at, no matter how low the morals of contemporary society become. God wills that we be holy: "This is the will of God, even your sanctification" (4:3).

Fourth, Paul wrote this epistle to correct some wrong ideas about the second coming of Christ. Some of the Thessalonians needed to learn that the promise of the Lord's return was not an excuse for idleness. They had the idea that since the Lord was coming back they did not need to work. They simply lived off the kindness of those who did work. Thus Paul prefaces his major exposition of Christ's return with the plea "to do your own business, and to work with your own hands" (4:11). Later, in 2 Thess. 3:10, he will remind them of his teaching while he was among them that if any man would not work, neither should he eat. In other words, looking for the Lord's return is not stargazing. It is not idleness. Some urgently needed to learn that.

Others needed to learn from the doctrine of the Lord's return the truth about their loved ones who had died in Christ and about whom they were obviously greatly worried. Paul addressed one of the most comforting passages in the New Testament to them on this subject: "But I would not have you to be ignorant, brethren, concerning them which are asleep, that ye sorrow not, even as others which have no hope. For if we believe that Jesus died and rose again, even so them also which sleep in Jesus will God bring with him. For this we say unto you by the word of the Lord, that we which are alive and remain unto the coming of the Lord shall not prevent them which are asleep. For the Lord himself shall descend from heaven with a shout, with the voice of the archangel, and with the trump of God: and the dead in Christ shall rise first: then we which are alive and remain shall be caught up together with them in the clouds, to meet the Lord in the air: and so shall we ever be with the Lord. Wherefore comfort one another with these words" (1 Thess. 4:13–18).

Fifth, Paul wrote this epistle because he desired to ensure that the church was well ordered and well disciplined: "We beseech you, brethren, to know them which labour among you, and are over you in the Lord, and admonish you; and to esteem them very highly in love for their work's sake. And be at peace among yourselves" (5:12–13). He wanted the church to be a fellowship of involved and caring Christians led by the Spirit, in their personal lives and their public worship, working out a blameless testimony for the glory of the Lord Jesus Christ. The great admonitions of 5:14–26 clearly show that was his burden.

Obviously, then, this is an important epistle. It is a small book, with only five brief chapters. However, they are chapters with great themes. For example, here more than in any other book Paul speaks of "the brethren," twenty-one times in all. Another seven times he speaks individually of "a brother." True love, fellowship, community, and a family unity are the marks of the Christian church. Another major emphasis appears from the apostle's repetition of the verb "to know." This is an epistle of Christian assurance. Our *election* is assured (1:4). The *efficacy of the gospel* is assured (1:5). The *experience of grace* is assured (2:1): "[You] know our entrance in unto you, that it was not in vain." Our *emancipation from sin's dominion* is assured (4:2, 4, 5). Our *expectation* is assured, for our Lord Jesus Christ is certainly coming back again (5:2).

That theme of the return of Christ is another major emphasis of the epistle. In every chapter there is a reference to the second coming of Christ. Alongside that teaching Paul lays great emphasis on Christian living. That is the major practical theme of the book. In this study we will take these two themes together, because they are the essence of the message of 1 Thessalonians. Combining the thought of the second coming of Christ with that of Christian living, as Paul does repeatedly in this book, we perceive a basic but beautiful truth: **we should live our entire Christian life in view of the Lord's return.** Paul defines five things about the Christian life in terms of the Lord's return.

THE CHARACTER OF THE CHRISTIAN LIFE

First, he defines the character of the Christian life in terms of Christ's return. He says, "Ye turned to God from idols to serve the living and true God; and to wait for his Son from heaven" (1:9–10). Here he defines Christian living as waiting for God's Son from heaven. By waiting we testify that this life is an interim. It is just a brief period we have to serve Christ. It is not our final state. We should always remember this. We are in the world, and we have to work and prosper in it so as to be able to support ourselves, our family, and the work of God. However, we must not become so involved in the things of this world that we forget that this life is but an interim period. We must live with eternity's values in view. The basic character of our time on earth is that it is a time of waiting for the Lord Jesus Christ to return to earth from heaven. How then are we to live in this interim period? What does waiting mean for the Christian? Obviously it is not the waiting of idleness, but of involvement. This waiting is active, not passive. Paul makes clear three ways in which we are to wait.

We are to wait in expectancy. That is inherent in the very verb "to wait." It denotes an active expectation of the Lord's coming. We are to live on earth with our eyes on heaven, daily crying with John the apostle, "Even so, come, Lord Jesus" (Rev. 22:20). What we do should be done in the light of the fact that Christ is coming. That is true expectancy.

Then we are to wait in evangelism. Paul rejoiced that this is how the Thessalonians waited for Christ: "From you sounded out the word of the Lord" (I Thess. 1:8); "ye turned to God from idols to serve the living and true God" (v. 9). This tells us how we are to wait. We truly wait for Christ's return only as we actively serve Him by taking the gospel to those who are lost. We have been saved to serve by reaching others who are still in the state from which Christ has rescued us. If we really believe that Jesus is coming again we will give ourselves to evangelism in the light of that coming.

We are also to wait for the Lord with an exemplary life: "Ye were ensamples to all that believe in Macedonia and Achaia" (1:7). As John put it, "Every man that hath this hope in him purifieth himself" (1 John 3:3). Sin dims the vision of the Lord's return, which the Scripture presents as a powerful promoter of holiness. However much a person knows of the prophetic Scriptures, he is not "waiting" for Christ unless he is living a life of exemplary piety.

THE CONDUCT OF THE CHRISTIAN LIFE

That leads us to the second thing Paul defines in terms of Christ's return: the conduct of the Christian life. In 1 Thess. 2:11–12 he says, "We ... charged every one of you ... that ye would walk worthy of God, who hath called you unto his kingdom and glory." Here the conjunction of the two thoughts, Christian conduct and the return of Christ, is very clear. The same is true in 3:12–13: "The Lord make you to increase and abound in love one toward another, and toward all men, even as we do toward you: to the end he may stablish your hearts unblameable in holiness before God, even our Father, at the coming of our Lord Jesus Christ with all his saints." The expectation of the Lord's return will affect our conduct in every sphere of life—in the church, in the home, and in the world. We may summarize all Paul's commands regarding our conduct under three simple heads.

First, *walk* in the light of the Lord's return. "Walk worthy of God" (2:12). Christians are at times perplexed about what is right and what is wrong. There is one very simple question we can ask ourselves when we are discerning between right and wrong: what is worthy of God? Our walk should be such as will glorify God by reflecting both His love and His holiness. The apostle puts the same truth in a different way in 4:1: walk so as to please God. What pleases Him is true holiness. In 4:12 Paul gives yet another command about our walk: "walk honestly," especially in the area of morality and marital fidelity (4:3–6). This is the kind of holy walk living in the light of the Lord's return promotes.

The second command regarding our conduct is to *work* in the light of the Lord's return: "Study to be quiet, and to do your own business, and to work with your own hands, as we commanded you" (4:11). The word *Lord* appears twenty-five times in 1 Thessalonians and another twenty-one times in 2 Thessalonians. So in eight brief chapters Paul speaks to the Thessalonians forty-six times of Christ as our Lord. No other New Testament book makes such frequent reference to Christ as Lord. Why does Paul lay such a powerful emphasis on this truth in this epistle? Surely it is because here his major theme is the second coming of Christ and our response to that truth. The returning One is the *Lord,* a term which stresses the position of His waiting saints as servants. The Lord Jesus told the parable of the talents (Matt. 25:14–30) to show that those who truly wait for His return work as good and faithful servants, employing the talents the Lord has given them for His glory.

The third command regarding our conduct is to *watch* for the Lord's return. "Let us not sleep, as do others; but let us watch and be sober.... Let us, who are of the day, be sober, putting on the breastplate of faith and love; and for an helmet, the hope of salvation" (5:6, 8). What does it mean to watch? Negatively, it means not to be intoxicated by worldly pleasure (5:7) or to be deterred by worldly persecution (3:3). Positively, it means to maintain the highest spiritual standards in personal, church, and public life (5:12–22). "Blessed are those servants, whom the lord when he cometh shall find watching" (Luke 12:37). *Walk, work,* and *watch:* these are the key words that describe the conduct of the Christian life in terms of the Lord's return.

THE COMFORT OF THE CHRISTIAN LIFE

The third thing Paul defines in terms of Christ's return is the comfort of the Christian life. The word *comfort* appears five times in the Authorized Version's translation of 1 Thessalonians. The Greek verb may also be translated "exhort" or "beseech." It appears eight times in the epistle and has the idea of calling alongside. When John 14:16

speaks of the Holy Spirit as the Comforter, the Greek term is *Paraclete,* one called alongside. The word comes from the same root as the verb we are considering. Thus the comfort Paul describes is the comfort given by one coming alongside to help us. One of the most famous passages in the New Testament on the subject of comfort is 1 Thess. 4:13–18. After stating the Christian's hope in the Christ who died, rose again, and is soon to return to receive and glorify His people, Paul says, "Wherefore comfort one another with these words." Here is the comfort of the people of God described in terms of the coming of Christ. The return of Christ is firmly based on His death and resurrection, and therefore our comfort at His coming is based on His death and resurrection: "If we believe that Jesus died and rose again, even so them also which sleep in Jesus will God bring with him." We find comfort in a backward look to the finished work of Christ. We find comfort also when we look down into the grave and see death for what it really is: It is a sleep—not for the soul but for the body. Dying in Christ is like lying down in the bosom of God, a resting in Christ in perfect peace, free from enervating care. Sleep does not last forever. Sleepers must awake. And so Paul's metaphor in 4:13 teaches us that at the coming of the Lord there will be a glorious resurrection of the saints who have died. Thus we also find great comfort in looking forward to the coming of our Saviour and our gathering together unto Him.

What comfort Christians have! They can look back without shame and guilt, knowing that their sins are under the blood of Him who died and rose again. They can face death without fear, knowing that to be absent from the body is to be present with the Lord (2 Cor. 5:8). They can look forward without doubt, for they know they will rise to meet their returning Saviour in the air.

Everlasting, perfect glory is our destiny. This is the hope every Christian has. This is the joyous light that penetrates even the darkness of the tomb. That is why Paul could cry, "O death, where is thy sting? O grave, where is thy victory?" (1 Cor. 15:55). That sting has been forever removed because the Lord has ransomed His people from the power of the grave (Hos. 13:14) and has appointed them to life eternal with Him. Not much wonder Paul said, "Wherefore comfort one another with these words."

THE COMPLETENESS OF THE CHRISTIAN LIFE

The fourth thing Paul defines in the light of Christ's return is the completeness of the Christian life. In 1 Thessalonians he addresses three things that deeply concern us: life, death, and judgment. These things challenge every one of us, both saved and unsaved. They are unavoidable. To the sinner they are words of doom and gloom. He is dead even as he lives, "dead in trespasses and sins" (Eph. 2:1). When physical death is added to that spiritual death it leads him out into eternal death, the second death, or eternal, painful separation from God. Who, in such a case, can look forward to the judgment of God? Who can joyfully anticipate Christ's awful dismissal of the ungodly, "I never knew you: depart from me" (Matt. 7:23); "Depart from me . . . into everlasting fire" (Matt. 25:41)? No man without Christ can look forward to the judgment. However, for a believer it is altogether different. We have seen that the second coming of the Lord Jesus Christ relates to the Christian's life and death. Now we must add that it also relates to his judgment: "God hath not appointed us to wrath, but to obtain salvation by our Lord Jesus Christ, who died for us, that, whether we wake or sleep, we should live together with him" (1 Thess. 5:9–10). God has not appointed us to wrath. We will never hear that awful sentence, "Depart from Me." God has appointed us to eternal salvation, and we shall certainly obtain it because "he which hath begun a good work in [us] will perform it until the day of Jesus Christ" (Phil. 1:6). That denotes the true completeness of the Christian's life. He lives his life in the foreglow of Christ's coming. When he dies, he dies in the sure hope of the resurrection. Then he faces judgment with the certainty that he will never be in hell. Here is the completeness of the Christian life: our life, our death, and our judgment, seen in the light of the coming of Christ, form a united, joyful testimony to our salvation and security in Christ.

THE CROWN OF THE CHRISTIAN LIFE

The final thing Paul defines in terms of Christ's return is the crown of the Christian life. "What is our hope, or joy, or crown of rejoicing? Are not even ye in the presence of our Lord Jesus Christ at his coming? For ye are our glory and joy" (1 Thess. 2:19–20). We should each ask himself these questions. What is my hope? What is my joy? What is my crowning achievement? And we should answer in the light of eternity, for many of the things in which men take such pride now will be of little or no significance when the Saviour comes. Paul tells us that in the light of Christ's return his crown of achievement is the crown of having faithfully presented Christ to sinners for the salvation of their souls. The true crown of rejoicing is the souls we bring to heaven. What else can we bring from earth to heaven? We must leave all the world's boasted pleasures and treasures behind us. The only things we can take with us to glory are the souls we have won for our Saviour. Why then do so many professing Christians live as if the only worthwhile achievement in this world is carnal rather than spiritual? Why do they invest so much time, effort, and money in things they admit are but for a moment and practically ignore the work of reaching the lost with the gospel? The great achievement of this life is to take the things God has given us—jobs, money, houses, health, strength, talent—and use them to bring the lost to heaven, to the glory of Jesus Christ.

> *Only one life, 'twill soon be past;*
> *Only what's done for Christ will last.*

2 Thessalonians
A Sane View Of The Second Coming

The Thessalonians were being shaken out of their minds

◆

by foolish prophetic theories. Paul taught them a lesson

◆

of undying importance: a sane view of the subject of

◆

Christ's second coming will protect Christians from

◆

many dangerous delusions.

*I*t takes very little to give Satan a way to hurt the work of a good church. The Thessalonians had a good church. However, its very existence was being threatened because of some foolish theories about the second coming of Christ. The Thessalonian believers were new Christians who displayed remarkable spiritual growth. They had a warm spiritual fellowship in a church marked by abounding love and overflowing zeal. They were actively evangelistic and boldly engaged in missionary outreach. They were undaunted by fiery trials and afflictions, unmovable and always abounding in the work of the Lord. In the face of great tribulation they stood courageously for the Lord Jesus Christ. In a word, the church in Thessalonica was one of the greatest success stories of the New Testament church. Yet the people who could not be moved by external opposition were being *shaken out of their minds* (as 2:2 literally means), disturbed by internal commotions—all because of wild theories about the second coming of Christ.

Solomon tells us that there is nothing new under the sun. Certainly the passage of almost two thousand years since New Testament times has not made Christians and churches any wiser on this score. They still tend to allow themselves to be divided and distracted by some new prophetic theory. Paul's appeal to the Thessalonians should speak as clearly to us as it did to them. His aim in this epistle is very clear. He states it in 2:1–3: "We beseech you, brethren, by the coming of our Lord Jesus Christ, and by our gathering together unto him, that ye be not soon shaken in mind, or be troubled, neither by spirit, nor by word, nor by letter as from us, as that the day of Christ is at hand. Let no man deceive you by any means." How careful we should be to guard the faith, fellowship, and continued usefulness of the church of Christ! Paul must have felt that as he penned these opening verses of chapter 2. Here he states the aim of the entire epistle and sets forth its central message in bold terms: **A sane view of the doctrine of the second coming of Christ will protect us from many dangerous deceptions and delusions of the devil.** Let us follow Paul's argument.

THE PROMISE OF THE LORD'S RETURN

The first point he makes is that God has given His church the glorious promise of Christ's return. Chapter 1 speaks of this: "To you who are troubled rest with us, when the Lord Jesus shall be revealed [or, at the revelation of the Lord Jesus] from heaven" (v. 7). That is the great subject of the commencement of this epistle. As He came the first time He will come the second time, just as literally, just as physically. However, whereas He came the first time in humiliation and obscurity, He will come the second time in public honour and majesty. He will come not to die for sin as the Man of sorrows but to judge it as the King of glory.

The revelation of the Lord Jesus Christ from heaven affects both saints and sinners, and chapter 1 sets out to show us how. First, *the revelation of Christ will bring rest for the saints:* "To you who are troubled rest with us" (v. 7). The Thessalonian believers were deeply troubled. As soon as they were saved a great storm of affliction broke upon them. They continued to suffer bitter persecution. To them Paul announced the significance of the return of Christ: God would give them rest at the revelation of the Lord Jesus Christ from heaven with the angels of His power. The word *rest* signifies a relaxation, an easing, or a loosing of the cords of affliction that were so tightly drawn around them. He assured them that the saints will find a release from the afflictions of earth at the glorious revelation of Christ. That puts an end to the controversy that has raged in the church as to when the apostles taught the Lord would come back for His people. Some Liberals contend that in 1 Thessalonians Paul taught the church to expect to be caught up to meet Christ at any moment. However, they argue, Paul discovered his mistake and developed his view of the second coming to postpone the time of Christ's return and to dull the expectation of his readers. It must be admitted that 2 Thessalonians does not hold out the expectation of an immediate return of Christ. Where the Liberals are wrong is in imagining that 1 Thessalonians does hold out such a hope. It does not. There is no discrepancy.

Dispensationalists, who are far removed from Liberals on the theological spectrum, also insist that 1 Thessalonians teaches an "any-moment" return of Christ. They often refer to it as the "any-moment rapture of the church," or the secret rapture of the church. Paul's clear statement that the church will find rest at the glorious revelation of Christ, not at a secret return some seven years earlier, destroys any such notion. Dispensationalists seek to evade the force of this argument by saying that Paul was speaking about two different comings in his two Thessalonian epistles. However, Paul clearly scotches that idea, for he places "our gathering together unto him" (2 Thess. 2:1), which is a clear reference to the "rapture" of 1 Thess. 4:16, at the revelation of Christ from heaven with His mighty angels, with flaming fire taking vengeance on them that know not God. In other words, he knows nothing of any coming of Christ prior to His glorious appearing. That is when the church will rest from its earthly afflictions. This is the "blessed hope" (Tit. 2:13) of the church of Christ, the one and only second coming of the Lord Jesus Christ. The conflict between the world and Christ's faithful witnesses will continue. We need to gird on our spiritual armour (Eph. 6:10–18) and expect no relaxation of spiritual warfare before our Lord returns. And He will return. Let that assurance comfort and motivate us.

One glimpse of Christ at His return will repay all the toil of battle.

In 2 Thess. 1:10 Paul says that Christ will come "to be glorified in his saints, and to be admired in all them that believe." What does "to be glorified in his saints" mean? The simplest suggestion is that the word *in* means "by means of" or "through." That is a frequent usage of the word. At His coming Christ will show His glory through the instrumentality of His saints, or by means of what He does for His saints. The Old Testament has a direct parallel. In Exod. 14:4 the Lord said that He would do certain things to Pharaoh and He would be glorified in Pharaoh. The Greek translation of the Old Testament uses exactly the same phrase as Paul does in 2 Thess. 1:10. God said, "I will be glorified in Pharaoh." How was He glorified in Pharaoh? What He did to Pharaoh brought honour to His name. He showed His glory by what He did to Pharaoh. That supplies the best key to understanding what Paul meant when he said that at His return Christ would be glorified in His saints. What He does to His saints at His coming will show His glory. What will He do to them? John tells us, "Now are we the sons of God, and it doth not yet appear what we shall be: but we know that, when he shall appear, we shall be like him" (1 John 3:2). In 1 Cor. 15:51–53 Paul spoke of this glorious change: "We shall not all sleep, but we shall all be changed, in a moment, in the twinkling of an eye . . . . This corruptible must put on incorruption, and this mortal must put on immortality." The Lord Jesus, therefore, will make our most inglorious body like His own glorious body (Phil. 3:21). In doing so, He will bring everlasting glory to Himself.

Paul goes on to say that Christ will be "admired in all them that believe." The word *admired* means He will be wondered at, or marvelled at. Saints will marvel. Sinners will marvel. Angels will marvel. Devils will marvel. Heaven, earth, and hell will wonder at what the Lord has done for His people. Think of that scene. It is impossible for us to form any just conception of it. But think of this: We were born in sin and shapen in iniquity. We were vessels fitted by their own wickedness for wrath and destruction. Now saved by grace, washed in the blood of Christ's atonement, reconciled to God, and glorified to be made like unto Christ, with a body that is fit for the immediate presence of the eternal Deity, we will be a cause for all the universe to wonder at the glory of divine grace. Here is a glory that outshines the sun. Here is an act of grace that far outstrips any act of God's creative power in the entire history of the universe. Christ will be marvelled at. The Lamb will have great glory because of what He has done in us.

That is God's promise to the saints. There will be rest for them at the coming of the Lord Jesus Christ. That is how the return of the Lord affects them.

The revelation of Christ also affects sinners. The wrath of God will be revealed against sinners at the coming of Christ. In 2 Thess. 1:7–9 Paul spells out what the wrath of God means. His robust words, literally translated, describe "the revelation of the Lord Jesus from heaven with the angels of His power, in a flame of fire, awarding vengeance on them that do not know God, and on those that do not obey the glad tidings of our Lord Jesus Christ: such shall pay a penalty, eternal destruction from the face of the Lord and from the glory of His strength." That is the message of Christ's second coming for sinners. What a message it is! What a serious thing it is for anyone to despise the gospel! This is a word specifically for sinners who have received the gospel. I do not think that it is necessarily a word for every sinner in the world at the day of the coming of Christ. I do not think that it is addressed to those who have never heard the name of Christ. There are other Scriptures that apply to them, but this is written specifically to speak to the consciences of people who have heard the gospel. They know the glad tidings. They have the Word of God before them. They know that God sent His Son into the world, not to condemn the world, but that the world through Him might be saved. They know that Christ died for our sins according to the Scriptures, was buried, and rose again the third day according to the Scriptures. They know the gospel invitation, "Come unto Me, and I will give you rest." Yet they despise the message. They throw it away as something of no importance. For all such people Paul has a solemn word. Jesus Christ is coming again. This time He will not come as a babe and be laid in a manger. He will not come as a Jewish itinerant preacher, to be mocked and scourged and spat upon and crucified. He will come with His mighty angels in flaming fire to administer the judgment of Him who said, "Vengeance is mine; I will repay."

Christ's second coming has a message for saints and for sinners. Its message for sinners should do certain things to the saints. First, it should make us intensely earnest in our dealings with sinners. It should drive us to our knees. It should energize us to seek to bring them to know the Saviour. Second, it should give us boldness. Here we see that we need never fear the face of puny men. How easily frightened we are. Yet man's power is as nothing when confronted with the power of God. Christ's return in power and glory will demonstrate this, and if we grasp that fact we will be able to say with the psalmist, "I will not fear what man will do unto me." Rather we will serve the Saviour in the power of God's grace and in the might of His Spirit, rejoicing in the fact that the Lord has given us the promise of His victorious return.

DELUSIONS AND DECEPTIONS ABOUT THE
LORD'S RETURN

Throughout church history some have misrepresented the promise of Christ's return and have deceived many. In Thessalonica there were some deluded teachers who insisted that the day of Christ was "at hand" (2:2). Some commentators hold that the Greek text should be translated, "The day of Christ is present," that is, has already come. That, however, appears to be a misunderstanding. The false teachers Paul was talking about were not saying that Christ had already returned but that He was just about to return. What they were saying was, "We have worked out the doctrine of the second coming and have unlocked the mystery of the time of Christ's return. The date is almost here. The day of Christ is upon us." Their claimed authority for all this is very interesting. They claimed a threefold divine authority, but it was all a deception.

Their first authority was *mishandled Scripture.* Paul speaks of a "letter as from us" (2:2). Some people were reading into his first epistle to the Thessalonians things that Paul had never intended and that an honest grammatical reading of the words would never yield. They went to that epistle with their own desires and ideas, forced some support out of its statements, and then presented the results as Scripture. Always be very careful of people who misuse Scripture to prove a prophetic viewpoint, especially when they make very large deductions from very slender premises. This is a common error, and it is not limited to any one school of prophetic interpretation. Dispensationalists are guilty of it with their invention of a two-stage second coming, one "for" and one "with" the saints. Postmillennialists are just as guilty when they foist their theory that in prophecy a year stands for a day. Amillennialists are guilty when they invent all sorts of spiritualized meanings to avoid the plain sense of much of Old Testament prophecy. Beware of accepting mishandled Scripture as an authority on any subject. When people mishandle Scripture they turn the truth of God into a lie. That is what happened in Thessalonica, and sadly it continues all too frequently today.

A second authority cited by the false teachers in Thessalonica was *erroneous preaching.* Paul refers to a "word" claimed to have come from him. This was a pretended exposition of Paul's teaching. Beware of preaching that is more imposition on the text than exposition of it. I once heard a great preacher trying to establish that the church would not be on earth during the period of the great tribulation. To prove his point he quoted 1 Thess. 5:4 as follows: "Ye, brethren, are not in darkness, that that day should overtake you." Most of his hearers believed he had faithfully expounded Paul's meaning. He had not. He had imposed his own idea on the apostle's words. Paul had written, "Ye, brethren, are not in darkness, that that day should overtake you *as a thief.*" Those three little words make all the difference. The Millerites, from whom the Seventh-Day Adventist movement came, dated Christ's return in 1843, and when that did not occur, re-dated it in 1844. The self-styled Jehovah's Witnesses date the beginning of the end time at 1799 and say that "the day of the Lord" began in 1914. Indeed, they assure us, the Lord Jesus Christ came back again to cleanse His temple in 1918, and so commenced "the day of our Lord Jesus Christ." Some orthodox Christians have fallen into similar follies, setting 1988, or 1992, or 1994, or 1996, or 2000 as the year of our Lord's return. All these people claim to be expounding God's Word and obtaining their information from it. Obviously they are not. Christians need to remain alert to escape deception. Be sure you are receiving a biblical exposition, not a human imposition.

The third claimed authority of the false teachers in Thessalonica was a "spirit," or *a spirit communication,* that is, a communication purporting to be a vision or prophecy straight from heaven. I recently heard a man who claimed to have died and gone to heaven, where he had received a vision of Christ. In fact, he had received more than a vision. He had met Christ face to face. He spoke of all the things the Lord had told him. I do not know if the man was a liar, or a charlatan, or merely deluded. He claimed that Jesus had told him what He did not tell Paul, or James, or Peter, or even John on the island of Patmos, something He never tells us in the Bible, namely, the exact time of His return. The spirit behind this man's claim was certainly not the Holy Spirit, and with the passing of the time he predicted for Christ's return his vision has proved to have been false. Many people were mightily impressed by that man's claim. Let us never forget the true standard of judging truth: "To the law and to the testimony: if they speak not according to this word, it is because there is no light in them" (Isa. 8:20). We would save ourselves from many prophetic deceptions and delusions if we would stick to God's Word.

The sad thing about all the misrepresentations of the promise of Christ's return is that they bring great harm to the cause of God. In Thessalonica people were "shaken out of their minds." They could no longer think straight. They were unable to think the gospel through and apply it to daily life. Some of them had given up working, so sure were they that Christ was at the door. They had fallen down on the basic Christian ethics by which they should have been living. If Paul had not stepped in and checked it, the delusion would have destroyed the church in Thessalonica. It would have wreaked havoc with the faith of God's people. Those who were saying, "The day of Christ is upon us; it is about to happen at any moment" would have felt betrayed when it did not happen. They would have begun to question the whole gospel. This is the real wickedness of all these prophetic deceptions. They bring the gospel and even the doctrine of the blessed hope into disrepute and undermine the faith of God's people.

THE BEST DEFENCE AND OFFENCE AGAINST DECEPTIONS

The plain teaching of the Word of God is our best defence and our best offence against Satan's deceptions and delusions. The order of prophetic events in 2 Thessalonians chapter 2 is clear. We would do well not to impose any theory or system on what God's Word says here, but rather to let it determine our system. In this chapter there are three A's that summarize the order of prophetic events.

The *Apostasy*—"That day shall not come, except there come a [lit., *the]* falling away [or, apostasy] first" (2:3).

The *Antichrist*—"That man of sin [shall] be revealed, the son of perdition .... Then shall that Wicked be revealed ... even him, whose coming is after the working of Satan" (2:3, 8, 9).

The *Appearing* of Jesus Christ—"The coming of our Lord Jesus Christ" (2:1) will not take place until the first two have occurred.

That is the order. The apostasy and the antichrist are very deceptive and will appear to many as something good, and even Christian. Paul warns (2:9–12) that the man of sin will come "with all deceivableness," or with every form of deceit. He will bring with him "strong delusion" and will back his claims "with all power and signs and lying wonders."

Nor is all this merely for the future. The mystery of lawlessness is already at work (2:7), for while antichrist is yet to come, there are many antichrists even now (1 John 2:18). For the moment there is One who restrains the mystery of lawlessness (2 Thess. 2:6), but when the time comes for the man of sin to be revealed, the restraints will be removed.

This is a solemn warning. Already, millions have fallen for the deception of the great apostasy. They welcome the unbiblical, antichristian doctrines and pretensions of Romanism and the ecumenical movement. A powerful support for both of these has come from the Charismatic movement, with its emphasis on signs and wonders. Nowadays, many professing Christians will follow almost anyone and anything that appears to be validated by a miracle. But Deut. 13:1–3 and Matt. 7:22–23 prove that many miracles are not of God. Certainly the miracles of the great apostasy and of the man of sin are not of God. Those who have disobeyed Scripture and have swallowed a lie because it came with a miracle will have no defence against the pretensions of the apostasy and the antichrist in their final and most powerful manifestation. Those who insist on judging all things by God's written Word will have no difficulty in separating "the precious from the vile," as Jer. 15:19 puts it. They are already doing so and can see through the deceitful claims of false religion, especially in the three powerful movements mentioned above. All who take seriously what the Bible says about the coming of our Saviour and what precedes it should be careful to identify the spirit of antichrist in its present mode of working so as to have no fellowship with it (Eph. 5:11).

The man of sin and all he represents will ultimately fail. He will fail because Christ cannot fail. The Lord Jesus is coming again. When He comes, He shall "consume [the man of sin] with the spirit of his mouth, and shall destroy [him] with the brightness of his coming" (2 Thess. 2:8). We must live in the light of this reality. Then shall we have rest, relaxation, and glory. Until then, in the light of Christ's coming and our gathering together unto Him, Paul gives us four divine commands:

Stand (2:15)—"Therefore, brethren, stand fast, and hold the traditions which ye have been taught, whether by word, or our epistle."

Supplicate (3:1)—"Finally, brethren, pray for us, that the word of the Lord may have free course, and be glorified, even as it is with you."

Separate (3:6)—"Now we command you, brethren, in the name of our Lord Jesus Christ, that ye withdraw yourselves from every brother that walketh disorderly, and not after the tradition which he received of us."

Serve (3:13)—"But ye, brethren, be not weary in well doing."

We could not sum up these duties better than in the terms of Paul's prayer for the Thessalonians in 3:5: "The Lord direct your hearts [lit., guide your hearts in a straight line] into the love of God, and into the patient waiting for Christ." With our hearts full of His love for us we will patiently await our Lord's return, safe from the delusions and deceptions with which Satan would derange and distract us.

We have the promise of Christ's coming. Others may misrepresent it, but let us take Scripture's sane view of it. Knowing that Jesus is coming again, leaving the timing to Him, let us boldly face the forces of apostasy and antichristianity. Until the day of Christ's appearing dawns and the shadows flee away, let us stand, let us supplicate, let us separate in holiness unto God, and let us serve Him with undiminished zeal.

CHAPTER
15

1 Timothy
The Church, The Pillar And Ground Of The Truth

The church of God must keep itself pure in doctrine

♦

and in practice so that it may support the truth of God

♦

and not weaken or obscure its testimony.

I am going to ignore the controversy which scholarly unbelief has used to surround the authorship and the date of this epistle and the other pastoral epistles, 2 Timothy and Titus. I will simply say that there is no sane or spiritual reason to doubt that Paul wrote these epistles as, when, and why the text of the epistles indicates.

1 Timothy is a very brief letter, six short chapters, directed by the apostle Paul to young Timothy, the minister of the church in the city of Ephesus. Timothy was Paul's personal choice to be the minister there. The apostle recognized the immense importance of the Ephesian church. It was strategically positioned. It was a very important church in a very important place, and a great deal depended on the behaviour and the success of the gospel workers there. So Paul was not surprised when he noted that the church in Ephesus was attracting the attention of certain heretics and deniers of the gospel of the free grace of God. He had warned the Ephesian elders to expect an infiltration by enemies of the gospel: "Take heed therefore unto yourselves, and to all the flock, over the which the Holy Ghost hath made you overseers, to feed the church of God, which he hath purchased with his own blood. For I know this, that after my departing shall grievous wolves enter in among you, not sparing the flock. Also of your own selves shall men arise, speaking perverse things, to draw away disciples after them" (Acts 20:28–29). That warning predated Paul's letter to Timothy by some years. Now the foreseen danger had become a reality, and he learned that certain Judaizers had com e int͘o the church seeking to overthrow the gospel of salvation by grace received by faith in Christ alone. They were seeking to make certain works of the law necessary to salvation. Then they wanted to be "teachers of the law" (1 Tim. 1:7), a single word in the Greek that is used in the Gospels to describe the doctors of the law, Pharisees who opposed the Lord Jesus. That was the name claimed by the pharisaical type of people who had come right into the church. They were seeking to undo all that Paul had done in bringing the gospel of free grace to the Gentiles. They were seeking to bring the Gentiles who had received Christ by faith under the yoke and bondage of the Jewish law.

When Paul realized what was happening, he desired Timothy not to accompany him to Macedonia, but to go and pastor the work in Ephesus. He writes in 1:3–4, "I besought thee to abide still at Ephesus, when I went into Macedonia, that thou mightest charge some that they teach no other doctrine, neither give heed to fables and endless genealogies, which minister questions, rather than godly edifying which is in faith: so do." Paul wanted Timothy to stay and get the work on a sure foundation and thereby defeat the schemes of the Judaizers. He knew that the battle with error was only beginning. In 4:1 he warns, "The Spirit speaketh expressly, that in the latter times some shall depart from the faith, giving heed to seducing spirits, and doctrines of devils." He goes on to describe those doctrines of devils, warning Timothy and the Ephesians that what they were seeing was just the first line of the devil's attack. That attack would develop not only in Ephesus but throughout all the churches in an effort to undo the gospel of God and bring in the doctrine of devils. You expect to find the doctrine of devils in heathen religions. But we do not expect demonic doctrine to be put forth in the name of Jesus Christ. That was what Paul was warning about: men speaking the devil's white lies, hypocritically pretending to be preaching the truth of God. Paul could see this developing. He desired Timothy, and with him every true pastor and every true church, to take a stand on the word of God's truth, to lift up its standard, and to oppose the encroachments of error however difficult that may be. It was certainly not an easy task for Timothy, but it was what he undertook in assuming pastoral responsibility in Ephesus. The battle lines were drawn; there could be no pulling back. That fact sets the tone for the epistle and dictates its content.

If we were to analyse the epistle we may divide it into two main parts. Chapters 1 and 2 deal with *sound doctrine versus satanic delusions*.

Chapters 3 to 6 deal with *sound instruction* (especially how to rule the church) *versus satanic intrusions*.

Paul works everything around those two sections. However, as in all these studies, it is not the analysis of the book that interests us so much as its central message. What is the core message of 1 Timothy? Remember that it is one of the pastoral epistles, which are directed to Timothy and Titus to instruct them how they should behave in the church, how others should behave in the church, and how the church should behave in the world. The pastorals are especially aimed at teaching how the church is to be guided and guarded so as to be a good witness for Jesus Christ in an age of apostasy. Their messages, therefore, are very much needed today.

To help us grasp the core message of 1 Timothy we will note a unique and very telling statement in 3:15. Here Paul gives his reason for writing to Timothy: "If I tarry long, that thou mayest know how thou oughtest to behave thyself in the house of God, which is the church of the living God, the pillar and ground of the truth." This is the key to the central message. The church is the pillar and ground of the truth. It is not to be a playground for heretics. The church of Rome tries to make this statement say that the truth depends on the church, that the church has the power to define doctrine by its own authority. The fallacy of that position is clear. The church is described, defined, and delineated in the Scriptures. Apart from the Scriptures we would never know what the church is or what it is intended to be. It is both logical and theological nonsense to make the church the ground of truth in the sense that it has the authority to define what is to be believed. The words *ground* and *pillar* mean the stay and the support of the truth. What Paul means is very simple. The church of God in this world is the upholder of the truth. Let us grasp that clearly. That is the basic function of every true church of Jesus Christ. There are many important tasks for the church to perform, but everything else is subservient to her fundamental responsibility to uphold the truth of God in Christ. This is so important that it is a defining mark of a true church. How may we recognize a true church? A true church of Christ upholds the truth of God.

From Revelation 2:1–7, which is also addressed to the church at Ephesus, we learn that it is possible to have orthodoxy without much love. That is dangerous. A church can be orthodox and yet pass out of existence under the judgment of God because it has lost its love for Christ. However, without orthodoxy we have nothing. Nowadays there is a lot of fuzzy thinking that goes something like this: "They are not very orthodox, but they have great spirit. They have a great love for the Lord Jesus and for one another." Without Christian orthodoxy churches may display human virtue, but they can have no fruit of the Spirit. Orthodoxy is simply believing what God says as the core of the gospel. Where people deny the heart of the gospel they have no Christianity at all. The church is the pillar and the ground of the truth. Paul's argument of this truth is very simple, but very important. **The church must keep itself pure in doctrine and in practice so that it may support the truth of God and not weaken or obscure its testimony.** In order to accomplish this the church of Christ must do three things.

DEFINE THE DEPOSIT

First it must define the deposit. *Deposit* is a technical term Paul uses for the message of Christ. In 1 Tim. 6:20 he says, "O Timothy, keep that which is committed to thy trust." The word *keep* means guard. "That which is committed to thy trust" is a single word that simply means the deposit. Obviously if Timothy was to guard the deposit he had to know what it was. Paul defines it very clearly here in this epistle. He uses certain telling terms by which he means to define the deposit. Six times he uses the word *doctrine* with the definite article. He also uses it without the article, but on six occasions he speaks of "*the* doctrine." Again, nine times he speaks of "the faith," and four times he speaks of "the godliness." The use of the definite article in the phrases "the doctrine," "the faith," and "the godliness" indicates that the apostle is using these terms technically or theologically as definitions of the deposit.

"The doctrine" is the content of the deposit. In other words, the gospel is the doctrine we are called upon to teach. But what is the gospel? In 1:11 Paul terms it "the glorious gospel of the blessed God, which was committed to my trust," or literally, "the glad tidings of the glory of the blessed God with which I was entrusted." He proceeds to expound the leading truths of this gospel in 1:15; 2:5–6; and 3:16. This last text is one of the greatest definitions of the gospel in the New Testament, and we will therefore take it first.

Paul introduces the definition with this formula: "Without controversy [literally, confessedly] great is the mystery of godliness." Here then is the essence of the Christian confession: "God was manifest in the flesh, justified in the Spirit, seen of angels, preached unto the Gentiles, believed on in the world, received up into glory." In this definition Paul sets forth six fundamental truths of the gospel.

The first fundamental of Christianity is that Jesus Christ is God incarnate. John 1:1, 14 teaches this in the clearest possible terms: "The Word was God. . . . And the Word was made [became] flesh, and dwelt among us, (and we beheld his glory, the glory as of the only begotten of the Father,) full of grace and truth." The glorious truth of the gospel of the blessed God is that what man could not do, God did for him. Man could never reach up to God, so God reached down to man. Man could never work his way from earth to heaven, so God stepped down from heaven to earth. Man could never unite himself to deity, but God came and took into personal union with Himself a true human nature. This is the miracle of the incarnation.

One of the recurring questions asked about the Lord Jesus during His ministry was, "Who is this?" (see Luke 5:21; 7:49; 8:25 Greek; 9:9). That is the most important question any man can face. Who is Jesus Christ? Some say He was a carpenter from Nazareth. Some say he was merely a Jew who lived two thousand years ago. Some say He was a great teacher, even the greatest of teachers. Others say He was the ideal man. Clearly, however, none of these answers goes far enough. Who is this who forgives sin? Who is this who raised the dead? Who is this who went to the cross and the third day rose again from the dead in fulfilment of His own word, "I have power to lay [my life] down, and I have power to take it again" (John 10:18)? The answer is, this is God manifested in the flesh. That is the first fundamental of Christianity.

The second is that He was "justified in the Spirit." There are two possible ways to understand this. Some interpret it to mean that Christ was vindicated in His own spirit. While it is obviously true that He felt vindicated in Himself in all He said and did, Paul's phrase in 1 Tim. 3:16 refers rather to the action of the Holy Spirit. The Holy Spirit set His seal to everything that Jesus Christ did, especially by His resurrection from the dead. He most emphatically justified Him—He bore testimony that Jesus Christ is righteous (1 John 2:1) and just (Acts 3:14; 7:52; 22:14). And the Spirit justified the Saviour by declaring His righteousness the sole ground of our justification and acceptance with God. It is as the righteous one that Christ stands as our advocate with the Father (1 John 2:1). It is by bearing that witness that the Spirit justifies—or declares the righteousness of—the Lord Jesus.

The third fundamental truth of the gospel is that the Saviour was "seen of angels." Commentators differ greatly over the significance of this clause. One thing, however, appears to be certain: it was only in the incarnate Son that angels ever actually looked upon eternal deity. We may also see a reference to God's sovereign grace. The angels knew that when some of their number fell, God's Son did not provide any means of redemption; yet He went so far as to become flesh to save fallen men. Not much wonder Peter says the angels desired to look into this subject (1 Pet. 1:12).

The fourth fundamental truth Paul mentions is that Christ was preached unto the Gentiles. Christianity is unique. It is the only worldwide religion and has the only universal gospel. Though our Lord lived, died, and rose again among the Jews, His gospel is equally fitted for the Gentiles, indeed for people of every kind. Well did the Samaritans say of the Lord Jesus, "This is indeed the Christ, the Saviour of the world" (John 4:42).

The fifth fundamental truth of the gospel is that Christ is "believed on in the world." Here is the glorious success of the gospel. Across the world, from every class, colour, tribe, and nation, God is drawing out a people unto Himself. Millions have believed. Millions more will yet believe to the saving of their souls.

Nor will their trust be misplaced, for the sixth fundamental truth of the gospel is that Christ was "received up into glory." Every other professed deliverer will prove a disappointment. Not so with Christ. God has highly exalted Him (Phil. 2:9), and therefore "he that believeth on him shall not be confounded" (1 Pet. 2:6). This is the mystery of godliness.

In 1 Tim. 1:15 Paul shows the gospel to be a message of grace: "This is a faithful saying, and worthy of all acceptation, that Christ Jesus came into the world to save sinners; of whom I am chief." I have mentioned Christ's coming into the world. Here is the purpose of that coming: "Christ Jesus came into the world to save sinners." This message of grace is addressed to sinners. It brings to them the good news of salvation. It addresses sinners in all their need with a statement of the power and purpose of Christ to save them. It does not set before sinners any demand that they do anything to make themselves salvable or acceptable in the sight of God. It does not even tell them that Christ is willing to help them get to heaven. Rather, it says He came to save them. That is the message of grace.

In 2:5, 6 Paul adds the third strand to his exposition of the glorious gospel: "There is one God, and one mediator between God and men, the man Christ Jesus; who gave himself a ransom for all, to be testified in due time." God is holy. Men are depraved. How then can sinners draw near to God? How can they ever find acceptance with Him? The answer is, through Jesus Christ, the Mediator between God and men. Here we see the beauty of the gospel. The Mediator is God and satisfies God. Yet He is man and therefore can stand in the place of men. He took our place, paid our debt, and fully wrought out the righteousness which God demanded. Putting one hand on the throne of God and the other on the head of the sinner, He reconciles God and man in Himself. He is the Mediator between God and men.

This is the doctrine that is the content of the gospel deposit: the mystery of godliness, the message of grace, and the mediation with God. No treatment of the gospel is adequate that fails to do justice to these great themes.

"The faith" is our conviction about the deposit (1:19; 3:9; 4:1; etc.). Paul did not speak about the gospel as a matter of doubt or debate. The faith is the body of truth we believe on the authority of the revelation of God. It is not the cunningly devised fables of man. It is not even a mixture of divine truths and human opinions. No! The Christian faith is God's objective truth, unmixed with human error, given to us through the instrumentality of men supernaturally inspired by the Spirit of God for the task.

Let it be clear, there is such a body of doctrine. The modern notion that we can have true Christianity without the doctrine of the deity of Christ, or His virgin birth, or His miracles, or His atoning death and resurrection, is utterly foolish. The notion that we can have true Christianity without the Bible truth of justification by grace alone, through faith alone, in the merits of Christ alone, is equally foolish.

So is the idea that the content of the faith is constantly changing. This is the teaching of Romanism with its claims that the pope and the church have the power to define doctrine, even though there is no foundation for it in Scripture. The faith was delivered once and for all (Jude 3). It is God's unchangeable truth.

The body of truth that comprises the gospel is received by faith, that is, by a personal conviction wrought in our hearts by the Holy Ghost.

The gospel is divinely logical, but it is not received by bare logic. It establishes the sacraments of baptism and the Lord's Supper, but it is not received by the reception of the sacraments. It calls for action, but it is not received by works. The gospel can be received only by faith—a faith that engages our logic and stirs our hearts to obedience, but that is chiefly marked by its utter conviction of the truth as it is in Christ Jesus and its consequent trust in Him alone for salvation.

"The godliness" is the consequence of the gospel deposit (1 Tim. 3:16; 4:8; 6:5, 6). The gospel produces real holiness of life. Nothing else can. Men may clean up their lives, but only the gospel can produce real holiness. A faith that fails to do this is counterfeit. Nowadays, even some Fundamental churches make it a point of orthodoxy that a new life of holy obedience is not a necessary mark of saving faith. According to them, saving faith does not necessarily lead to a change of life. Repentance is merely a mental decision that does not necessarily lead to holy action. If that were the truth we would have to throw away half of our New Testament. The gospel received in the heart produces godliness.

The deposit is the doctrine. That doctrine is called the faith. And that faith produces the godliness. We must know this truth before we can ever stand up for it. And we must define it as the inspired apostle does if we are to stand up for it. Nowadays in New Evangelicalism, which more and more resembles old-fashioned unbelief, there is a lot of "redefining" taking place. New Evangelicals are redefining the terms *inspiration* and *inerrancy* as applied to Scripture. They believe these doctrines, they assure us, but when they have redefined them they present an inerrant Bible that is full of errors. Some of them are even redefining what it means to be a Christian or an evangelical.

Others are redefining the very gospel and the mission of the church. The craze to "contextualize" the message for one group after another may produce a gospel that will be acceptable to various nationalities, cultures, and subcultures, but it usually bears only a faint resemblance to the gospel as preached by the apostles. Today's buzz word is *relevant*—we need a relevant message, presented by a relevant method, with relevant music, etc. What we should be concerned about is a scriptural message presented by scriptural means. Then, and only then, may we expect scriptural results. This is not a day to *redefine* the deposit but to define it in its God-given terms.

GUARD THE GOSPEL

Our second responsibility is to guard the deposit. In 5:21 Paul says, "Observe these things." In 6:20 he adds, "O Timothy, keep that which is committed to thy trust." In both texts the verb is the same. It means to guard. Timothy was to "guard the deposit," as 6:20 may be translated. There would be attempts to steal it, ruin it, and corrupt it. That situation has never changed. Some people want to ritualize the gospel, some want to socialize it, some want to rationalize it, and some want to politicize it. We are called upon to guard the gospel. Paul says, "I am set for the defence of the gospel" (Phil. 1:17). He commands Timothy to "war a good warfare" (1 Tim. 1:18). In 4:1 he warns that there will be doctrines of demons in the church. What are we to do? We should hold faith in a good conscience (1:19). That means to hold to the whole truth of the gospel of grace that presents a free salvation which we can receive only by faith.

The most dangerous attacks on the gospel come from an unlawful use of the law (1:7–10). The law is good if a man uses it lawfully. There are two extremes that appear in the unlawful use of the law. First there is the extreme of legalism. That is what the people in Ephesus whom Paul was combatting were promoting. They wanted a return to a system of rituals that had been fulfilled in Christ. Some have a worse form of this extreme, for they want to impose a system of man-made regulations that have no warrant in Scripture by which to bind the consciences of God's people. Legalism is not the way to holiness. It is the way to defeat.

Then there is the opposite extreme, one that is very popular today. It is the extreme of antinomianism. This denies any obligation to the law of God. Some people are selective. They accept the obligations that suit them and reject others that do not—especially the observance of the Christian sabbath. But who has the right to abrogate any of the ten commandments, when their Author has not done so?

Legalism and antinomianism are unlawful uses of the law. The law is good if we use it lawfully to expose sin, to cause conviction and show sinners their need of Christ, and to show the unchanging standards of holiness God expects from His people. It is never to be presented as a way of salvation. It cannot replace or even modify the gospel of free grace. That is something we must guard jealously. Guard the gospel.

TEACH THE TRUTH

The church's third duty as described by Paul in this epistle is to teach the truth. Teaching figures very largely in Paul's admonitions. Elders must be "apt to teach" (3:2). In 4:6 he reminds Timothy of the "good doctrine, whereunto thou hast attained," or "the good teaching which thou hast closely followed." In 4:11 and 6:2 he commands Timothy to teach. Ignorance is fatal to the church's ministry. Today there is a famine of "the word of the truth of the gospel." As a result, Christians and churches are weak. We certainly need preachers who will teach the truth whatever the cost.

Paul gives a good example of what is needed. In this epistle he deals with the church and its government and with believers and their manner of life. He applies the truth to both. We may sum up his meaning in his command to teach the truth. Teaching the truth involves more than the mere mention of the doctrines of truth. We have already noted the importance of orthodox doctrine, but when Paul gave Timothy and the elders the command to teach he meant them to *conduct the church in an orderly way.* He lays a great deal of emphasis on a "good" or "pure" conscience (1:5, 19; 3:9) in contrast with a "conscience seared with a hot iron" (4:2). Eleven times he uses the word *pistos,* usually translated "faithful." The gospel is faithful (1:15) and produces faithful people (1:12; 3:11). Evidently the reflection of the gospel in the lives of those who profess to believe it was very important to the apostle. It should be to us. We are not to teach the truth merely in words but by our works. By precept and example we are to impress on all men the full implications of God's saving truth. And, of course, to do that we must live our lives by the light of that truth. Paul makes that the standard for church office bearers. Conforming their own lives to the truth of the gospel, they govern the church by the same standard.

Teaching the truth also involves *separating from heretics and hypocrites.* The two epistles to Timothy contain fourteen distinct calls to separation, six of them in 1 Timothy: 1:3–7; 4:1–7; 5:22; 6:5, 11, 20. The message is plain. If we teach the truth of the gospel and hold our conscience captive to the Word of God, we will run into opposition. We will have to separate from those who oppose the gospel or who compromise it. That is not a popular stance today, but it is the stance demanded by God's truth. That truth defines our personal and church conduct and fellowship. Any fellowship that involves compromising the truth of the gospel is wrong. The gospel calls us to separation because in everything the church of Christ must be "the pillar and ground of the truth."

Here, then, is our calling. By our message, our ministry, and our manner of life we must hold forth God's unchanging truth. It still does the work in men it has always done. Three times Paul says, "This is a faithful saying," or "Faithful [true, or trustworthy] is the word." Let us be sure to be faithful in defining, defending, and declaring the truth, and God will be faithful to use it to bring men to life in Christ and to defeat the devices and delusions of the devil.

Thus shall we glorify our God. This is the supreme end of our existence. Paul voiced that sentiment in 1:17: "Now unto the King eternal, immortal, invisible, the only wise God, be honour and glory for ever and ever. Amen." Again, in 6:15–16 he speaks of Him as "the blessed and only Potentate, the King of kings, and Lord of lords; who only hath immortality, dwelling in the light which no man can approach unto; whom no man hath seen, nor can see: to whom be honour and power everlasting. Amen." Every true Christian and every true church echoes these sentiments. We will actually promote the glory of our God and King as we remain pure in doctrine and practice and support the testimony of God's truth in the world.

2 Timothy
The Changing Of The Guard

Young ministers should take up the torch of truth and

♦

continue the work of faithful men whose earthly service

♦

is over. Thus Paul deals with the proper function of a

♦

minister. Describing him as a soldier, a striver, a

♦

husbandman, a student, a workman, a servant,

♦

a teacher, a preacher, a sufferer, and a soulwinner,

♦

he charges him to be faithful to God.

*T*here is a very clearly marked progression of thought from 1 Timothy to 2 Timothy. 1 Timothy deals with the proper function of the church. In 2 Timothy Paul deals with the proper function of the minister in the church. Any study of these epistles must take note of this shift of emphasis. What the Lord says to the church and to the minister is very important. Ministers must see clearly not only what the church ought to be and do, but what *they* ought to be and do. Similarly, churches need to understand their responsibilities before God, and they should especially keep in mind that a good minister labours in the light of the judgment seat. He is the messenger of God. He is not the cat's-paw of the congregation. While he is to be the servant of all, he is not to be the puppet of the congregation, or of any faction in the congregation. Churches ought to remember that ministers are not given to them to do what *they* want, but rather to stand among them as the mouthpiece of God to be a continual voice for the Lord in their ears. That is certainly how Paul saw the functions of ministers and churches.

It is interesting and instructive that Paul's last letter before his martyrdom should deal so largely with the office and duty of the Christian minister. He describes the minister of the gospel in various ways. In chapter 2 he calls him a soldier (v. 3), a striver (v. 5), a husbandman (v. 6), a student of the Word of God who as a good workman knows how rightly to divide the Word of truth (v. 15), and a servant and teacher (v. 24). In chapter 4 he speaks of him as a preacher (v. 2) and as a sufferer and a soulwinner (v. 5). In all these capacities the minister of Jesus Christ is to be a man of the Word. He must be a man of vital godliness, one who is not entangled with the affairs of this world. He must be a man of courage and integrity who will stand for God and God's truth whatever the personal cost may be. He must be faithful to his Lord whether men will hear him or not. When men have itching ears and crave to hear something different, something new, he must be immovable from the old gospel of free grace in Jesus Christ.

This was Paul's charge to Timothy, and it is his charge to every preacher and every aspiring preacher. It is by these standards that every professed servant of God will be judged. We have a foretaste of that judgment in the more than two dozen references Paul makes to various people by name. Noting the apostle's comments on these people, one preacher termed 2 Timothy "a veritable judgment seat." In charging Timothy Paul sets up the abiding standards for the Christian ministry. These are the things that really count in God's service. Paul felt this very deeply. He was at the point of death. More clearly than ever he could see what really mattered in life—and that was to be the kind of man for God he describes in this epistle.

He says, "I have fought a good fight, I have finished my course, I have kept the faith" (4:7). His race was finished, his warfare accomplished. But the work of God must go on. When Moses died God had to raise up a Joshua. When Paul died He had to raise up a Timothy. That is why Paul's final letter was such an impassioned plea to Timothy, a young minister, to take up the torch of the gospel and to advance the cause of Christ in the world. That is the great burden of 2 Timothy. I think of this epistle as **the changing of the guard.** Paul was dying, and Timothy was rising up to stand in his place, at least in some measure. Paul deals with his subject in a very straightforward way.

THE NEED FOR FAITHFUL MINISTERS IS GREAT

First, the need for faithful ministers is great. One reason for the need is that *the old guard is passing.* The death of faithful ministers leaves a gap young men must rise up to fill. In 1:12, 13 Paul refers to his imminent death and the responsibility it would place on Timothy: "For the which cause I also suffer these things: nevertheless I am not ashamed: for I know whom I have believed, and am persuaded that he is able to keep that which I have committed unto him against that day. Hold fast the form of sound words, which thou hast heard of me, in faith and love which is in Christ Jesus." He does the same thing in chapter 4: "Watch thou in all things, endure afflictions, do the work of an evangelist, make full proof of thy ministry. For I am now ready to be offered, and the time of my departure is at hand" (vv. 5–6). See how he joins the two things. He says, "Timothy, I am dying. My day is over. My generation of preachers is finished. Now it is time for you to step forward. It is time for you to be in the front line, to take up the torch of the cause of Jesus Christ our Lord."

The passing of the old guard always emphasizes the church's need for faithful ministers. The great old preachers who blazed a trail for God, who did a work for God that still stands, either have passed away or are passing away. There is an urgent need for young men, for new stalwarts to arise and carry on the work of God into the next generation. So the passing of the old guard accentuates the need for faithful ministers.

The fact that *we live in perilous times of rampant apostasy* also shows the need for good ministers. "This know also, that in the last days perilous times shall come" (3:1–7). Those perilous times have come. They are upon us. They are no longer in the future; they are here. Men are lovers of themselves. They are "covetous, boasters, proud, blasphemers, disobedient to parents, unthankful, unholy, without natural affection, trucebreakers [the same word appears in Rom. 1:31, where it is translated "implacable"], false accusers, incontinent, fierce, despisers of those that are good, traitors, heady, highminded, lovers of pleasures more than lovers of God; having a form of godliness, but denying the power thereof" (3:2–7). In "perilous times" apostasy runs riot in the church. Paul warned, "The time will come when they will not endure sound doctrine; but after their own lusts shall they heap to themselves teachers, having itching ears; and they shall turn away their ears from the truth, and shall be turned unto fables" (4:3–4). Such apostasy can be met only by faithful ministers of Christ.

Each generation faces a new onslaught from a new crop of apostates. Each generation, therefore, needs a new race of godly preachers. We cannot fight today's battles in the strength of men who fought well in their own day but are now dead. We celebrate their memory and make use of their labours, but *our need is for new men of the old school,* men of the apostolic mould, who will "guard the deposit." We need a race of preachers on fire for God, who know God personally and who have the power of the Holy Ghost in their ministries. We need a race of preachers who do not fear the face of man, who will go across the world with the gospel and endure hardship as good soldiers of Jesus Christ. We need a new race of Christian pioneers, young men who have died to the world's claims and attractions and who are ready and willing to serve their Saviour whatever the cost. There is the need for a new generation of such preachers. May God raise them up.

THE DUTY OF FAITHFUL MINISTERS IS SOLEMN

The second thing we will notice is that the duty of faithful ministers is solemn. You could preach verse by verse through 2 Timothy proving this point, but there are three things that I will say to sum all this up.

First, *the Christian minister must prove the gospel:* "I am appointed a preacher, and an apostle, and a teacher of the Gentiles. For the which cause I also suffer these things: nevertheless I am not ashamed: for I know whom I have believed, and am persuaded that he is able to keep that which I have committed unto him against that day" (1:11–12). Paul had a personal experience of Jesus Christ, and he preached out of that experience. It is usually true that the level of spiritual life in a congregation will not exceed the level of spiritual life in the minister. A spiritually dead minister has a deadening effect. A faithful minister of Christ must have a proven personal experience of God's grace. It is said that a new minister in the parish in which Thomas Carlyle lived asked the famous writer what the parish most needed. Carlyle's reply was memorable: "Sir, this parish most needs a man who knows God other than by hearsay." A minister must prove the gospel in his personal experience.

Then, *he must preach it.* Paul says, "I charge thee therefore before God, and the Lord Jesus Christ, . . . preach the word" (4:1–2). The context of this charge is important. "From a child thou hast known the holy scriptures, which are able to make thee wise unto salvation through faith which is in Christ Jesus. All scripture is given by inspiration of God, and is profitable for doctrine, for reproof, for correction, for instruction in righteousness" (3:15–16). Now then, says Paul, preach the Word. It is inspired, so preach it. We have an inspired book, a God-breathed book, a living book. Therefore let us preach it. "Preach *the Word*," not merely preach around and about the Word. Expound the Word. That is what Paul is telling young Timothy. Be a man who can go to the heart of the Word. Do not be afraid of the Word; let it speak for itself. Never be ashamed of what it says. Too many people are either afraid or ashamed of the unvarnished teachings of Scripture. Not long ago I heard a preacher expounding Ephesians chapter 1. He was dealing with election and predestination. These words obviously frightened him. He pretended to be expounding what Paul had written, but having read Eph. 1:4–5, without a single Scripture reference to warrant his idea, he said, "God chose us *all* at Calvary, everybody in the world, and it is now up to us as to whether we endorse or reject the choice of God." A faithful minister cannot treat the Bible like that. He must preach it as it is. While he does not understand everything that is in the Bible, he must be ready to accept everything it teaches. He has no cause to fear anything in Scripture. It is true. It is inspired.

Preach it, because its message alone can make men wise unto salvation. I would to God preachers would always remember that. For example, there is a place for illustration in preaching. However, all too often the illustration becomes the sermon. Sermons are frequently a string of little stories to make people laugh or cry at the right time to produce the reaction the preacher wants. An illustration, Spurgeon said, is to be like a window that lets light into a building. The sermon is the building; the illustration is the window. Too many preachers have sermons that are all window and no substance. That is not preaching the Word.

Faithful ministers must preach the Word in all seasons: "Be instant in season, out of season" (4:2). They must preach it with urgency: "Be instant" means to be urgent, especially in giving the gospel to sinners. Paul tells Timothy to "do the work of an evangelist" (4:5). He was to be urgent in his dealings with sinners. One of the marks of the preaching of George Whitefield was the urgency with which he preached. In every time of genuine revival there was an intense urgency in every sermon. Christians went to sinners not to give them a mere theory form or even a bare form of a doctrine. With all the urgency of people who knew the reality of sin and of eternity, they brought sinners face to face with God's law and God's love. They showed them the glory of Christ and pleaded with them to repent and be converted. There never was a greater pleader in the pulpit than Whitefield. As a Calvinist who wrote a famous treatise on God's sovereign election, he pleaded with tears that sinners should flee to Christ. Faithful preaching of the Word has to have real urgency.

We have a great gospel to preach: "[God] hath saved us, and called us with an holy calling, not according to our works, but according to his own purpose and grace, which was given us in Christ Jesus before the world began, but is now made manifest by the appearing of our Saviour Jesus Christ, who hath abolished death, and hath brought life and immortality to light through the gospel" (1:9–10). Christians have the message for this world of sin and shame, suffering and death. It is the message of the Christ who died and in dying abolished death, who rose from the dead to open the way to glory. It is the message of the Christ who is the Saviour of perishing sinners. With such a message Christians must not be silent. They must "be instant" and preach the gospel with urgency.

They must preach it with personal application: "Rebuke, reprove, exhort with all longsuffering and doctrine" (4:2). Faithful preaching does not simply inform the intellect. It must do that, but it must do much more. It must stir the emotions, reach the conscience, and storm the stronghold of the will. That is the task of faithful preachers.

He who would apply the Word of God to others must apply it first to himself. He must preach as one who must soon give account to God: "I charge thee therefore before God, and the Lord Jesus Christ, who shall judge the quick and the dead at his appearing and his kingdom." What a solemn thing it is to preach the Word of God! Soon this preacher will meet the Lord and will render an account of his stewardship. Woe to me in that day if I have feared the face of man and therefore have obscured the face of God. Woe to me if out of deference to man I have compromised the truth of the gospel of God. The duty of the preacher is solemn. He must prove the gospel, and he must preach the gospel.

Third, *he must preserve the gospel.* Paul warns that the time will come when people will not endure sound doctrine (4:3). That time has come. Most churches do not want sound doctrine. They crave entertainment instead of exposition. They prefer emotional experiences to the evangel. That is sad, because the gospel produces the deepest and most satisfying emotional experiences. Emotionalism apart from the exposition of the great truths of the gospel is both dangerous and wrong. Experience that flows from a grasp by faith of the glories of the gospel will be profound and lasting. It will be holy and healthful to the soul. However, since so many people want to short-circuit the gospel and satisfy their emotional or spiritual needs with sensual stimuli—like crowd hysteria, repetitive "worship" jingles, or, at the other extreme, priestly rituals and liturgy—the faithful preacher must hold fast the gospel (1:13). He must not be moved from it and must pass it on in all its purity to those who come after him: "The things that thou hast heard of me among many witnesses, the same commit thou to faithful men, who shall be able to teach others also" (2:2). That is a vital criterion for judging any man's ministry. There are two things every preacher must face at the end of his ministry: Did I hold fast the gospel? Did I pass that gospel on in its undiluted purity to those who came after me? Paul says that is the duty of the minister.

It is no easy task. It will involve tough spiritual warfare. That is why Paul admonishes, "Thou therefore endure hardness, as a good soldier of Jesus Christ" (2:3). In 4:5 he adds, "Watch thou in all things, endure afflictions, do the work of an evangelist, make full proof of thy ministry." Only as ministers are faithful to Christ and His gospel, whatever opposition or affliction may arise on that account, can they fully carry out their service, as this verse literally reads. It is their solemn duty to do no less. They must fight a good fight, keep the faith, and finish the course (4:7), or, to use the words of Christ to the church in Smyrna, they must be faithful unto death (Rev. 2:10).

THE STANDARDS FOR CHRISTIAN MINISTERS ARE HIGH

The standards for Christian ministers are high. Paul gives us a clear statement of those standards in 2 Timothy chapter 2. We may particularly note five ways in which he shows ministers the standards of true faithfulness.

First, the Christian minister is to *live out the gospel of free grace:* "Be strong in the grace that is in Christ Jesus" (v. 1). It is easy for a minister to preach grace to others and not live by it himself. It is easy for him to tell others that looking unto Jesus by faith is the way to triumph in the battles and difficulties of life while he himself pursues his ministry in a spirit of frustration and defeat. The work of a minister may so isolate him that he feels he carries the burden of his work for God alone. If the work prospers he feels that it prospers in spite of him. If the work fails to prosper he feels it is because of him. That becomes a crushing, soul-destroying burden. The man of God must know how to live out the gospel of grace by faith in Jesus Christ.

He must *be separated in his personal life:* "No man that warreth entangleth himself with the affairs of this life" (v. 4). John Calvin wisely commented on this verse: "Every one who wishes to fight under Christ must relinquish all the hindrances and employments of the world and devote himself unreservedly to the warfare. . . . Paul speaks to the pastors of the church . . . . First, let them see what things are inconsistent with their office, that, freed from those things, they may follow Christ. Next, let them see, each for himself, what it is that draws them away from Christ; that this heavenly General may not have less authority over us than that which a mortal man claims for himself over heathen soldiers who have enrolled under him."

The faithful minister must *be dedicated in his service.* Paul says, "I suffer trouble, as an evil doer, even unto bonds; but the word of God is not bound. Therefore I endure all things for the elect's sakes, that they may also obtain the salvation which is in Christ Jesus with eternal glory" (vv. 9–10). Paul was suffering but remained dedicated to Christ and His cause. The faithful minister must labour in the certainty that the Word of God cannot fail. The assurance of the success of his message will keep him dedicated even when he is enduring the most intense affliction for his faith.

He must *be diligent in ministering the Word of God:* "Study to show thyself approved unto God, a workman that needeth not to be ashamed, rightly dividing the word of truth" (v. 15). *Study* means to be diligent. "Rightly dividing the word of truth" does not mean to divide it up into many different dispensations with various gospels and tests for divine acceptance. That would not be rightly dividing the Word of truth. Indeed, it is wresting the Word of truth. Rightly to divide the Word of truth is to take this Word, to apply it to every man in his own situation, and to give to every man what is his due portion. The preacher of the gospel must be diligent in ministering the Word.

The faithful minister must also *be a holy vessel in God's house* (vv. 20–21). In a great house there are not only vessels of gold and of silver, but also of wood and of earth. There are some to honour and some to dishonour. "If a man therefore purge himself from these, he shall be a vessel unto honour, sanctified, and meet for the master's use, and prepared unto every good work." Some people think Paul meant that if we purged ourselves we would all be vessels of gold or silver. That is not what he says. In every great house there are some vessels of gold, some of silver, and others of wood or of clay. Each has its usefulness. There are some functions for which a golden goblet, or a silver salver, would be of no use. The spiritual implication is plain. We do not all have the same capacity or gifts, but we can all be useful to our Saviour. It is up to the Lord in His sovereignty to make us the kind of vessels He wants us to be.

However, all faithful servants of the Lord must be vessels unto honour. They must be clean vessels. "If a man therefore purge himself from these, he shall be a vessel unto honour." That is true not only of ministers, but of every Christian who would serve the Lord acceptably.

According to verse 24, faithful servants must put away everything that hinders their service: "The servant of the Lord must not strive; but be gentle unto all men, apt to teach, patient, in meekness instructing those that oppose themselves; if God peradventure will give them repentance to the acknowledging of the truth." Faith in Christ that produces separation from sin, dedication to God, diligence in service, and holiness of life—purity, gentleness, patience, and meekness—is what constitutes a true servant of God. God has set the standard high.

THE REWARDS OF FAITHFUL MINISTERS ARE GLORIOUS

The rewards the Lord gives to faithful ministers are glorious. Paul refers to these in 4:6–8: "I am now ready to be offered, and the time of my departure is at hand. I have fought a good fight, I have finished my course, I have kept the faith: henceforth there is laid up for me a crown of righteousness, which the Lord, the righteous judge, shall give me at that day: and not to me only, but unto all them also that love his appearing." There is something very special about a testimony from the edge of the grave. People can express all sorts of beliefs while they think they have a long time to live. When you are facing death, however, it is a very different thing. If your religion is not good enough to die by, then it is not good enough to live by. Paul was dying, and as he faced a violent death, knowing that it could come at any moment, he rejoiced that he was ready to die. He was looking forward to heaven. How blessed to be able to finish the course with such joy! What an encouragement this was to Timothy and all the other young ministers to remain faithful to the gospel!

But Paul's testimony has a much wider application than to Timothy. It speaks to all of us. We must all die. It may be nearer than we think. The great question is, do we have Paul's testimony?

Think of this. Paul says *he has no fear:* "God hath not given us the spirit of fear; but of power, and of love, and of a sound mind" (1:7). He has no fear of death, of judgment, or of eternity. Further, he says *he has no shame:* "I am not ashamed" (1:12). What a testimony! It is as if he said, "My sin is under the blood. My guilt is purged away. I am justified freely by the grace of God. I have believed the gospel to the saving of my soul. I have committed my life to Christ. I have not done everything perfectly, but I am covered by the blood of His atonement and the garment of His righteousness, and I am not ashamed. I am not ashamed to stand for God before men, and I am not ashamed as I go out to meet my God, because Christ is my righteousness."

He also says *he has no doubt:* "I know whom I have believed" (1:12). He has no doubt about the salvation of his soul. He says, "I know whom I have believed." Not *what* but *whom*—it is not a mere head knowledge of doctrines about Christ that saves, but Christ Himself. Only He can give a well-grounded assurance like Paul's.

As he writes his last letter Paul has no doubt about his work. He was laying down his life work and was about to present it to God. He was not perfect in his work, but he had no doubt that he had made the right choice, he had done the right thing, he had lived in the right cause, and he had served the right Master.

Paul tells us he has no doubt about the gospel. He says, "He is able to keep that which I have committed unto him against that day." He refers to the *deposit* we noted in 1 Timothy. He says, "He is able to keep the deposit," the gospel of His Son. Paul had exhorted Timothy to guard the deposit. Now he says God will guard the deposit. He will keep the gospel. He will stand up in His own cause and defend His own Son. He will publish His own truth and give success to His servants so that the gospel of Jesus Christ will not be preached in vain.

Paul also testifies that he has no doubt about eternity. "That day" would hold no surprises. The Lord who saved him would keep him and bring him safely home to heaven. As he says in 4:18, "The Lord shall deliver me from every evil work, and will preserve me unto his heavenly kingdom: to whom be glory for ever and ever."

Facing death, Paul adds one final strand to his testimony. He says *he suffers no loneliness:* "At my first answer no man stood with me, but all men forsook me: . . . notwithstanding the Lord stood with me, and strengthened me" (4:16–17). The Word of God says, "Woe to him that is alone when he falleth" (Eccles. 4:10). Woe to the man who is alone when he comes to die. Death is the loneliest valley in the world. Humanly speaking, we must die alone. Earth's nearest and dearest friends must leave us to face the last enemy alone. But Paul's testimony is the happy assurance of every Christian. We may honestly and confidently say, "I am not alone. Men may not be able to come with me into the valley of the shadow of death, but David's Shepherd is my Shepherd. 'Yea, though I walk through the valley of the shadow of death, I will fear no evil: for thou art with me; thy rod and thy staff they comfort me.' He will not ask me to cross Jordan alone." Such was Paul's testimony. Let us each one ask himself, is this my testimony?

Paul's testimony calls every one of us to lay hold of Christ. Make sure you are saved. It also calls every Christian to take up the torch, to take our stand, and to dedicate ourselves wholeheartedly to our God. There is an urgent need for faithful servants. Their duties are solemn. The standards required of them are high. But the rewards are glorious. Let us lay ourselves open to the service of our Saviour, to be fully used for His glory.

17

Titus

The Truth According To Godliness

Titus spells out the responsibilities of both the church's

♦

eldership and its membership. It contains many

♦

striking expressions to expound the "sound doctrine"

♦

of "God our Saviour" and to show how Christians

♦

should live according to the truth that is according

♦

to godliness.

*T*itus is the last of the three pastoral epistles. 1 Timothy focuses attention on the office and the function of the church. 2 Timothy focuses attention on the office and the function of the minister. Now Titus combines both those ideas as Paul sets forth the will of God for the good order of the church in its internal government and in its external testimony. In addressing these subjects, the apostle clearly states the responsibilities both of the eldership and of the membership of the church. To both Titus was to be "a pattern" (2:7), giving them an example of the power of "sound doctrine" to convict the contradictors of the gospel (1:9) and to instruct believers how they ought to adorn the profession of the gospel with holy living (2:10).

It is remarkable that the Holy Spirit chose to have this epistle written to Titus when he was the minister of the church in Crete. This is an epistle that tells God's people how to live in the fulness and victory of the Holy Spirit in vital Christian living. Now, Crete was a very difficult and unpromising situation for a church. The Cretians had a bad reputation: "One of themselves, even a prophet of their own, said, The Cretians are always liars, evil beasts, slow bellies. This witness is true" (1:12–13). "Evil beasts and lazy gluttons"—this was certainly a scathing indictment. And, says Paul, that reputation was well deserved. The island people provided no hospitable soil for the gospel and its good seed. But Paul had a firm conviction in his heart. He believed that the grace of God that could save and transform him could do the same for anybody anywhere. And he was not disappointed. When he preached the gospel in Crete, he saw people saved. Some of these people from this evil, bestial background received Jesus Christ and were formed into a living church of the living Christ.

Despite the fact that they had just been saved out of such a wicked environment, Paul's new converts were expected to manifest the gloriously transformed lives of saints. They were no longer sinners. They were now saints, and Paul expected them to live like saints, not like sinners. He fully expected them to live up to the standard of the gospel.

Obviously, there were many difficulties in the way of his vision being realized. Some of those difficulties were inside the church. Some were outside the church. But none of them was allowed as an excuse for a lack of vital godliness. There is no excuse for Christians living unholy lives. That is what Paul makes clear in this epistle. When a man is saved, though he may have come from a very wicked background, he is a new creature in Christ. He may have battles to fight and enemies to face that many other newborn Christians know nothing about. Still, Paul's contention is that a new creature will always manifest the new life he has in Christ. The man in whom the Spirit of God dwells is bound to show some evidence of transformation.

Internally, the church of Jesus Christ must have a scriptural order and discipline, and externally, it must through its members have a testimony that adorns the gospel of Christ. Even in a place like Crete, that church must and will, by the grace of God, live to the highest standards of godliness. What an encouragement for us today, as we seek to serve the Saviour in an increasingly vicious society! And what a challenge! It challenges our indolence and the easy way in which we make the immoral state of society an excuse for our own spiritual impoverishment. This epistle challenges us to realize there is no excuse for an individual believer, or a church, living any other way but in the victory and holiness of the risen Christ. This is the message of spiritual power we find in Paul's epistle to Titus.

There are many striking phrases and statements in Titus. One of them is "God our Saviour." The three chapters of this book contain six occurrences of the word *Saviour* (1:3, 4; 2:10, 13; 3:4, 6). That theme runs throughout the epistle. Thus we are not at all surprised to find that Paul sets forth the great fundamentals of the gospel as the basis of his message of challenge and hope to the church. First, he emphasizes the deity of our Lord Jesus Christ. In 1:3, 4 we read, "[God] hath in due times manifested his word through preaching, which is committed unto me according to the commandment of God our Saviour; to Titus, mine own son after the common faith: grace, mercy, and peace, from God the Father and the Lord Jesus Christ our Saviour." Our Saviour is God. In 2:13 there is one of the most striking of all the Bible's testimonies to the deity of the Lord Jesus Christ: "Looking for that blessed hope, and the glorious appearing of the great God and our Saviour Jesus Christ." The demands of Greek grammar limit us to one understanding of this verse. No other is possible: we are waiting for the blessed hope, namely, the glorious appearing of Him who is the great God our Saviour, Jesus Christ. The great God is our Saviour Jesus Christ, and Jesus Christ our Saviour is the great God. That is the clear teaching of the inspired apostle in this epistle. Any gospel that is not based on the absolute divinity of Jesus Christ is not even faintly related to the gospel of the Word of God.

This epistle has other striking statements. G. Campbell Morgan called attention to what he termed the two epiphanies, or the two appearings. The first is *the epiphany of grace:* "For the grace of God that bringeth salvation hath appeared to all men" (2:11). "After that the kindness and love of God our Saviour toward man appeared" (3:4). When did this epiphany of grace begin? Luke 1:78–79 supplies the answer: "The dayspring from on high hath visited us, to give light to them that sit in darkness and in the shadow of death, to guide our feet into the way of peace." The epiphany of grace came with the epiphany or the appearing of the Lord Jesus Christ. The appearing of grace was the appearing of Christ, who is grace incarnate. Paul writes to Titus about a second epiphany, *the epiphany of glory.* Think again of Tit. 2:13: "Looking for that blessed hope, and [or, even] the glorious appearing of the great God and our Saviour Jesus Christ." There is an epiphany of grace at the first coming of Christ; there is an epiphany of glory at the second coming of Christ.

Between them, 2:14 makes clear, there is the doctrine of the atonement. "[Our Saviour Jesus Christ] gave himself for us, that he might redeem us from all iniquity, and purify unto himself a peculiar people, zealous of good works." Here is the framework of the gospel: Jesus Christ, the Son of God, came into the world to be our Saviour. That was His appearing in grace. Then He went to the cross to die as our atoning sacrifice. Finally, since He is risen from the dead and ascended back into heaven, He is coming again in glory. These are great fundamental truths of the faith.

The question is, how does this theology lead us to the experience of salvation? Paul answers by showing that the way of salvation is by grace through faith. Faith presupposes a body of truth to be accepted. In other words, by the grace of God we lay hold of Christ as He is set forth in the gospel. Through faith we are justified and assured of eternal glory. Paul combines all these elements in his statement in 3:4–8: "After that the kindness and love of God our Saviour toward man appeared, not by works of righteousness which we have done, but according to his mercy he saved us, by the washing of regeneration, and renewing of the Holy Ghost; which he shed on us abundantly through Jesus Christ our Saviour; that being justified by his grace, we should be made heirs according to the hope of eternal life. This is a faithful saying, and these things I will that thou affirm constantly, that they which have believed in God might be careful to maintain good works." Here are all the elements of the way of salvation—*God* saves, the *Holy Spirit* regenerates, so that we are justified and made heirs of God, all on the merits of *Jesus Christ* our Saviour, whom we receive by faith, not works. This is what Paul calls "sound doctrine," or, to use the words of the very first verse of the epistle, "the truth which is after [or, according to] godliness." This is what the epistle is all about. Having established the fundamentals of the faith, Paul proceeds to expound his central theme, which is **living according to the truth which is according to godliness.** He calls us to do three things about the truth which is according to godliness. First, we should *acknowledge* it (1:1). Second, we should *adorn* it (2:10). Finally, we should *advance* it (1:9f; 3:10). These are the only reasons Christians and churches have to live.

ACKNOWLEDGE THE TRUTH

First, then, we are to acknowledge the truth which is according to godliness: "Paul, a servant of God, and an apostle of Jesus Christ, according to the faith of God's elect, and the acknowledging of the truth which is after godliness" (1:1). Christianity—including our personal salvation—commences with an honest reception of the factual and theological statements of the gospel. We have mentioned the fundamental doctrines of the faith. No one can be a Christian without an honest belief in those truths. It is often said that saving faith is more than mere intellectual assent to the truth of the gospel; it is a personal trust in the One who is the truth. True, but there can be no personal trust in Christ without an intellectual assent to the doctrinal propositions of the gospel. The Neo-Orthodox fancy that we may having a saving encounter with Christ apart from any doctrinal or dogmatic statement of belief is utter folly. Christ is revealed in the gospel of truth. We must acknowledge that truth if we are to be saved. Nothing can take the place of this acknowledgment, for without it there is no faith, and where there is no faith there is no salvation (Mark 16:16). Good works cannot replace acknowledgment of the truth of the gospel. Such works are not good, for godliness and truth cannot be separated.

That truth must be *acknowledged,* honestly received for the truth it is, not merely professed in a thoughtless or meaningless way. Where it is acknowledged it will produce godliness. Paul's words in Tit. 1:1 make it very clear that truth produces godliness in those who receive it. What is godliness? Godliness is living according to the truth of the gospel. Anything less is sinful licence. Anything more is a legalistic curtailment of liberty. Empty professors are content with their profession, even though behind the façade they have a heart of corruption and a life of wickedness, without any real interest in the glorious holiness of Jesus Christ. Such people are yet in their sins. Yet they find their way into Christian churches. There were people like this in the church in Crete, and Paul showed Titus how to identify them: "They profess that they know God; but in works they deny him, being abominable, and disobedient, and unto every good work reprobate" (1:16). Empty professors show their hypocrisy by their ungodliness, but believers are different. They cannot be like that. As acknowledgers of the truth that is according to godliness, they have certain marks about them. Their behaviour befits sound doctrine (2:1). It reflects what they believe. Their behaviour befits holiness (2:3), or, to give the words their literal significance, their behaviour befits "sacred ones," meaning either sacred things or sacred persons. Christians' behaviour reflects what they are in Christ. They are saints. It is also in harmony with the holy things they deal with, for example, the Word of God, the testimony of Christ, the place of prayer, and the Lord's Table.

This is how to acknowledge the truth which is according to godliness.

ADORN THE TRUTH

The second thing we are to do is to adorn this truth. "Adorn the doctrine of God our Saviour in all things" (2:10). How may we adorn the truth? Surely, the way in which we adorn the truth of the gospel is by living our lives in accordance with it. We adorn the gospel when it governs the way we live. It is the will of God for His people to live such lives. Christ died to produce this result: "Who gave himself for us, that he might redeem us from all iniquity, and purify unto himself a peculiar people, zealous of good works" (2:14). The entire gospel of grace teaches us "that, denying ungodliness and worldly lusts, we should live soberly, righteously, and godly, in this present world" (2:11, 12).

Many years ago a preacher gave this illustration of what it means to adorn the doctrine of God our Saviour. Imagine a musician with a sheet of music from a great composer. To most people it is merely a collection of symbols that convey little or nothing. If the musician simply shows the sheet music to his audience he is not really doing very much to set the message of the composer before the people. To do that he must practise with great dedication. He must seek to understand and reproduce the composer's message with sounds that move our souls. Then, said the old preacher, he is adorning the message the composer placed on the page. Though the analogy is far from complete, we may learn from the illustration. It is not enough for us simply to set the page of Scripture's message before men. Do not misunderstand. The Bible is the living Word of God, and it is a good thing to distribute it to men. The point is, however, that Christians should not only show men the page of truth. They should show them the power of truth. They should adorn the truth they profess. How may we do that? The answer is, we adorn it with godly living. There is an old saying, "I would rather see a sermon than hear one any day." Let us certainly sound out the Word with our lips, but let us sound it just as loudly with our lives. Paul makes this point very forcibly by his repeated reference to "good works" (1:16; 2:7; 3:1, 8, 14).

Good works are *the qualification for the eldership of the church.* "A bishop must be blameless, as the steward of God; not selfwilled, not soon angry, not given to wine, no striker, not given to filthy lucre; but a lover of hospitality, a lover of good men, sober, just, holy, temperate; holding fast the faithful word as he hath been taught, that he may be able by sound doctrine both to exhort and to convince the gainsayers" (1:7–9).

Good works are *the mark of the membership of the church.* "This is a faithful saying, and these things I will that thou affirm constantly, that they which have believed in God might be careful to maintain good works" (3:8).

Good works are *the rule for the fellowship of the church.* "A man that is an heretick after the first and second admonition reject; knowing that he that is such is subverted, and sinneth, being condemned of himself. . . . And let ours also learn to maintain good works for necessary uses, that they be not unfruitful" (3:10–11, 14).

Thus, godliness is expected of all classes of Christians. Chapter 2:1–10 speaks of the old men and women, of the young men and women, of the wives, of the pastors, of the elders, and of the slaves, who together comprised the church in Crete. Every class of Christians should be godly. They should be holy in every circumstance and situation—in the church, in the home, in the place of employment, and in public life. This all-encompassing godliness is the biblical mark of true Christians enjoying the fellowship of a true New Testament church.

It is also to be the standard for the government of the church. Elders are to be holy men, and as holy men they are to uphold holy standards of belief and behaviour for the whole church. But "there are many unruly and vain talkers . . . whose mouths must be stopped" (1:10, 11). That is as true today as it was in apostolic times. Such people threaten the peace and the usefulness of the church. To deal with them, Paul advises, "Ordain elders" (1:5), holy men who will govern the church according to the holy Word of God. The elements in good church government, therefore, are sound doctrine, sound discipleship, and sound discipline, according to the Word of God and administered by men who themselves personally exemplify all three. It is only then that a church and its members adorn the doctrine which is according to godliness.

ADVANCE THE TRUTH

Finally, we are called to advance this truth which is according to godliness. This is our ever-present concern. Every believer must have this concern. The gospel faces many "gainsayers," or contradictors (1:9). It is attacked by the peddlers of works-righteousness, vain talkers who labour to destroy the doctrine of free grace and reinstate a doctrine of works (1:10). It is also sullied by hypocrites: "There are many unruly" (1:10). The truth according to godliness is also assailed by heretics (3:10).

In many churches nowadays such people have freedom to pursue their sin, without discipline. Churches are too "loving" to act scripturally against them. But love at the expense of truth is not love. God's truth and our testimony to it before the world are precious things. The advancement of truth must be our great concern. That is why Paul says gainsayers must be convicted, hypocrites must be silenced, and heretics must be rejected. We must maintain the truth and testimony of the gospel in all their pristine purity. We are called to do battle against the enemies of the gospel. How can we do battle? By sound doctrine and by holy living. Both belief and behaviour are vitally important to the Christian church in its work of advancing Christ's truth. Someone has said, "Christianity cannot fly on one wing." Belief without behaviour is like an aeroplane trying to fly with one wing. Behaviour without belief is like an aeroplane trying to fly with the other wing. It cannot be done. We must have the two wings. Let us mount up upon them.

Like the church in Crete, we are called to stand for God in a very difficult time, in the midst of great wickedness. The surroundings grieve us, but they are no excuse for our powerlessness or our carelessness. We can and should advance the truth of the gospel where God has placed us.

Three statements will summarize all we have covered in this study:

The power of the church depends on God's revealed truth.

Revealed truth produces vital godliness.

Vital godliness, therefore, is the greatest evidence of the operation of revealed truth in the church.

Acknowledge the truth according to godliness. *Adorn* the truth according to godliness. *Advance* the truth according to godliness by our words and by our works. Can we be content to do anything less with "the doctrine of God our Saviour"?

18

Philemon
Grace Triumphant

Philemon is the story of the restoration of Onesimus,

◆

runaway slave, to his master after Paul had pointed him

◆

to Christ. It tells how Paul desired Philemon to treat his

◆

restored slave and shows how the gospel undermined the

◆

evil of slavery. It also shows how grace triumphs in the

◆

lives of believers to enable them to conform their lives to

◆

the gospel of Christ, and ultimately to transform the

◆

society in which they live.

*T*he appeal of Paul's letter to Philemon is in the pictures that it conjures rather than in the precise definitions of the faith in which the apostle usually traded. Philemon was a man of considerable social stature, a prominent member of the church in the city of Colosse, and he had a slave by the name of Onesimus. *Onesimus*—and this is vital to an understanding of the epistle, which is largely a play upon the word—means profitable, though clearly this particular slave had not lived up to his name. It would appear that he had defrauded his master and had then run off, ending up in the throngs of the city of Rome, where Paul was a prisoner. In some way, possibly because conviction of his sin had set in, possibly through fear of being found out, or, as some commentators think, possibly through meeting Epaphras, then on a visit to Rome from Colosse to see Paul, Onesimus came under the ministry of the imprisoned apostle. That ministry bore great results. The Lord laid hold of the heart of the runaway slave and made him a new creature in the Lord Jesus Christ.

Immediately Onesimus began to live up to his name. He became very profitable to Paul in the bonds and fellowship of the gospel—so much so, indeed, that the apostle would have loved to keep him with him in Rome. We learn from verses 23 and 24 that Paul had a company of prominent men with him. It says a great deal for Onesimus's usefulness to Paul that despite the fact that he had Epaphras, Marcus, Aristarchus, Demas, and Luke with him, the apostle would have dearly loved to keep this new Christian, this runaway slave. However, he decided to send him back to his legal master. Roman law was extremely severe on runaway slaves, even to the point of putting them to torture and death. And it was illegal to harbour a runaway slave. I think that though Paul does not specifically mention those things in his letter to Philemon, they must have been in his mind. The safety of Onesimus must have weighed heavily with him. There was an even greater reason for sending Onesimus back—his desire to induce Philemon to free this slave. That above all things led Paul to send him back to Colosse.

With him he sent Tychicus (Col. 4:7), and together Tychicus and Onesimus carried the Colossian epistle to the church. Onesimus also carried this personal letter from the apostle Paul addressed chiefly to Philemon, but also meant for the eyes of his family and of the church which met in his house. If you read it with any understanding, you will see that it is, in the nicest sense of the word, a begging letter. The apostle was not a proud man and was very happy to take his place humbly before Philemon, pleading. As an apostle he could have commanded Philemon to do what he desired in this matter. However, as "Paul the aged," now the prisoner of the Lord Jesus Christ, he pleaded the cause of

Onesimus, whom, said he, "I have begotten in my bonds." Paul requested Philemon to do three things. First of all, he requested him to receive Onesimus as he would receive Paul himself. Second, he requested him to place any debt against the name of Onesimus to Paul's personal account. He said, "I will repay it," but added, in effect, "However, do not forget, you owe me a lot, even your own soul." In other words he was saying, "Brother, cancel the debt." The third thing he requested of Philemon was to treat Onesimus no longer as a slave, but as a brother beloved.

In Col. 4:1, in the general epistle to the church, Paul wrote to all slave-holding masters and gave them a general order. He commanded that all masters should supply what was just and equitable to all their slaves. That was the general order from the apostle. At the very least, no matter what Roman law permitted by way of punishment, Philemon had to do that to Onesimus. That was his Christian duty. But Paul wanted more than mere duty from Philemon. He wanted more than basic justice from him. He wanted grace, and that is why he said, "I am sending this slave back to you in order that you may receive him, not as a slave any longer, but as a brother." Even that was not enough. In verse 21 Paul expressed his confidence in Philemon's obedience that he would do even more. That can mean only one thing, and it certainly would have meant only one thing to Philemon—Paul expected him to give Onesimus his legal freedom.

That must have sounded a very extreme request to the people of those days, but Paul was using this God-given opportunity to begin to educate them and the entire church of Jesus Christ as to how the gospel was going to attack the evil of slavery and the hellish trade in the souls of men. Greek and Roman society ran on slave labour. In fact, the number of slaves in most cities outnumbered the number of free citizens anything from 4 to 10 to as many as 20 to 1. Masters had absolute rights over their slaves, who, according to Roman law, had no rights whatsoever. They were the mere chattels of their owners, and those owners had no responsibility to them. They acted according to what they perceived would make the slaves most useful or profitable to them. However, no matter what Roman law permitted, the question was, how could a Christian possess a Christian brother as he would possess a lump of stone or an animal on the hoof? How could a Christian make one who is Christ's free man his slave? Roman law saw no difficulty in those things, just as the laws of many other nations throughout history have seen no difficulty. However, Paul expected Philemon to live not by Roman law, but by the principles of the gospel of Jesus Christ.

In doing this, Paul recognized that Philemon would undoubtedly make a loss in a worldly sense. He would lose property. He would lose free labour. He would lose money, even the money that Onesimus had stolen from him. Paul addresses that in verse 20. He says, "Yea, brother, let me have joy of thee in the Lord." These words literally mean, "Brother, I wish to make a profit of you." In other words, "I acknowledge you are going to lose out in this, but there are some things that are more valuable than money, and the bodies and souls of men are among them." Actually, Paul's choice of words in verse 20 is a lovely touch. The Greek verb in the first line of this verse, "Let me have joy of thee," is just another form of the word *Onesimos*. We may paraphrase Paul's appeal as follows: "Brother, be an Onesimus unto me. Do not think in terms of worldly profit, but think in terms of spiritual and eternal profit. Treat this runaway slave as you would treat me if I were to come today. Treat him no longer as a slave, but as a brother. Forgive all his debt, and if you want your money back, I will pay it. Give this man his freedom." I do not for one moment think that Paul was disappointed in Philemon's response. When Paul finally revisited Colosse, as I am sure he did—verse 22 certainly shows that he expected to—I have no doubt that he found the former master and the former slave equally profitable to Christ and His church in the bonds of the gospel's love and service.

Now, as we have already noted, this is a book, not of great theological definitions, but of beautiful pictures. As you read it now with the background story in mind, you will be able to see some of those pictures and perhaps be able to imagine some that are not actually delineated for us. There is the picture of a thieving runaway slave, skulking through the streets of the city of Rome where thousands of other slaves were doing the same thing, hoping and trusting that he would avoid detection. There is the constant gnawing of fear: Will somebody see me? Will somebody turn me in? Onesimus was a criminal on the run, and the gallows loomed large at the end of the run. Then there is Paul, a prisoner, labouring not initially to restore Onesimus to Philemon, but to bring him to Christ. Then what a picture! Can you see Paul the great apostle—the greatest scholar, the greatest theologian, the greatest preacher in the world—humbly bowing beside this runaway slave to lead him to the Lord Jesus Christ? And what a picture of transformation when the slave becomes the servant of Christ and immediately is profitable in the gospel. Then there is the picture of his return. Onesimus returned to Colosse with all the uncertainty that entailed. You can picture Philemon's amazement as Onesimus comes back with Tychicus, not in bonds, but absolutely freely, not now as an enemy, but as a brother in Christ. And perhaps the most powerful of all the pictures here, and one of the most powerful pictures in all the New Testament, is of Philemon and Onesimus worshipping and working, not as master and slave, but as equals and as brothers in Jesus Christ. Philemon, then, is a book with lovely pictures. So I want us to think of the message of this book as simply **Pictures of Triumphant Grace.** In four places in Philemon we trace these pictures.

GRACE IN THE LIFE OF ONESIMUS

As I have indicated, Onesimus was a slave. He was not only a slave, he was a thief, and he was a runaway, condemned by the law to torture and death if his master so decided. Then this slave suddenly was transformed by the renewing, saving grace of God. There was a point in his life when the runaway thief and slave bowed the knee to Jesus Christ and was absolutely, instantaneously, and irrevocably transformed. He became a new creature in Christ. We see this new creature growing in grace and in the knowledge of the Lord Jesus Christ, so that he can stand amongst great men of God. His name can be placed alongside some of the leading servants of Christ in the New Testament. He is making giant steps in the faith, so that Paul, the greatest of all Christ's servants, longs to have him by his side. Paul is at home in his company. Paul can talk with him; he can work with him; he can pray with him; he can fellowship with him. What a transformation! What a triumph of the grace of God!

That triumph is nowhere more clearly seen than in Onesimus's willingness to return to Colosse to face his past, to make restitution if his master so decided, even with his very life. He had no guarantees; he had a letter from Paul, but no guarantees. Yet for the sake of Jesus Christ, for the testimony of Christ—even though both he and Paul could and would argue that the whole institution of slavery was a wicked invention—he would go back, possibly at the cost of his life. That was the power of grace in the life of Onesimus. The runaway slave had become a devoted servant of Jesus Christ.

In a sense, the testimony of Onesimus is the testimony of every Christian. We were all slaves, slaves of sin, thieves who had taken every gift of God and had turned it to the service of the devil, runaways from divine justice, under condemnation of eternal death. Yet one day the grace of God caught up with us; brought us to our knees and to the place of repentance; washed us in the precious blood of the Lamb; put away our guilt, our sin, and our shame; brought us from darkness to light, from death to life, from damnation to justification; reconciled us to God; and made us profitable in the service of Christ. The God who could call the angels to His service and send them on His commissions took guilty, hell-deserving, wretched sinners such as you and I and has made us profitable in the service of Jesus Christ. That is triumphant grace, just as in the life of Onesimus.

If your life is out of control, as this man's was, and your heart is alienated from God, then I tell you that there is mighty, soul-saving, life-transforming power in the gospel of Jesus Christ. You do not need anything but grace to save a soul. You do not need any other power but the power of the love and the mercy of God in Jesus Christ to transform a sinner into a saint. It does not take a year, it does not take a month, it does not take a week—it takes but an instant of time for God's grace to bring a sinner into eternal salvation. Oh, if you are not saved, take your place at the feet of Jesus, where Onesimus the runaway slave took his place, and calling on the name of the Saviour, you too will pass from death unto life. So the first picture of triumphant grace is in the life of Onesimus.

GRACE IN THE LIFE OF PAUL

The second is in the life of Paul as he appears in this epistle, and that may be seen in three ways.

The first thing that shows me the power of grace in Paul's life is that *he saw the value of a soul,* even the soul of a runaway slave. Paul was a man of his own time. The marvel of inspiration is that though it was written at a particular point in history, the New Testament transcends history. It is not a prisoner of its historical and cultural environment. But Paul was. Paul was a child of his age. Left to himself, he would not have transcended the norms of his age. It was grace that made him transcend those norms. Paul looked at Onesimus, and he did not see a slave on the run. He saw a soul on its way to hell, and he longed to see that soul saved. It is very easy for us to say that, but it was contrary to all the thinking of his age. Even the greatest philosophers in ancient times had no concept of the human dignity of a slave or of the value of his soul. The two greatest of the Greek philosophers were, I suppose, Aristotle and Plato. Aristotle used all the power of his mighty intellect to define the institution of slavery and to spell out the intrinsic worthlessness of slaves. And even Plato's *Republic* wrought the institution of slavery right into the fabric of what he thought was the ideal society. They could see no value in a slave. A slave was a nobody, a nothing. Now Paul lived in times when the philosophy of such men informed the whole moral climate. But Paul did not accept the nonsense the philosophers taught. When Onesimus stood before him, he did not look upon him as a slave, but as a soul. Unlike Aristotle and Plato, Paul knew the plague of his own heart. He also knew that the grace and power of God that had saved him could save anybody. He himself was a recipient of grace. Paul had no illusions about himself. When he looked at Onesimus he saw a man who was not one whit more worthy of hell than he was. When he looked inside himself, he saw the power of grace. He saw what the transforming gospel of

Christ could do, and so, as he felt the grace of God, he had a great love for souls as souls. He did not care who they were, what their station was, what their background was, what their nation was, what their race was, or what their religion was. He had a great love for souls as souls. He was not particularly worried about their legal position or about their standing in society. He was not even particularly worried about the strictures of the law against him for harbouring this slave during the time he was seeking to win him for Christ. Paul had grace in his heart.

The man who feels the miracle of saving grace in his own soul is one who will always have a love for the souls of others. People who can give up sinners and let them perish without a thought or a care have little or no experience of the power of triumphant grace in their own lives. When you have felt the grace of God, you will have a love for souls. Some people think that a passion for souls comes through lurid descriptions of the debased condition of the ungodly. That may stir us for a little time, but no more. Others think that a passion for souls comes from a vision of hell. That certainly is better. An ever-present conviction of the terrors of a lost eternity should provide a strong impetus to every Christian's desire to reach the lost. However, even that will not last. There is one thing will give us a love for souls, and that is a knowledge of the love of Christ for us. When we feel how deep in sin we were without Christ, and when we grasp the truth that our only worth is bestowed by the gracious hand of God in sending Christ to save us, then His love will kindle a love for souls within our heart. Many old-time preachers used to pray that the Lord would live His life through them, love the souls of men through them. In other words, they were saying, "Lord, so possess my mind that I will think of people as Christ thinks of them, that I will look on sinners as Christ looks on them, that I will look on the great cities of this world as Christ looked on the cities of His day, that I will weep over the erring one with the tears of Christ, and that I will have the burden for perishing sinners that broke the heart of the Saviour." Paul had a love for souls, even the most debased and the most despised.

We see the grace of God in Paul in a second way: *he treated others as the Lord had treated him.* Verses 17 to 19 form one of the loveliest passages in all the New Testament. "If thou count me therefore a partner, receive him as myself. If he hath wronged thee, or oweth thee ought, put that on mine account; I Paul have written it with mine own hand, I will repay it." The verb in verse 18, "put that on mine account," appears in only one other place in the New Testament, and that is Rom. 5:13. There it is rightly translated "impute." That is one of the key verses, one of the key words, in Paul's whole description and discussion of the doctrine of justification. *Impute.* Now keep that in mind as you read verses

17 and 18 again. Dr. Scofield has a beautiful note in the Scofield Bible at this particular point. This is what he says: "Verses 17, 18 perfectly illustrate imputation: 'Receive him as myself'—reckon to him my merit; 'If he hath wronged thee or oweth thee ought, put that on mine account'—reckon to me his demerit." There is, in summary form, the whole doctrine of justification. Paul had experienced this. Indeed, this was the heart of his whole ministry. In his letters he constantly preaches justification, emphasizing the two great points he makes in verses 17 and 18. What are they? They are that our Lord Jesus Christ says, "Father, reckon the demerit of the sinner to Me, and reckon My merit to Him. Make Me sin for him, and make him righteousness in Me. Let Me bear the shame, the agony, the suffering, and the punishment, and let him, the poor sinner who believes in Me, enter into all that I purchased by My righteousness." This truth of the imputation of our sin to Christ and of His righteousness to us is the glory of the gospel. Paul loved this theme. He preached it constantly. Some of the greatest texts in the New Testament are his expositions of it (see, for example, Rom. 3:23–26; 5:17–19; 2 Cor. 5:21). He felt the power of this gospel in a very personal way.

That being so, how could he treat other people by a different standard? Paul treated Onesimus as Christ had treated him. I would say that is one of the greatest triumphs of grace in any man's life. Men frequently call Christ's command in Matt. 7:12 "the golden rule": "Whatsoever ye would that men should do to you, do ye even so to them." That is a wonderful rule of life. We ought never to forget it. Treat other people as you would have them treat you. That is a high and noble standard, but here Paul goes even further and says, "I will treat other people as God in Christ has treated me."

What a difference it would make in every area of life if we would only live by that standard! If husbands and wives would live by it, they would transform their homes. The church and society generally would feel the impact. When we live our lives in the home in the constant realization of what Christ has done for us, when we look at our partners in life as being in Christ and see the glorious grace Christ has bestowed upon them, we will treat them as those who are in Christ. We will treat them as Christ has treated us. Nothing will deal with the problems that mar marital relations as quickly and comprehensively as this.

The same holds true in the church. If we would only treat one another as we are conscious of how Christ has treated us, what a difference it would make! In public life also, especially in the work place, we should treat others as Christ has treated us. That is grace.

There is a third way in which grace is pictured in Paul's life, and that is that *he saw every circumstance as an opportunity for service.* Paul by this time was an old man. He refers to himself as "Paul the aged, and now also a prisoner of Jesus Christ," or *for* Jesus Christ. His great labours for the gospel had been cut short. Indeed, for some years now he had lain a prisoner, first in Judaea and now, after an arduous journey, in Rome. To the human gaze it was all a great defeat. We might well have expected to find Paul in Rome a frustrated and angry man, chafing at his inactivity. In fact, we would have found a contented man bearing a vibrant testimony for his Lord. You see, Paul looked at things through the filter of grace. His attitude was, "I am a prisoner, yes, but I am not a prisoner of Nero. I am a prisoner of Jesus Christ. It is Christ who sent me to Rome. The Lord Jesus stood by me and said, 'As thou hast testified of me in Jerusalem, so must thou bear witness also at Rome' (Acts 23:11). So the Lord sent me here." During his second imprisonment he wrote something which no doubt he felt in his first imprisonment: "I suffer . . . even unto bonds; but the word of God is not bound" (2 Tim. 2:9). So there was Paul, in jail, a prisoner. The man who had been accustomed to constant activity, seeing churches built, souls saved, and who had seemed to enjoy perpetual revival, was now shut up in a very restricted sphere of service. His testimony, however, was as strong as ever: he was in prison because the sovereign Christ sent him there to be a witness for Him. His Word was not bound, so Paul would keep working for Him whatever the circumstances. Whether he won a hundred souls for Christ, or only one, he was happy to serve the Lord wherever He put him. That was Paul's attitude. The result? One day a runaway slave came into his presence, and Paul pointed him to Christ. As he says, he begot him in his bonds. That indeed was grace. He accepted the circumstances of life as the provision of the all-wise providence of the Lord and sought to use them to serve Him.

We are all creatures of reaction. We react to circumstances so much that the slightest change in them leads to a great change in our mood. A great change in our mood leads to a great change in our ability to pray, to study, to witness, or to stand. We are rejoicing in the Lord, but then we suffer a financial loss, or a family problem, or a physical affliction, and suddenly our joy all but disappears. We feel as if God has forsaken us. Why did God allow that to happen? We become so discouraged that we almost quit praying except to lament our circumstances. In all such situations there are questions we should ask ourselves: Is the grace of God any less than before? Is the merit of the blood of Christ any less than before? Are the love, mercy, and kindness of the Saviour any less? Is the assurance of heaven any less? The grace to accept our circumstances as dispensed by the hand of a sovereign Lord in order that we may use them for the glory and honour of the Lord Jesus Christ is triumphant grace indeed.

GRACE IN THE LIFE OF PHILEMON

Not only do we see the triumph of grace in Onesimus and in Paul, but we see it in the life of Philemon. When Paul wrote to Philemon, he was already a saved man (vv. 5–7). Grace had made him a man of God. Those verses paint for us the picture of what a man of God ought to be. He is a man of love. He is a man marked by love and faith toward Christ and toward the saints. We cannot have love for Christ if we do not have love for the saints. We are not living by faith in Christ if our faith is not affecting the lives of the saints. There is no such thing as our living in fellowship with God if we are living out of fellowship with God's people. Paul recognized Philemon as such a man of God. He rejoiced at all the good things in him that brought such consolation to the saints. Grace had made Philemon a truly great man of God.

Grace had given him a godly home (vv. 1–2). Apphia was a godly wife for this beloved and busy servant of Christ, and Archippus, most commentators believe, was his son and probably the pastor of the church in Colosse (4:17). So grace had given Philemon salvation. Grace had given him a godly home with a good wife and a son in the service of Christ. Now Paul was saying, "The grace that has begun a good work in you is going to triumph in a greater way than ever." I believe it did.

Grace enabled Philemon to live above the demands of the flesh. He was only human, and when he saw Onesimus coming, no doubt his flesh thought of vengeance or punishment. That happens to all of us. It happens in our homes. The old man insists on his "pound of flesh." That is always a cause of much sorrow. When Christian homes get into trouble it is not because there is a lack of power in the gospel. It is because men and women who name the name of Jesus Christ are living by the flesh and not by the faith. It is the same in a church. When a Bible-believing church divides itself, it is because Christians are living by the flesh and not by the faith. Paul was asking Philemon—and I believe he obeyed with joy—to live above the flesh.

Then he asked him to do something that was perhaps even more difficult. He asked him to live above the demands of his "rights." Philemon could have turned to the page of Roman law which said Onesimus had no right to freedom. In fact, if Philemon spared his life, Onesimus should have been grateful to him for the rest of his days. Philemon could very easily have said, "There is the law. That is my civil right." In effect Paul says, "Forget about your civil rights and start living by faith." One of the most difficult things for people to do is to get beyond what carnal men have defined as their rights. Someone has observed that there is so much emphasis nowadays on rights that nobody seems to be at all interested in duty. There are certain rights, clearly defined in the Word of God, that are worth standing for. However, when we simply stand up for "our rights" out of regard for personal gain and greed, no matter what the cost, or the hurt, to others, we effectively deny the gospel.

We should also note that Paul asked Philemon to live above the opinions of men. There were other slave owners in his church fellowship and all around him in society. To adopt Paul's plan for Onesimus would leave Philemon open to all sorts of suspicion from those slave owners. However, Paul was asking him to live solely for the glory of the Lord, free from the tyranny of what men think or say. That is no small freedom. Only a clear view of our Saviour can allow us to live in it. We need to have such a clear sight of His face that we will never again fear the face of man.

Philemon knew the triumph of grace because he lived above the flesh, above the demands of his rights, and above the opinions of men. Thus he glorified God. This is the heart of this epistle, and of all true Christianity. Such godliness was incomprehensible to the world in Philemon's day. It still is incomprehensible to the world in our day. The mark of a man who is in fellowship with the Lord is that he will walk as Philemon walked. That is the triumph of grace in a Christian.

GRACE IN THE LIFE OF THE CHURCH

Finally, we must move from the lives of the individuals, Onesimus, Paul, and Philemon, to see the triumph of grace in the life of the church. The church met in Philemon's house. Archippus probably was Philemon's son and the pastor of the church. Philemon was a leading member. There were other slave-holding masters in the church (Col. 4:1), and there were slaves in its membership (3:22). That is a very significant fact. The church received slaves into full membership. That was one place, no matter what society dictated, where there were no second-class citizens, or no citizens and noncitizens. They worshipped together as equals before God. That was already happening in the church in Colosse. They saw their fellowship as being in Christ, not as something fragmented by the divisions of contemporary society.

Much of the trouble in churches comes from what people bring from outside to the inside. They transplant the mindset of the world into the church. All too often they bring the pressures, the mores, and the desires of the world into the church. They allow the divisions of society to break up what should be the united fellowship of the church of Christ. Let us put ourselves in the Colossian church. There is a free man and beside him there is a slave. They are worshipping as equals, as brothers in Christ. According to Roman law there is a huge disparity between them. By law the slave is nothing, is worth nothing, and has nothing. He is no more worthwhile than a flea or a dog. Yet citizens and slaves sit together. They drink the same cup of communion. They celebrate the same glorious love and grace of God in Jesus Christ. That is one of the most powerful pictures in the whole New Testament.

That new Christian view of society changed the world. The church was under the law, and yet it lived superior to the law. The result of that was that the grace of God in the lives of Christians like those in Colosse ultimately affected the law and changed it for the better. The early church did not make it its concern to address the social evils of the day. Christians staged no protests. They wrote no letters to their senators. They did not make changing the society by political means their aim. If they had done that, the church would immediately have become a mere political and social pressure group, and it would have been dispensed with as such. Rather, the early Christians had confidence in the power of the gospel to transform lives in such numbers as to change the entire fabric of society. When you are seeing three thousand people saved one day, and five thousand people saved another day—when you can go into a town and in one day see enough people saved to start a thriving church, so that from being a very small group of people you are spreading at a tremendous rate across the world—you will have confidence in the power of your gospel. The early church had such confidence. It was not misplaced. Christian preachers changed the world. Through their ministry the whole system of slavery ultimately fell to the ground.

I trust we will grasp that lesson. There are things we can do that early Christians could not, because we have a different legal and constitutional framework in which to work. If you can write a politician and put enough pressure on him that he will do right because he is afraid of losing your vote, then write and pressure him. However, let us never forget that the church's power to transform society depends directly on its experience of the grace of God in each of its members. If we do not have enough grace to transform our lives, our homes, and our church meetings, how can we pretend that we have the power needed to change the world? The power to change society depends on the power of grace experienced to change ourselves. This is the lesson the church in Philemon's house learned. That they learned it so well was the real triumph of grace in them. Wonderful indeed is the grace of Jesus. It is triumphant grace to save sinners, to set the servants of God on fire for God whatever their circumstances, and to give the church the power to be God's salt in society to change what otherwise must remain beyond remedy.

Hebrews
The Better Way

Hebrews addresses the difficult subject of the

◆

transition from Judaism to Christianity. The gospel is

◆

the completion and fulfilment of the Old Testament

◆

revelation. It therefore replaces the Old Testament

◆

types and shadows with God's full and final word to

◆

men in His Son, Jesus Christ.

A mong the many features that make Hebrews an outstandingly important book, one is preeminent.[†] Many have noted the superior Greek style and the passionate theological argument of this carefully and beautifully crafted treatise. But of far more significance is the book's greatest characteristic: Hebrews is the only book in the New Testament that formally and fully addresses the difficult transition from Judaism to Christianity that perplexed so many Jewish believers. Thousands of Jews had confessed the Lord Jesus Christ as Saviour. However, the Jewish temple was still standing; its worship and sacrifices continued as before. That raised a great question: what is the precise relationship of Christ and His gospel to the temple and its worship? The answer to that question was not widely understood. When it was grasped it was vehemently opposed by Jews zealous for the law.

It appears that the first man to face the question in a profound way was Stephen. That was the main reason he was murdered. Stephen in many ways was a Paul before his time. He was the first Christian leader to start spelling out the true relationship of the Old Testament temple and its worship with the New Testament gospel of the Lord Jesus Christ. After Stephen's death the Holy Spirit used Paul to develop what Stephen had begun to teach. Not surprisingly, the Jews, including many Christian Jews, looked on Paul with the same suspicion they had harboured against Stephen. They misrepresented and persecuted him, and the chief reason was that it was he who spelled out theologically the precise relationship between the temple and the gospel. In doing so, the apostle made it clear that there were contentious issues that were of little immediate consequence. In those areas he was content to allow Jewish converts to have their conscience. He preached tolerance in things that are not of the essence of the gospel. However, when it came to the great fundamental doctrines of the gospel, Paul was adamant that both Jewish and Gentile believers had to grasp the truth that Christianity was not merely a form of Judaism. He made it clear that there was an unbridgeable gulf between the gospel as preached by the apostles of Christ and what the Jewish leaders presented as the message of God. The Jews, misunderstanding the law, preached salvation by works. The gospel is the message of free grace through faith in the merits of Jesus

---

[†]The feature that usually receives first consideration is the fact that the writer does not introduce himself by name. This, along with other internal marks of the book, has led to prolonged dispute over the author's identity. The apostle Paul has been generally accepted as the writer, and that is the position assumed in this study. However, it is not essential to our understanding of the central message of the book. For a very brief statement of the authorship dispute, see the additional note at the end of this chapter.

Christ. Just as clearly as Romans, though from a different perspective, Hebrews clears away the heresy of works-righteousness and establishes the all-sufficient merits of Christ. That is what makes it a book of such abiding importance.

Hebrews was written to Jewish believers. It is because they forget this fact that many people have great difficulty in interpreting some passages in the book. Those Jewish believers were under intense pressure from their countrymen to repudiate Christ and to return to the temple and all the ritual of Judaism. Thus in writing to them the apostle Paul opens up the Old Testament in a unique way to show the superiority and the finality of God's saving revelation in Jesus Christ.

When we read this book we should particularly note certain key words and expressions. For example, seventeen times Paul employs the word *heaven(s)*, or *heavenly*, to show that the gospel deals with the spiritual realities typified by the earthly patterns of Old Testament worship. He uses the word *eternal* fifteen times to show the permanence of those realities in contrast with the passing forms of the Old Testament. Fourteen times Paul uses the word *perfect*, and again he is contrasting Christ and His gospel with the imperfect, shadowy forms of the Old Testament. Thirteen times he uses the word *better*. In a way that word supplies the key to understanding the entire book. For example, we have a better persuasion (6:9), a better priesthood (7:7), a better hope (7:19), a better covenant (7:22), better promises (8:6), better sacrifices (9:23), a better reward (10:35), a better country (11:16), and a better resurrection (11:35). Clearly the apostle wants to convey the idea of the superiority and finality of God's saving revelation in Jesus Christ. All these words set the tone for the central message of the book: **the gospel is the completion and the fulfilment of the Old Testament's revelation.**

If we understand that truth, we will grasp both the meaning and the value of the Old Testament and of the New Testament. If we do not, we will understand neither. We must understand that the New Testament does not merely replace the Old. The New Testament is not new in the sense of being unrelated to the Old. It is rather its fulfilment, its completion, and its perfection. In many ways we may look on Heb. 10:9 as the key text to the argument of the entire epistle: "Then said he, Lo, I come to do thy will, O God. He taketh away the first, that he may establish the second." Throughout the epistle there is a taking away of one thing and the development of another thing out of it, and its establishment in the place of the thing removed. This is the peculiar emphasis of Hebrews. God takes away the first, that He may establish the second. The entire Old Testament economy provides the historical background and basis for the New Testament revelation of the gospel. The New Testament economy is the necessary and perfect development of the Old Testament. What is that saying? It is saying simply, the Old has run its course. The Old Testament as Scripture is still the Word of God, but it must be understood in the full light of the New Testament. What does the Old Testament really mean? It means what the New Testament says it means. The function of the Old Testament, therefore, is to set forth by means of type and prophecy, and by way of illustration, the greater glory of the New Testament. Thus the book of Hebrews—and this is one of its major themes—makes it a crime punishable by eternal death to repudiate Christ and return to the sacrifices of the Old Testament. Think of that for a moment. In the Old Testament period, people came under God's wrath by refusing the sacrifices, but now that Christ has come, people will come under God's wrath if they hold on to the Old Testament sacrifices. Why is that? It is because the Old Testament sacrifices were prophetic types, and the Lord Jesus Christ is their perfect fulfilment. When we have sunlight we do not need candlelight. When we have the substance, we do not need mere types. The remaining usefulness of those types is that they help us understand the meaning of the New Testament. Thus for people now to repudiate the gospel and go back to the temple and its sacrifices is a damning step. That is what Hebrews is all about.

In pursuing the truth that the gospel of Jesus Christ entirely fulfils and replaces the Old Testament types and shadows, Paul takes four logical steps in an argument that shows that *Jesus Christ is God's full and final word to men.* These four steps sum up the whole book.

First, the basis of the gospel is the person of the Lord Jesus Christ.

Second, the person of the Lord Jesus Christ establishes the value of His work.

Third, the value of the work of Christ proves Him to be God's final word to men and the sole way of salvation for them.

Fourth, God's final word in Christ can never be repudiated by true believers.

That is the argument of the book of Hebrews.

THE BASIS OF THE GOSPEL IS THE PERSON OF THE LORD JESUS CHRIST

Here we are dealing with the first two chapters. They are thrilling chapters. The opening verses of the book are some of the grandest and most majestic utterances God has ever put in human language. The great truth of chapter 1 deserves such glorious words. That great truth is that the Lord Jesus Christ is God. The Father says to the Son, "Thy throne, O God, is for ever and ever" (v. 8). That is a plain statement. The Father addresses the Son as *God.* He also addresses Him as Lord:

"Thou, Lord, in the beginning hast laid the foundation of the earth; and the heavens are the works of thine hands" (v. 10). What is the grand truth of chapter 1? Jesus Christ is God.

The grand truth of Hebrews chapter 2, however, is that Jesus Christ is man. Verses 5–9 speak of Christ's incarnation, and verses 14–15 expand upon that theme: "Forasmuch then as the children are partakers of flesh and blood, he also himself likewise took part of the same; that through death he might destroy him that had the power of death, that is, the devil; and deliver them who through fear of death were all their lifetime subject to bondage." The great truth of chapter 1 is that Jesus Christ is God. The great truth of chapter 2 is that Jesus Christ is man. By these two statements Paul establishes the truth that the person of the Lord Jesus Christ is the basis of the gospel. We must look at this doctrine in rather more detail.

Jesus Christ is God. "Thy throne, O God, is for ever and ever." Throughout the first chapter Paul presents multiple proofs of this truth. Jesus Christ is the *Son* of God (vv. 2, 8). "All things are made by [or, through] him" (John 1:3). He reflects the glory of His Father: "Who being the brightness of his glory, and the express image of his person" (Heb. 1:3). The idea is of the radiance that bursts out of a brilliant light. The Son is the effulgence of His Father, the outraying, or outshining, of His fulness and glory. He bears the stamp of His Father's nature, for He is "the express image of his person." He upholds all things by the word of His power (v. 3). What a statement that is! Colossians 1 says the entire creation is held together in and by the person of Jesus Christ. The whole universe is in constant motion, from the largest star to the smallest cell, and the motion is controlled so that it fulfils the purpose of God. How is it done? It is held together by the Lord Jesus Christ, who upholds all things by the word of His power. He is the Lord of the angels, and the angels worship Him (vv. 4–6). He is the creator of the starry host. As a man would fold his garment, so in His time the sovereign God, Jesus Christ, will fold up this whole heaven as a vesture. Truly our Saviour is God. That truth lies at the heart of the gospel.

But then, chapter 2, He is man. According to verses 14 and 15, He became a man in order to be able to deliver us from sin. Sin could be dealt with only by a sacrificial death. Death could be defeated only by one dying and rising again, thus bursting the bands of death. God cannot die. In order to make a sacrifice through death to destroy him that had the power of death, the Son of God took into a personal union with Himself a true humanity. As a result, without ceasing to be God, He became a true man. Thus He has two distinct natures in one perfect person forever, without humanizing His deity and without deifying His humanity. Jesus Christ is truly God yet truly man and thus became the Saviour of sinners. He died, He rose from the dead, and now "we see Jesus, who was made a little lower than the angels for the suffering of death, crowned with glory and honour" (v. 9). He is the Captain of our salvation, that is, the *author* of our salvation whose sufferings perfectly fitted Him to lead His people to glory (v. 10). He is also our great High Priest: "Wherefore in all things it behoved him to be made like unto his brethren, that he might be a merciful and faithful high priest in things pertaining to God, to make reconciliation [or rather, *propitiation]* for the sins of the people. For in that he himself hath suffered being tempted, he is able to succour them that are tempted" (vv. 17–18). This is the doctrine of the person of Jesus Christ. This is the basis of the gospel.

THE PERSON OF CHRIST ESTABLISHES THE VALUE OF HIS WORK

Paul was not interested in discussing deep theology as an intellectual game. Having stated the deep and mysterious truth about the complex person of Christ, he immediately comes to the very heart of the gospel. Hebrews is a book—and in the first two chapters Paul sets the tone for the whole book—of outstanding gospel statements made in connection with the doctrine of the person of Christ. "God . . . hath . . . spoken unto us by his Son" (1:1, 2). The Son "by himself purged our sins" (1:3). The price of that purging was His vicarious "suffering of death" (2:9). He is the author of salvation for His people (2:10) and their "merciful and faithful high priest" (2:17).

Having laid this foundation in the opening chapters, in the body of the book the apostle goes on to give a detailed exposition of the work of Christ. The fact that Jesus Christ is God manifested in the flesh clearly establishes the value of what He has done.

He is the great Prophet: God has spoken unto us by His Son (1:1). Men or angels may be God's messengers, but obviously no man or angel can be compared with the Son of God as a vehicle of divine revelation. Thus Paul proceeds to show the superiority of Christ, the Prophet over all other prophetic messengers. He is superior to angels (1:4–14), to Moses (3:3–6), and to Joshua (4:8). Jesus Christ is the great Prophet. That truth lends terrible force to the words of 2:1–3: "Therefore we ought to give the more earnest heed to the things which we have heard, lest at any time we should let them slip. For if the word spoken by angels was steadfast, and every transgression and disobedience received a just recompence of reward; how shall we escape, if we neglect so great salvation; which at the first began to be spoken by the Lord, and was confirmed unto us by them that heard him?" If God fulfilled His word and judged those who rejected the revelation of His grace through angels and men, how much more severely will He judge those who have heard the gospel of the Son of God and have counted His blood as an unclean thing? Jesus Christ is the great Prophet. That is not an empty academic notion, but a truth in the light of which we are all going to live either in heaven or in hell for all eternity. If He is God and man and He has come to speak to us and show us the way of life and bring us into eternal salvation, it behoves us to receive His word.

Christ is also the great Priest, in which capacity Paul contrasts Him with Aaron. He portrays Christ's priesthood as a "better priesthood." The exposition of this truth takes up the heart of the book (chapters 5–10). The priesthood of Christ is better than Aaron's as to its *primacy,* because Christ is a priest "after the order of Melchisedec" (5:10), who came before Aaron (7:1–9). Christ's priesthood is better because of its *permanence.* How long was Aaron a priest? He was a priest for only a limited period of time. Then he handed his priesthood to Eleazar his son, who served for a few years and handed it on to Phinehas his son. So Aaron's priesthood was a transferable priesthood whereas Christ's is untransferable (7:24). Christ's priesthood is better than Aaron's because of the *promises* relating to it: "He is the mediator of a better covenant, which was established upon better promises" (8:6).

Also, as a priest, Christ has better *power.* In himself Aaron had no power. His office was endowed with various divine rights and powers because it was typical of the priesthood of the coming Christ. In contrast, the Lord Jesus Christ possessed full power to accomplish once and for all the redemption Aaron's work could merely typify. In 9:8–12 we read of the impotence of Aaron's work and the omnipotence of Christ's work to effect salvation: "The way into the holiest of all was not yet made manifest, while as the first tabernacle was yet standing: which was a figure for the time then present, in which were offered both gifts and sacrifices, that could not make him that did the service perfect, as pertaining to the conscience; which stood only in meats and drinks, and divers washings, and carnal ordinances, imposed on them until the time of reformation." That is as far as Aaron's priesthood could go. Christ's priesthood, on the other hand, is fully able to accomplish salvation: "But Christ being come an high priest of good things to come, by a greater and more perfect tabernacle, not made with hands, that is to say, not of this building; neither by the blood of goats and calves, but by his own blood he entered in once into the holy place, having obtained eternal redemption for us." In the Old Testament the washings and the sacrifices purged the flesh. They made a man ceremonially clean to come in to the worship of the tabernacle. But they could not touch the conscience. But the blood of Jesus Christ purges the conscience: "If the blood of bulls and of goats, and the ashes of an heifer sprinkling the unclean, sanctifieth to the purifying of the flesh: how much more shall the blood of Christ, who through the eternal Spirit offered himself without spot to God, purge your conscience from dead works?" (9:13–14).

That is not to say that no believer in the Old Testament had a clear conscience. He did. Abraham's conscience was obviously clear when he was justified. David's conscience was clear when he wrote those words at the beginning of Psalm 32. He was justified. But Old Testament believers were not justified by the offerings and washings of the Aaronic priesthood. Their conscience was purged by God's Spirit, looking forward to the merit of the blood of Jesus Christ the true High Priest. It is only through the merit of His blood that any man can have his conscience purged. That is the value of the work of Christ. It truly effects salvation. Christ's death once and for all satisfied God and put away sin.

In 10:1–3 Paul argues that a sacrifice that really effects these things would never need to be repeated. The fact that Aaron's sacrifices needed constant repetition proves their ineffectiveness. Christ's sacrifice needs no repetition. It has real power to save: "Every priest standeth daily ministering and offering oftentimes the same sacrifices, which can never take away sins: but this man, after he had offered one sacrifice for sins for ever, sat down on the right hand of God .... For by one offering he hath perfected for ever them that are sanctified" (10:11–12, 14).

Here is the heart of the gospel: Christ, who is truly God and truly man, is our great Prophet. Here is the value of Christ's work: He is our great Priest, who reconciled us to God by His blood and now intercedes for us on the basis of that blood atonement. Now we are in a position to see the force of the third major point in Paul's argument.

THE VALUE OF CHRIST'S WORK PROVES THAT HE IS GOD'S FINAL WORD AND THE ONLY WAY OF SALVATION FOR SINNERS

This is the testimony of the entire Bible. Even the Old Testament, with all its clearly temporary, symbolic, and typical rituals, points to Christ. What is the meaning of the Levitical offerings? Their true meaning is that Christ alone can atone for sin by the shedding of His own blood. Heb. 7:25 interprets the fulfilment of the Old Testament's typology to teach that Christ "is able also to save them to the uttermost that come unto God by him." All the Levitical offerings pointed forward to Him, so that without Christ, therefore, the Old Testament would be incomplete. Unless there is a fulfilment of all its foreshadowings, the Old Testament stands discredited. That is a very strong statement, but it does not overstate Paul's argument. God has sent Christ as His once-for-all sacrifice for sin. Christ is God's final word of salvation to men. "God, who at sundry times and in divers manners spake in time past unto the fathers by the prophets, hath in these last days spoken unto us [once and for all] by [or, in] his Son" (1:1–2). He is God's final word, and therefore He is God's only way of salvation.

Now see what that does to resolve the question of the relationship between the temple and the gospel. First, the Old Testament is a genuine revelation of God. Second, that revelation became progressively clearer as the Lord developed His purpose through the history of His people. Third, what we have from the Old Testament to the New Testament is not a development from error to truth, but a development from truth as seen by moonlight to truth as seen by sunlight. Fourth, the Old Testament, therefore, was never intended to be permanent as to its forms and rituals. Its principles and doctrines are permanent and unchangeable, but the forms in which they were expressed were temporary and symbolic. They were mere shadows which Christ and His gospel cast before them. Fifth, from this it follows that the proper interpretation of the Old Testament is to find out what permanent gospel truth is expressed by its temporary and symbolic forms.

The Old Testament is entirely misunderstood, it is misrepresented, unless it is accepted for what it truly is: a light that leads to Christ. That is why Hebrews makes the very strong argument that for anybody to set up the Old Testament and its passing, temporary forms in place of God's permanent revelation in Jesus Christ—for anybody to give up the once-for-all sacrifice of Christ for the continual offerings and washings of the Old Testament—is soul-destroying heresy. While as yet Christ had not come, those temporary forms were fine. They pointed to Him. However, now that Christ has come, for anybody to hold on to them is to repudiate all that God has said and done in His Son.

Furthermore, and this directly affects our churches, for anybody to mix the shadowy forms of Old Testament ritual with the spiritual reality and finality of the New Testament and its gospel is to deny the sufficiency of Christ. That is a major part of the apostasy of Roman Catholicism. In almost every detail Roman ritual transplants the Old Testament ritual into the New Testament church and thereby subverts the gospel. What is the Roman priesthood but an attempt to revive the Levitical priesthood that offers propitiatory sacrifices to appease the wrath of God and stand between the people and God? The entire system of ritualism, Roman or otherwise, is an attempt to join the shadows of the Old Testament with the realities and the final form of the New Testament. In Paul's terms, that is to fall from grace. It is to deny the sufficiency of Jesus Christ, because He is God's final word and sole way of salvation.

How are we to benefit personally from that saving word? The answer to that question forms the final step in Paul's argument.

GOD'S FINAL WORD IN CHRIST CAN NEVER BE REPUDIATED BY TRUE BELIEVERS

"Now the just shall live by faith: but if any man draw back, my soul shall have no pleasure in him. But we are not of them who draw back unto perdition; but of them that believe to the saving of the soul" (10:38–39). There is something a true believer in Jesus Christ cannot do, and there is something he will do.

What True Christians Cannot Do

True believers can sin. They can fail. We are all living examples of that. But a true believer in Jesus Christ cannot repudiate the Saviour for any other way of salvation. Paul says, "If any man will draw back"—that is, if any man will give up Christ and return to the Old Testament sacrifices and pin his hopes for heaven on those rather than on Christ—"my soul shall have no pleasure in him." Empty professors may draw back, but, says Paul, "We are not of those who draw back." True believers can never give up Jesus Christ for any other way of salvation.

This is the key to understanding the dire warning of chapter 6 and chapter 10. Chapter 6 has plagued many Christians' consciences, especially if they feel they have failed the Lord. After a period of coldness, or disobedience, or even some degree of backsliding, they come to chapter 6 and feel condemned without hope. "For it is impossible for those who were once enlightened, and have tasted of the heavenly gift, and were made partakers of the Holy Ghost, and have tasted the good word of God, and the powers of the world to come, if they shall fall away, to renew them again unto repentance; seeing they crucify to themselves the Son of God afresh, and put him to an open shame" (vv. 4–6). This appears to condemn all who fall to a hopeless doom. But does it? The Word of God does not contradict itself. That Word explicitly calls upon erring Christians to make confession of their sin and promises forgiveness (1 John 1:9–2:2). Hebrews 6 cannot contradict that. So what does it mean? Remember that it was written to Jews who were being tempted to give up Christ. The sin that Paul is constantly dealing with in the book of Hebrews is not just any sin. It is the sin of repudiating Christ. For example, when he says, "Forsake not the assembling of yourselves together, as the manner of some is," he is not merely saying, make sure you are in church on Sunday. No doubt that is included and no doubt it is sin for God's people wilfully and wantonly to absent themselves from the worship in God's house. But that is not strictly what Paul was discussing.

What he was referring to was forsaking the assembly, forsaking the church, forsaking the gospel, forsaking Christ in order to go back to the synagogue and the temple. That is the sin of the book of Hebrews. True Christians can never give up Christ, but people may profess faith in Christ, come into the church, and derive many benefits from their profession. They may be wrought upon physically, emotionally, and even in their conscience and in their spirit. They may be appear to be Christians, but if they give up Christ they are not saved—they never were saved and never will be saved. That is what Paul teaches. If people give up Christ, how can they ever get to heaven? Who else can take them to heaven? Can the blood of a bull or a goat get them into heaven? If they give up the blood of God's Son, how can they ever receive forgiveness of sin? That is the meaning of the warning of chapter 6. The same is true of the warning of 10:26–29: "If we sin wilfully after that we have received the knowledge of the truth, there remaineth no more sacrifice for sins." The wilful sin is the sin of apostasy from Christ.

While those warnings were specifically given to Jewish Christians, they have a solemn application to Gentiles as well. There are false professors in Gentile churches too. Hebrews has an urgent message for us all. Pay particular attention to its repetition of the word *lest*. That is a word of warning. In 2:1 we read, *"Lest* at any time we should let them slip." Chapter 3:12 says, "Take heed, brethren, *lest* there be in any of you an evil heart of unbelief." Chapter 4:1 commands, "Let us therefore fear, *lest*, a promise being left us of entering into his rest, any of you should seem to come short of it." We are to consider Christ *"lest* ye be wearied and faint in your minds" (12:3), "looking diligently *lest* any man fail of the grace of God; *lest* any root of bitterness springing up trouble you, and thereby many be defiled; *lest* there be any fornicator, or profane person, as Esau, who for one morsel of meat sold his birthright" (12:15–16). It is one thing to be a professor. It is another thing to be a Christian. It is one thing to join the church. It is another thing to be in Christ. Professors can and always will give up Christ for something else, but God's people cannot do that.

What True Christians Will Do

What will they do? Chapter 11 tells you what they will do. God's people, true believers, are not of those who draw back. They are of those who believe to the saving of the soul, and therefore they will live as God's people have always lived, by faith in the promise of God in Christ. How to live by faith is the great lesson we learn from the eventful records of the Old Testament. Hebrews 11 summarizes most of the Old Testament and applies its message. What are we to learn from Abraham and the rest of the Old Testament saints? We are to learn that they lived by faith in Jesus Christ. That is what we too are called to do. What is the Christian life? It is the life of faith. What is the life of faith? It is living out the gospel, so that what we believe concerning Christ governs all we are and do.

The closing chapters of Hebrews show what this means. *Christ is our leader; follow Him.* "Seeing we also are compassed about with so great a cloud of witnesses, let us lay aside every weight, and the sin which doth so easily beset us, and let us run with patience the race that is set before us, looking unto Jesus the author and finisher of our faith" (12:1–2).

Christ is our altar; feed off Him. "We have an altar, whereof they have no right to eat which serve the tabernacle" (13:10). What does it mean to feed off Christ? It means to get our minds focused on His person, which is the basis of the gospel, on the value of His work, on the final word that God has spoken in Him, and on the sole way of salvation God has provided in Him. It is to meditate on Christ, to think upon Christ, and to apply the truth of Christ to our hearts until it forms how we live and act. Christ is our leader; follow Him. He is altar; feed off Him.

Finally, *Christ is our Saviour; fellowship with Him.* "Wherefore Jesus also, that he might sanctify the people with his own blood, suffered without the gate. Let us go forth therefore unto him without the camp, bearing his reproach" (13:12–13).

How should a Christian live? He should live out the gospel. Why? Because Jesus Christ is God's full and final word to men. All God has to say to us is in Christ. He is the object of our faith. We cannot give Him up. The Jewish believers who first received this epistle could not repudiate Him in favour of the temple and its ritual. They had heard His word and experienced the power of His blood. They must live and die in the light of that reality. So must we. And He who saved us is able to give us the grace and power we need to live according to God's last word to men: "Now the God of peace, that brought again from the dead our Lord Jesus, that great shepherd of the sheep, through the blood of the everlasting covenant, make you perfect in every good work to do his will, working in you that which is well pleasing in his sight, through Jesus Christ; to whom be glory for ever and ever. Amen" (13:20–21).

Additional Note on the Authorship of Hebrews

Paul's authorship of the book was generally accepted—though with some dissent—until the time of the Reformation. Erasmus, Luther, and Calvin all rejected it. Luther proposed Apollos as the writer. The chief argument against Pauline authorship is the Greek style in which the book is written. It is highly cultured and quite distinct from the usual style of Paul's epistles. To Calvin that argument was decisive, and most modern commentators are of the same opinion. However, it is easy to make too much of the stylistic argument. John Brown thought that little dependence could be placed on it.

> Variety of subject is calculated to produce variety of style; and there is not a greater dissimilarity between the Epistle to the Hebrews and the other Epistles of Paul, than there is between the Gospel, the Epistles, and the Apocalypse—all of them the admitted writings of the Apostle John.

There are strong arguments in favour of Paul's authorship.

First, the language of 10:34; 13:18–19, 23 clearly leaves the impression that the writer is Paul.

Second, Peter, the apostle to the Jews and one who addresses himself to Jewish Christians (1 Pet. 1:1), explicitly states that Paul wrote to the same people (2 Pet. 3:15). Thus we know Paul did write an epistle to Jewish Christians.

Third, given these facts we can appreciate Brown's argument:

> There can be little doubt, that when they [the original recipients] gave copies of the Epistle to other churches, they did not conceal the name of the writer; and if a tradition be found early received and generally prevailing, unless there be very strong internal evidence of its falsehood, the probability is that that tradition is true. Such a tradition we find prevailing towards the end of the second century, and since that period it has been generally received in the Christian Church. That tradition ascribes the Epistle to the Apostle Paul as its author.

20

James

A Faith That Works

What is the true relationship between faith and works?

♦

The New Testament has only one answer: A living faith

♦

in Christ produces a faithful life for Christ. A fruitless

♦

faith is dead, and dead faith is not saving faith.

A ll too often Christians study James from a merely defensive point of view. They usually start off by defending its authorship. There is no good reason to doubt the traditional view that the James who penned this epistle was the brother of Jude, author of the penultimate book of our New Testament, and that they are the same James and Jude who were brothers of our Lord Jesus Christ (Matt. 13:55). However, since radical critics dispute this view, orthodox believers have felt compelled to spend inordinate time and effort in defending it.

Mostly, however, their effort goes into defending the orthodoxy of the book. In doing so, the thrust has usually been to establish what James does *not* teach, namely, salvation by works. Some statements of James ring strange in the ears of those who have studied the epistles of Paul. For example, in Romans 3 Paul teaches that we are justified by faith alone, while James says, "Ye see then how that by works a man is justified, and not by faith only" (2:24). That sounds like a flat contradiction of Paul, though careful study shows it is not. What James is actually teaching is that faith that has no fruit is dead and therefore cannot save. Paul taught the same thing. It is worth noting that James, in emphasizing the necessity of works, speaks of those who are rich in faith, while Paul, in emphasizing the necessity of faith, speaks to Timothy of those who are rich in good works.

The polemical or defensive arguments are undoubtedly very important, but as a treatment of the book of James, they are woefully inadequate. We must go on to establish positively what this book does teach. James has a very strong and positive theology. It is what is called an ethical theology. It deals with down-to-earth, practical issues. There is deep doctrine in this book, but it is not expounded as, for example, in Paul's epistles. However, James builds his ethical teaching on the very same doctrinal foundation as Paul and the other apostles.

Let us take an example. Critics point out that James uses the name of the Lord Jesus Christ only twice in his entire epistle, and he does not refer by name to the Holy Spirit, unless 4:5 is taken to refer to Him. The critics use these facts and James's supposed lack of evangelical doctrine to theorize that this is a Jewish treatise doctored to appear like a Christian epistle. The truth is far different. The doctrinal foundation of James is far from flimsy. In 2:1 James speaks of "the faith of our Lord Jesus Christ." While he does not systematically expound that faith, he does lay down the elements in it that are necessary for his call to Christian living. We may mark four fundamental theological themes upon which James bases his ethical appeal.

Fourfold Revelation of God

First, there is a fourfold revelation of God. He is "the Father of lights" (1:17). That is a wonderful title describing God as the Creator of all the heavenly bodies, the One who said, "Let there be light," and there was light. He is "God, even the Father" (3:9). In context, that describes Him as the Creator of all men. He is the "lawgiver" (4:12), a title which establishes man's moral accountability to Him. Finally, He is "the Lord of sabaoth," or the Lord of hosts (5:4), a title which shows His sovereignty over angels, devils, and men.

Threefold Revelation of Christ

That revelation of God is followed by a threefold revelation of the person of Christ. In 2:7 James sets the tone of his Christology when he speaks of "that worthy name by the which ye are called." He gives us three wonderful descriptions of that worthy name. First, he uses the full title, the Lord Jesus Christ (1:1; 2:1). That speaks of Christ as our Saviour. James adds the title "the Lord of glory" (2:1), which speaks of Christ as our God. In 5:9 James speaks of Him as our Judge. Christ our Saviour, our God, and our Judge—that is the Christology on which the book is built.

Doctrine of Scripture

James also displays a well-developed doctrine of Scripture. Chapter 1 has multiplied references to the Word of God. It is the Word of truth (1:18). It is the ingrafted, or the implanted, Word (1:21). It is the perfect law of liberty (1:25). The Scripture is the royal law (2:8). Such descriptions are not accidental. They form part of a careful statement of the orthodox doctrine of Scripture as the very, authoritative Word of God. This becomes even clearer when James proceeds to describe the supernatural power of the Word. It is like a mirror (1:23–25). It can show a man what he really is. It is also the instrument God uses in the new birth (1:18). And it is the implanted seed God uses to produce the fruit of salvation in the lives of His believing people (1:21).

Doctrine of Salvation

This epistle also has a very definite doctrine of salvation. It teaches the doctrine of the sovereignty of God in regeneration. "Of his own will begat he us with the word of truth" (1:18). It teaches the doctrine of divine calling: "that worthy name by the which ye are called" (2:7). Finally, James gives a careful dissertation on the divine method of justification (2:14–26). Upon this theological basis James proceeds to echo the teaching of the Lord Jesus Christ in the Sermon on the Mount. It is a very profitable study to mark the parallels between the Sermon on the Mount and the epistle of James. Again and again James echoes, applies, and expounds the very words of the Lord Jesus in that sermon. As he does so, he follows one great central theme. It is simply this: **godly practice is the identifying mark of God's people.**

Writing probably a mere fifteen to twenty years after the death of the Lord Jesus Christ, James was addressing Jewish believers with very specific concerns on his mind. Two things were special concerns.

First, *he was concerned about the church's place in the world.* The converts to whom he wrote were under great pressure. Their faith was constantly tested: "Knowing this, that the trying of your faith worketh patience" (1:3). "The trying of your faith" simply means "your tested faith." How was their faith being tested? Rich men dragged these poor Jewish Christians before the courts and blasphemed the name of the Lord Jesus Christ by which they were called (2:6–7). Wealthy landowners employed them to reap their fields and proceeded to defraud them of their rightful wages. Worse still, at times, either by working them to death or by some other form of cruelty, they killed some of God's people (5:4–6). So these Jewish believers were under tremendous pressure—poor, worked to death, dragged into court, defrauded of their wages, and in some cases murdered. In such circumstances, James urged them to be patient: "My brethren, count it all joy when ye fall into divers temptations; knowing this, that the trying of your faith worketh patience. But let patience have her perfect work, that ye may be perfect and entire, wanting nothing" (1:2–4). *Patience* means steadfast endurance. How were these believers to find strength to endure with steadfastness such trials as they were experiencing? James addresses this in 5:7–11. In a word, he directed them to get their eyes on Christ, and especially on His coming as the Judge of all. In this James echoes the uniform message of the entire New Testament. Christians obtain strength to run their race "looking unto Jesus" and receive grace not to faint by "consider[ing] him that endured such contradiction of sinners against himself" (Heb. 12:2–3).

Clearly, some to whom James wrote were failing in this grace, and that led him to voice his second concern. Not only was he concerned about the experience of the church in the world, *he was also concerned about the world getting into the church.* There seemed to be an attitude of "If you can't beat them, join them" getting into the church. Some were falling into open worldliness. In 1:27 James speaks of "pure religion." In many ways that expression is the key to the whole book. "Pure religion and undefiled before God and the Father is this, To visit the fatherless and widows in their affliction, and to keep himself unspotted from the world." This was his concern, that God's people would remain unspotted from the world. The force of the word *unspotted* may be gauged from 1 Pet. 1:19, where it describes the purity of Christ as the Lamb of God. James became even more forceful in 4:4: "Ye adulterers and adulteresses, know ye not that the friendship of the world is enmity with God? Whosoever therefore will be a friend of the world is the enemy of God." That is very strong language, but it was justified. Worldliness in the church is a matter of the gravest concern.

James's twin concerns make his epistle a very relevant book for us today. Are these not the two concerns that must be upon our minds, the experience of God's people in the world, and the danger of the world getting into the church? James spells out a variety of ways in which worldliness does its deadly work. Instability and unbelief that hinder prayer (1:8) are an example of worldliness at work. Fawning upon the rich and spurning the poor (2:1–4) is a blatant form of worldliness. The sins of the tongue are another form of worldliness (3:1–12; 4:11–12; 5:9). Carnal folly that leads to violent disputes is yet another form of worldliness (3:13–4:3). Bitter envy and strife are "earthly, sensual, devilish." It is no wonder that where there are such "wars and fightings" in a church God refuses to answer prayer: "Ye ask, and receive not" (4:3). Worldliness shows itself in yet another way, by a boastful, careless arrogance about the future: "Go to now, ye that say, Today or tomorrow we will go into such a city, and continue there a year, and buy and sell, and get gain: whereas ye know not what shall be on the morrow" (4:13–14). This carnal spirit shuffles God over to the sidelines. It places Christ and His gospel away in the background.

There is one other form of worldliness James deals with. This is the sin that he repeatedly exposes and condemns, the sin of professing a faith that fails to produce good works (1:22–27; 2:14–26). Failure to put into practice what we profess to believe is the ultimate form of worldliness.

Here are James's two concerns—the church in the world, and the world in the church. Addressing these twin concerns, James expounds his central theme in a very simple but very far-reaching manner. I have stated that the theme is that godly practice is the identifying mark of God's people. If we rephrase that slightly it will help us to grasp the force of James's argument. He is arguing that **a living faith produces a faithful life.** He was scandalized by a profession of faith that allowed the professor to have low standards of personal behaviour. James could not accept the reality of a Christianity that was a mere lip service. So, pursuing his theme, he makes three very simple points.

JUSTIFIED BY A FAITH THAT WORKS

James first makes the point that we are justified only by a faith that works. Chapter 2:18 is the key to the whole argument: "A man may say, Thou hast faith, and I have works: show me thy faith without thy works, and I will show thee my faith by my works." How can we show our faith to another person? We cannot see the heart of another. We can only see his works. Thus we cannot show our faith except by our works. James says, "I will show thee my faith by [or, out of] my works." He is speaking of works that flow out of faith. He is speaking of a faith that produces works. He is not saying we are saved without faith; he is saying we are saved by faith that produces works. He is not speaking or arguing in any sense against the apostle Paul. He is not speaking of a man who is unsaved working to merit the favour of God and enter into justification by virtue of his works. No. He is speaking of people who profess to have been justified by faith, and he argues that if they do not have good works to prove their faith, they do not have any justifying faith at all. That is his argument. His reference to Abraham proves that this is his meaning. "Was not Abraham our father justified by works, when he had offered Isaac his son upon the altar? Seest thou how faith wrought with his works, and by works was faith made perfect? And the scripture was fulfilled which saith, Abraham believed God, and it was imputed unto him for righteousness" (2:21–23). James is referring to Abraham's willing obedience to offer up Isaac at the command of God (see Genesis 22). He says, "Faith wrought with his works, and by [or, out of his] works was faith made perfect" (v. 22). In this way the Scripture was fulfilled in its statement, "Abraham believed God, and it was imputed unto him for righteousness" (v. 23). But that imputation took place *before Isaac was born* (Gen. 15:6). Clearly, then, Abraham's works recorded in Genesis 22 were not the cause of his justification but the result and the proof of it. Abraham had faith. How do we know he had faith? Because faith worked. James argues, Abraham's faith was a working faith; therefore it was a living faith. Therefore it was a justifying faith. A faith that does not produce works is dead and useless: "What doth it profit, my brethren, though a man say he hath faith, and have not works? can faith save him?" (2:14). The force of the Greek is much stronger than "Can faith save him?" That is not really the question James is asking. There is a definite article before the word *faith,* and the construction of the sentence is such as to lead us to expect a negative answer. In the Greek text, then, James's question is, "If a man says he has faith, but he has no works, that faith cannot save him, can it?" Surely not. That faith which produces no works, which is all in words but does not humble the soul to submit to the holiness of God and to follow Christ in obedience, is not faith at all. It is dead. It is make-believe. It is a devilish counterfeit. That faith damns; it does not save. That faith cannot justify.

If ever there were a message that needed to be preached again in the twentieth century, that is the message. Paul preached that message. Both Paul and James are agreed. We are justified only by a faith that works.

Churches are filled with people who have walked the aisle, signed a card, raised their hand, joined the church, or otherwise made a profession. These things are legitimate in their place, if they are expressions of a heart humbly accepting Christ on Christ's terms as Lord and Saviour. In themselves, however, they are worthless. It is time to obey the Scripture: "Let a man examine himself." Let us face the challenge of God's word, "Show me thy faith." Woe to the man whose faith has no fruit. That faith cannot save him, can it? No. We can be justified only by faith that works.

SANCTIFIED BY A FAITH THAT WORKS

The second great truth that James establishes in expounding his theme is that we are sanctified only by a faith that works. This takes up most of the book. A faith that works governs our attitude to everything around us. James deals with six things to which faith will govern our attitude.

First, *faith governs our attitude to the world.* James's argument is that only by a faith that works can we escape the worldliness he condemns so fully. How do Christians escape worldliness? Not by legalism. Not by mere will power. They escape worldliness by a faith that works. That faith will enable God's people to bear the *pressures* of the world. That is what chapter 1 is all about. It will also enable them not to be intimidated by the *people* of the world (chap. 2). Faith in Christ also enables Christians to eschew the *practices* of the world (chap. 4). So faith governs our attitude to the world.

It also governs our attitude to worship (2:1–11; 5:13–18). It will destroy partiality in the church. It will also lead to prayer in the church. Here are two of the most persistent problems in church life—sinful divisions among God's people and lack of powerful prayer. How are these to be overcome? It does not take any high-powered seminar or program. It simply takes the activity of faith, Christians living according to what they profess to believe.

Faith will govern our attitude to the Word of God (1:22–25). James makes the attitude of faith to the Word of God very clear. We may set forth its teaching as follows:

The will of God is set forth in the Word of God.

The Word of God is not merely a proposition to be believed; it is a law to be obeyed.

This law is a royal law of liberty.

This liberty is not license to sin; it is freedom to be holy.

This holiness is the hallmark of true Christianity.

Thus true Christianity is expressed by a life in accordance with the Word of God.

That is the attitude of a working faith to the Word of God.

If we have that attitude to the Word of God, that same *faith will govern our attitude to our own words* (3:1–12; 4:11; 5:9, 12). James places a strong emphasis on the Christian's words. All too often we pride ourselves in the vices we avoid and the virtues we profess, while being capable of the most destructive criticism. We use our tongue as a weapon. Let us govern our tongue by our faith. What we truly believe must be evident in what we say and how we say it. Sadly, we are not perfect in this matter, just as we are not perfect in anything else we do, but nonetheless that must be the prevailing standard of the child of God. That is faith at work.

Faith also governs our walk (4:1–5:11). How should we walk? Paul says we walk by faith, not by sight. James teaches the very same thing. Anything else is worldliness, which is spiritual adultery, because it is idolatry. If we fail to walk by faith we are guilty of putting something above our God. If we are walking with the devil, we are not believing in God. Believing and behaviour cannot be separated. Our faith must direct our feet.

Faith also governs our witness (5:19–20). If we have a faith that works, we cannot sit back and allow the lost to perish without hearing the gospel. Who can turn a sinner from the error of his way? A man who has such a working faith in Christ. Soulwinning is not a work for academics for whom the gospel is merely a matter of speculation. It is a work for evangelists who know whom they have believed and whose lives are living proofs of Jesus' power to save.

In these six ways faith works in our sanctification.

GLORIFIED BY A FAITH THAT WORKS

We will be glorified only by a faith that works. Twice in chapter 5 James raises the thought of not being condemned: "Grudge [or, murmur] not one against another, brethren, lest ye be [or, in order that ye be not] condemned: behold, the judge standeth before the door" (v. 9). "Swear not, . . . let your yea be yea; and your nay, nay; lest ye fall [or, in order that ye may not fall] into condemnation" (v. 12). James has been dealing with people who say they are saved, but who act in a way that contradicts their profession. They have great profession but very little performance. He has been expounding to them the reality that justifying faith is a working faith that will produce holiness in their lives. Now, as he comes to the end of the epistle, the apostle is thinking about eternity. The final judgment is weighing heavily on his mind. He realizes that people who profess faith in Christ but whose faith produces no spiritual fruit are going to be condemned on the day of judgment.

Therefore he introduces this caution, "lest ye be condemned." His message is clear: be careful that you have a faith that works, because only by a faith that works will you escape condemnation. Entrance into heaven is only through a faith that works. We must never settle for anything less. Why? There is one very simple reason. God will not. Others may. We are not going to be judged by how we relate to the prevailing standard of morality. We are not going to be judged by how we appear in comparison with the rest of this world's sinners. There is one Lawgiver, and by the standard of His law we shall be judged. Only Christ has satisfied that law. Only in Him, therefore, can we find safety from its condemnation. And we can enter into Christ only by a living faith. God will accept nothing but a faith that works, for that alone is a true and living faith in a true and living Saviour.

1 Peter
The Trials And Triumphs Of True Christians

Christians should live in happiness and holiness despite

◆

all their trials because God has saved them and sealed

◆

them for heaven through the Lord Jesus Christ.

The new Christians to whom Peter wrote this epistle were Jews. That meant that they had to endure suspicion from both the Gentiles and the Jews. The Gentiles called them atheists because they refused to worship the gods that made up the heathen pantheon. The Jews looked on them as apostates, dangerous detractors from the glory of Moses. Victimized by both Jews and Gentiles, these new Christians came under intense, immense, and insistent pressure. In writing to them, therefore, the apostle Peter dealt with matters of the most basic importance to them and their testimony. He gave them clear doctrinal instruction along with forthright practical guidance and uplifting spiritual encouragement to raise them out of the mental and spiritual oppression caused by relentless persecution. In doing all this the apostle expounded the fundamental doctrine and the fundamental duty of a Christian. The fundamental doctrine is the doctrine of salvation (1:1–2:10), and the fundamental duty is subjection to the Lord in all things, what we may call holiness unto the Lord under all sorts of conditions and circumstances (2:11–5:14). By interweaving these three strands of thought—the distress caused by persecution, the doctrine of salvation, and the duty to be holy and submissive—Peter produces his central message. He sets it forth in 5:6–11: "Humble yourselves therefore under the mighty hand of God, that he may exalt you in due time: casting all your care upon him; for he careth for you. Be sober, be vigilant; because your adversary the devil, as a roaring lion, walketh about, seeking whom he may devour: whom resist steadfast in the faith, knowing that the same afflictions are accomplished in your brethren that are in the world. But the God of all grace, who hath called us unto his eternal glory by Christ Jesus, after that ye have suffered a while, make you perfect, stablish, strengthen, settle you. To him be glory and dominion for ever and ever. Amen." We may paraphrase this message: "We as Christians are called to endure much hardship in the world, but God has saved us and sealed us for heaven through the Lord Jesus Christ. He will, therefore, sustain us in all our cares and conflicts. In the light of all this, what is our duty? We should live in humility, in holiness, and in the confident hope of Christ's eternal glory." We may summarize the theme even more briefly: 1 Peter is a book that is all about **the trials and the triumphs of true Christians.**

WHAT A TRUE CHRISTIAN IS
A Product of Sovereign Grace
Peter takes a great deal of time to show what a true Christian is. The epistle is full of this theme. We are sinners by nature; we are Christians by grace. That is how Peter teaches what a true Christian is. At the very commencement of the book Peter sounds the note of sovereign grace. In

1:2 he shows that a Christian is one chosen by God the Father, sanctified (effectually called) by the Holy Spirit, and rendered acceptable to God by the merits of the blood of Christ: "Elect according to the foreknowledge of God the Father, through sanctification of the Spirit, unto obedience and sprinkling of the blood of Jesus Christ." The election of the Father, the sanctification (or effectual call) of the Spirit, the sprinkling of the blood of Jesus Christ, the sacrifice of Calvary, are the reasons we are Christians.

We are Christians because God set His love upon us in the decree of eternal election. Left to ourselves none of us would ever choose God or His Christ. We would rather go the way our depraved nature leads us. We are Christians, not because we had some spark of goodness within us but because God sovereignly loved us when there was nothing lovable about us. He set His love upon us when there was no reason to do so outside of the goodness of His own will and good pleasure. That purpose of God not only chose us but chose us in Christ. There is a sense in which God only ever chose one man, the Man Christ Jesus. The Father calls Him "mine elect" in a preeminent way. It is in Him, through Him, because of Him, and unto Him (for His glory) that God set His love upon us.

The purpose of the Father leads Peter directly to the sacrifice of the Son. In 1:20 we read that Christ was the Lamb "foreordained before the foundation of the world" to be the sacrifice for our sins. The sacrifice of the Son receives a great deal of attention in this epistle. We "were not redeemed with corruptible things, as silver and gold, from [our] vain conversation . . . but with the precious blood of Christ, as of a lamb without blemish and without spot" (1:18–19). A true Christian is a person redeemed by the blood of the Lamb. From 2:24 we learn that Christ not only purchased our redemption but expiated all our sin: "Who his own self bare our sins in his own body on the tree." Furthermore, He reconciled us to God by His blood: "Christ also hath once suffered for sins, the just for the unjust, that he might bring us to God" (3:18), reconciled by the blood of the Lamb. What is a Christian? A Christian is one who is the object of God's sovereign love. He is one for whom the Lord Jesus Christ died on Calvary's cross. He is one who is reconciled to God by the blood of the Lord Jesus Christ.

A Christian is also one who has been sanctified (set apart) by the Holy Spirit (1:2). The Holy Spirit does this by effectually calling a person out of a state of sin and death into one of grace and acceptance with God: "But ye are a chosen generation, a royal priesthood, an holy nation, a peculiar people; that ye should show forth the praises of him who hath called you out of darkness into his marvellous light" (2:9).

That is a sovereign, omnipotent call. It carries with it the power of God to effect what it commands. This effectual call of the Spirit not only tells dead sinners they need life; it gives them life. God's word of life to Jerusalem (Ezek. 16:6) is a perfect description of His effectual call: "When I passed by thee, and saw thee polluted in thine own blood, I said unto thee when thou wast in thy blood, Live; yea, I said unto thee when thou wast in thy blood, Live."

Here is what a Christian is. He is a sinner transformed by the grace of the triune God—chosen, not for any good in him, but by divine fore-ordination (for the inspired definition of foreknowledge see Acts 2:23, where the construction of the Greek shows that foreknowledge and predeterminate counsel are the same thing), redeemed by the precious blood of Christ, and regenerated by the Holy Spirit.

A New Relationship

The result of this transformation is a new relationship with the Lord, which Peter proceeds to explore. *Christians are God's temple:* "Ye also, as lively stones, are built up a spiritual house, an holy priesthood, to offer up spiritual sacrifices, acceptable to God by Jesus Christ" (1 Pet. 2:5). When Moses raised the tabernacle, the glory of the Lord filled it. When Solomon raised up the temple, the glory of the Lord filled it. God concentrated His glorious presence there because that was uniquely His dwelling place on the earth. The church is uniquely the dwelling place of the Almighty. The body of every individual Christian is the temple of the Holy Ghost (1 Cor. 6:19). We are God's temple, indwelt by "the spirit of glory and of God" (1 Pet. 4:14).

Christians are God's people: "Ye are a chosen generation, . . . an holy nation, a peculiar people" (2:9). Chosen by God, born of His Spirit, and purchased by Christ, Christians are the special people of God. They are His holy nation. They are His peculiarly purchased people, the people of His possession. They confess, "This God is our God," and know that God says, "This people is My people—the true Israel of God." That is the greatest privilege on earth. Christians are God's people.

They are also God's priests: "Ye . . . are . . . an holy priesthood, to offer up spiritual sacrifices, acceptable to God by Jesus Christ. . . . Ye are . . . a royal priesthood" (vv. 5, 9). As God's priests, Christians enter into His presence to worship, to minister, and to serve through the merits of the blood of the Lord Jesus Christ. They have access to the very throne of God. They do not offer sacrifices for sin—Christ offered one sacrifice for sin forever. Their sacrifices are the praise and worship of their lips (Heb. 13:15), the sacrifice of a broken and a contrite heart (Ps. 51:17), and the living sacrifice of a body consecrated to His service (Rom. 12:1).

These are the results of the grace of God in making us Christians. Here is what a Christian really is. Now, this raises the question, am I a Christian? *Christian* is the most misused word in the English language. According to some, a Christian is one born in a so-called Christian nation. There is no such thing in this world. Others imagine that if they belong to a Christian church they must be Christians, if they have been baptized with Christian baptism they must be Christians, if they have taken the sacrament of the Lord's Supper they must be Christians. None of these things makes a person a Christian.

The Marks of a Christian

Peter tells us that there are various marks that evidence a Christian. For example, he insists that a Christian is one who has been *born again:* "Blessed be the God and Father of our Lord Jesus Christ, which according to his abundant mercy hath begotten us again" (1 Pet. 1:3). Again, he says, "[We have been] born again, not of corruptible seed, but of incorruptible, by the word of God, which liveth and abideth for ever" (1:23). In 2:2 he describes those to whom he writes as "newborn babes." To be born again is to be made a new creature in Christ. It is to be made a partaker of the divine nature (2 Pet. 1:4).

A Christian is also a *believer.* He has a saving faith in Jesus Christ. Peter describes God's people as those "who by [Christ] do believe in God, that raised him up from the dead, and gave him glory; that your faith and hope might be in God. Seeing ye have purified your souls in obeying the truth through the Spirit" (1 Pet. 1:21). A Christian's faith is not in self, or in the church, or in the sacraments, or in anything that man can say or do. Rather, it is in Jesus Christ, who died and rose again. A Christian is one who receives the truth of the gospel and responds to it with the obedience of faith. That is what marks a man as a Christian. Many people profess to have been born again, but they do not believe in the blood atonement of Jesus Christ, or in His bodily resurrection. Those who profess to be born again while treating the essential truths of the gospel with unbelief have never been born of God's Spirit. They are yet unregenerate. All born-again people are believers in the gospel of Christ.

Many others make a profession of faith on the ground of which they assure themselves that they have been born again though they lack credible evidence of true, saving faith. There is one acid test that Peter gives us to show if our professed faith is a living, saving faith. It is this: *a believer is a lover of Jesus Christ.* If a man is born again, he will believe in the person and the work of Jesus Christ, and if he believes in the person and work of Jesus Christ, he will love the Lord Jesus. Peter lays great stress on this: "Whom having not seen, ye love" (1:8). "Unto you therefore which believe he is precious" (2:7). To the unbeliever Christ is a stumbling stone and a rock of offence (2:8). There is no beauty in Him that would make unbelievers desire Him. They perceive no preciousness in Christ. Any man to whom Christ is not precious is not a Christian. He may clean up his life, join the church, get baptized, sing in the choir, and even ascend the pulpit, but he is not a Christian. A Christian is born again; he is a believer; he is a lover of Jesus Christ.

How To Become a Christian

That raises the additional question, how may a sinner become a Christian? Peter answers that for us. The way to become a Christian is, first, by *obeying the call of the gospel.* This is the certain result of electing and regenerating grace (1:2). The saving purpose and power of God are "unto obedience." In other words, the Father's election and the Spirit's sanctification are for our obedience and sprinkling of the blood of Jesus Christ. God calls us to obey the gospel and come to be washed in the blood of the Lamb. That obedience of faith is essential for salvation: "Ye have purified your souls in obeying the truth" (1:22). The apostle is not saying we become Christians as the result of a life of obedience. What he teaches is that we become Christians by obeying the call of the gospel and receiving Christ on the terms the gospel presents. The gospel commands us to repent and believe on the Lord Jesus Christ. It calls us to acknowledge that He is the Son of God who came into the world to be the Saviour of sinners, that His blood alone can reconcile and redeem us to God, and that He rose from the dead. Then it tells us to call upon Him to be our Saviour. That is the call of the gospel. Obey it and you will be saved. That is the same thing as saying, "Believe on the Lord Jesus Christ, and thou shalt be saved" (Acts 16:31). This is faith in who Christ is, what He has done, and what His work has done, can do, and will do for us. To change the terminology, Peter says this obedience of faith is coming to Christ like a lost sheep: "Ye were as sheep going astray; but are now returned unto the Shepherd and Bishop of your souls" (1 Pet. 2:25). There are other passages of Scripture which speak of the Shepherd seeking us as lost sheep, but remember, these are only figures of speech. We are not actually sheep. Therefore Peter, without contradicting the great truth that the Shepherd seeks the lost, says that we are rational creatures of God who have a responsibility to do what is right, to respond obediently to the call of the gospel. We are morally responsible for the decision that we make when the gospel of Jesus Christ is presented to us. Therefore, people who are like sheep who are going astray should return unto Christ, the Shepherd and Bishop of their souls. This is how a sinner becomes a Christian. He turns to Christ.

When he does so he rejoices that his very coming to Christ is the evidence of God's sovereign grace extended to him. When he comes, he is assured by God's Word that God will fully save him. He will keep him by His power through faith (1:5). He will strengthen and develop the returning sinner so that he will grow from being a newborn babe to being a full-grown Christian (2:2). He will comfort him amid the trials of life: "[Cast] all your care upon him; for he careth for you" (5:7). And, as we have already noted, every Christian becomes a priest: God will give every returning sinner an exalted place of service and usefulness in the work of the gospel.

Having seen what a true Christian is, and considered the implications of Peter's statements on the subject, we can now proceed to his teaching on how a true Christian lives.

HOW A TRUE CHRISTIAN LIVES

A true Christian lives in the light of who and what he is. That simplifies life for a Christian. A Christian really should not need a long list of dos and don'ts. That is not to say that there are no dos and don'ts. There are, but the fundamental rule of the Christian life is to live in the light of who we are and what we are in Jesus Christ. That will give you a direct answer to many of the questions we face. In recent years the media have been full of the scandals of the British royal family. People clearly think that royalty should not live in immorality—that their royalty demands a higher standard than others have to meet. In a way, the logic of this sentiment is right. However, earthly royalty is fallen and depraved like every other part of mankind. Royal flesh is just as wicked as common flesh. But Christians are the true royalty. We are a *royal* priesthood. We are the children of the King of kings. We should live in the light of what we are. We should live like the royal family of heaven on earth.

This means we live in *happiness*. Dr. Martyn Lloyd-Jones called a miserable Christian a contradiction in terms. That is not to say Christians cannot weep or be saddened by events. What it says is that despite their circumstances, Christians should be inwardly and fundamentally happy. They should be a contented people. They should be a rejoicing people: "Ye greatly rejoice, though now for a season, if need be, ye are in heaviness through manifold temptations" (1:6). Peter's readers were under severe mental, emotional, and spiritual pressure. Their trials were deeply disturbing. "But," says Peter, "you greatly rejoice in the great truths of the gospel, despite all the things that would naturally depress you." The things in which they rejoiced amid their distresses were the great gospel truths listed in the opening verses of the epistle—election, regeneration, the blood atonement of Christ, the new birth, a living hope through a risen Saviour, an inheritance incorruptible and undefiled in heaven, the keeping power of God, and the certainty of ultimate salvation. However dark life's pathway, God's people have cause for joy. Amid all the troubles they face, the great truths of the gospel never change and never fail. Therefore, they live in happiness.

Christian should also live in *holiness:* "As he which hath called you is holy, so be ye holy in all manner of conversation" (1:15). "Laying aside all malice, and all guile, and hypocrisies, and envies, and all evil speakings, as newborn babes, desire the sincere milk of the word, that ye may grow thereby" (2:1–2). "As strangers and pilgrims, abstain from fleshly lusts, which war against the soul" (2:11). To these commands to be holy Peter adds the call to follow the example of the Lord Jesus Christ (2:21). This holiness must reach into every sphere of life. Peter refers to our life in the world, in the church, and in the home.

Christians should live in happiness and holiness. They should also live in *humility.* Five times Peter calls on Christians to submit and subject themselves to the ordinances of their rulers (2:13), to their masters (2:18), to their husbands (3:1), and to their elders (5:5). Finally, Peter adds a crowning call: "All of you be subject one to another, and be clothed with humility: for God resisteth the proud, and giveth grace to the humble. Humble yourselves therefore under the mighty hand of God, that he may exalt you in due time" (5:5–6).

Christians should also live in *hope:* "Gird up the loins of your mind, be sober, and hope to the end [or, hope perfectly] for the grace that is to be brought unto you at the revelation of Jesus Christ" (1:13). What an encouragement! Our Saviour is coming back again. Soon He will be revealed from heaven in all His glory. That is our "blessed hope" (Tit. 2:13). It thrills our hearts and stirs our souls to serve the Lord with patience and joyous expectancy.

In the light of the kind of life true Christians lead, Peter now faces an urgent question.

WHY A TRUE CHRISTIAN SUFFERS

Why do true Christians suffer? Very simply, because *the world cannot understand them or their Christianity* (1 Pet. 4:4): "They think it strange that ye run not with them to the same excess of riot." Christians are "strangers and pilgrims" in the earth (2:11). The world cannot understand God's pilgrims and therefore persecutes them.

Again, Christians suffer because *they are called to bear the cross of Christ* (2:21). It is the cross that leads to the crown. Another reason Christians suffer is that *tested faith brings glory to God* both now and eternally (1:7). Now it is a testimony to sinners. Eternally it brings praise to the Lord's name.

HOW A TRUE CHRISTIAN OVERCOMES ADVERSITY

Peter not only shows us why Christians suffer, he also shows how they overcome. We have already noted the force of 1:6: "Wherein ye greatly rejoice, though now for a season, if need be, ye are in heaviness through manifold temptations." In effect he says, "Christian, even though you are in darkness, sometimes tempted to despair, when it is too painful to look in or to look out, then look up! Rejoice in the Lord." That is the key. Chapter 4:1 is very similar: "Arm yourselves likewise with the same mind" as the Christ who suffered and died in the flesh. In other words, "Think as Christ did about obedience and suffering." If we do that, we will not "think it . . . strange concerning the fiery trial . . . as though some strange thing happened unto [us]" (4:12), but will rejoice inasmuch as we are partakers of Christ's suffering (5:1).

A Christian can rejoice amid his sufferings and trials because he looks at his present situation through the filter of the past and of the future. He considers what the triune God has done for him and rejoices in that saving work. He considers what his Saviour is going to do for him, something no present tribulation can take away from him. Peter puts it like this: "The God of all grace, who hath called us unto his eternal glory by Christ Jesus, after that ye have suffered a while, make you perfect, stablish, strengthen, settle you" (5:10). Here is the key to a stable, strong, well-founded and well-grounded life. The backward look at what God has done for us and the forward look at what He will certainly do for us is what enables us to overcome all the distractions of present troubles and to live as Peter commands in 4:19: "Let them that suffer according to the will of God commit the keeping of their souls to him in well doing, as unto a faithful Creator."

That is how a true Christian triumphs over trouble. And his greatest triumph is still to come.

THE TRUE CHRISTIAN'S REWARD

We have thought about the Christian's trials. We have seen some of his triumphs in the midst of those trials, but there is a final triumph, the destiny of every child of God. Peter says we are born again "unto a lively hope" (1:3). What is that hope? It is the hope that comes "by the resurrection of Jesus Christ." The Lord Jesus said, "Because I live, ye shall live also" (John 14:19). Here is the ground of our assurance: our hope rests in the One who died and rose again from the dead as He had promised. He proved He had power over life and death. By His resurrection He proved His claim to be the great "I am," the Son of God, the Father's full and final revelation to men. Christ died, Christ lives, and in Him we live also. Because of that we have an incorruptible inheritance (1 Pet. 1:4), and He is coming back soon to lead us into the full possession of it. Peter says we are partakers of His glory (5:1), whom God "hath called . . . unto his eternal glory by Christ Jesus" (5:10). This is the climax of God's grace. This is the pinnacle of the Christian's triumph.

Without grace it would have been a very different story, as it will be for those of you who reject the Saviour. Salvation is neither cheap nor easy. That is why Peter asks, "What shall the end be of them that obey not the gospel of God? And if the righteous scarcely [or, with difficulty] be saved, where shall the ungodly and the sinner appear?" (4:17–18). The doom of sinners further accentuates the grace of God in the salvation of His people. Despite their sufferings and trials, Christians are born for glory. They triumph now and eternally in the triumph of their Lord.

2 Peter
Crushing The Challenge Of Apostasy

Apostasy has always been the most powerful and

◆

destructive foe of God's work and God's people.

◆

That makes Peter's message particularly significant:

◆

the challenge of apostasy will be crushed by a true

◆

knowledge of Christ in God's people.

*S*econd Peter was Peter's last word to God's people. According to 1:14 he was very soon to lay down his life for his faith as the Saviour had prophesied. As he faced death the apostle had no fear for himself. He had caught a sight of the glory of God in the face of Jesus Christ, and he knew that he was assured of a place with His Saviour in glory. However, as this epistle shows, he had great concern for the wellbeing and witness of the church of Christ. Paul had prophesied to the Ephesian elders that after his departing "grievous wolves" would enter into the flock, wicked perverters of the Word of God, who would not spare the flock but would viciously rend the people of God. Such apostates had already begun to surface in many parts of the apostolic church, and that is what concerned Peter as he penned this final message.

The identity of the particular enemy within the church described in 2 Peter has been the subject of almost endless speculation. Some people think that Peter was combatting the earliest form of what became known as the Gnostic heresy. Others believe—and there is a lot to be said for their view—that the epistle deals with the Nicolaitans, who are mentioned in Rev. 2:6, 15. Whatever the exact name of the enemy Peter has in mind, the same evil brood was active in Corinth, in Colosse, in the rest of Asia Minor, and over the wide area Peter addresses in his two epistles (see 1 Pet. 1:1).

Obviously this was a widespread heresy. The leading beliefs and practices of its promoters are very evident from 2 Peter. These were people who denied the sovereign Lordship of Christ (2:1). They lived in open debauchery and blatant immorality, even at the love feasts and communion services of the church (2:13–14). They were crafty and full of high-sounding doctrine (2:18). They were skilful in perverting the doctrine of free grace to make it an excuse and license to sin (3:16). They openly scoffed at the doctrine of the second coming of the Lord Jesus Christ as the Judge and the King (3:3–4). They pretended to pay deference to the Bible, but they constantly perverted and twisted the Scriptures to support their own iniquitous theories (2:1–3; 3:16). These people were both persuasive and destructive. Thus Peter issued one of the most devastating critiques of apostasy ever penned (chaps. 2, 3) with the clear aims of exposing the apostates for what they really were and of giving instruction to God's people in the face of the threat they presented.

In doing all this Peter constantly calls the believers back to basics. He calls on them to keep in mind the great truths of the gospel. Five times he speaks of the need for them "to have these things always in remembrance" (or an equivalent expression): 1:12, 13, 15; 3:1, 2. This is his theme throughout the book. Everything that these Christians had was based on the gospel, and so Peter wanted to get them back on to a solid gospel foundation. Let us try to understand his argument.

In effect, he says to God's people, "You have come to a knowledge (a key word in this book) of the Lord Jesus Christ as your Saviour and Lord. Everything you are and have, and everything you ever hope to be or have, depends on that, that you know Him. This knowledge of Christ places certain demands upon you. The first of these demands is that you grow in knowledge ever more deeply, that you come to know Christ more and more. It also demands that you grow in every part of your Christian life, because growth is the essential sign of life. It is only as you live in the knowledge of Christ that you can be said to be living the Christian life at all."

So knowledge is vitally important. But knowledge presupposes a sure foundation. You cannot have knowledge without the sure foundation of truth upon which it rests. Our knowledge does in fact have a sure foundation, because it rests on the authority of the Old and New Testaments (1:19–21; 3:15–16). Scripture is essential to saving faith. Faith must rest upon Scripture or it is not a saving faith at all. The enemies of the gospel are fully aware of the importance of Scripture. That is why they deny and corrupt it. By these methods they introduce heresies of destruction and turn souls away from the purity of the gospel (2:1–3). This is nothing new. There were false prophets in Old Testament times. It happened in Israel, and it still happens in the church. There are always false prophets who sound very plausible, but they are nonetheless discernible as false prophets. False prophets are always unscriptural in their doctrine and usually unclean in their lives. They are arrogant scoffers who set themselves and their opinions above the prophets of the Old Testament and the apostles of the New Testament. For various reasons they do not like the thought of Christ's coming again (3:3–4). However, God has always judged this kind of wickedness. He will do it again.

Meantime, what are we to do? We must be patient. We must remember the rock of Scripture upon which we stand. We must repudiate every deviation from that Scripture, and we must ensure that we ourselves are ever more deeply rooted in the Scripture and its certainty. The best answer to apostates is a people whose knowledge of Christ is deep, real, and constantly increasing. Such people do not provide fertile ground for the ideas of apostates. They are rather the most capable instruments God has to expose them and put them to flight. Let us then "grow in grace, and in the knowledge of our Lord and Saviour Jesus Christ" (3:18).

In a nutshell, that is Peter's argument. We may sum it all up in one sentence. What Peter teaches here is that **the challenge of apostasy will be crushed by a true knowledge of Christ in God's people.** As he develops this theme he calls upon God's people to recognize four things.

THE FAITH OF THE GOSPEL

First, Peter calls on us to recognize the faith of the gospel. He speaks eloquently of the exercise of our faith for salvation and for Christian living. But trust must always have truth to trust in. That is exactly what the gospel of Scripture provides. Peter was concerned that God's people would not forget this. In 1:12 he says, "I will not be negligent to put you always in remembrance of these things, though ye know them, and be established in the present truth." The "present truth" means simply "the truth which you now have." In effect he says, "Keep in mind the truth you have received in the gospel. Do not depart from it." It is a cardinal error in God's people to imagine that spiritual maturity means growing beyond the fundamentals of the gospel. On the contrary, Christian development is but a further and fuller understanding of the very heart of the gospel of Jesus Christ. Nowadays, while Christians rush to try one new method of Christian growth after another, the great central truths of the person, work, and blood atonement of Christ, justifying grace, and the power and exercise of faith in that grace are all but ignored as if they were only for babes. The very opposite is the case. We must be established in the present truth.

But what is that truth? Peter has already given a wide-ranging statement of it in his first epistle. In this second epistle he is content to restate some of the major points controverted by the apostates of his day. He sums up the essence of the gospel in 1:16 as "the power and coming of our Lord Jesus Christ." In other words, the Lord Jesus Christ whose majesty Peter witnessed privately on earth is coming back again, powerfully and publicly. That is the very heart of the gospel. He was once manifested to put away sin. He will be manifested the second time without sin unto salvation. That is a fundamental doctrine, first because it establishes the person of Christ as divine, and second because it clearly shows the full results of His work. Let us look at those two things—the person and the work of Christ—a little more closely.

The apostolic doctrine of the person of Christ is the heart of the gospel. He is our Lord and Saviour (2:20). He is our God and Saviour (1:1). In this text the expression "the righteousness of God and our Saviour Jesus Christ" does not make a distinction between the person of God and the person of our Saviour. The construction of the Greek is very clear. It has only one meaning: our Saviour Jesus Christ is God. So Christ is the Lord and Saviour. He is our God and Saviour. He is also the Son of the Father (1:17). Therefore, His power is utterly divine (1:3). This, in summary, is the doctrine of the person of Christ.

Flowing from it is the doctrine of the work of Christ. In his very first statement of Christ's person Peter introduces the idea of His work (1:1):

"Simon Peter, a servant and an apostle of Jesus Christ, to them that have obtained like precious faith with us through the righteousness of God and our Saviour Jesus Christ." This is a most important statement. Peter is saying what Paul teaches throughout his epistles: it is by the righteousness of Christ that we receive faith and salvation. Some commentators deny that *righteousness* here has any forensic meaning. They exclude any reference to the imputed righteousness of Christ. One modern American evangelical commentator says that the word simply means justice or fairness. According to him Peter is teaching that God is no respecter of persons, and so in fairness He has granted us faith and salvation. This is mere invention, and a most dangerous invention at that. The righteousness that is mentioned is not the attribute of God's eternal justice. It is specifically the righteousness of Jesus Christ, which has the usual meaning of His obedience in life and death on our behalf to make us acceptable to God. Furthermore, it is not fairness but grace that saves sinners. "God in fairness gave us all faith and salvation" is a sentiment nowhere taught in Scripture. It was God's grace that made Him reach out to us. To say it was fairness rather than the vicarious righteousness of Christ that brought us faith and salvation inevitably leads to the notion of a divine obligation to sinners—that God owes them His salvation, otherwise He would not be fair. Such a notion is obnoxious to Scripture. Peter's teaching is far different: through the righteousness, that is, the obedience in life and death, of Jesus Christ, we receive faith and salvation.

Here, then, is the essence of the gospel. The second Person of the trinity, the eternal Son of the Father, became our Lord and our Saviour, and through His righteousness we have received faith and salvation. This same Jesus is coming again to inaugurate the day of the Lord. This, according to Peter, is the message of the gospel—remember it and do not be shifted from it.

THE FOUNDATION OF THE FAITH

The second thing Peter calls on us to remember is the foundation of the faith of the gospel: "We have also a more sure word of prophecy; whereunto ye do well that ye take heed, as unto a light that shineth in a dark place, until the day dawn, and the day star arise in your hearts: knowing this first, that no prophecy of the scripture is of any private interpretation. For the prophecy came not in old time by the will of man: but holy men of God spake as they were moved by the Holy Ghost" (1:19–21). This is a very critical passage in the New Testament, indeed, one of the most important passages in all the Bible on the subject of the inspiration of Scripture. There are two suggested interpretations.

Many modern commentators hold that the passage simply means that after seeing Christ's majesty at His transfiguration (v. 16), Peter, James, and John felt the prophecies of the Old Testament to be surer, or more confirmed, than ever. Thus their preaching was not based on myths but on God's confirmed word. A second interpretation, perhaps more widely held, is that having testified to what he had seen and heard on the Mount of Transfiguration, Peter continues, "We have also a more sure word of prophecy. We have the written Word of God. If you doubt my report of what I saw and heard, then listen to the Old Testament Scripture. It is God's written Word. The false teachers who so arrogantly withstand us must equally reject the Old Testament Scriptures to establish their peculiar doctrines."

Whichever interpretation we take, it is clear that Peter intends us to grasp the fact that the Scriptures are the inspired Word of God. No Scripture prophecy originated with the prophet who bore it: "Knowing this first, that no prophecy of the scripture is of any private interpretation" (v. 20). For a long time the Church of Rome used this text to support the notion that no individual could come privately to the Bible to interpret it. He had to have the interpretation of the Church. But that is not what Peter teaches. The word *interpretation* speaks of the origin of Scripture, not our understanding of it. No Scripture sprang from the private ideas of any of the prophets: "For the prophecy came not in old time by the will of man: but holy men of God spake as they were moved by the Holy Ghost" (v. 21). This written Word of God is the secure foundation for our faith.

So tenaciously did Peter hold to this truth that he would not make what he personally saw and heard on the Mount of Transfiguration a basis to establish anything that could not be established from the written Word of God. Theologically that is one of the most important things in this book. A doctrine had to be scriptural to be Christian. Peter included the New Testament writings, mentioning especially the writings of Paul, in his definition of inspired Scripture. Clearly, however, he saw the writings of the apostles as developments of Old Testament prophecy, founded on it and agreeable to it. Here is the foundation for our faith. It is not tradition. It is not the views, visions, or plausible ideas of men. The old Reformation slogan still holds good: *"Sola Scriptura."* By Scripture alone can we establish gospel truth.

THE FIGHT FOR THE FAITH

The third thing Peter calls on us to remember is the fight for the faith. Many Christians nowadays are unwilling to engage in what Paul termed "the good fight" of faith. To engage in theological conflict is to invite the scorn of this ecumenical age. People who fight for the faith are likely to be reviled as unloving or judgmental. The spirit of the age is one of theological compromise. We should not, we are told, divide over doctrine. We must all learn to worship and work together, whether Roman Catholic or Protestant, evangelical or liberal—that is the spirit of the age. Peter's position was entirely different. He says we must remember that there is a fight for the faith.

That fight starts at the very point he has been so concerned to establish, the place and purity of the Word of God. The apostates and false teachers in Peter's day attacked the Scripture's place as God's authoritative standard of faith and practice. Apostates and heretics still attack God's Word. They do so in one or other of the following ways: first, by denying biblical truth, for example on the person and work of Christ; second, by speaking their own high-sounding words and vain pretensions (2:18); and third, by twisting the Scriptures and perverting them to suit their malignant purpose (3:16). Any time we have any or all of these attacks on Scripture, we have apostasy. This is an ongoing fight, and Christians must be aware of the challenge.

The leading characteristics of the apostasy of Peter's day are all too obvious today, and often they are accepted as entirely Christian. Consider the following features of the apostasy Peter fought and see if they are not alarmingly widespread in churches nowadays.

The denial of Lordship to their professed Saviour by people who claim to be Christians (2:1). Is it not a badge of evangelical orthodoxy in many Bible-believing churches that you can take Christ as your Saviour while refusing Him as your Lord? For years now American evangelicalism has been rocked by the "Lordship salvation" controversy. To many the denial of the Lordship of Christ is no more than a lack of spiritual maturity. To Peter it was a heresy of destruction.

Making the gospel of grace an excuse for sin (3:16; 2:21–22). Peter's opponents argued that since God chose us and saved us without reference to our works, how we live cannot affect our standing in grace. Therefore it does not matter how we live. Against them Peter argued that to take the doctrine of free grace, which is entirely scriptural, and make it a license to sin, is apostasy. Thus he calls those who teach such things "spots . . . and blemishes, sporting themselves with their own deceivings while they feast with you; having eyes full of adultery" (2:13, 14). People who make grace a cloak for sin are yet strangers to grace, for though it is without any work of ours to merit it, grace always produces works as its inevitable fruit.

Selling the eternal for the temporal (2:15). An overemphasis on the here and now and the devaluation of the rewards of grace in eternity are characteristic of apostasy. It is a telltale sign of a heresy of destruction that it ignores the rewards and punishments of eternity and uses religion merely or chiefly as a means of temporal profit or pleasure. Yet, though this is something Peter fought, nothing is more commonly accepted in our day.

Advocating friendship with the world (2:15). As Balaam brought the Moabitesses into the camp of Israel and led God's people into the disastrous compromise of Baal-peor, many false prophets in the church are busy trying to remove all the barriers between the church and the world. "The friendship of the world is enmity with God" (James 4:4). James tells us it is spiritual adultery, which means it is idolatry. It is apostasy.

Making salvation merely "this worldly" and not ultimately "other worldly" (3:3–4). Peter's words were directed at those who scoffed at the blessed hope of Christ's return. To them salvation was mainly a thing of this age. The church always has to face this danger. The idea that salvation deals mainly with the here and now is the fundamental tenet of the social gospel, of social justice theology, and of liberation theology. Each of these, in its own way, interprets redemption in social and political terms, usually to the exclusion of such biblical doctrines as vicarious atonement and eternal life with Christ in heaven. Obviously God's people must have a conscience about the social needs of their fellow men. Every great advance in the social wellbeing of mankind has sprung from the spread of the gospel. Nevertheless, we must never mistake the gospel for anything that is merely "this worldly." We may feed a man. We may clothe him, educate him, give him a job, endow him with all sorts of political rights, and still leave him on the broad road to eternal ruin.

The Lord hates this apostasy. He fought against it throughout the period of the Old Testament (chap. 2). He will do so again. So what should our attitude to such apostasy be? We should be as opposed to it as our Saviour is. We should have no part of it or fellowship with it. Rather, we should oppose it and "earnestly contend for the faith" (Jude 3).

THE FRUIT OF THE FAITH

The final thing Peter calls on us to remember is the fruit that faith must produce in the lives of Christians. Gospel faith makes demands of us. A faith that makes no demands of us is a false faith. A cynic once said that the Christian experience is "an initial spasm followed by chronic inertia." Sadly, there is all too much truth in that as far as most professing Christians are concerned. But true gospel faith is not like that. It is fruitful. Note how Peter stresses this fact. He says, "Make your calling and election sure" (2 Pet. 1:10). Clearly spiritual fruit is the evidence of spiritual faith. In 3:11 Peter asks, "What manner of persons ought ye to be in all holy conversation and godliness?" In the verses that follow he answers his own question. The climax of that answer is found in verses 17–18: "Beware lest ye also, being led away with the error of the wicked, fall from your own steadfastness. But grow in grace, and in the knowledge of our Lord and Saviour Jesus Christ."

How are we to do that? Peter gives us the answer in 1:5–7: "And beside this, giving all diligence, add to your faith virtue; and to virtue knowledge; and to knowledge temperance; and to temperance patience; and to patience godliness; and to godliness brotherly kindness; and to brotherly kindness charity." J. A. Bengel, the famous German commentator, said of these verses, "Each step gives birth to and facilitates the next. Each subsequent quality balances and brings to perfection the one preceding." *Add* is a lovely word. It comes from a word signifying the leader of a stage chorus or dance, or a sponsor at the Athenian drama or music festivals. Rich men vied for the privilege of defraying the expenses of the chorus on such occasions. That is the word that Peter uses. Clearly, Christians must be willing to grow in grace whatever the cost. But there is another thought in the word *add.* The graces of the Christian life are like so many parts of a beautiful chorus. They blend together to produce a balanced and harmonious experience of Christ that gives us what Moses called "days of heaven upon the earth."

Christian life starts with faith. We are justified by faith (Rom. 5:1) and become the children of God by faith (Gal. 3:26). He who has no faith in Christ is lost (Mark 16:16). Faith is God's initial gift of grace to us (2 Pet. 1:1, where *obtained* means obtained by gift; Eph. 2:8). Everything else proceeds from this.

Peter says, "Add to your faith virtue," or "By your faith supply virtue." "Supply" is a good translation of the verb, as is clear from 1:11, where it is translated "minister." *By your faith supply virtue,* or goodness, or excellence. What is excellence? The word here means that which fully expresses what we are meant to be. The excellence of a sword is that it is sharp and it pierces. Without these qualities it is not a good sword. What is the excellence of a Christian? Peter gives us the answer in verses 3–4: Christ has called us to glory and virtue, and His divine power has given us exceeding great and precious promises, making us who have escaped the corruption and filthiness of the world partakers of the divine nature. That is why we are Christians. The excellence of a Christian is to walk in goodness unto glory. This is the gospel answer to the downward pull of the old man in all of us.

By your goodness supply knowledge, or practical wisdom, "which distinguishes the good from the bad and shows the way of flight from the bad" (Bengel). This is the answer to the deceptiveness of temptation.

By your knowledge supply temperance, or self-control. It is by a practical knowledge of the Word of God that we are be able to exercise godly self-control. Temperance is the gospel answer to the dangers Christians face from the pleasures of the world. Those pleasures are very seductive and can quickly master us. We need that self-control which one writer defined as "submission to the control of the indwelling Christ."

By your self-control supply patience, or endurance, or perseverance. Here is the answer to the dangers Christians face from the pain the world inflicts upon us. Perseverance is "the temper of mind which is unmoved by difficulty and distress, and which can withstand the Satanic agencies of opposition from the world without and enticement from the flesh within" (T. Green).

By your perseverance supply godliness, or reverence, the fear of God and respect for His people. This reverence will save us from the fear of man and set us free to serve the Lord and His church.

By your godliness supply brotherly love. He who does not love his brother whom he has seen certainly does not love God whom he has not seen. Brotherly love is the gospel safeguard against bitterness and division. We are called to separate from apostates but not from those of like precious faith.

By your brotherly love supply charity, which is love at its spiritual summit. It is love for God and love from God. It has its root in what God is, what He has done for us, and what He has made us. It is a fixation of mind and will for the good of its object. It is such a love for our Saviour as compels us to live for Him according to His Word and to eschew everything that is unworthy of His name.

This is the fruit of faith. It is not perfect in any Christian, but it is present in every Christian. Peter desired his readers to keep that in mind. If they would remember the faith of the gospel, understand its foundation in the Word of God, and commit themselves to fight for its purity against all destructive heresy while producing its fruit in vital godliness, they would never fall a prey to the deceptions of apostasy.

That is Peter's message to us. All around us apostasy is deepening. If it were possible, its deceptions would destroy the very elect. To overcome it we must get back to basics, to the pristine faith of the gospel. Only by a true knowledge of Christ can Christians crush the challenge of apostasy.

23

The Epistles of John
Christian Profession Tested And Proved

John's epistles present one of the most penetrating

♦

examinations of Christian profession in all the Bible

♦

and show what the biblical evidences of true Christianity

♦

really are. John expounds the essence of true Christianity:

♦

the Lord Jesus Christ brings His people into a fellowship

♦

with God that is exclusive to true believers and that

♦

shapes their attitudes both to false professors and to

♦

genuine Christians.

*T*he three epistles of John are closely related. The first is the final general epistle of the New Testament. The other two are personal letters, each of a single chapter. These two brief books pick up and illustrate parts of the main argument of the first epistle. Thus we may profitably consider their central message as one. That is not to say that there is not a distinctive emphasis in each epistle. There is.

In 1 John the theme is the fellowship of those who have been born of God. They walk in light before the Lord and in love among their brethren. Any other walk professing to be Christian betrays the hypocrisy of the professor. Thus 1 John gives seven tests of religious profession and seven marks that assure believers of the genuineness of their profession. In that assurance they enjoy their fellowship with God in prayer and look forward with confidence to Christ's return.

The theme in 2 John is the rejection of deceivers: "Whosoever transgresseth, and abideth not in the doctrine of Christ, hath not God. He that abideth in the doctrine of Christ, he hath both the Father and the Son. If there come any unto you, and bring not this doctrine, receive him not into your house, neither bid him God speed: for he that biddeth him God speed is partaker of his evil deeds" (vv. 9–11). The argument is very simple: "If you are abiding in the doctrine, you have the Father and the Son; you are in fellowship with God. But fellowship with God presupposes separation from the enemies of God. It presupposes separation from deceivers and from antichrist." In a day when ecumenical evangelists demand that we accept and support the integration of believers and heretics or apostates to sponsor what purports to be the gospel of Christ (but is not), we need to remember this teaching. The Bible calls not for integration with, but for separation from, apostasy. God's Word commands us not to fellowship with apostates even in what appears to be a good cause. The end does not justify the means. We are not Jesuits. We are Christians. The only thing that justifies the means we adopt is the Word of God and obedience to that Word.

The theme of 3 John reverts to the positive aspect of Christian fellowship. While we must maintain a sturdy rejection of apostates, we must equally maintain a hearty reception of God's faithful servants: "We therefore ought to receive such, that we might be fellowhelpers to the truth. I wrote unto the church: but Diotrephes, who loveth to have the preeminence among them, receiveth us not. Wherefore, if I come, I will remember his deeds which he doeth, prating against us with malicious words: and not content therewith, neither doth he himself receive the brethren, and forbiddeth them that would, and casteth them out of the church. Beloved, follow not that which is evil, but that which is good. He that doeth good is of God: but he that doeth evil hath not seen God.

Demetrius hath good report of all men, and of the truth itself: yea, and we also bear record; and ye know that our record is true" (vv. 8–12).

Combining the themes of the epistles, we may say that their central message is that the Lord Jesus Christ brings His people into a spiritual fellowship which is exclusive to true believers. This naturally raises serious questions: Who are true believers? How may we recognize them? Indeed, how may we know that we are true believers? The epistles of John give us very full answers to these questions.

John gives us seven statements of purpose to explain why he wrote. They are all summed up in his declaration in 1 John 5:13: "These things have I written unto you that believe on the name of the Son of God; that ye may know that ye have eternal life, and that ye may believe on the name of the Son of God." Thus these epistles show us plainly how we may be sure we are true believers.

They do so by drawing a series of stark contrasts between true Christians and false professors. These antithetical statements are a feature of the epistles. The apostle does not mince words. He speaks of Christ and antichrist, of God and of the world, of light and of darkness, of the truth and of the lie, of righteousness and of sin, of life and of death, of love and of hatred, of those who believe and of those who believe not, of those who confess Christ and of those who deny Christ. He calls believers the children of God. He calls unbelievers the children of the devil. He says that true believers will have confidence before Christ at His coming, while false professors will have shame. He describes the Lord Jesus Christ as the righteous One, the Head of the whole family in heaven, and Satan as the wicked one, with the whole world in his hand. The ultimate statement of the contrast between believers and empty professors is 1 John 5:12: "He that hath the Son hath life; and he that hath not the Son of God hath not life."

In the light of such contrasts we are not surprised to find that John probes deeply into the professions of those who claim to be Christians. He exposes some who had gained entrance into the church as deceivers and as enemies of Christ. The particular people John had in mind were some of the earliest proponents of what came to be known as the Gnostic heresy. Gnostics made loud professions of superior knowledge and spiritual experience. They presented themselves as the elite of the church. John showed that in fact they had no place in the church. They were not Christians at all.

John's exposure of the Gnostics goes far beyond the limited confines of that ancient sect. His method of exposing them was to show the fundamental nature of true faith in Christ and set it side by side with empty profession. He gives us seven tests of religious profession. We will look more closely at these in due course. For the moment it is enough to point out that John establishes clear and objective grounds on which to judge a person's profession of faith in Christ. Alongside his seven tests of profession he gives seven grounds of assurance, using such expressions as "Hereby ye know," or "By this we know."

All this gives us a clear insight into the central theme and purpose of the epistles of John. Here **religious profession is probed and proved.** In developing this theme the apostle builds one truth upon another, as follows:

First, true Christians enjoy a real fellowship with God in Christ.

Second, this fellowship with God produces true godliness.

Third, this true godliness produces a well-grounded assurance of salvation.

That brings us full circle: fourth, assurance of salvation produces confidence to enjoy our fellowship with God in victory over the world.

That is the outline of John's thought in this first epistle. Let us consider it in detail.

CHRISTIANS HAVE FELLOWSHIP WITH GOD

True Christians enjoy a real fellowship with God in Christ. John gives as one of his reasons for writing that "ye also may have fellowship with us: and truly our fellowship is with the Father, and with his Son Jesus Christ" (1 John 1:3). He at once develops the theme of fellowship with God: "If we say that we have fellowship with him, and walk in darkness, we lie, and do not the truth: but if we walk in the light, as he is in the light, we have fellowship one with another, and the blood of Jesus Christ his Son cleanseth us from all sin" (vv. 6–7). The root meaning of the word translated "fellowship" is sharing. From that it develops to mean "intimacy of association on the basis of something or some things in common." That is as true of the English word *fellowship* as it is of the Greek *koinonia.* It is the idea of an intimacy, friendship, association, and knitting of hearts on the basis of something or some things the participants have in common. It is therefore a beautiful word to express a Christian's relationship with God in the Lord Jesus Christ. It is a glorious truth that we have fellowship with God because of what we have in common with Him. At first that sounds too much for mere men to claim. However, John's message is that we share in His life. The very name given to the Lord Jesus Christ (1:2) is "eternal life." That is how John commences his first epistle. He ends it by saying, "We are in him that is true, even in his Son Jesus Christ. This is the true God, and eternal life" (5:20). Peter says that we are made partakers of the divine nature (2 Pet. 1:4). We are not made part of God, but He communicates to us the life that is in Christ Jesus. Not only do we share in His life but also in His light and His love (1 John 1:7; 2:5). So on the basis of what we have from Him, we have fellowship with God.

This fellowship is established by God's action, not ours. It is very important that we understand this. However much the religions of men disagree in points of detail, they all agree on one thing, that is, on man's seeking to establish a participation with or in the infinite by means of what he is or what he does. Every false religion ultimately betrays itself by this: it leaves the onus upon man to establish that fellowship, that relationship with God. The gospel is altogether different. It says that fellowship with God must be on account of His action. John puts it like this: "In this was manifested the love of God toward us, because that God sent his only begotten Son into the world, that we might live through him. Herein is love, not that we loved God, but that he loved us, and sent his Son to be the propitiation for our sins" (4:9–10). He adds, "We love him, because he first loved us" (v. 19). No man can ever enter into fellowship, or obtain a saving relationship, with God on the basis of his works, or morality. No man can take any credit for the salvation of his soul. The world says, "Do this and live." God says there is nothing for a sinner to do to be saved. Jesus Christ has done it all. We do not obtain our salvation by doing but by resting. We do not achieve fellowship with God by activity, but by faith in the finished work of the Lord Jesus Christ. The call of the gospel to the sinner who is perishing in his sin is to abandon all hope in the flesh and to embrace Christ as He is freely offered in the gospel. Every sinner who comes by faith to Christ will be saved and will enter into fellowship with God, because it is established by God's action and not by ours.

This brings us back to the point that we have fellowship with God on the basis of something in common. What God and the believer have in common is that *both are satisfied with Christ.* There is a beautiful picture of this truth in the peace offering of the Old Testament. Part of the peace offering was burned on the altar: God was satisfied. The offerer also ate a part of the sacrifice: the believer was satisfied. God and man were satisfied with the same sacrifice. All this found its fulfilment in the sacrifice of Christ, whom the Father sent "to be the propitiation for our sins" (4:10). That sacrifice satisfied God's righteous wrath, His justice, and His holy law. It equally satisfied our need. God and the believer meet around the altar of Christ's cross. We have fellowship.

We have fellowship with Christ because He and His people are graciously united so that *we share in His merits.* John puts it beautifully in chapter 4:17: "As he is, so are we in this world." That is one of the deepest and greatest statements in the Bible. It means essentially the same as Eph. 1:6: "He hath made us accepted in the beloved." Though we are yet in the world and are afflicted by faults and temptations, we are in Christ. God invests us with the merit and standing of our righteous Head. He is God's Son; we are God's children. He is the object of the Father's love; so are we. God sees us in Him and treats us as possessors of His merit.

We have fellowship with God through Jesus Christ because *we have been born of God and His seed remains in us* (1 John 3:9). *Seed* has been variously understood by commentators. Some see it as a reference to divine life, or to the Holy Spirit, or to the Word of God. In fact, all three ideas appear in 1 John. His life (3:14–15), His Word (2:14), and His Holy Spirit (4:13) abide within us.

John further describes our fellowship with God in terms of *the Holy Spirit's working in us to teach and guide us:* "Ye have an unction from the Holy One, and ye know all things. . . . The anointing which ye have received of him abideth in you, and ye need not that any man teach you" (2:20, 27). Bishop Westcott points out that the anointing refers not to "the act of anointing, but that with which it was performed." Anointing was usually performed with oil. Here it speaks of the Holy Spirit. At His baptism Christ was anointed with the Holy Spirit (Matt. 3:16; Acts 10:38). Believers also receive the anointing of the Spirit (2 Cor. 1:21–22). The result of that anointing is that "ye know all things." This does not mean that Christians are omniscient and have no further need of instruction. Rather, it means that all that Christians need to know is in the gospel. They have no need of any human theory, for they have the revelation of God in His Son. The Holy Spirit has the special ministry of revealing Christ and of leading His people into His truth (John 14:26; 15:26; 16:13–15). It is common nowadays for preachers to give the impression that while the gospel is necessary for salvation, we need to progress beyond it if we are to come to grips with the complex problems of modern life. Thus they introduce all sorts of psychological theories. The Word of God says the very opposite: "Ye have an unction from the Holy One." We who have an anointing of the Holy Spirit do not need anything beyond the gospel. There God has given us everything we need for life, for death, and for eternity. We do not need Christ plus something else. We need Christ. The incarnation, the virgin birth, the sinless life, the perfect obedience, the atoning death, the bodily resurrection of Jesus Christ, His current intercession, His coming again in glory, our justification by grace through faith, our acceptance with God, our peace with God—these are the "all things" that Christians know. There is no knowledge in the world superior to, or comparable with, the knowledge of the gospel. Other subjects—accountancy, languages, law, etc.—are legitimate fields of study, but the knowledge of the gospel is the only thing that equips us for life here and hereafter.

Here, then, is our fellowship with God in Christ: it is established by God's action, procured by the merits of the blood of the Lord Jesus Christ, with whom we are in vital union so that we are justified freely by His grace. His seed and life remain within us, and His Spirit teaches, guides, and directs us. This fellowship with God has certain characteristic marks.

First, it is *biblical:* "That which we have seen and heard declare we unto you, that ye also may have fellowship with us" (1 John 1:3). He expounds this further in 4:6: "We are of God: he that knoweth God heareth us; he that is not of God heareth not us. Hereby know we the spirit of truth, and the spirit of error." Clearly, those who know God hear His inspired messengers. In other words, the fellowship we have with God is biblical. That was the first mark of the new converts at Pentecost: "They continued steadfastly in the apostles' doctrine" (Acts 2:42). Fellowship with God is always biblical. John emphasizes this in his three epistles by his multiplied references to "the truth." Twenty times he uses the word *truth,* with another seven references to *true.* Clearly John intends to set forth an objective basis to judge the claims men make for their fellowship with God. Anything that is unbiblical does not spring from fellowship with God.

In John's day Gnostics claimed all sorts of spiritual insights and experiences, professedly the results of fellowship with God. John argued that the unbiblical nature of their theories proved they did not have fellowship with God. We need to remember that argument today. Citing special visions—and even physical visits to heaven—as their authority, some Charismatic preachers have taught some wildly unbiblical nonsense. One of America's most celebrated Charismatic evangelists said that each person of the trinity was Himself a trinity, so that there really were "nine of them." The same preacher and another Charismatic leader have argued vehemently that from all eternity God essentially has a material body. This preacher also assures us that Adam was a superman who could fly intergalactically. These unbiblical fantasies and heresies do not proceed from fellowship with God. The closer we become to the Lord, the more biblical we will be.

Fellowship with God is also *joyful:* "These things write we unto you, that your joy may be full" (1 John 1:4). The Bible knows nothing of that dismal religion that too many people think is Christianity. The Bible takes note of the sorrows and sufferings of God's people, but it also teaches us of a joy in Christ that is unspeakable and full of glory, a joy that endures through the bleakest circumstances of life.

When we know that God is our Father and Christ is our Saviour, that His blood has made propitiation for our sins, that the Holy Spirit abides within us and we are in living fellowship with the living God, and that heaven is our home for all eternity, we have a fulness of joy the world cannot remove or destroy.

Fellowship with God is also *progressive:* "If we walk in the light, as he is in the light, we have fellowship one with another" (1:7). John here makes an important distinction. We *walk* in the light. God *is* in the light. Walking speaks of progression. The more we walk in the light, the deeper will be our fellowship with Him who "is light, and in him is no darkness at all" (1:5).

Fellowship with God is also *holy:* "If we walk in the light, as he is in the light, we have fellowship one with another, and the blood of Jesus Christ his Son cleanseth us from all sin" (1:7). Walking with the Lord in the light of His Word, we will know the constant cleansing of the precious blood of Christ. Living in the constant experience of the power of the blood of Christ is a perfect way to describe the fellowship God has established for His people in His Son.

FELLOWSHIP PRODUCES GODLINESS

This fellowship produces true godliness. Sinful living and fellowship with God do not go together. Some people in John's day professed deep fellowship with God but were wicked in both doctrine and practice. John calls them deceivers and antichrists. In his first epistle he goes to great lengths to expose this kind of false profession. Seven times in the epistle he says, "If we say," or "He that saith," or "If a man say." This is the sevenfold test of religious profession we noted earlier. As each one of us stands before these texts of Scripture, the supreme question is whether our teaching and behaviour are consistent with each other and with the apostolic proclamation that God is light and in Him is no darkness at all. Here are the seven tests. They plainly expose the perverse claims of the deceivers of John's day. They are just as potent in our day.

The first perverse claim John answers is that sin does not hinder fellowship with God: "If we say that we have fellowship with him, and walk in darkness, we lie, and do not the truth" (1:6). The second perverse claim John answers is that sin does not exist in our nature; we are naturally good. He replies, "If we say that we have no sin, we deceive ourselves, and the truth is not in us" (1:8). The third perverse claim John deals with is that sin is not really sin. John's opponents had developed a neat little philosophy to enable themselves to live wickedly without feeling guilt. They wanted to redefine their actions so as to avoid what God's Word teaches about sin. John answered their claimed innocence:

"If we say that we have not sinned, we make him a liar, and his word is not in us" (1:10). The fourth false claim John answers is that obedience to God's commandments is not essential to knowing God. John replies, "He that saith, I know him, and keepeth not his commandments, is a liar, and the truth is not in him" (2:4). The fifth perverse claim John deals with is that an un-Christlike walk is no evidence against our being in Christ. To this John replies, "He that saith he abideth in him ought himself also so to walk, even as he walked" (2:6). The sixth perverse claim John deals with is that we may be in the light of God while living in the darkness of hatred toward His people. John rejects this: "He that saith he is in the light, and hateth his brother, is in darkness even until now" (2:9). The final perverse claim John deals with is that we can love God while hating our brother. John shows the impossibility of this: "If a man say, I love God, and hateth his brother, he is a liar: for he that loveth not his brother whom he hath seen, how can he love God whom he hath not seen?" (4:20).

Here are seven great texts, seven great tests of Christian profession. In each of them the Word of God contradicts the claims of empty professors. A man who makes any of these empty professions shows by doing so that he is not born of God, for "whosoever is born of God doth not commit sin; for his seed remaineth in him: and he cannot sin, because he is born of God" (3:9). This does not teach that a true believer can never commit any sin, because John has already made it clear that if we say we have no sin, or that we have not sinned, we are liars. What it means is that he that is born of God cannot practise sin. That is the force of the present tense: he cannot constantly and habitually live in the practice of sin. The verse also carries the idea of sinning for sin's sake, making sin the great end of one's life. A man who can live happily in sin has never been born of God or brought into fellowship with Him, because fellowship with God produces godliness.

A very good summary of the godliness of which John speaks in his epistles is *Christlikeness*. Six times in the first epistle he uses the word *kathos*, "even as," to shows the Christian's likeness to Christ (2:6; 3:2, 3, 7, 23; 4:17).

We are to walk as Christ walked (2:6). We are to be pure as Christ is pure (3:3). We are to do righteousness as Christ did (3:7). We are to love one another as Christ commanded (3:23). Christlikeness is the heart of godliness, and godliness is the proof that we have fellowship with God.

GODLINESS PRODUCES ASSURANCE

The third main step in John's argument is that godliness produces in us a well-grounded assurance of salvation. How can a man know he is saved? What gives any of us the right to say, I am saved? There are various possible answers. On one level assurance arises from simply taking God at His Word. "Him that cometh to me I will in no wise cast out" (John 6:37). We may put the argument here in the form of a syllogism. Major premise: The Lord will not cast out any who come to Him. Minor premise: I have come to Him. Conclusion: Therefore He will not cast me out. So long as we understand "coming to Christ" as the Bible means us to, that is a very safe way to reach assurance of salvation.

There is another possible answer to the question of assurance. Paul says, "The Spirit itself beareth witness with our spirit, that we are the children of God" (Rom. 8:16). The immediate witness of the Holy Spirit to our spirit assures us that we are saved. But remember, the Spirit is the Spirit of truth, the One who inspired the Bible. As we have already noted, any claimed experience of the ministry of the Spirit must be according to Scripture. Revelation chapters 2 and 3 show that the message of Scripture is the witness of the Spirit: "He that hath an ear, let him hear what the Spirit saith unto the churches" (2:7, 11, etc.). When the Spirit bears witness with our spirit, He does so by applying the Scriptures to our heart.

That brings us to John's answer to the question of assurance. Eight times in the first epistle he uses the clauses, "Hereby we know," or "Hereby ye know," or "By this we know" (1 John 2:3, 5; 3:19, 24; 4:2, 6, 13; 5:2). Here is how we may know we are saved. The words of 3:18–19 are of particular value: "My little children, let us not love in word, neither in tongue; but in deed and in truth. And hereby we know that we are of the truth, and shall assure our hearts before him." When what we say we believe is expressed by what we do and how we live, when our faith produces works, when our profession produces Christlikeness, we may justly claim that the Spirit bears witness that we are the sons of God. We can assure our hearts before Him. This is the very same message as Paul's in 2 Cor. 5:17: "Therefore if any man be in Christ, he is a new creature: old things are passed away; behold, all things are become new." The evidence of a new life is assured proof of the new birth. Godliness and Christlikeness are evidences that give us a well-grounded hope and assurance of salvation.

This talk of evidences is not meant to degenerate into the bondage of morbid introspection. There are Christians who fail to enjoy full assurance because they seem to look more to their evidences than to Christ. Our godliness is never perfect in this life. Can we never then have perfect assurance? We can and we should. Christ is perfect, and our trust is in Him. That is why John writes, "If our heart condemn us, God is greater than our heart, and knoweth all things" (1 John 3:20). This is spoken for our comfort. There are times when the conscience of the truest Christian will condemn him, but, John argues, "When your heart condemns you, God is greater than your heart. He sees all things. He not only sees the thing in which you have failed. He also sees that He has put within you His Spirit, that He has united you to Christ, and that He has imputed to you the perfect righteousness of Christ. He sees the merits of Christ by which He is bringing you to heaven. God is greater than your heart. So be at peace in Christ." Our assurance is not based ultimately on how we live, but on Christ who enables us to live for Him at all. He has made us new creatures. Thus we can assure our hearts that we are ready for heaven.

CONFIDENCE TO ENJOY FELLOWSHIP AND VICTORY

The final step in John's argument brings us full circle: assurance produces confidence to enjoy our fellowship with God in victory over the world. John lays great emphasis on Christian confidence: "Beloved, if our heart condemn us not, then have we confidence toward God. And whatsoever we ask, we receive of him, because we keep his commandments, and do those things that are pleasing in his sight" (3:21–22). "And this is the confidence that we have in him, that, if we ask any thing according to his will, he heareth us: and if we know that he hear us, whatsoever we ask, we know that we have the petitions that we desired of him" (5:14–15).

Here is our confidence. When we come to God in prayer we do not come as those who cry in the dark. We come with the confidence that He hears His people. We come with the confidence that He who has created within us a desire to live in a godly fashion in the enjoyment of fellowship with Him will satisfy that desire. When we lift up our hearts to Him according to His will, He will grant our petitions. What a difference it makes to our prayer life when we pray with the confidence of those who are assured of the Father's grace.

That is not to say that Christian living and praying will be easy. As we seek to live for God and enjoy fellowship with Him, we face some very real battles. The devil is against us. The wicked one is very strong in this world. The whole world lies in the lap of wickedness. But God's people are born to be victors over Satan and the world: "Whatsoever is born of God overcometh the world: and this is the victory that overcometh the world, even our faith. Who is he that overcometh the world, but he that believeth that Jesus is the Son of God?" (5:4–5). Those who have the assurance that they live in fellowship with God have confidence to live by faith in the world, enjoying victory over sin and Satan. This is what John meant in 3 John 2 when he spoke to

Gaius about his soul *prospering*. Our soul is prospering when it lives in fellowship with God and in victory over the world, the flesh, and the devil. This is that eternal life which Christ gives. This is that faith which saves and that fellowship which sanctifies.

So ends John's probing treatment of Christian profession. Having exposed false professors and assured true believers, he encourages the latter to live out their Christian testimony to the full: "Love not the world, neither the things that are in the world. If any man love the world, the love of the Father is not in him. For all that is in the world, the lust of the flesh, and the lust of the eyes, and the pride of life, is not of the Father, but is of the world. And the world passeth away, and the lust thereof: but he that doeth the will of God abideth for ever" (2:15–17). In the searching light of John's epistles, do we stand exposed or assured?

24

Jude

God's Answer To The Abomination Of Apostasy

The gospel faces its greatest threat not from outside the

♦

church, but from inside, from apostates. God is against

♦

all apostates and will have no mercy on them. He calls

♦

His people to expose and oppose them both by earnestly

♦

contending for the faith and by exemplifying its power in

♦

their lives and service.

J. Maxwell Coder had a good title for his commentary on the epistle of Jude. He called it *The Acts of the Apostates.* That is certainly a title which goes to the very heart of the book. It is interesting that the final two books of the New Testament deal extensively with the subject of apostasy. Jude warns the people of God against an apostasy that was just beginning to emerge in those early days of the Christian church. In the book of Revelation the Lord reveals the final form of that apostasy. In Revelation apostasy no longer poses as a stealthy intruder but struts across the world's stage as the official religion of the nations. It will ultimately employ every vicious form of persecution in an effort to eradicate the truth of God from the earth. Not only will it signally fail to do that, but it will ultimately crash before the glory of the returning Christ.

All this should alert us that apostasy is a very vital subject. That has always been the case, but it is even more so as we approach the end of the age. That means that no Christian ministry can be faithful to Christ if it ignores the pervasive threat of apostasy to the gospel. To put it mildly, it is wrong to adopt the notion so prevalent today, that we must be so positive that we are afraid to identify error lest we appear negative. In the church it is easy to attack humanism. According to the Bible, however, humanism is not, was not, and never will be the great threat the church has to face. God's Word says apostasy is the real threat to the gospel. Paul told Timothy about this apostasy: "If thou put the brethren in remembrance of these things, thou shalt be a good minister of Jesus Christ, nourished up in the words of faith and of good doctrine, whereunto thou hast attained" (1 Tim. 4:6). A minister who is silent on the subject of apostasy has no right to be thought of as a good minister. He may be a popular minister. He may be a talented minister. He may appear a successful minister, but according to the Holy Ghost he is not a good minister if he is not willing to alert God's people to the danger of apostasy. That is how vital the Bible makes this subject.

This epistle was written by a man by the name of Jude or Judas. Here is a divine irony. Judas is a name forever associated with apostasy and betrayal. Judas, the apostate, the betrayer, sold the Christ of God. God chose another Judas to sound the gospel message and the note of alarm to warn the church against apostasy. This Jude or Judas, the brother of James, was of the family of Mary and Joseph, and therefore a half-brother of the Lord Jesus Christ. Like James, despite his family relationship with the Saviour, he calls himself "the servant of Jesus Christ" (v. 1). Jude wrote mainly to Jewish believers. It is obvious that he was greatly alarmed at the intrusion of apostates into the church. Peter had already written to warn of this apostasy, and Jude took up his warning as a matter of urgency.

He had intended to write a very different sort of letter, one that dealt with the salvation all Christians have in common. Preaching on apostasy is not really the joy of any good preacher's heart. It is much nicer to preach on justifying grace, the glories of the offices of the Lord Jesus Christ, and other great central themes of the gospel. That is what Jude had intended to do. He puts it very bluntly. He says, "I gave all diligence [or, using all diligence] to write unto you of the common salvation, it was needful for me to write unto you, and exhort you that ye should earnestly contend for the faith" (v. 3). Here then is Jude's theme: God's people have a great salvation set forth in what he calls "the faith which was once delivered unto the saints." The greatest danger to that faith comes not from the outside but from the inside. It comes from apostates who have professed the faith but now seek to corrupt it while remaining among God's people. Jude makes it clear that God is against apostates and will have no mercy on them. God's people likewise should expose and oppose these same apostates. In this ecumenical age when we are told that to be Christian you must love everything and everybody indiscriminately, that does not sound very loving or very Christian. But Jude's definition of Christianity was the right one. The modern definition is wrong. If we love the Lord then we will say with David, the man after God's own heart, "I hate them [God's enemies] with perfect hatred" (Ps. 139:22). Can we love God and yet love what God hates? Can we love Christ and yet be willing to go along with what puts Him to an open shame? No, no. God is against apostates, and so must His people be. The little epistle of Jude guides our opposition as it reveals **God's answer to the abominations of apostasy.** Keep in mind that Jude sounds two great notes in his message. He is going to sound these notes right throughout his epistle: salvation in Christ, and apostasy from Christ that seeks to corrupt the faith of the gospel. Thus he expounds the faith and exposes the threat that apostasy poses to it.

THE FAITH DEFINED

"The faith which was once delivered unto the saints" (v. 3), or "your most holy faith" (v. 20), refers not to the human act of believing but to the body of revealed truth in which one believes to the saving of his soul. Jude mentions some of the elements in this gospel message: "the common salvation" (v. 3), "the love of God," "the mercy of our Lord Jesus Christ unto eternal life" (v. 21), escape from "the fire" (v. 23), and preservation by the power of God "to present you faultless before the presence of his glory" (v. 24). Here then is the faith as Jude defines it: it is the scripturally revealed message of the person and work of the Lord Jesus Christ, by whom alone God gives sinners salvation from sin's penalty and brings them to enjoy eternal life and glory in His presence forever.

At the heart of this faith is the truth that Jesus Christ is God. Jude warns against those who deny "the only Lord God, and our Lord Jesus Christ" (v. 4). This is one of the most important verses in the New Testament in its testimony to the person of Christ. Literally, it speaks of "denying the only Master, our Lord and our God, Jesus Christ." Jude calls Christ "the only Master"—the Greek word gives us the English word *despot*—because He is our sovereign Ruler. The only Master is our God and our Lord, Jesus Christ. That is the Person who is at the heart of the gospel, the Person who is revealed in "the faith which was once delivered unto the saints," the Son of the Father. The gospel clearly presents the trinitarian faith. Christianity is trinitarian; antitrinitarianism is antichristian. Verse 1 speaks of "God the Father." Verse 4 clearly speaks of the Son, who though truly man is yet our Lord and our God, and yet who is distinguished from the Father (v. 1). Then verse 20 speaks of the Holy Spirit. Father, Son, and Holy Spirit: "These three are one God, the same in substance, equal in power and glory" (Shorter Catechism).

Jude summarizes Christ's work under the term *mercy* (v. 21), divine favour brought to us through all the Saviour did for us in His life, death, and resurrection. *Mercy* is a word that carries the idea that Christ's work deals with our sin despite the fact that we naturally deserve God's judgment. Here is the essence of the gospel. It is the story of a Saviour who came down from heaven to save us from "the fire" (v. 23) and bring us to "the presence of his glory" (v. 24). This is the only gospel that saves souls. Nothing else can set a sinner free. That is why Jude starts off by showing what the gospel actually does for men. He writes to them "that are sanctified by God the Father, and preserved in Jesus Christ, and called" (v. 1). The order of the words as Jude wrote them has caused interpreters a great deal of difficulty. The calling governs all that follows. It comes first, though it stands at the end in Jude's order of words. He is writing to those that are *called.* That is the first thing. The gospel comes to men as God's call. He who has the sovereign right to command comes tenderly to call us to Himself. He comes with pleading tones. God's pleading is powerful because when He effectually calls, He exercises the necessary power to give effect to His call—He not only asks us to come to Him, He brings us.

He calls, and then He *sanctifies,* or separates unto Himself those whom He calls. This is the same order of events as Paul notes in Rom. 8:29-30. And then He *keeps* those whom He sanctifies. He is able to keep them from falling and to present them faultless in heavenly glory. Calling, separating, and keeping are all divine acts. This is what the Lord does through the gospel. This is God's salvation. He effectually calls us and thereby separates us unto Christ. By means of that separation He preserves us "for Jesus Christ." This idea of preservation surfaces again in the stirring benediction with which this epistle climaxes: "Now unto him that is able to keep you from falling, and to present you faultless before the presence of his glory with exceeding joy" (v. 24). The word *keep* is a different word from *preserved* in verse 1. It is a word that speaks of guarding. The result is the same. God reserves, preserves, and keeps His people for Jesus Christ. How does He do it? He stands guard over them, to bring them to heaven with exceeding joy. This is the faith that Jude defined.

THE FAITH DENIED

The body of this epistle deals with the subject of the denial of the faith (vv. 4–16). Jude feels the necessity to put before God's people a stern reminder of the curse of apostasy. The entire New Testament is very insistent on doing the same thing. In His parable of the wheat and the tares the Lord Jesus warns us of the activity of an "enemy" in seeking to corrupt the work of God (Matt. 13:24–30). In His great message about the end times in Matthew 24 He warns, "Many false prophets shall rise, and shall deceive many" (v. 11). Worse still, "There shall arise false Christs, and false prophets, and shall show great signs and wonders; insomuch that, if it were possible, they shall deceive the very elect" (v. 24).

In his farewell speech to the elders of the church at Ephesus Paul warned, "After my departing shall grievous wolves enter in among you, not sparing the flock. Also of your own selves shall men arise, speaking perverse things, to draw away disciples after them" (Acts 20:29–30).

In Gal. 1:6–9 Paul writes, "I marvel that ye are so soon removed from him that called you into the grace of Christ unto another gospel: which is not another; but there be some that trouble you, and would pervert the gospel of Christ. But though we, or an angel from heaven, preach any other gospel unto you than that which we have preached unto you, let him be accursed. As we said before, so say I now again, If any man preach any other gospel unto you than that ye have received, let him be accursed." That is a strong statement that shows the inroads of apostasy into the church even in apostolic times.

Paul warns in 2 Thess. 2:3 concerning the coming of the Lord Jesus Christ, "That day shall not come, except there come a falling away [lit., the apostasy] first." Writing to Timothy, Paul repeats this note of warning: "The Spirit speaketh expressly, that in the latter times some shall depart from the faith, giving heed to seducing spirits, and doctrines of devils" (1 Tim. 4:1). In 2 Tim. 3:6–8 he alerts Timothy to the certainty that "in the last days" (v. 1) there would arise men with "a form of godliness, but denying the power thereof." He goes on to describe them: "For of this sort are they which creep into houses, and lead captive silly women laden with sins, led away with divers lusts, ever learning, and never able to come to the knowledge of the truth. Now as Jannes and Jambres withstood Moses, so do these also resist the truth: men of corrupt minds, reprobate concerning the faith."

Paul adds further solemn warnings against apostasy in Tit. 1:10–11, 16, and in Heb. 6:4–6; 10:26–29, 39. Peter adds his warning (2 Peter 2), as does John (1 John 2:18–19; 2 John 9–11).

This last text spells out the proper response a Christian should make to all apostates: "If there come any unto you, and bring not this doctrine, receive him not into your house, neither bid him God speed: for he that biddeth him God speed is partaker of his evil deeds." We must expose and oppose apostasy, which denies the heart of the gospel. That is the message. The New Testament writers are not dealing with minor differences of opinion. There were differences of opinion on nonessential matters in the early church. In those cases the apostles were willing to give liberty of conscience to each believer. For example, reading Romans 14, we find that Paul was not a man to major upon minors. The New Testament stands against building little things up into great things to divide the body of Christ unnecessarily. But when dealing with a fundamental departure from the faith, Christ and His apostles were uncompromising. That is why Jude speaks in such strong terms.

The apostasy Jude describes is a wilful and wicked rebellion against God and His gospel on the part of ungodly men who profess to be Christians. This is an evil that creeps into the church by stealth (v. 4). That is always the way apostasy operates. The modernistic and rationalistic apostasy that has devastated entire denominations did not arise overnight. Nor did it openly and honestly set itself up in opposition to the Scriptures. No, it was advanced by creepers who stealthily intruded into the church and who gradually spread their poison, destroying many. As Jude shows, apostasy has its own agenda and its own agents, and it perpetrates the most abominable actions that Satan can conceive, all with the purpose of robbing the gospel of its saving power and confusing the souls of men to their eternal destruction. That is why Jude's language is so very severe. Radical disease calls for radical surgery. That is what this epistle performs on the cancer of apostasy.

Starting at verse 4, Jude constructs a powerful indictment of apostasy. First, he lists *five marks that define the essence of apostasy*. Apostates creep in by stealth, dishonest and serpentlike, with the family characteristic of their father the devil clearly upon them. They fulfil the biblical predictions as to their character, methods, and message: they were "before of old ordained," or prewritten. They are "ungodly men," a description that occurs five more times in verses 15 and 18—they lack the fear of God that would give them wisdom and restrain them from the wickedness of their demonic doctrines. They "[turn] the grace of our God into lasciviousness," either by rejecting the truth of justification by free grace on the ground that it will lead to loose living (as the Church of Rome has always done), or by using grace as a license to sin (cf. Jer. 7:8–10). Finally, they deny the only Lord God, our Lord Jesus Christ, for apostasy is essentially an attack upon His person and/or His work. These are the five marks that define the essence of apostasy.

Second, Jude gives *three illustrations that demonstrate the end of apostasy* (vv. 5–7). The Israelite unbelievers in Moses' day denied the faith by wanting to go back into Egypt, and they died in the wilderness under the wrath of God. The angels that sinned and kept not their first estate were the first of all apostates: they are "reserved in everlasting chains under darkness unto the judgment of the great day." Sodom and Gomorrah are the third illustration of the end of apostasy, "suffering the vengeance of eternal fire."

Third, Jude presents *three acts that denote the excesses of apostasy* (vv. 8, 10). They "defile the flesh." They "despise dominion [or, lordship]." They "speak evil of dignities [or, blaspheme glories]." Considering these excesses, the apostle condemns apostates as brute beasts who blaspheme anything that is above the level of their own bestial nature.

Fourth, Jude names *three men as examples of apostasy*. He speaks of "the way of Cain," "the error of Balaam," and the gainsaying of Korah (v. 11). Here are examples of apostasy. *The way of Cain* was the doctrine of works instead of grace. Cain denied the blood, rejected the lamb, and presented the works of his own hands as the ground of his acceptance with God. *The error of Balaam* was the doctrine of compromise and integration with false religion. If Balaam lived today he would probably be made the president of the World Council of Churches. Certainly his repudiation of the separation of God's people from the heathen practices and worship of the surrounding nations is still rampant in parts of the professing church (Rev. 2:14).

The gainsaying of Korah is the usurpation of Christ's sole mediation. Korah rejected Moses' and Aaron's sole right to the place God had given them. In that place they stood as pictures of Christ, the sole Mediator between God and men. The apostasy of Korah denies Christ's unique mediation, perhaps not removing it altogether but putting other mediators alongside Him—as Rome does by exalting Mary to be co-redemptrix and co-mediatrix and by inventing a host of saints to act as intercessors for us in heaven.

Fifth, Jude gives us *five word pictures that denounce the effects of apostasy* (vv. 12–13). Apostates "are spots [or, hidden rocks] in your feasts of charity"—though they sit with you at the Lord's Table they are hidden but deadly dangers that will bring your work to shipwreck. They are clouds without water, seducing you with false promises. They are trees without fruit, displaying, like the fig tree in Matt. 21:19, an empty and fruitless profession. Apostasy has never produced one saint, or built one church, or witnessed one revival. It is entirely without the fruit of the Spirit of God. Jude also calls apostates "raging [or, wild] waves of the sea, foaming out their own shame," to denote the furious shame of apostasy. Finally, he calls them "wandering stars, to whom is reserved the blackness of darkness for ever" to show the rebellion and ruin of apostasy.

From all this it is clear that the virulent enmity of apostasy is focused on "the faith." It especially hates the sovereign preeminence of God, our Lord (v. 4). It is marked by a deliberate decision to break the bounds He has set. For example, the angels who apostasized *broke the bounds of the sphere their Creator had given them.* This has a clear parallel in the attempts of churches that have departed from the faith to adopt the agendas of such movements as radical feminism and the homosexual revolution—both of which are blatant attempts to break the sphere the Creator has allotted to men and women.

Sodom and Gomorrah deliberately *broke the bounds of God-ordained morality* with their sodomy and moral perversion. Once again we must note the modern parallel within the professing church. One major denomination after another has reconciled or attempted to reconcile the wicked immorality of the sexual revolution with its profession of Christianity. This is apostasy.

Cain, Balaam, and Korah *broke the bounds of revealed doctrine.* Departure from the central tenets of the gospel is often labelled progressive. It is not. It is regressive. It is the apostasy that turns the truth of God into a lie and worships and serves the creature and his vain delusions instead of the Creator who has given us His unsullied truth.

From these examples we may discern the campaign now being conducted by apostates at the highest levels of the major denominations of Christendom. In many cases denominations that once stood firmly for God's truth have fallen irretrievably under the control of apostates. According to Revelation 17 the situation is going to get worse. But apostasy is doomed to ultimate failure. As Paul said, "The foundation of God standeth sure" (2 Tim. 2:19). It is with confidence, therefore, that Christians should take their stand for the faith. That is the final part of Jude's message.

THE FAITH DEFENDED

There are two ways in which the faith is defended. First, *by God's people,* and second, *by the Lord Himself.*

We are to "earnestly contend for the faith" (v. 3). Contending is one very necessary way for us to defend it. There is another way, as verses 20–23 show, and that is to exemplify the power of the faith for which we contend: "But ye, beloved, building up yourselves on your most holy faith, praying in the Holy Ghost, keep yourselves in the love of God, looking for the mercy of our Lord Jesus Christ unto eternal life. And of some have compassion, making a difference: and others save with fear, pulling them out of the fire; hating even the garment spotted by the flesh." Here Jude shows us five major areas of life and service in which we must clearly show the power of the gospel at work.

Edification. We must not only contend for the faith but build our very lives on its truth.

Supplication. Praying in the Holy Ghost is praying under the direction of the Spirit, pleading the glorious truth of the gospel's promises and the powerful merit of Christ's blood. If our faith does not lead us to pray, it is suspect.

Motivation. The love of God in Christ is the believer's true motivation. That is what stirs our love for Him (1 John 4:19) and constrains us to serve Him (2 Cor. 5:14).

Expectation. Awaiting our Saviour's mercy unto eternal life is allowing the certainties of our faith to keep us "steadfast, unmoveable, always abounding in the work of the Lord" (1 Cor. 15:58).

Evangelization. This is the work of pulling sinners out of the fire. If we believe what we say we believe, we must have compassion on the lost and seek to win them for Christ. The best answer to apostasy is the power of the Holy Ghost to bring sinners to the Saviour.

Second, not only is the faith defended by God's people but *by the Lord Himself.* He does so by judging apostasy and the apostates who promote it. He judges them even in this life (Jude 5–7). He will judge them at the return of Christ (vv. 14–15).

He judges them in yet another way: He completes His purpose despite all apostates say or do (vv. 24–25). He will bring His people to glory. That is the ultimate success of the gospel, and it demonstrates God's final verdict on apostasy.

Thus Christians can contend with confidence. Their knowledge of the power of the faith which was delivered to them and which they defend against the ever-present attack from apostates is the best answer to the abominations of apostasy.

25

Revelation

The Unveiling Of Christ

Revelation teaches us to live on earth in the light of

◆

what the Lord is doing in heaven. It is the message of the

◆

victory of Christ over Satan and his hosts. What a

◆

glorious theme! Christ is glorified. Christ is ruling.

◆

Christ is coming. Therefore, Christians, rejoice, because

◆

we overcome in His victory and will reign with Him.

There are four schools of interpretation of the Revelation: the preterist, the historist, the idealist, and the futurist.

The preterist sees the book rooted in the time John wrote it. The beast is the Roman emperor, and the various visions depict the experiences of the church under Roman rule. The apocalyptic symbols are the writer's way of describing the horrors of Roman persecution and his hope of the utter defeat of the empire. Thus the Revelation deals with the evils of Rome and portrays Jewish history up to the fall of Jerusalem. According to some preterists, the book also goes on to describe the fall of the Roman empire.

The historist, or the presentist, sees the Revelation as an unfolding of the history of the church in the world. The various symbols are events that either have come to pass or will yet come to pass. For example, many historists have taken the locusts of the fifth trumpet to represent the Moslem hordes who poured into Europe during the sixth through the eighth centuries. Similarly, the four angels bound in the Euphrates (9:14) represent the spread of Turkish power. Historist interpreters see the Revelation as ultimately portraying the victory of the gospel in the world, leading to a worldwide reign of grace followed by a brief apostasy before the return of Christ.

The idealist, or spiritualist, sees the visions of the Revelation as representing spiritual principles, not specific historical events. Idealists see the book as a series of parallel segments that describe the entire Christian era. They explain the various apocalyptic symbols as portraying the spiritual warfare that is being waged in the world. They especially use the symbols of Christ's victory as the message of God to beleaguered Christians to look beyond their apparent difficulties and see that they are in reality more than conquerors.

The futurist sees most of the Revelation as predictive prophecy dealing with the end time leading up to the return of Christ to reign on the earth. They take 1:19 and 4:1 as stating very definitely that the book is genuinely predictive. They also insist that many of the prophecies cannot be said to have been fulfilled at any time in church history, and therefore remain to be fulfilled. They also note that the great judgments of the book bring us time and again right up to the coming of the Lord. The terminus of all the book's prophecies is the coming of Christ and the proclamation that He has taken the kingdoms of this world and will reign in power over the nations.

These four schemes yield three very divergent millennial views. The preterist and historist schools lead to postmillennialism, the theory that Christ's return will come after the millennial fulness of the church. The idealist interpretation leads to amillennialism, the idea that there is no future millennial period predicted to occur either before or after the return of Christ. An idealist sees the thousand-year period of Revelation 20 as a picture of the entire period of the history of Christ's church. The futurist interpretation yields a premillennial understanding of the Revelation—that is, that there will be a thousand-year reign of Christ on the earth after His return.

At first all this seems hopelessly confused and confusing. Personally, I am more and more convinced that as an ultimate system of interpretation, only futurism does justice to the book. To see the Revelation as having been entirely fulfilled in the first century (or soon thereafter) as the preterist does is untenable. To see it as the historist does is to demand a very extensive education in extrabiblical history before the message of Scripture can be enjoyed. It also keeps one's beliefs in a state of flux, for the longer the world goes on, the more the historist must revamp his interpretation of the symbols of Revelation. The same Scripture data must be constantly stretched to cover more and more time and events. To see Revelation as the idealist does stretches the imagination. If this book does not intend to portray actual historical events, we may well despair of ever making sense out of it.

And yet the main idea in each of these schools is precious. With the preterist I am glad to see Revelation as addressing the concrete needs of first-century Christians. The book is rooted in the situation they were facing. In the catastrophes that ended the apostolic era, I can discern prefigurations of the upheavals of the end time. With the historist I am happy to see the great predictions of this book casting foreshadows throughout history. It is vital to see God's hand in all history. With the idealist, I rejoice that the spiritual principles by which God will work out the events of the end time are the very same as He constantly employs. The result of the warfare between heaven and hell is always the same, so that the message of Revelation has instant and constant encouragement for God's people in their struggles in the world.

Whichever interpretation we adopt, the theme of the book is clear—*the unveiling of Christ.* That appears from the very first line of the book. The unveiling is the revelation of which Christ is either the great subject or the great Mediator. Indeed, perhaps we may include both ideas, since each is certainly supported by the text of the book.

Revelation is addressed to seven churches in Asia Minor. These were actual churches. We are not sure why only these seven are named, except that they are representative of the state of all the churches. Such churches as these exist in every age.

Christ is the main speaker in this book. Indeed, it is His last word to His churches. That lends added solemnity and importance to it. Christ's last word to His church is an unveiling of Himself. This unveiling of Christ is a vision to encourage, instruct, and guide the church, and to keep her faithful to her Lord and Master. The Revelation was never meant to be a handbook of extravagant end-time speculations. It has a message about the end time, but its purpose is to point God's people to Christ at all times. Thus we must not use this book to focus on the beast and on the dragon, and so on. These and other figures are all here, but each of them must be seen in the light of Christ, the great central figure. It is all too easy to forget this. In reading this book we tend to get caught up with the fantastic imagery and try to visualize what John describes. That is impossibly difficult to do. Here there are lamp stands with stars in the middle of them; horses and their riders; living creatures in heaven and wild beasts on earth; a woman clothed with the sun and the great red dragon, her adversary; a beast with seven heads and ten horns and a woman riding upon his back; a book with seven seals, which are broken to reveal tremendous events in earth and heaven; seven trumpets and seven vials; an army of locusts like battle horses, but with faces like men and hair like women, whose king is Apollyon, the angel of the bottomless pit; Babylon, the harlot of the beast, and the new Jerusalem, the bride of Christ. In the face of such vivid symbolism we are tempted to isolate each part and try to explain it as if it stood alone, forgetting that the role and the meaning of every character in this drama can be understood only in its relation to the great central character, the Lord Jesus Christ.

With all that in mind, how may we state the central message of the book? Remember, this was written to seven churches in Asia, and through them to the whole church of Christ. It had a message for them in their day. It was intended to have an immediate impact upon the people to whom it was written. Those churches were facing many differing kinds of problems in this world. What was the book saying to them? It was bringing them a wonderful message: what is now happening in the world is not the last word. The authorities who rule are not the final power. Behind all the events of earth there is a great spiritual conflict, and in that conflict Jesus Christ is the victor. He is executing the purpose of God in all the developing affairs of time. That purpose is the continuation and consummation of what He did at Calvary. That consummation will be reached when Jesus, who died and rose again, returns as King of kings.

Here, then, is the central message of the book. It is not mere academic theory. Men have made Revelation such a battleground for their theories that they miss Christ in it. The people to whom this book was written were living people of real flesh and blood. They were fighting real battles. They were facing real enemies. They were suffering real

persecution. They were enduring real trouble, and they needed something to touch them, to encourage them, and to lead them on with God.
Thus Revelation is a book with a vital message, and it gives us grace to
go on with God to final victory. It teaches us to live on earth in the light
of what the Lord is doing in heaven. We should write that over the whole
book of the Revelation. We may not understand all the imagery and
symbolism, but at least we can understand this. Let us repeat it and
learn it well: Revelation teaches us to live on earth in the light of what
the Lord is doing in heaven. It does so by constantly alternating the
scene between heaven and earth. That structure is not an accident; it is
deliberate, and it yields a major lesson. What occurs on earth does not
just happen. It is the result of what goes on in heaven. We naturally tend
to fasten our eyes upon what we can see on earth. But things are not
what they seem. William Hendriksen, an amillennial commentator, puts
the matter beautifully: "The theme of the book is *The Victory of Christ
and of His People over the Dragon (Satan) and his Helpers.* . . . The
beast that comes out of the abyss *seems* to be victorious . . . . In reality it
is the believer who triumphs . . . . Throughout the prophecies of this
wonderful book the Christ is ever pictured as the Victor, the Conqueror.
. . . He conquers death, Hades, the dragon, the beast, the false prophet,
the men who worship the beast, etc." If the devil appears to be getting
the victory, it is only an appearance. The reality is altogether different
from the appearance. The devil is not the conqueror. The New Age
movement is not the victor. Communism is not the winner. Nor
is Romanism, nor ecumenism. The Victor is Christ, with those who
believe in Him. So here is the message: **Christ is glorified! Christ is
ruling! Christ is coming! Therefore, rejoice, because we are over-
comers, and as such we will reign with Christ.**

CHRIST IS GLORIFIED!

Christ is risen from the dead. That is the first great truth upon which
the book of the Revelation is built. God's people at the time of writing
were facing very hard circumstances. They were being bitterly persecuted
(1:9). Some were facing imprisonment and even death itself (2:10, 13).
John himself had been banished to the isle of Patmos because of his testimony to Christ (1:9). Despite all this, John had a message of victory,
and it started with this: Christ is risen from the dead. He recounted the
vision he had received on that special Lord's day when he was "in the
Spirit" and heard behind him the voice as of a trumpet saying, "I am
Alpha and Omega, the first and the last" (1:10, 11). Turning to see the
speaker, the apostle saw a vision of the Lord Jesus Christ in the midst
of His churches. The Saviour said, "I am he that liveth, and was dead;

and, behold, I am alive for evermore, Amen; and have the keys of hell and of death" (1:18). This same Jesus could therefore say to the saints in Smyrna, "Fear none of those things which thou shalt suffer: behold, the devil shall cast some of you into prison, that ye may be tried; and ye shall have tribulation ten days: be thou faithful unto death, and I will give thee a crown of life. He that hath an ear, let him hear what the Spirit saith unto the churches; He that overcometh shall not be hurt of the second death" (2:10–11). Only the risen Christ could give that assurance. He is not in the tomb but on the throne. He is the sovereign Ruler and Lord of all. He says, "I am Alpha and Omega, the beginning and the end, the first and the last" (22:13; 1:8). He cannot fail. Even if we die, our death is a blessing: "Blessed are the dead which die in the Lord" (14:13). He will raise us from the dead (20:4–5). Once we are convinced that we serve the risen Christ, the Lord of life, death, and eternity, we will not fear men or circumstances but will be faithful unto death.

Christ is risen. That is what put fire in the early church. That is what made Peter, the man who in a time of weakness cursed Christ, a veritable giant who could face life and death, indeed all hell, rather than turn against his Saviour. That is what puts backbone in our witness. It is what makes the witness of the church unanswerable. Christ is risen and ascended to glory.

CHRIST IS RULING

The risen Christ is ruling from heaven. As a futurist and a premillennialist, I must admit that premillennialists have often made the mistake of so emphasizing the coming reign of Christ on earth that they have lost sight of the fact that He is now reigning in heaven. The future aspect of His kingdom in no wise detracts from the reality that the risen Christ is now ruling from heaven.

Revelation makes this clear in two ways: *He is working in His church on earth* (chapters 2 and 3). He walks among the churches. He has a word appropriate to each of them. His was not some general message, but one particular to the needs of each church. Ephesus was the *loveless* church (2:1–7) that needed to repent. Smyrna was the *little* church, but rich toward God (2:8–9). Pergamos was the *lax* church that allowed the doctrine of Balaam, compromise with this idolatrous world (2:12–17). Thyatira was the *libertine* church that harboured Jezebel (2:18–29), a plain type of the false and worldly religion that is creeping in among God's people. Sardis was the *lifeless* church, having a name to live but dead (3:1–6). Philadelphia was the *loving* church (3:7–13), and Laodicea was the *lukewarm* church, neither cold nor hot (3:14–22). Each church was different from the others, but the Lord Jesus had a command for every one of them. He also had a promise for each overcomer. Chapters 2 and 3, then, show us that the Lord Jesus is working in His church on earth.

The rest of the book shows that *Christ is working for His church from heaven.* That is the meaning of the seals, the trumpets, and the vials. Beyond the visible there is the invisible. Behind the natural there is the supernatural. Presiding over all that is happening on earth there is the throne of God. Read Revelation 4 and 5. Presiding over it all is the throne of God, and "in the midst of the throne" is the Lamb, our Saviour. That is always true throughout history. It is very especially true in the end time, when Satan seems to be victorious. In the end time men can see great catastrophes, but the truth is that these catastrophes are really only our Saviour, the Lamb, opening the seals of the book of God's purpose for the world. Now more than ever before we need to look beyond the apparent, the visible, and see the great spiritual reality that from heaven Christ is working out God's ultimate purpose for the earth. God has not forsaken His people. Remember who opens the seals. It is the Lamb, and thus according to Revelation He conquers Babylon, the beast, the dragon, and the final amalgamation of nations who gather together at Armageddon. All things are under His control. What a comfort for God's people!

Christ is risen. Christ the risen One is ruling from heaven. That leads us to the third strand in the glorious argument of this book.

CHRIST IS RETURNING

The ruling Christ will return to earth: "Behold, he cometh with clouds; and every eye shall see him, and they also which pierced him: and all kindreds of the earth shall wail because of him" (1:7). In 11:15–17 we read, "The seventh angel sounded; and there were great voices in heaven, saying, The kingdoms of this world are become the kingdoms of our Lord, and of his Christ; and he shall reign for ever and ever. . . . We give thee thanks, O Lord God Almighty, which art, and wast, and art to come; because thou hast taken to thee thy great power, and hast reigned."

Chapter 20:11–15 paints a solemn picture of that coming: "I saw a great white throne, and him that sat on it, from whose face the earth and the heaven fled away; and there was found no place for them. And I saw the dead, small and great, stand before God; and the books were opened: and another book was opened, which is the book of life: and the dead were judged out of those things which were written in the books, according to their works. And the sea gave up the dead which were in it; and death and hell delivered up the dead which were in them: and they were judged every man according to their works. And death and hell were cast into the lake of fire. This is the second death. And whosoever was not found written in the book of life was cast into the lake of fire." The book ends with yet another assurance of Christ's return: "Surely I come quickly. Amen. Even so, come, Lord Jesus" (22:20).

What a comfort to the church is the second coming of Christ! Tragically, many Christians make the doctrine of Christ's return a theological football, a mere subject of contention. In so doing they are in danger of denying God's people the comfort of the Lord's coming. There are people who would compass the earth to make a convert to their doctrine of a pre-, mid-, or post-tribulation coming of Christ, who yet miss the real comfort of the fact that Christ is coming again. That comfort begets holiness. The Revelation reinforces John's message in his first epistle: "Every man that hath this hope in him purifieth himself, even as he is pure" (1 John 3:3). We cannot believe that Jesus is coming again and live in a wicked and worldly fashion.

Not only does the doctrine of Christ's second coming have a message of comfort and holiness for the church. It also brings a word of challenge and condemnation to the world. Rev. 6:12–17 is one of the most terrible portions in all the Word of God: "I beheld when he had opened the sixth seal, and, lo, there was a great earthquake; and the sun became black as sackcloth of hair, and the moon became as blood; and the stars of heaven fell unto the earth, even as a fig tree casteth her untimely figs, when she is shaken of a mighty wind. And the heaven departed as a scroll when it is rolled together; and every mountain and island were moved out of their places. And the kings of the earth, and the great men, and the rich men, and the chief captains, and the mighty men, and every bondman, and every free man, hid themselves in the dens and in the rocks of the mountains; and said to the mountains and rocks, Fall on us, and hide us from the face of him that sitteth on the throne, and from the wrath of the Lamb: for the great day of his wrath is come; and who shall be able to stand?"

Again in 19:11–15 we read of the Lord's coming: "I saw heaven opened, and behold a white horse; and he that sat upon him was called Faithful and True, and in righteousness he doth judge and make war. His eyes were as a flame of fire, and on his head were many crowns; and he had a name written, that no man knew, but he himself. And he was clothed with a vesture dipped in blood: and his name is called The Word of God. And the armies which were in heaven followed him upon white horses, clothed in fine linen, white and clean. And out of his mouth goeth a sharp sword, that with it he should smite the nations: and he shall rule them with a rod of iron: and he treadeth the winepress of the fierceness and wrath of Almighty God."

We have already noted the passage in 20:11–15 describing the great white throne at which the Lord will arraign every sinner of every age in history and will judge them for their sins. Only the Lamb who died to redeem His people from their sins (5:9) can save sinners from that awful judgment and its sentence, "the second death," in the lake of fire forever: "Whosoever was not found written in the book of life was cast into the lake of fire." The ruling Christ will return to earth. What a comfort to redeemed saints! What a condemnation to unconverted sinners!

CHRIST WILL REIGN FOREVER

The final truth of Revelation is that the returning Christ will reign forever. We have noted 11:15: "The kingdoms of this world are become the kingdoms of our Lord, and of his Christ; and he shall reign for ever and ever." In 20:4–6 we have the same truth expressed. Christ and His people with Him will reign a thousand years. After that, of course, is eternity with its never-ending glory of the new heavens and the new earth.

In the light of Christ's assured reign we should remember His promise: "To him that overcometh will I grant to sit with me in my throne, even as I also overcame, and am set down with my Father in his throne" (3:21). Could we have any greater encouragement to be faithful? Here is a vision to breathe courage into a fainting people.

We come full circle. Let us use the book of the Revelation, not primarily to parade our knowledge of symbols and mysteries—about which we do well to pray humbly for wisdom—but to fill our minds with Christ. Revelation is the unveiling of Christ. This is Christ's final word. This is how we are to look at all theology, all history, and all prophecy. Christ is risen; Christ is ruling; Christ is returning. Therefore, let us rejoice and be faithful, for we who now reign with Him in grace will soon reign with Him in government and in glory. That is the real heart of the message of the book of the Revelation. Could we end our study of the essential messages of the New Testament books on a better note?